An Introduction to B
Northern Ireland

An Introduction to Business Law in Northern Ireland

2nd Edition

Lisa Sturgeon, LLB

Chartered Accountants Ireland

Published in 2016 by
Chartered Accountants Ireland
Chartered Accountants House
47–49 Pearse Street
Dublin 2

www.charteredaccountants.ie

ISBN: 978-1-910374-70-2

Typeset by Datapage
Printed by CPI Group (UK) Ltd, Croydon, CR0 4YY

FSC
www.fsc.org
MIX
Paper from
responsible sources
FSC® C013604

Table of Contents

Chapter 1

AN INTRODUCTION TO LAW

Introduction

The legal system of Northern Ireland has evolved from a wide variety of sources which have developed it into the system that it is today. Northern Irish law is also significantly influenced by United Kingdom (UK) law and European Union (EU) law.

Until June 2016, EU law always took precedence over both UK law and Northern Irish law. However, the outcome of the UK referendum on 23 June 2016 on whether or not to remain in the EU, and the UK's decision to leave the EU, will alter this position. How, exactly, it remains to be seen. EU law will still stand in Northern Ireland until the UK ceases to be a Member State of the EU, which means that Northern Ireland will continue to abide by EU treaties and laws.

TYPES OF LAW

Within the Northern Ireland legal system, a number of different types of law can be distinguished:
- common law and equity;
- statute law;
- private law and public law; and
- criminal law and civil law.

Common Law and Equity

Common law is a legal system based on Anglo-Saxon principles. Common law developed following the Norman invasions of England in 1066 and Ireland in 1169. Before this, Ireland was governed by Brehon law, which was a legal system based on traditional custom. However, following the Norman invasion, Ireland became subject to the common law system. In essence, the application of law was made by judges who travelled around the country dispensing justice in order to keep the King's peace. These judgments became known as 'the King's courts'. The aim of these courts was to centralise the administration of justice and to create a system which was common to the whole country.

A crucial feature of common law is the doctrine of **judicial precedent**. This doctrine, which is explained more fully below, states that once judges have made a ruling on a particular point of law in a higher court, judges in lower courts must follow this rule if dealing with the same point in subsequent cases.

Prior to 1875, there were three courts to handle three broad categories of case:
1. cases involving the King's interest in the maintenance of law and order were dealt with by the Court of King's Bench;
2. taxation cases were heard in the Court of Exchequer; and
3. disputes involving only 'common' (here meaning private) individuals went to the Court of Common Pleas.

However, there were many disputes that could not be dealt with in these three courts. Petitions sent to the King to settle such cases were referred by him to his Chancellor for justice to be done. From this practice another court emerged: the Court of Chancery. The tradition thus developed that justice dispensed by the Court of Chancery was '**equity**', while the justice dispensed by the King's other courts was '**common law**'. It was not until 1875 in England, and 1877 in Ireland, that common law and equity could be administered in one and the same court. Until then, the two types of law had to be kept quite separate. Hence, equity added to and improved on the common law by introducing the concept of fairness.

The interaction of equity and common law had a number of significant advantages. For example, the Court of Chancery considerably developed the law relating to trusts and mortgages. Furthermore, it also developed a number of **discretionary remedies**, which included the following:
* **Specific performance** – this is an order of the court compelling a person to perform an obligation existing either under a contract or trust.
* **Injunction** – this is an order of the court compelling or restraining the performance of some act.
* **Rectification** – this is an order of the court in relation to the alteration of a document to reflect the parties' true intentions.
* **Rescission** – the remedy of rescission aims to restore parties to the position they were in prior to the contract being formed, i.e. their pre-contract state of affairs.

Statute Law

In addition to law created by judicial precedent, the other main source of law is statute law or 'Acts of Parliament' (more commonly referred to as 'primary legislation'). Acts of Parliament also provide authority for numerous Orders,

Rules and Regulations, which are called 'secondary legislation'. (Primary and secondary legislation are considered in more detail below, under Sources of Northern Ireland Law.)

Private and Public Law

Private law is the area of law that deals with the relationships and interactions between businesses, customers, employees and other private individuals, groups and organisations. (Private law is the main source of law discussed in this book.)

Public law, on the other hand, regulates relationships between individuals and public bodies such as councils and local authorities. For example, the branch of public law called constitutional law is concerned with the role and powers of our State institutions, how we are governed and what our civil liberties are. (*Note:* this area of law does not have great significance for the purposes of a business law course.)

The key distinction between public law and private law rests upon who brings a case if a wrong has taken place. In public law, it is the State that takes up the case when a wrong is committed. For example, the Health and Social Services Trust has a duty to investigate if pupils fail to attend school regularly or are suffering or at risk because of a lack of parental care. Under private law, it is the individual who brings the case. For example, private law applications can be made in the course of domestic proceedings and matrimonial causes or where parents are otherwise in dispute about their children.

Criminal Law and Civil Law

Criminal Law

Criminal law is a branch of public law. Criminal law outlaws acts that are considered to be contrary to public order and society's interests. Criminal acts are called **offences**.

As it is the community that suffers as a result of a criminal law being broken, the state is therefore the prosecutor in a criminal case. The police take the initial decision to prosecute, but this decision will then be reviewed by the Public Prosecution Service (PPS). Anyone convicted of a criminal act will be fined, imprisoned or served with a community-based punishment.

Criminal cases that are formally reported are cited in the form '*R. v. Smith*', where the 'R' stands for *Rex* or *Regina* (*Rex* being Latin for King, *Regina* for Queen, or 'the Crown'). The prosecution is brought in the name of the Crown.

Civil Law

Civil law is a branch of private law. Civil law governs disputes over the rights and obligations of persons dealing with each other. The outcome of a civil action will be compensation for the injured party. Different terminology is used in civil cases to that in criminal cases. For example, the person bringing a case in a civil claim is called the 'plaintiff' and the person against whom they are bringing the claim is called the 'defendant'. In citations, reported civil cases cited are, therefore, referred to as, for example, *Smith v. Jones.*

Some types of behaviour can constitute both a crime and a civil wrong. The criminal part of the incident will be dealt with in a criminal court, while the civil part of the incident will be tried in a civil court. It is the standard of proof that is the crucial distinguishing feature between a criminal and civil claim. In a criminal case, in order to convict someone accused of a crime, the prosecution bears the burden of proving an accused guilty; hence the phrase 'innocent until proven guilty'. The standard for the burden of proof, in a criminal trial, is 'beyond reasonable doubt'.

In a civil case, a plaintiff must prove their case 'on the balance of probabilities'. As the standard of proof is higher in a criminal case than in a civil case, this means that cases are more difficult to prove in the criminal courts. In effect, this means that in some circumstances an individual can be found guilty of a civil wrong but not a criminal wrong because of the higher standard of proof required.

The following table illustrates the comparison between civil law and criminal law in Northern Ireland.

Table 1.1 Comparison of Criminal Law and Civil Law in Northern Ireland[1]

Criminal Law		Civil Law
Prosecution		Civil action
Parties		
Prosecution (State) Defence		Plaintiff Defendant
Objective		
Punishment – as well as incapacitation, retribution, deterrence, rehabilitation		Compensation Ceasing the unwanted action Specific performance

[1] From Vaeni MacDonnell, *An Introduction to Business Law* (2nd edition, Chartered Accountants Ireland, 2015).

Table 1.1 *(Continued)*

Criminal Law		Civil Law
Tests applied to determine liability		
Beyond all reasonable doubt		Balance of probabilities
Finding		
Guilty Not guilty		Liable Not liable
Commencement of proceedings		
State/PPS by summons or indictment		By way of pleadings Representatives of the State
Penalties/Remedies		
Fines Imprisonment Probation orders Community service orders, etc.		Damages Injunctions Court orders Account for profits etc.
Courts		
Magistrates' Court		County Court

SOURCES OF NORTHERN IRELAND LAW

Legislation

Legislation is a key source of law. In Northern Ireland, legislation is passed by the Northern Ireland Assembly and the Parliament of the United Kingdom. Until 1973, the Parliament of the United Kingdom was completely sovereign. However, in 1973 the United Kingdom entered the European Community and, therefore, under the Treaty of Rome, is now obliged to ensure that Northern Ireland/United Kingdom law is in line with the Treaty itself and with any Directives issued in Europe.

In order to understand how legislation is passed in Northern Ireland, it is necessary to understand the difference between the Northern Ireland Assembly and the Parliament of the United Kingdom (often referred to as 'Westminster'). The Northern Ireland Assembly is the Parliament for Northern Ireland. It was created by the Northern Ireland Act 1998 and it has the power to legislate on a wide range of matters which have not been reserved to the Parliament of the United Kingdom. Matters in Northern Ireland are either 'reserved' or 'delegated'. Reserved matters are matters that continue to be dealt with by the Parliament of the United Kingdom under the terms of the Northern Ireland Act 1998 (for example, policing and justice). Delegated matters are matters that have not been retained by the Parliament of the United Kingdom; these include education and employment and learning.

In Northern Ireland, three broad types of legislation exist: primary, secondary and Orders-in-Council.

Primary Legislation

Primary legislation consists of Acts of Parliament or 'statutes'. As stated above, in Northern Ireland matters are either reserved to the Parliament of the United Kingdom or are delegated to the Northern Ireland Assembly. Only the Parliament of the United Kingdom can legislate on the reserved matters. The Northern Ireland Assembly has the power to make Acts that legislate on delegated matters.

In order for an Act to be passed by Parliament, there is a set process that must be followed. Initially, a proposal for legislation is brought by a member of the Government. In the Parliament of the United Kingdom, the first step is for a Government Bill to be introduced into the House of Commons. Following this, the successive stages of dealing with the Bill are as follows:

Stage One: The first reading of the Bill takes place at stage one. At this stage, the first draft of the Bill is published and is laid before the House of Commons. No debate takes place on the Bill at this first stage.

Stage Two: At stage two, there is a general debate on the merits of the Bill within the House of Commons. This is known as the Second Reading of the Bill and no amendments are made to the Bill at this stage.

Stage Three: Stage three of an introduction of an Act of Parliament is known as the Committee Stage. At this stage, the Bill is examined by a Standing Committee of about 20 members of the House of Commons. These members will be representative of the main parties within the House of Commons and, among these members, will be those who specialise particularly in the relevant subject to which the Bill relates. Amendments to the Bill are suggested before it progresses to the Report stage, which is the final stage of the introduction of the Bill.

Stage Four: Stage four is known as the Report stage. Any detailed amendments recommended at the Committee stage are given further consideration within the Report stage before the Bill progresses to the House of Lords for approval. A similar process takes place in the House of Lords.

If any amendments arise, the Bill is sent back to the House of Commons for further approval. An Act comes into force on the day on which it receives Royal Assent. An Act ceases to have effect only on the day it is repealed by another Act.

Secondary Legislation

Secondary legislation is derived from primary legislation. The purpose of secondary legislation is to set down law, as outlined in an Act of Parliament, in more detail. The power to do this is given in the Act itself and the delegated legislation can take various forms. Local authorities can be given statutory powers to make bye-laws. Rules of Court may be made by the judiciary to control court procedure. Professional regulations concerning certain occupations (such as accountancy, law, etc.) can be delegated to authorised bodies (such as the Law Society for Northern Ireland, Chartered Accountants Ireland, etc.).

Orders-in-Council

The third type of legislation in Northern Ireland are 'Orders-in-Council'. These are made when the Queen assents to proposals put to her by senior ministers appointed by Privy Councillors. For most of the period from 1972 to 2007, much of Northern Ireland's legislation was made by Orders-in-Council. This was done under the various Northern Ireland Acts 1974–2000. An Order-in-Council usually has the following form:

> "Her Majesty, in pursuance of [relevant section of primary legislation], is pleased, by and with the advice of Her Privy Council, to order, and it is hereby ordered, as follows: …".

Judicial Precedent

The doctrine of judicial precedent is also an important source of Northern Irish law. The doctrine, which is sometimes referred to by the Latin phrase '*stare decisis*' (Latin for 'stand by things that have been decided'), states that a lower court is obliged to follow a higher court's decision in a similar case unless the previous decision can be distinguished (see the section on the courts system, below). In essence, a higher court can overrule a previous decision by a lower court. However, this means that the higher court is changing the law from that point of time onwards. (It does *not* mean that the losing party in the earlier decision, which may have been taken years previously, can now have that decision reversed.)

The highest court in Northern Ireland's legal system is the Supreme Court. The decisions of the Supreme Court are binding on all the other courts in Northern Ireland. Although, generally speaking, the courts in Northern Ireland are not bound by decisions in other jurisdictions, such decisions can provide persuasive authority that may influence, from time to time, Northern Ireland judges in applying the law in this country. Typically, the courts look at the decisions of other Commonwealth jurisdictions such as England, Australia and Canada.

There are a number of advantages to the concept of judicial precedent. First, it provides certainty, as the law is decided fairly and predictably. Secondly, judicial precedence is an important form of guidance to judges – judges set down their reasoning for their decision and this reasoning gives guidance to future judges when making a decision with the same legal issues. Thirdly, judges recognise that circumstances and economic climates change over time. This makes judicial precedent extremely flexible, as judges can factor in these concepts when arriving at a decision. Indeed, what may have been a fair decision 50 years ago may no longer be a practical decision in today's society. Finally, judicial precedent is extremely practical. When legislation is set, it does not have the benefit of having been tried and tested in court. Hence, judicial precedent helps to interpret legislation from a practical point of view through its application and analysis of everyday case law.

Judgments made by judges contain a *'ratio decidendi'* or simply the 'reason for deciding' the case. The *ratio decidendi* is the part of the case that will bind lower courts to that decision. The doctrine of judicial precedent permits lower courts to follow higher court decisions only if the higher court decision raises issues similar to the facts of the lower case. As such, this makes it essential for lawyers to deduce, from every reported case upon which they rely to support their case, the precise reason why this case may be used as an authority for their case.

In addition, throughout the course of their judgments, judges often make comments that do not have a direct bearing on the main point of the case. Such comments are *'obiter dictum'*, which literally means 'something said by the way'. Essentially, therefore, only the *ratio decidendi* of a case is binding.

Statutory Interpretation

Despite the best intentions of those who have drafted it, every piece of legislation passed is subject to different interpretations by different judges. This arises because of two factors:

1. **Ambiguity** – this is caused by error in drafting whereby the words used are capable of two or more literal meanings.

2. **Uncertainty** – this arises where the words of a statute are intended to apply to a range of factual situations and the courts must decide whether the case before them falls into any of these situations.

Three Canons of Construction

Over time, three approaches have developed to interpreting statutes:
- the literal rule,
- the golden rule, and
- the mischief rule.

These rules have become known as the '**Three Canons of Construction**'.

The literal rule states that the words used in any piece of legislation passed by Parliament must be given their literal or usual meaning, even if the result appears to be at odds with that which Parliament intended.

For example, the Restriction of Offensive Weapons Act 1959 made it an offence to "offer for sale" certain weapons including "flick knives". In *Fisher v. Bell* (1961), a shopkeeper who displayed the knives in his window was found not guilty of the offence. Although he had displayed the goods and accepted offers from customers to buy the goods, and subsequently sold the goods, he had not offered them for sale.

The golden rule states that the literal rule must be followed unless to do so would produce an absurd result. For example, in the case of *Re Sigsworth* (1935), a mother, who had not made her will, was murdered by her son. The Administration of Justice Act 1925 provided that, in the event that someone does not leave a will, under the rules of intestacy the next of kin should receive the estate. In this situation, this would have meant that the son would have inherited his mother's estate as he was the next of kin. The court held here that the golden rule should apply to prevent the absurd situation of the son, in these circumstances, receiving the estate.

The mischief rule states that where a statute is passed to remedy 'a mischief', or a point or gap in the law that has been causing confusion, the court must adopt the interpretation that will have the effect of remedying the mischief in question. Therefore, courts are permitted to look at the law prior to the enactment of the statute in order to establish what the defect was that the legislation was intended to remedy.

Other Assistance in Statutory Interpretation

The Interpretation (Northern Ireland) Act 1954 is often referred to when statutes are being interpreted. It defines certain terms found frequently in legislation. For example, the Act states that the use of masculine terminology in a statute is taken to include the feminine terminology and it further states that, if a word is singular, it also includes plurals. The Act also deals with such problems as the meaning of 'month'.

'Intrinsic aids' are also perceived as a help in statutory interpretation. Intrinsic aids include the long title of an Act as it gives guidance on the Act's general objective. The preamble of an Act is said to direct a judge as to its intentions and objects. Statutes often have side notes in their margins which are also a useful tool in statutory interpretation.

Similarly, 'extrinsic aids' also assist in statutory interpretation. Extrinsic aids include the following:
1. Reports of the Law Commission, Royal Commissions and the Law Reform Committee, and other official documents.
2. *Hansard*, the official journal of UK Parliamentary debates. This journal will include the original speech that first introduced a Bill. The case of *Pepper v. Hart* (1992) said that it is acceptable for judges to look at the original speech introducing a Bill for assistance in statutory interpretation.

The Courts System in Northern Ireland

The Supreme Court

The highest court in the UK is called the Supreme Court. It is based in London and is presided over by the Lord Chancellor with a staff of 12 Justices of the Supreme Court. The Supreme Court acts as the ultimate appeal court for all courts throughout the United Kingdom (with the exception of criminal cases in Scotland). Permission must be given from the Court of Appeal to take a case to the Supreme Court. Furthermore, cases heard in the Supreme Court are usually high-profile cases or cases that will have a significant impact upon the law.

The Court of Judicature of Northern Ireland

The Court of Appeal, the High Court and the Crown Court together make up the Court of Judicature of Northern Ireland. The most important judge in Northern Ireland is the Lord Chief Justice of Northern Ireland (Sir Declan Morgan QC at the time of writing). He assigns work to the judges of the various courts. The Court of Appeal consists of the Lord Chief Justice and three other judges called Lords Justices of Appeal. A case in the Court of Appeal will usually be heard by three judges, always sitting in Belfast, although some matters may be dealt with by two Lords Justices of Appeal and some incidental matters by one judge sitting alone. A jury is never involved.

The High Court of Justice in Northern Ireland

The High Court of Justice deals with the hearing of the more important civil cases in the first instance, as well as some appeals from the inferior courts. The High Court consists of the Lord Chief Justice, 10 other judges and seven High Court Masters. These 10 other judges are officially called '*Puisne*' judges, meaning a judge inferior in rank to the Lord Chief Justice. They may sit in any of the divisions of the High Court, although some judges are seen as particularly expert in one or other divisions. (The divisions of the High Court are further discussed below.)

Usually, all High Court cases will be heard in public, although a judge can ask that the court room be cleared if very private matters are to be discussed. A few High Court cases, mostly libel cases, are tried by a judge and jury. (Juries in civil cases consist of seven people and are now used quite rarely.)

The division in which a case in the High Court is dealt with depends upon the type of subject matter involved. There are three divisions of the High Court. The first division is called the 'Queen's Bench Division'. This division is for claims in contract or tort and for all matters not assigned by legislation to another division. The second division is called the 'Chancery Division', which is for types of claims dealt with as equity business in the county courts and for bankruptcies and claims involving breach of copyright. The third division is called the 'Family Division'. This division involves every type of claim concerning family matters, including the wardship of children, determination of a person's legitimacy and the administration of the property of a psychiatric patient.

The High Court also contains the Divisional Court, which is a sort of Appeal Court within the Queen's Bench Division and which mainly hears applications for '*habeas corpus*', i.e. a claim that a person's detention in custody has no legal justification, or judicial review.

In addition, the High Court also has six separate offices, which are managed by a High Court Master. The six offices are:
- Queen's Bench and Appeals
- The Chancery
- Bankruptcy and Companies
- Care and Protection
- Taxation
- Enforcement of Judgments

High Court Masters exercise a very important function in the High Court, both in an administrative and in a decision-making capacity. High Court Masters are either solicitors or barristers who have been appointed to manage matters of the High Court which, by statute or under Rules of Court, do not fall to a judge. For example, the Queen's Bench, Chancery and Bankruptcy Masters deal mainly with all of the interlocutory work and any applications that fall within their jurisdiction. In certain circumstances, they can also try actions sitting as a 'Judge in Chambers'. An appeal against their decision usually lies to a judge.

The Crown Court

The Crown Court is a branch of the Court of Judicature of Northern Ireland that sits at nine venues throughout Northern Ireland and is the court for more serious criminal trials. The main part of a trial takes place in the Crown Court after the defendant has been committed for trial by the Magistrates' Court. The Crown Court can be presided over by the Lord Chief Justice, a Judge of the Court of Appeal, a High Court Judge or a County Court Judge. In all cases, there will be a jury of 12 people. The role of the judge is to explain the relevant law to the jury. The jury listen to all the evidence, decide which alleged facts are true, and find the accused person guilty or not guilty based on the law explained to them by the judge.

Certain serious criminal offences, called *scheduled offences* (a scheduled offence is one liable to be committed by terrorists) are heard by a judge sitting alone or 'Diplock Courts' as they have been called.

The Subordinate Courts

The County Court The main administrators in County Court Divisions are called '*Chief Clerks*' (formerly known as Clerks of the Crown and Peace). In Magistrates' Courts, they are called '*Clerks of the Petty Sessions*'.

In Northern Ireland, there are seven County Court Divisions. As of July 2016, there are 18 County Court Judges, four District Judges and 21 District Judges of the Magistrates' Courts. Although County Courts are almost exclusively civil courts, they still hear appeals from criminal cases tried summarily in the Magistrates' Courts. A 'summary' trial in the Magistrates' Court is one that takes place without a jury. Judges who sit as County Court Judges frequently also sit as Crown Court Judges for criminal cases.

District Judges, who were formerly known as Circuit Registrars, assist the County Court Judges and exercise jurisdiction in the Small Claims Courts.

They may also hear undefended County Court claims and frequently sit as County Court Judges to hear other claims.

It is important to note that a County Court is restricted both as to the size and type of case that it can hear. The County Court is where everyday civil disputes are heard. Examples of potential County Court claims include:

- cases in tort or for breach of contract where the amount claimed is less than £30,000;
- actions for the recovery of land or disputes as to ownership of land where the rateable value is less than £1,000;
- disputes as to the validity of a will;
- undefended petitions for divorce; and
- applications for liquor licences.

The Small Claims Court The Small Claims Court is a separate type of County Court procedure where District Judges deal with claims for less than £3,000, usually relating to debts or private disputes. Certain proceedings, such as accident or personal injury claims, which cannot be dealt with through the Small Claims procedure, must go to the County Court in the normal way. Most of the claims in the Small Claims Court are by business or commercial organisations, usually for non-payment of hire purchase instalments, money owed or goods delivered. The aim of the Small Claims Court procedure is to deal as quickly as possible with disputes with a minimum of formality and expense. The parties do not need to be legally represented and cannot, except rarely, recover their legal costs from one another.

Magistrates' Court The 'Petty Sessions' is the official name for the Magistrates' Court. The Lord Chancellor gives directions as to the days on which the petty sessions are to be held and as to the hours of sitting. As well as these regular sittings, Magistrates' Courts sit at intervening times (i.e. 'out of petty sessions') whenever it is necessary for them to do so.

There are 17 petty sessions venues in Northern Ireland. The judges who preside in the courts of petty sessions are called District Judges. However, in the Family and Youth Courts (which are specially constituted types of Magistrates' Courts and which deal specifically with criminal matters in relation to children), in addition to the District Judge, there must also be two lay Magistrates (one of whom must be a woman). Lay Magistrates were a recommendation of the Northern Ireland Criminal Justice Review and were introduced into Northern Ireland in April 2005. Lay Magistrates are people with no formal legal qualifications and the intention behind having Lay Magistrates is to foster stronger links between the courts and the community.

The Magistrates' Court has a very wide jurisdiction, both criminal and civil. It deals mainly with less serious criminal offences, such as driving offences. It also handles committal proceedings for the more serious criminal cases and hear, some civil disputes. The main types of civil case that a Magistrates' Court can hear are:

- domestic and family cases;
- claims to recover small debts;
- claims to deprive someone of occupation of land; and
- applications for licences.

Other Statutory Legal Officials in Northern Ireland

Apart from the judiciary, in Northern Ireland there are a number of other legal officials and statutory offices who exercise a particular role and function. The **Public Prosecution Service (PPS)** brings prosecutions for indictable criminal offences like murder, as well as for such lesser criminal offences as it considers should be dealt with by the PPS. The PPS's office represents the Crown in all criminal cases in the Crown Court, the Court of Appeal and the House of Lords. For these purposes, the PPS retains the services of three senior and three junior Crown Counsel (barristers) and the PPS's office functions as the solicitor for these barristers.

The Crown Solicitor provides legal assistance to government departments and some other public bodies. Most of the work of the Crown Solicitor's Office is to do with civil rather than criminal matters. Usually, this work involves litigation because the office represents government departments when they are sued by members of the public.

The Official Solicitor represents the interests of litigants in cases where they would not otherwise be adequately protected, such as those involving children or persons who are in custody for contempt. The Official Solicitor must conduct such investigations and provide such assistance as may be authorised by the Rules of the Supreme Court or required by any direction of a court to assist in the due administration of justice.

Appeals

The following table illustrates the hierarchy of courts in Northern Ireland's legal system.

Figure 1.1: The Hierarchy of Courts in the Legal System of Northern Ireland[2]

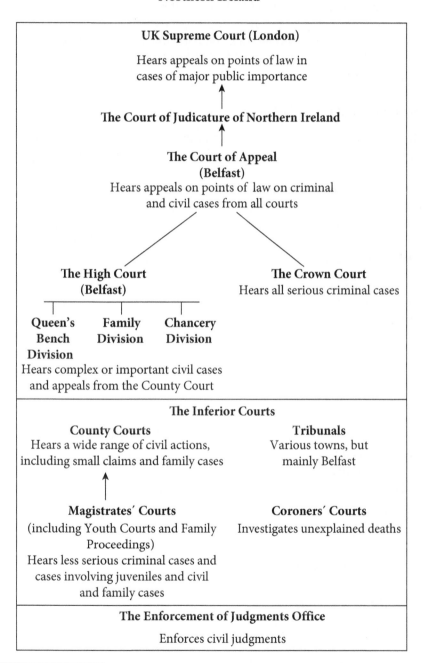

UK Supreme Court (London)

Hears appeals on points of law in cases of major public importance

The Court of Judicature of Northern Ireland

The Court of Appeal (Belfast)

Hears appeals on points of law on criminal and civil cases from all courts

The High Court (Belfast)

Queen's Bench Division   Family Division   Chancery Division

Hears complex or important civil cases and appeals from the County Court

The Crown Court

Hears all serious criminal cases

The Inferior Courts

County Courts

Hears a wide range of civil actions, including small claims and family cases

Tribunals

Various towns, but mainly Belfast

Magistrates' Courts

(including Youth Courts and Family Proceedings)

Hears less serious criminal cases and cases involving juveniles and civil and family cases

Coroners' Courts

Investigates unexplained deaths

The Enforcement of Judgments Office

Enforces civil judgments

---

[2] Brice Dickson, *The Legal System of Northern Ireland* (Fifth Edition, SLS Legal Publications (NI) 2005).

Alternative Dispute Resolution in Northern Ireland

Alternative dispute resolution (ADR) is an alternative way of sorting out disputes without having to resort to court. Going to court can be expensive, slow and stressful, and people often complain that it is not an experience they enjoy. ADR is an alternative to this and involves a process of conciliation, mediation, arbitration or other regularity bodies.

Mediation and Conciliation

Mediation and conciliation are much the same thing. Both involve an independent third party (the mediator or conciliator) helping parties with a dispute to try to reach an agreement. The Law Society of Northern Ireland holds a panel of certified mediators who are listed at www.mediateni.com. The role of the mediator is to help discussions run smoothly and to manage and ensure fairness in the process. The mediator is also there to facilitate those in dispute to find a solution. Mediation is particularly successful in areas of family law, employment law, partnership disputes and other areas where parties have ongoing relationships.

Mediation works on the premise that it is 'without prejudice'. This means that what is said in mediation cannot later be referred to in a court of law. If mediation is successful, an agreement is executed, at which point it becomes binding. However, if mediation is not successful, parties are free to return to court to let a judge resolve any dispute.

Arbitration

Arbitration is an alternative means of dispute resolution to litigation in the courts. It involves an independent arbitrator who hears both sides of a disagreement and then makes a decision. An arbitration hearing is similar to a court case in that it normally involves pleadings and a full hearing based on the law of evidence applicable to court proceedings.

The arbitration process is confidential and arbitration is binding. This means that once the parties have decided to use it and the process has begun, they usually give up their right to seek a resolution of the matter elsewhere, such as in a court or tribunal.

Ombudsman Schemes

There are a number of Ombudsman Schemes in Northern Ireland. They provide an independent and impartial review into determination of complaints by public and private organisations.

The role of an ombudsman is to investigate cases of maladministration. An ombudsman is usually referred to as a means of last resort when all internal avenues have been exhausted. An ombudsman will only investigate a case where an individual has suffered personal injustice, hardship or financial loss because of the action, or lack of action, of a particular organisation. The complaint must be brought by the person who has suffered the injustice, hardship or loss. It should be noted that an ombudsman cannot investigate a decision made by an organisation; they can only investigate the way in which a decision was reached.

In Northern Ireland, there are different types of ombudsmen:
- the Northern Ireland Ombudsman, who investigates complaints about Northern Ireland Government departments, local councils and other public bodies, including registered social landlords, the Northern Ireland Housing Executive, and health and social services;
- the Parliamentary and Health Service Ombudsman, who investigates complaints about national public bodies and certain other public bodies not covered by the Northern Ireland Ombudsman;
- the Financial Ombudsman Service;
- the European Ombudsman;
- the Ombudsman for Estate Agents;
- the Police Ombudsman for Northern Ireland; and
- the Prisoner Ombudsman for Northern Ireland.

EUROPEAN UNION LAW

The European Union

The United Kingdom joined the European Union (EU) in 1973. By becoming a member of the EU, it effectively signed three treaties, namely:
1. The European Economic Community Treaty – 'The EEC Treaty' or the 'Treaty of Rome';
2. The European Atomic Energy Treaty – 'EURATOM'; and
3. The European Coal and Steel Community Treaty – 'The ECSC Treaty'.

The ECSC Treaty had been signed by the six original members of the European Union (EU) on 18 April 1951. The six original members were Belgium, France, Germany, Italy, Luxembourg and the Netherlands. The EURATOM Treaty was signed in Rome in 1957, as was the Treaty of Rome. The Treaty of Rome aimed to establish an Economic Community or Single European Market in which people, goods and capital could move without restriction across national borders in Europe. The provisions of the original EEC Treaty have been amended twice: first in 1986 by the Single European Act 1986 and again in 1992 by the Treaty on European Union, or the 'Maastricht Treaty' as it became known after the city where it was signed on 7 February 1992.

The Maastricht Treaty established a framework for intergovernmental co-operation in the fields of:
1. foreign and security policy; and
2. justice and home affairs.

As a result of this, the European Union is now often said to comprise three pillars. The first pillar is concerned with European Union law; the second pillar deals with common, foreign and security policy; and the third pillar is concerned with greater co-operation in justice and home affairs.

At the time of writing there are 28 Member States of the European Union: the original six plus Austria, Bulgaria, Croatia, Cyprus, the Czech Republic, Denmark, Estonia, Finland, Greece, Hungary, Ireland, Latvia, Lithuania, Malta, Poland, Portugal, Romania, Slovakia, Slovenia, Spain, Sweden and the United Kingdom.

European Union Institutions

There are four main institutions of the EU:
- the European Commission;
- the Council of the European Union;
- the European Parliament; and
- the European Court of Justice.

The principal functions of each institution are now considered below.

The European Commission

The Commission is led by a President and is divided into approximately 20 Directorates-General (or DGs as they are sometimes known). European Commissioners work alongside the President. Each Commissioner is appointed within a Member State of the European Union and is chosen by the unanimous agreement of the government of the Member States. Each Commissioner is responsible for an area of European Union policy.

Specifically, the European Commission has three main functions. The Commission's first function is to supervise and monitor the implementation of EU law. The second function is to initiate proposals for legislation. It formulates policy and forwards legislative proposals to the Council of Ministers for approval. The third function of the European Commission is to discharge various administrative responsibilities. In other words, the Commission works closely with national administrations to ensure that all regulations passed by the Council of the European Union are being carried out in the Member States.

The Council of the European Union

The Council of the European Union can be described as the primary legislative body of the EU. Although the European Commission has the power to forward legislative proposals, no legislative proposal can be passed without the assent of the Council of the European Union. In effect, it makes the final decision to adopt new Community legislation. The Council of the European Union is not a permanent body. It meets only for a short period of time each year. Accordingly, continuity is provided to the Council's work by the Committee of Permanent Representatives (COREPER). COREPER is a permanent body with permanent staff. Their function is to work behind the scenes to scrutinise and examine the various proposals submitted by the Commission before they go before the Council itself.

The European Parliament

The European Parliament consists of over 600 members who are directly elected by citizens of the Member States. Members of the Parliament are known as MEPs and they serve for five years, after which time they may stand for re-election.

Although the European Parliament does not have the same kind of legislative functions ordinarily associated with national parliaments, it does play an important role as a co-legislator in the EU. It exercises direct political control over the European Commission. For example, it has the power to question the activities of the Commission or Council in written or oral questions, thereby establishing a system whereby EU policies are discussed in the Parliament. Finally, the European Parliament has important powers in the context of approving the Community's budget. For example, the European Parliament can reject (for good reasons) a draft budget submitted to it by the Commission or Council.

The Court of Justice of the European Union

The Court of Justice of the European Union (CJEU) is based in Luxembourg and has supreme authority in all matters relating to the interpretation, validity and effect of EU law. The CJEU is made up of judges from each of the Member States of the EU. The judges are assisted by Advocates-General. Advocates-General are not judges of the CJEU but are legally qualified. The function of the Advocate-General is to present a reasoned opinion on cases brought before the CJEU, in open court, in order to assist the court in making its final decision in a case. After the opinion of the Advocate-General is presented, judges are free to decide whether to follow it or to hand down a different opinion. It is important to note, however, that in most cases the court does follow the opinion of the Advocate-General.

The CJEU sits either as a full court or in chambers. The chamber consists of a smaller number of judges hearing a case and the advantage of having cases heard in chambers is that the court can hear a greater number. If cases were always heard by the full court, it would take a lot longer to get through court lists. It should be noted that the CJEU is completely different from the European Court of Human Rights. The CJEU sits, as stated above, in Luxembourg. It is concerned only with the body of EU law. On the other hand, the European Court of Human Rights, by contrast, sits in Strasbourg and is concerned with the interpretation of the European Convention on Human Rights and with the protection of human rights and fundamental freedoms.

The Scope of European Union Law

The scope of EU law is extraordinarily wide ranging and affects many areas of law relevant to businesses in Northern Ireland and elsewhere throughout the EU. These areas include contractual matters, sex discrimination, employment law, environmental issues, consumer protection, agricultural law, health and safety law, etc. It can be a common misconception that the relevance of EU law is minimal. In the last 10 years, for example, a significant number of Regulations have been passed that come directly from EU legislation.

As stated in the introduction to this chapter, the UK's decision to leave the EU, as a result of the referendum on 23 June 2016, will have an impact on the relevance of EU law in Northern Ireland. For the immediate future, EU law will stand in Northern Ireland until the UK ceases to be a Member State of the EU. At the time of writing, when exactly that will happen no-one really knows. For the UK to leave the EU, the UK will have to invoke Article 50 of the Lisbon Treaty, from which time it will have two years to agree to the terms under which it is splitting from the EU. The difficulty is that Article 50 has never been used before and there is uncertainty as to how it will work in practice. It could take longer than two years for the UK to leave. Only time will tell. Until such time as the UK officially leaves, it is therefore still bound by EU law.

Types of Legislation

Treaties

The primary source of EU law are the Treaties of the European Union. The main Treaties governing the European Union have been set out at the beginning of this section. They also include: the Single European Act 1986; the Treaty of Maastricht 1992; the Acts of Accession of Austria, Sweden and Finland 1994; the Treaty of Amsterdam 1997; the Treaty of Nice 2001; the Treaty of Accession 2003; the Treaty of Accession 2005; and The Treaty of Lisbon 2007.

Legislation passed by the EU institutions is known as a secondary source of EU law. Article 189 of the EEC Treaty of 1957 defines the various types of secondary legislation, i.e.:

- Regulations;
- Directives; and
- Decisions.

Regulations

Regulations are of general application. This means that they are binding in their entirety and are directly applicable in all Member States without the need for further national legislative action. The purpose of Regulations is to obtain uniformity of law throughout the Member States. For example, the EU Customs Regulation 1383/2003 came into force on 1 July 2004. It is a Regulation laying down measures to prohibit the release for free circulation, export, re-export or entry for a suspensive procedure of counterfeit or forfeited goods.

Directives

Unlike Regulations, Directives do not have immediate binding force in all Member States. They are addressed to Member States, requiring the national parliaments to make whatever changes are necessary to implement the Directive within the specified time. For example, Council Directive 95/46/EC of 24 October 1995 gave effect to a Directive on the protection of individuals with regard to the processing of data and the free movement of such data. This Directive became the Data Processing Act 1998 in the UK.

Decisions

Decisions are binding on those to whom they are addressed. They may be addressed either to a Member State or to an individual or to an institution. For example, in 2015, the EU issued a Decision on the EU participating in the work of various specified counter-terrorism organisations.

Nature of European Union Law and its Implementation in Northern Ireland

The two concepts that are most important, both for a general understanding of EU law and, in particular, the implementation of EU law in the UK, are **direct applicability** and **direct effect**.

Direct Application of EU Law

The term 'direct application' is specifically used in Article 189 of the EC Treaty, which states that a Regulation shall be "binding in its entirety and directly applicable in all Member States". In stating this, the Treaty seeks to ensure that Regulations are applicable simultaneously and uniformly throughout the EU. Thus, Regulations become law within each of the Member States of the EU simply by being adopted by the Member States, and without any need for national re-enactment.

Direct Effect of EC Law

Unlike 'direct application', the concept of 'direct effect' is expressed nowhere in the Treaties of the EU. Rather, it has evolved through the case law of the CJEU. The concept of direct effect was first brought to the fore in the *Van Gend En Loos* case in 1963. Until this point, it was not thought possible to rely directly on provisions of EU law before national courts. However, in this case, the CJEU ruled that Community provisions may create rights and obligations that are enforceable by the individuals before their national courts. However, also in this case, the CJEU held that, in order to be directly effective, a provision had to be clear and precise, unconditional and require no further legislation to be enacted by the Member States or the EU institutions.

Direct effect takes two forms:
- vertical direct effect, where individual rights can be enforced against a national Member State; and
- horizontal direct effect, where individual rights can be enforced against other individuals.

HUMAN RIGHTS LAW

"We hold these truths to be self-evident, that all men are created equal, that they are endowed by their creator with certain unalienable rights, that among these are life, liberty and the pursuit of happiness."

(from the American Declaration of Independence)

This was the essence of human rights set out in 1776 by the 'Founding Fathers' of the United States of America. However, the concept of human rights has developed considerably since the days of 1776 and continues to develop as society changes.

The decolonisation of much of the world in the 20th Century and the newly independent countries formed, for example in the British Commonwealth, saw an increasing trend for countries to adopt constitutions which detailed the human rights of their citizens. Indeed, the most important single impetus to the spread of human rights thinking was provided by World War II and its aftermath.

The Nuremberg Trials, at which Nazi leaders were arraigned for crimes against humanity, set a key precedent for the development of human rights.

The European Convention on Human Rights

The European Convention on Human Rights (ECHR) is a treaty of the Council of Europe, which was set up after World War II with the aim of re-establishing democratic government in Europe. At a meeting in The Hague in 1948, the Congress of Europe established the 10-member Council of Europe, whose statute read:

> "Every member of the Council of Europe must accept the principles of the rule of law and the enjoyment by all persons within its jurisdiction of human rights and individual freedoms."

This founding statute was signed in May 1949. One of the main objectives of the newly formed Council was to draft a Human Rights Charter. The Convention for the Protection of Human Rights and Fundamental Freedoms was signed in November 1950 and entered into force on 3 September 1953.

Some rights contained in the ECHR are absolute in that there are no circumstances in which the rights can be overridden, whereas other rights are qualified in as much as the exercise of these rights is subject to limitation clauses prescribed by law. Article 3 (the prohibition of torture, inhuman and degrading treatment or punishment); Article 4(1) (prohibition of slavery); and Article 7 (prohibition on the retrospective application of criminal law) are all examples of absolute rights. In contrast, Article 8 (the right to respect for private and family life, home and correspondence); Article 9 (freedom of thought, conscience and religion); Article 10 (freedom of expression); and Article 11 (freedom of assembly and association) are all qualified rights and are subject to limitations and specific circumstances.

Although Britain was one of the first members of the Council of Europe to sign up to the ECHR and accept its jurisdiction, it did not allow people in the United Kingdom to take cases to Strasbourg until 1966, and it did not take legislative action to incorporate Convention rights into domestic law until the Human Rights Act was enacted in 1998.

The Human Rights Act 1998

The Humans Rights Act 1998 made the ECHR enforceable in all UK courts from 2 October 2000. The Act gave certain provisions of the ECHR and its protocols legal status in UK law. In effect, it means that all public authorities are bound by the provisions of the ECHR. Public authorities include Government departments, local authorities, courts and schools. The Human Rights Act also requires that existing rights and obligations, including those under statute, should be interpreted in a way that is consistent with the Convention. The Human Rights Act specifically acknowledges the principle of Parliamentary sovereignty by providing that, where a court decides that a legislative provision is incompatible with the ECHR, "a declaration of incompatibility" may be made but that it is then for Parliament to decide whether the provision should be changed. Tony Blair commented that the Human Rights Act 1998 was intended to:

> "give people in the United Kingdom opportunities to enforce their rights under the European Convention and British Courts rather than having to incur the cost and delay of taking a case to the European Human Rights Court in Strasbourg."[3]

The Commission on Human Rights

The original structure for the enforcement of the ECHR involved a preliminary screening procedure, which was in the hands of a European Commission on Human Rights, based in Luxembourg. The Commission was empowered to receive from any State party to the Convention any allegation of a breach of the Convention by another State party. The Commission could also receive petitions from any person, group of individuals or non-governmental organisation claiming to be the victim of a violation of the Commission. However, this was amended by the Contracting States with effect from 1 November 1998 so as to do away with the Commission and put all stages of the procedure for determining human rights applications in the hands of the European Court of Human Rights at Strasbourg.

The European Court of Human Rights

The European Court of Human Rights, which sits in Strasbourg (not to be confused with the Court of Justice of the European Union, which sits in Luxembourg), has the job of interpreting the European Convention on Human Rights.

The court structure involves three different types of bodies: committees, chambers and a Grand Chamber. The bulk of the court's work is carried out in chambers, which each comprise seven judges. Committees, comprising three judges appointed from the chamber, have powers to strike out applications or declare them inadmissible.

The chambers include as a member the judge elected in respect of the State party whose conduct is being challenged or a substitute nominated by that State. Should the case before it raise a serious question affecting the

---

[3] *Childcare in Practice*, Volume 6, Issue 3. July 2000, pp. 288–294.

interpretation of the ECHR, or be likely to result in a decision inconsistent with previous judgments of the court, the matter can, if none of the parties objects, be referred to a Grand Chamber of 17 judges, which includes the President of the Court, his or her deputies and the Presidents of the Chambers. A case can also be referred to the Grand Chamber after judgment at the request of one of the parties. The case is referred to the Grand Chamber under this provision by a five-judge panel whose decision to reject is not appealable. The Grand Chamber can also hear a request from the Committee of Ministers of the Council of Europe for an advisory opinion on legal questions relating to the interpretation of the Convention.

Article 20 of the Convention states that the number of judges of the European Court of Human Rights shall equal the number of States adhering to the Convention. The judges sit as individuals and not as national representatives. They should be of high moral character and "must either possess the qualifications required for appointment to high judicial office or be jurisconsults of recognised competence". The judges are appointed for six-year terms and must retire when they reach the age of 70. Decisions of the European Court of Human Rights are binding on all the States involved in the case although, in practice, States wait some time before altering their national law to bring it into line with the pronouncements of the court. On occasion, the court may order a national government to pay compensation to an aggrieved party; however, in most cases, the decision that the Convention has been breached is deemed by the court to be a sufficient remedy. The ultimate decision for ensuring that the court's decisions are executed in the Member States concerned belongs to the Committee of Ministers of the Council of Europe.

Jurisdiction of the European Court of Human Rights

The European Court of Human Rights has compulsory jurisdiction over all matters concerning the interpretation and application of the ECHR which come about by way of interstate complaints, individual applications or an application for a ruling on the interpretation of the Convention. Applicants must have exhausted all domestic remedies and made their application within six months of the date on which those remedies were exhausted. Anonymous applications or applications concerning matters which have already been determined by the court or by some other international proceeding will not be entertained. Nor will the court consider applications incompatible with the ECHR or those that are manifestly ill founded or an abuse of the right of application.

One such area which has been tested in the European Court of Human Rights is that of dignity of life and assisted suicide. For example, in the case of *Pretty v. Director of Public Prosecutions* (2001), a terminally ill applicant wanted her husband to assist her to commit suicide at a time and in a manner of her choosing. However, the applicant was aware that her husband could be liable to prosecution under section 2(1) of the Suicide Act 1961, which makes it an offence to aid, abet, counsel or procure the suicide of another. In an effort to prevent her husband being prosecuted, the applicant asked that the Director of Public Prosecutions (DPP) not prosecute her husband as she believed that the offence was inconsistent with her right to life under the Convention (Article 2). However, the DPP could not give this promise to the applicant. The applicant subsequently brought a case to the European Court of Human Rights, contending that her rights under a number of Articles, including Articles 2 and 3 of the ECHR, were being infringed. The court held that the right to the dignity of life was not a right to die with dignity but a right to live with as much dignity as possible until that life reached its natural end. Therefore, the court concluded that the 1961 Act was not incompatible with the applicant's right under the ECHR.

A number of subsequent similar cases have been brought in the European Court of Human Rights and all have found that a right to the dignity of life is not a right to die with dignity. No doubt, there will be many similar cases brought to court that will receive similar attention.

References

- Catherine Barnard, *The Substantive Law of the EU: The Four Freedoms* (2nd Edition, Oxford University Press, 2007).
- Brice Dickson, "Legal Services" in Brice Dickson and Deborah McBride (eds), *Digest of Northern Ireland Law* (SLS Legal Publications (NI), 1995–1996).
- Brice Dickson, *The Legal System of Northern Ireland* (5th Edition, SLS Legal Publications (NI) 2005).
- Sharon Turner, "The Legal System of the European Community" in Brice Dickson and Deborah McBride (eds), *Digest of Northern Ireland Law* (SLS Legal Publications (NI), 1995–1996).
- John Wadham and Helen Mountfield, *Blackstone's Guide to the Human Rights Act 1998* (2nd Edition, Oxford University Press, 2000).

REVIEW QUESTIONS

(See Suggested Solutions at the end of this textbook.)

Question 1.1

ABC Accounting Services ('ABC') has contracted with IT Solutions Ltd. ('IT Solutions') for the past six years in relation to the implementation and servicing of its accountancy software systems. ABC has now decided to terminate the contract with IT Solutions and to employ its own in-house IT expert.

Requirement: ABC has recently discovered that an employee has been lodging client funds into his own personal account. ABC's solicitor has advised them that there are civil and criminal consequences for this action. Advise ABC on the distinction between criminal law and civil law. Your answer should also outline the various civil and criminal courts.

(Source: Chartered Accountants Ireland, CAP 1, Law for Accountants (NI),
Autumn 2008, Extract: Q4(c))

Question 1.2

Peter has been employed as an accountant with a pharmaceutical research company for the last 12 years. His contract describes him as an "independent contractor" and he receives payment at an hourly rate following the submission of monthly invoices, without the deduction of tax and social insurance.

The research company provides Peter with his own office, which is equipped with a computer, phone, fax and internet access. His normal hours of work are 9 am to 5 pm Monday to Friday. During his 12 years' employment, the research company has paid for Peter to undertake training and professional courses, he has regularly attended company social events, and is a member of the company's pension and medical insurance scheme.

Peter's contract requires him to obey all reasonable instructions, to comply with the company's employment policies, to sign a confidentiality agreement and to refrain from working for a competitor whilst in the employment of the company.

The company, which has recently been experiencing financial difficulties, called Peter to a meeting yesterday and informed him that they were terminating his contract with immediate effect. Peter asked whether he was entitled to any redundancy for the loss of his job, but the company informed him that redundancy only applies to employees and not independent contractors.

In light of recent difficulties at the research company, they have decided to update their employment policies to ensure that they comply with current legislation. In undertaking this review, they have discovered that most of the law governing protective leave in Northern Ireland is European in origin.

Requirement: Explain to the company the distinction between European Regulations and European Directives, outlining why the EU has the option of legislating in two different ways.

(Source: Chartered Accountants Ireland, CAP 1, Law for Accountants (NI),
Summer 2008, Extract: Q4(c))

Question 1.3

The Companies Act 2006 is a piece of primary legislation passed by the Parliament of the United Kingdom.

Requirement: Explain the process by which an Act of Parliament is passed.

(Source: Chartered Accountants Ireland, CAP 1, Law for Accountants (NI), Summer 2011, Extract: Q3(e).)

Question 1.4

Daffodil and Dandelions Ltd is involved in commercial litigation with a competitor for breach of some of their intellectual property rights. The case is listed for hearing in the High Court.

Requirement:
(a) Explain the composition of the High Court.
(b) List any THREE classifications of cases heard in the High Court.

(Source: Chartered Accountants Ireland, CAP 1, Law for Accountants (NI), Summer 2011, Extract: Q4(d).)

Question 1.5

ABC Ltd have heard that much of the legislation governing businesses today is generated from the European Union.

Requirement: Identify for ABC Ltd the types of legislation that exist within European Union Law.

(Source: Chartered Accountants Ireland, CAP 1, Law for Accountants (NI), Autumn 2011, Extract: Q4(c).)

Question 1.6

Sarah has worked at a university since 2000 as a clinical demonstrator within the biology department. On commencement of her employment, Sarah's contract stated that she was being employed under a 'contract for services'. Since her appointment, Sarah has worked for 12 weeks in the first semester, eight weeks in the second semester and four weeks in the third semester.

Before each semester commenced, she was always told the start and end time for classes. She was also given a teaching syllabus, told what was required in each class and had set hours each week. Sarah was also required to write an exam paper and after correction of exam papers she was required to be present at the exam board, where results were being reviewed and validated.

In September 2011, Sarah was told that the university would no longer be requiring her services and not to return for the next semester. Sarah is now considering suing the university for unfair dismissal, but she has been told, by a colleague, that she does not have a contract of employment but instead works under a contract for services and she cannot bring such a claim.

Sarah thinks that her claim is going to be heard in the High Court, but you have told her that employment matters are dealt with in the Industrial Tribunal.

Requirement: Explain briefly, to Sarah, the courts structure within Northern Ireland.

(Source: Chartered Accountants Ireland, CAP 1, Law for Accountants (NI), Summer 2012, Extract: Q2(d).)

Question 1.7

Your firm has acquired a new client, BlueSky Ltd. You are part of the team on the first audit of Bluesky Ltd. One of your tasks in the audit is to audit the travel expenses incurred by the company's management team in the past year. In so doing, you discover that Gary, the company's accountant, made numerous claims for trips abroad, which he claimed were work related. Further investigation has revealed that these trips were personal holidays and completely unrelated to his work. The firm's solicitor has advised that there could be both civil and criminal proceeding against Gary based on his fraudulent claims.

Requirement: Explain to BlueSky Ltd the distinction between criminal law and civil law, under any FOUR headings.

(Source: Chartered Accountants Ireland, CAP 1, Law for Accountants (NI), Autumn 2012, Extract: Q2(a).)

Question 1.8

Dylan has just discovered that a former employee is bringing an action against the college for damages for an accident that he sustained at work. The amount of damages sought by the employee is £20,000. Dylan is unsure as to whether this action will be heard in the High Court or the County Court.

Requirement:
(a) Discuss whether the above case will be heard in the High Court or the County Court.
(b) Discuss the Jurisdiction of the High Court.

(Source: Chartered Accountants Ireland, CAP 1, Law for Accountants (NI), Autumn 2013, Extract: Q1(c).)

Question 1.9

In order to establish her bakery business, Bella purchases a food processor from Premier Kitchen Supplies ('Premier'). When she was purchasing this item, Bella had a detailed discussion with one of the shop assistants and explained to her the various purposes for which this machine would be used. In particular, she informed the assistant that the food processor was for commercial use, and needed to be durable. Bella purchased the Kitchen Ninja 1400, based on the recommendations of the shop assistant. However, within one month of use, a number of issues arose with the machine. In particular, the rotator blade became blunt and the machine stopped mixing at high speeds. When Bella contacted the manufacturers of the Kitchen Ninja 1400, she explained the problems she was encountering with the processor, but they explained to her that this machine was only ever designed for non-commercial use and was unable to deal with the quantity and frequency of commercial use. Bella then contacted Premier about this issue, but they are refusing to deal with her, stating that the company operates a no-refunds policy. Bella is now considering bringing an action against Premier for breach of the Consumer Rights Act 2015.

When Bella contacted her solicitor about her problems with Premier, he informed her that if this case proceeded to litigation, precedent would be used to determine the meaning of merchantable quality and fitness for purpose. Bella does not understand the meaning of the word 'precedent' and seeks your advice.

Requirement: Define the meaning of the term 'precedent' AND discuss the rules of precedent, with reference to the hierarchy of the courts.

(Source: Chartered Accountants Ireland, CAP 1, Law for Accountants (NI),
Summer 2014, Extract: Q1(c))

Question 1.10

Explain the structure of the High Court within Northern Ireland.

(Source: Chartered Accountants Ireland, CAP 1, Law for Accountants (NI),
Autumn 2014, Extract: Q2(c).)

Question 1.11

Explain the role and court structure of the European Court of Human Rights.

(Source: Chartered Accountants Ireland, CAP 1, Law for Accountants (NI),
Summer 2015, Extract: Q1(c)).

Question 1.12

Harrison's architects have informed him that a statute prohibits the use of his leased premises for industrial purposes. Harrison does not consider his use to be industrial, but is aware that the term of this statute may be interpreted in a variety of ways, although he is unsure of the rules of interpretation.

Requirement: Advise Harrison on the THREE main methods of statutory interpretation that can be applied by the court.

(Source: Chartered Accountants Ireland, CAP 1, Law for Accountants (NI), Autumn 2015, Extract: Q1(g)).

CHAPTER 2

THE LAW OF TORT

Introduction to Tort Law

A tort is a **civil wrong**. If an individual commits a tort, it will enable the person who has suffered the wrong to claim redress in the civil courts. In society, it is inevitable that people will suffer injury, loss, damage or some sort of annoyance on account of the activities of others. The function of tort law is to establish whether or not the losses suffered by individuals have a remedy in the courts. Some areas of tort are covered by statute law (for example, the Occupier's Liability (Northern Ireland) Order 1987 (1987 No. 1280 N.I. 15)) while other areas of tort law are decided by case law (for example, defamation, trespass to a person, trespass to land, etc.).

It should be noted that the same set of circumstances can give rise to a civil claim (i.e. a claim in tort, which is within the area of private law) and a criminal offence (i.e. a public law matter). For example, a person can be prosecuted for assault and face a fine and/or imprisonment (public law remedy). The victim, who was assaulted, can sue the person who committed the tort, for monetary compensation, in the civil courts (private law remedy).

Examples of Tort

Negligence

Negligence is a tort that is concerned with the failure to exercise the care that a reasonable person would exercise. In *Blyth v. Birmingham Waterworks Co. Ltd* (1856), Baron Alderson defined negligence in the following terms:

> "Negligence is the omission to do something which a reasonable man, guided upon those considerations which ordinarily regulate the conduct of human affairs, would do, or doing something which a prudent and reasonable man would not do."

The tort of negligence is a very broad tort and is discussed in further detail below.

Defamation

The tort of defamation involves making a false and defamatory statement about another without lawful justification. Defamation can arise out of words spoken or written by someone, broadcasting, the Internet, caricatures, etc.

Nuisance

Nuisance is an activity that causes offence, annoyance or harm to others. Two types of nuisance exist: private and public. Private nuisance occurs when someone is adversely affected in the use or enjoyment of his land or of some right over or interest in land. Public nuisance is an act or omission which affects the community or a class of people at large.

Trespass

Trespass occurs when an individual directly interferes with the land or buildings in the possession of another.

Occupiers' Liability

Occupiers' liability is concerned with the loss sustained by persons at an occupier's premises. Liability to lawful visitors is covered under the Occupiers' Liability (Northern Ireland) Order 1957, while liability to non-visitors is covered under the Occupiers' Liability (Northern Ireland) Order 1987.

Vicarious Liability

An employer is responsible for damage caused by the torts of his employees acting in the course of employment. This is known as 'vicarious liability'; it is a form of strict liability because it arises from the employer–employee relationship. One example of vicarious liability is the common law duty owed by an employer to an employee to provide competent fellow workers. In an employment relationship, it involves an employer being liable for the wrongs committed by an employee where there is a sufficient connection with the employment. It arises even if the employer itself has committed no wrong. Vicarious liability most often occurs in employment relationships.

The Tort of Negligence

As stated above, the tort of negligence is concerned with the conduct of a reasonable person and the failure to exercise the care a reasonable person would exercise. A helpful analysis of negligence is found in the opinion of Lord

Wright in the case of *Lochgelly Iron and Coal Co. Ltd v. McMullan* (1934) in which he states:

> "... negligence means more than heedless or careless conduct, whether in omission or commission: it properly connotes the complex concept of duty, breach and damage thereby suffered by the person to whom the duty was owing."

The tort of negligence, therefore, comprises three elements:
1. *Duty of Care* This is concerned with whether there was a duty of care owed by one individual to another.
2. *Breach of the Duty of Care* This determines whether or not the duty of care which ought to have been exercised by one individual fell short of that which should have been adopted.
3. *Damage* This element assesses whether there was injury or loss sustained as a result of the breach of the duty of care.

1. Duty of Care

In order to sustain an action in tort, the first step is for the plaintiff to establish that a *duty of care* was owed by the defendant to the plaintiff. This is sometimes referred to as either the '**neighbour principle**' test or the '**proximity**' test.

The first case to establish this principle was *Donoghue v. Stevenson* (1932). In this case, the plaintiff drank a bottle of ginger beer manufactured by the defendant, which had been purchased by a friend for the plaintiff's consumption. The bottle containing the ginger beer was opaque. It was opened by the shopkeeper who supplied it and an amount of the drink was poured into a glass. The plaintiff took a drink from the glass. The plaintiff's friend thereafter poured the remainder of the ginger beer into the glass when a decomposing snail which had been in the bottle emerged. As a result, the plaintiff claimed that she had contracted a serious illness and sued the manufacturer in negligence. The basis of the plaintiff's claim was that the defendant had been negligent in that, as the manufacturer of a product intended for consumption, which product was contained in a bottle that prevented intermediate inspection, he owed a duty to her as the ultimate consumer of the product.

The decision of the House of Lords upheld the plaintiff's claim. The House of Lords decided that the manufacturer of products, which are sold in such a form as to show the intention to reach the ultimate consumer in the form in which they left the manufacturer, with no reasonable possibility of intermediate examination, and with the knowledge that the absence of reasonable care and the preparation or putting up of the products will result in injury to the consumer's life or property, owes a duty to the consumer to take reasonable care. The House of Lords held that the defendant had failed to take reasonable care and was therefore liable to the plaintiff for the injury which she sustained. The House of Lords further decided that a duty of care is owed to any person whom we can reasonably foresee will be injured by our acts or omissions. The court described such persons as 'neighbours'. It was held that the defendant could reasonably foresee that somebody apart from the original purchaser may consume this product and he was therefore held liable to the plaintiff. As Lord Atkin stated:

"[Y]ou must take reasonable care to avoid any acts and omissions which you could reasonably foresee would be likely to injure your neighbour. Who, then, in law, is my neighbour? ... persons who are so closely and directly affected by my act that I ought reasonably to have them in contemplation as being so affected when I am directing my mind to the acts and omissions which are called in question."

This 'neighbour principle' had a significant effect on the tort of negligence and shaped the way the law in this area was to further develop.

Development of the Neighbour Principle: the Anns Case The case of *Anns v. Merton London Borough Council* (1978) reviewed the development of the tort of negligence and marked a substantial change in judicial attitude towards the concept of duty of care. The issue in this case was whether a local authority was under any duty of care towards the owners or occupiers of a building constructed by builders within their area, with respect to the inspection of the property during the building process. In this case, the plaintiffs were lessees of flats which had been built by the first defendant. The issue of liability was whether or not the second defendant (the local authority) owed to the plaintiffs a duty of care arising from an inspection of the foundations of the building during the construction process. The plaintiffs argued that by failing to inspect properly the foundations of the flats, the local authority, through its employees, had been negligent. The plaintiffs argued that upon a proper inspection it would have been clear that the foundations were not of a sufficient depth.

In what has famously become known as the 'Wilberforce Test', the court established a two-stage test to decide whether a duty of care arises. This approach is as follows:

1. Does a sufficient relationship of proximity or neighbourhood exist between the alleged wrongdoer and the person who has suffered the damage such that, in the reasonable contemplation of the former, carelessness on his part may be likely to cause damage to the latter, in which case a *prima facie* duty of care arises?
2. If the first question is answered affirmatively, are there any considerations which ought to negate, reduce or limit the scope of the duty, or the class

of persons to whom it is owed, or the damages to which a breach of it may give rise?

However, this restatement of the neighbour principle was subsequently considered to be too expansive and was criticised for adopting an overly broad approach. Hence, in *Peabody Donation Fund v. Sir Lindsay Parkinson & Co. Ltd* (1984), Lord Keith doubted the universal applicability of the proximity test. This doubt was affirmed by the House of Lords in *Leigh and Sullivan Ltd v. Aliakmon Shipping Co. Ltd* (1986) and in *Curran v. Northern Ireland Housing Association Ltd* (1987).

In 1990, the decision in the *Anns* case was eventually overruled by *Murphy v. Brentwood DC*. In this case, the plaintiff claimed £35,000 from the defendant as compensation for the reduction in the value of his house, which resulted from defects in its design. The defective design had been approved by the Council. The plaintiff relied on the *Anns* case. However, the House of Lords unanimously overruled the *Anns* decision on the grounds that it did not proceed on the basis of established principles but introduced a potentially indeterminate liability covering a wide range of situations. It was held that the loss in this case was purely economic (not physical) and was not therefore within the scope of the duty of care owed by the defendant to the plaintiff.

The ultra cautious approach espoused in the *Murphy* case was further applied in *Caparo Industries plc v. Dickman* (1990). In this case, the plaintiff company sued two directors of Fidelity Plc and the accountants Touche Ross & Co, the auditors of Fidelity. The plaintiff had taken over Fidelity and alleged that the profits were much lower than shown in the audited accounts and consequently they had suffered financial loss. The House of Lords had to consider whether a duty of care was owed to persons who rely on the accounts to deal with the company or to buy and sell its shares. The House of Lords introduced a new three-stage test for establishing a duty of care which requires consideration of the following questions:
1. Was the harm caused reasonably foreseeable?
2. Was there a relationship of proximity between the defendant and the plaintiff?
3. In all the circumstances, was it just, fair and reasonable to impose a duty of care?

This approach differs to that laid down by Lord Wilberforce in *Anns*. In the *Anns* test, once proximity and foreseeability were established, a duty of care was presumed. However, the distinction in the *Caparo* test is that once relational proximity and foreseeability are established, a plaintiff must then go on to show that it is just and reasonable to impose a duty of care.

2. Breach of the Duty of Care

As stated above, the second element to the tort of negligence is breach of the duty of care. This is the extent to which the law requires a person to exercise reasonable care and skill to prevent harm to others. In order to establish whether or not a defendant breached the duty of care, an objective test is used, i.e. 'the reasonable man test'.

The 'Reasonable Man' Who is the 'reasonable man'? The case of *Hall v. Brooklands Auto Racing Club* (1933) summed up the reasonable man as being the average man, or the man on "the Clapham omnibus". Hence the ordinary reasonable man is very much a notional person and, indeed, the concept has been criticised due to the differing judicial interpretations of who is a reasonable man and what he may properly be said to be able to foresee.

The Objective Standard The standard of care expected of the reasonable man is objective. In every negligence case, it is left to the trial judge to determine what is reasonable and what could have been foreseen. The point is well illustrated by *Nettleship v. Weston* (1971) in which the defendant was a learner driver who crashed into a lamp post and injured the front-seat passenger. The defendant was convicted of driving without due care and attention but, initially, the plaintiff's claim was dismissed because the defendant had been doing her best to control the car. On appeal, however, the Court of Appeal held that the standard of care required of a learner driver is the same as that required for any other driver, namely that of a reasonably competent and experienced driver. The driver's incompetent best was not good enough. The defendant's driving had fallen below the standard and it was irrelevant that this was because of her inexperience.

Hence, in assessing what is reasonable conduct, regard must be had to the particular defendant in question, together with the circumstances of the case. In *Roberts v. Ramsbottom* (1980), the defendant collided head on with a parked vehicle, causing injury to its occupants. The defendant claimed that he was not liable because 20 minutes earlier he had unknowingly suffered a stroke. The defendant claimed that this affected his mind so much that he could not drive properly. It also meant that he could not appreciate that he was unfit to drive. The court, however, found that he did have sufficient awareness of his surroundings and traffic conditions to continue to control the car although in an inadequate way. It was held that, where a driver retains some control, even if imperfect, he must be judged by the objective standard of a reasonable driver. In the circumstances of this case, although the defendant was not morally to blame because of the nature of his symptoms, he had fallen below the objective standard and was therefore liable.

The objective standard that must be applied to the reasonable man can be further analysed by reference to foreseeable harm and the risk of harm.

Unforeseen Harm If a particular danger could not reasonably have been anticipated, the defendant has not acted in breach of his duty of care because a reasonable man would not take precautions against an unforeseeable consequence. Foresight of the consequence is measured by reference to knowledge at the time of the event. In *Roe v. Minister of Health* (1954), during the course of an operation, the plaintiff was paralysed by anaesthetic which had become contaminated by disinfectant. The anaesthetic had been kept in glass ampoules which were stored in the disinfectant and became contaminated by seepage through invisible cracks in the glass. At the time of the accident, in 1947, this risk was not known. The Court of Appeal held that the hospital authorities were not liable because the danger was not reasonably foreseeable. Lord Denning said that the court, "must not look at the 1947 accident with 1954 spectacles". However, he did state that it would have been negligent to adopt the same practice in 1954. Likewise, in *Glasgow Corporation v. Moore* (1943), the defendants were not liable for a spillage of scalding water because there was no reason to anticipate the accident and therefore no precautions were reasonably necessary. It is not necessary, however, for the particular damage that occurred to be foreseeable in a general way.

The Risk of Harm A defendant is not negligent if the damage was not a foreseeable consequence of his conduct. For example, in *Bolton v. Stone* (1951), the defendant cricket club was exonerated from liability when a cricket ball was hit out of the cricket ground onto the highway, striking and injuring the plaintiff. The possibility of such an event occurring was clearly foreseeable as balls had been hit from the ground before. However, the fact that this had happened only on very rare occasions (six times in 30 years), meant that the risk in the circumstances was one which a reasonable man could appropriately choose not to guard against. In the case, Lord Oaksey said:

> "the standard of care in the law of negligence is a standard of an ordinarily careful man but, in my opinion, an ordinarily careful man does not take precautions against every foreseeable risk. He can, of course, foresee the possibility of many risks but life would be almost impossible if he were to attempt to take precautions against every risk which he can foresee. He takes precautions against risk which are reasonably likely to happen. Many foreseeable risks are extremely unlikely to happen and cannot be guarded against except by almost complete isolation."

3. Damage

The third strand of the test for a plaintiff to bring a successful claim in tort is to show that the plaintiff suffered damage (i.e. injury or loss) and also that it was the defendant's wrongdoing which caused that injury or loss. In order to prove damage, **causation** must be established.

Causation Causation deals with the physical connection that links the defendant's negligence with the plaintiff's damage. The first issue to decide is whether the defendant's act or omission to act was the cause of the plaintiff's loss. The methodology that lawyers use to determine this issue is called the **'but for'** test. If the harm to the plaintiff would not have occurred 'but for' the defendant's negligence, then that negligence is the cause of the harm. This principle can be seen in the case of *Barnett v. Chelsea and Kensington Hospital Management Committee* (1969). In this case, the plaintiff went to the hospital complaining of vomiting and was sent away without being examined. He died shortly afterwards and the plaintiff's widow sued the hospital for negligence. The court held that the plaintiff had to show that 'but for' the actions of the hospital, her husband would not have died. The court found that the plaintiff would have died whatever action the hospital had taken and so the hospital, despite a careless examination, were not liable in the tort of negligence. Likewise, in *Robinson v. Post Office* (1974), a doctor's omission to test for an allergic reaction to an anti-tetanus vaccination was not causally related to the patient's subsequent reaction because the test would not have revealed the allergy in time.

It is more difficult to draw a conclusion using the 'but for' test where, rather than being based upon objective scientific proof, the court has to speculate as to what might have occurred had the defendant behaved in a different way. In *McWilliams v. Sir William Arrol & Co. Ltd* (1962), the plaintiff's occupation was as a steel erector. He fell to his death, during his employment, as he was not wearing a safety belt. Though his employers were in breach of a statutory duty to supply safety belts, the House of Lords held that they were not liable because it was probable that the deceased would not have worn the belt if it had been available. The deceased had rarely, if ever, used a safety belt in the past and so it was a natural inference that he would *not* have worn a belt on this occasion. Lord Reid commented that though it would not be right to draw such an inference too readily, because people do sometimes change their minds unexpectedly, the evidence in this case was "overwhelming".

This type of causation problem also arises in cases where a patient alleges that his doctor has been negligent in failing to disclose information about the risks of a proposed medical procedure. For example, in the case of *Sidaway v.*

Bethlem Royal Hospital Governors (1985), even if the plaintiff overcame the problem of establishing negligence, he still had to prove that, had the information been disclosed, he would have declined the treatment, thereby avoiding the risk.

It is for the plaintiff to prove, on the balance of probabilities, that the defendant's breach of duty caused the damage. In some cases, the precise cause of the damage may be unknown and this can be a particular problem with some types of medical condition. This also can place an impossible burden on the plaintiff. In *McGhee v. National Coal Board* (1972), the plaintiff, who worked at the defendant's brick kilns, contracted dermatitis. There were no facilities for washing off the brick dust after work and this materially increased the risk of contracting the disease. At the time, the current state of medical knowledge could not determine whether it was possible that the plaintiff would not have contracted the disease if he had been able to take a shower after work. The House of Lords held that it was sufficient for a plaintiff to show the defendant's breach of duty made the risk of injury more probable even though it was uncertain whether it was the actual cause. The case is noteworthy in that the plaintiff succeeded without having proved that the defendants had caused him any harm. They had merely increased the risk of injury to him.

Once the court has eliminated irrelevant factual causes by use of the 'but for' test, it must still consider which factual cause is to be regarded as the cause in law of the plaintiff's damage, namely, the cause for the purpose of attributing legal liability.

If there are two causes, each of which would be sufficient to cause the harm and which occur simultaneously, the practical solution is to say that both caused the harm. Where the two events are separated in time, it might be thought that the simple answer would be that the first event should be treated as the cause. Certainly, this is the case where it is the tort that comes second. In *Performance Cars Ltd v. Abraham* (1921), the defendant collided with the plaintiff's Rolls Royce and the damage would have necessitated a re-spray of part of the vehicle. However, the car had previously been damaged in the same position in an earlier accident and would have needed a re-spray to repair that damage. The defendant was not liable for the cost of the re-spray because having damaged an already damaged car, his negligence was not the cause of the loss. The decision in *Performance Cars Ltd v. Abraham* stems from the basic rule that the object of an award of damages in tort is to restore the plaintiff to the position he would have been in had the tort not occurred.

In *Baker v. Willoughby* (1970), the plaintiff's left leg was injured in a road accident caused by the defendant's negligence, and this affected his mobility and reduced his earning capacity. Subsequently, the plaintiff was shot in the same leg during the course of an armed robbery at his place of work and the leg had to be amputated. The defendant argued that the amputation obliterated the original injury so that he should have to compensate for the loss only up to the date of the robbery. Thereafter, the loss of mobility and earning capacity was the result of the shooting. The House of Lords, however, held that the defendant remained responsible for the plaintiff's initial disability after the date of the robbery and the amputation.

In the *Baker v. Willoughby* case, if the plaintiff had been able to sue the robbers, they would have been liable only for the additional loss that they had inflicted, not the whole disability. The defendant's argument would have left the plaintiff under-compensated because he would not have been compensated at all for the original injury after the robbery had occurred. It was clearly wrong that the plaintiff should fall between the two individuals in this way, receiving less in damages than he would have received had there been no interval between the two torts.

In *Jobling v. Associated Dairies Ltd* (1982), the facts were similar to *Baker v. Willoughby* except that the second event was not a wrongful act. In the *Baker* case, the second event, the robbery, was a wrongful act. In 1973, the plaintiff sustained a back injury as a result of his employer's negligence, which reduced his earning capacity by 50%. In 1976, he was found to be suffering from a disease unconnected with the accident, which prevented him from working at all. The House of Lords held that the defendants were liable only for the reduced earning capacity between 1973 and 1976 when the supervening disease terminated the responsibility. The decision in *Jobling v. Associated Dairies Ltd* is a policy-based one, and is based on the idea that the compensation for the period after the supervening illness would put the plaintiff in a better position than he would be in if he had never suffered the tortious injury.

Intervening Acts   Where the defendant's negligence forms part of a sequence of events leading to harm to the plaintiff and the act of another person intervenes between the defendant's negligence and the damage, the court must decide whether the defendant remains responsible or whether the acts can be regarded as breaking the chain of causation between the negligence and the damage, i.e. as '*novus actus interveniens*', which means 'new act intervening'. The result of a *novus actus interveniens* is to relieve the defendant completely from liability. This may be an act of the plaintiff himself or an act of a third party over whom the defendant has no control.

For example, in *Knightly v. Johns* (1982), the defendant, a motorist, negligently crashed his car, blocking a one-way traffic tunnel. A police inspector then told the plaintiff, a police constable, to ride the wrong way down the tunnel to stop motorists from entering. The plaintiff was injured when he struck a vehicle that was entering the tunnel. It was held that the defendant was not liable for the plaintiff's injuries since the plaintiff's accident was not a reasonably foreseeable result of the defendant's negligence.

Also, in the case of *Topp v. London Country Bus* (1993), the bus company left a bus unattended with the keys in the ignition for several hours. An unknown person stole the bus and drove it negligently, killing the wife of the plaintiff. It was held that, even if the defendants had been at fault, they were not responsible in law for the injury caused by the voluntary act of the third party since he was a complete stranger to them. Accordingly, there was no basis for interfering with the judge's decision. The act of the thief was a *novus actus interveniens* that broke the chain of causation.

Remoteness of Damage

Once causation has been established, the defendant may be able to escape payment for some or all of the damages claimed by showing that there was not a sufficiently close connection between the behaviour of the plaintiff and the damage suffered, i.e. that the loss is too remote. The law takes two different approaches here:

1. The first states that a defendant is liable for all the direct consequences of his own negligence, no matter how unusual or unexpected. This is essentially a test based on causation. Some independent intervening cause, either voluntary conduct or coincidence, would render the damage indirect.
2. The second test holds that a person is only responsible for consequences that were foreseeable.

Although, in theory, it is accepted that foreseeability is the correct test, in reality decisions as to exactly how foreseeable the consequences must be, in combination with the principles that a tortfeasor must take his victim as he finds them, means that the limits of actionability set by remoteness of damage lie somewhere between these two approaches. Thus, if the plaintiff would have suffered the same injury despite the defendant's conduct, he or she will not receive any compensation. Hence, the test for remoteness is objective. It does not matter what the defendant actually foresaw, but what a reasonable man would have foreseen as the consequences of the tort, had he applied his mind to it.

The test for remoteness was set out in *Overseas Tankship (UK) Ltd v. Morts Docks & Engineering Co. ("The Wagon Mound (No. 1)")* (1961). This case overruled *Re Polemis & Furness Withy & Company Ltd* (1921), which had stated that the defendant was liable for all loss, which was the "direct result" of the defendant's negligent act.

In *The Wagon Mound* case, an action was brought by the owners of a wharf against the owners of *The Wagon Mound* (a ship). This case attempted to introduce a cut-off point beyond which the defendant should not be liable. The ship had discharged oil into Sydney Harbour, which ignited when hot metal from welding operations being carried on in the harbour fell onto a piece of cotton waste floating in the oil. The court held that damage to the wharf by fouling was foreseeable, but not damage by fire, since oil on water does not usually ignite. The ignition of the oil only occurred because the hot metal fell onto highly combustible cotton waste. Such an event was not reasonably foreseeable.

The burden of proof, in negligence cases, is for the plaintiff to establish his case on the balance of probabilities. However, the principle of '*res ipsa loquitor*' ('the thing speaks for itself') states that, in some situations, a plaintiff will not need to prove a breach of the duty of care. The principle was first established in *Scott v. London & St Katherine Docks Co.* (1861–1873). In that case, the plaintiff was passing under a loading bay to a warehouse and six heavy sacks of sugar fell from the loading bay on the upper floor of the warehouse onto the plaintiff thereby causing him the injuries. There was no clear explanation as to how the sacks of sugar fell. The court upheld the plaintiff's claim and said that:

> "there must be reasonable evidence of negligence but, where the thing is shown to be under the management of the defendant, or his servants, and the accident is such as in the ordinary course of things does not happen if those who have the management of machinery use proper care, it affords reasonable evidence, in the absence of an explanation by the defendant, that the accident arose from want of care."

Likewise, in the case of *Mahon v. Osborne* (1939) a swab was left in a patient's body after an operation. Clearly, the patient could not prove a breach of duties since he was under an anaesthetic. However, the presence of the swab raised the inference of a breach of duty. The surgeon was unable to show that he had used reasonable care and was accordingly held liable.

This principle of *res ipsa loquitor* was again considered in the case of *Lloyd v. West Midlands Gas Board* (1971). In this case, it was held that a plaintiff establishes negligence where, even though it is not possible for him to prove precisely what was the relevant act or omission that set in train the events leading to the accident, on the evidence as it stands at the relevant time, it was more likely than not that the cause of the accident was some act or omission of the defendant or of someone for whom the defendant is responsible, which act or omission constitutes a failure to take proper care of the plaintiff's safety.

Negligent Misstatement

So far, our examination of the study of negligence has focused on how some-one can be liable for their act or omission to act, thereby resulting in damage to another individual. The courts, however, have also developed case law on liability for negligently making statements that cause economic loss to another individual. This type of negligence is called negligent misstatement.

It was the English case of *Hedley Byrne & Co. Ltd v. Heller & Partners Ltd* (1964) that established the principle of negligent misstatement. Heller & Partners were bankers to Easipower Ltd, which was a client of the plaintiff, who were advertising agents. Through their own bank, the plaintiffs made an enquiry to the defendants as to the financial standing of Easipower, mentioning an advertising contract for £1 million. The reply was headed "confidential for your private use and without responsibility on the part of the banker's officials". The letter said that:

> "Easipower was a respectably constituted company, considered good for its ordinary business engagements. Your figures are larger than we are accustomed to see."

Relying on this, the plaintiffs incurred expenditure on behalf of Easipower and lost £17,000 when the company went into liquidation. The plaintiffs alleged that the reference had been made carelessly and that the defendants owed them a duty to take reasonable care in giving this information. The House of Lords agreed that in the appropriate circumstances there could be such a duty. The defendants were not liable on the facts, however, because the disclaimer of responsibility made it unreasonable for the plaintiff to place reliance on the statement. Most importantly, the House of Lords set a precedent that auditors could be liable to persons whom they could foresee relying on the annual accounts that they had audited. The House of Lords referred to a "special relationship" (see below), which, in the view of Lord Reid, occurs:

> "where it is plain that the party seeking information or advice was trusting the other to exercise such a degree of care as the circumstances required, where it was reasonable for him to do that, and where the other gave the information or advice when he ought to have known that the enquirer was relying on him."

Lord Morris said that where a person is:

> "so placed that others could reasonably rely upon his judgement or his skill or upon his ability to make a careful enquiry, and a person takes it upon himself to give information or advice to, or allows his information or advice to be passed on to, another person who, as he knows or should know, will place reliance upon it, then a duty of care would arise."

Special Relationship

The crucial issue of what is a "special relationship" arose from the judgment in the *Hedley Byrne* case. It is apparent that the following requirements have to be satisfied:

1. the plaintiff must have relied on the defendant's skill and judgement or on his ability to make careful enquiry;
2. the defendant knew, or ought reasonably to have known, that the plaintiff was relying on him; and
3. it was reasonable in the circumstances for the plaintiff to rely on the defendant.

Since *Hedley v. Byrne*, the courts have used the concept of '**reasonable reliance**' as a way of placing limits on liability for negligent misstatements. Although knowledge or foreseeability of the plaintiff's reliance is necessary, it is not a sufficient criterion for limiting liability. For example, in the case of *Jebb Fasteners Ltd v. Marks, Bloom & Co.* (1983), it was held that auditors who prepared a company's accounts while knowing that the company was in difficulty and needed finance ought to have foreseen that a takeover was a possible source of finance, and that someone contemplating a takeover might rely on the accounts. Accordingly, the auditors owed a duty of care to that person in preparing the accounts. The accountant's duty would not extend, however, to "strangers of whom they have heard nothing and to whom their employee without their knowledge may choose to show their accounts". The defendants in *Jebb Fasteners* were held not to be liable because, even though the plaintiffs had relied on the accounts, this was not the cause of the loss because they would have taken over the company in any event. A plaintiff's reliance will only constitute a cause of his loss "as long as a misrepresentation plays a real and substantial part, though not by itself a decisive part, in inducing the plaintiff to act".

This view was reinforced in *Caparo Products Plc v. Dickman & Others* (1988) (as discussed above). To reiterate, the facts of this case were that on 8 June 1984, Caparo purchased 10,000 shares in Fidelity Plc. On 12 June, Fidelity's accounts for the year ending 31 March 1984 were issued to shareholders, including Caparo. Relying on those accounts, Caparo purchased a further 50,000 shares and subsequently made a successful takeover bid for Fidelity. In July 1985, Caparo brought an action against Touche Ross, the auditors of Fidelity, alleging negligence. Caparo alleged that Touche Ross owed a duty of care to investors and potential investors: they ought to have known that Fidelity's profits and share price had fallen and Fidelity required financial assistance and, therefore, they ought to have foreseen that Fidelity was vulnerable to a takeover bid, and persons such as Caparo might rely on its accounts in deciding whether to take over Fidelity and might suffer loss if the accounts were inaccurate. It was held by the House of Lords that, while it is foreseeable that investors may use published accounts to make investment decisions, the accountants who produce such accounts cannot be liable for losses if the results of the accounts are wrong. Indeed, as already stated above when discussing the development of the neighbour principle, the *Caparo* case set out the formula which is now used by the courts for determining a duty of care.

Professional Negligence

Professional negligence is not a distinct tort. Rather, it is a term applied to the liability of professional advisors to provide advice of a certain standard. In many instances, it may be a label for liability that arises under a more general heading, e.g. liability for negligent misstatements or economic loss.

Every professional body is governed by a set of standards that they must adhere to. If a professional adheres to those standards, he or she is likely to have a defence to a professional negligence case brought against them.

Barristers and Clients

The traditional view was that barristers did not owe a duty of care to their clients. This arose out of the fact that the Bar of Northern Ireland should remain free and independent. However, this thinking was abolished in the case of *Rondel v. Worsley* (1969), which established that there is a duty of care between a barrister and his or her client. However, when the barrister is acting in the role of an advocate, i.e. conducting proceedings before a court, this is not within the scope of any duty of care to the person whom he or she is representing. However, in the case of *Arthur J.S. Hall & Co. v. Simons & Others* (2000), the court held that it was no longer in the public interest that immunity for barristers remain in place. Hence, there is now a clarity of care even when before the court.

As indicated above, a barrister is not immune from a duty of care to his or her client when he is not acting as an advocate, meaning liability may ensue from an opinion given in chambers on a point of law or from paperwork drawn up by a barrister. This point was illustrated in the case of *Saif Alley v. Sidney Mitchell & Co.* (1980), where the defendant was found to be guilty of negligence. In this case, the barrister failed to institute proceedings on behalf of his client within the limitation period against certain defendants.

Solicitors and Clients

Unlike a barrister, a solicitor is in a direct contractual relationship with his client so he may also be liable to a client in tort as well as liable for breach of contract. Furthermore, a solicitor not only owes a duty of care to his client but also owes the duty of care to those persons who he knows will rely on his professional skill or who may suffer as a result of his carelessness (*Ross v. Caunters* (1980)).

In *Somasundaram v. M. Julius Melchior & Co.* (1988), the Court of Appeal took the view that it was an abuse of the process of the court to bring an action for negligence against solicitors where the action necessarily involved a collateral attack on the judgment of another court in a criminal or a civil matter. Solicitors were not, however, immune from suit in negligence in respect of their advice as to plain criminal proceedings.

A solicitor may not always be held to be negligent simply because a duty is held to exist. Indeed, many of the cases of professional negligence hinge more on breach rather than the scope of the duty owed. In *Booth and Andler v. Davey* (1988), a solicitor was held not to be liable in negligence in a transaction for the sale of land where, prior to the exchange of contracts, he read aloud to his clients the terms of the draft contract and gave them a copy to consider before signing it.

Likewise, in *Clarke v. Bruce Lance & Co. & Others* (1987), the Court of Appeal held that a testator's solicitors owed no duty of care to a potential beneficiary under a will to advise the testator that a particular transaction which the testator had entered into was likely to harm the potential beneficiary's interest.

Auditors and Accountants and Clients

Auditors and accountants have a duty of care to their clients and to their employers. This duty arises not only from the law of negligence, but also from the law of contract and from a fiduciary duty. As Lord Denning stated in *Candler v. Crane Christmas & Co.* (1951):

> "... to whom do these professional people owe this duty? I will take accountants, but the same reasoning applies to the others. They owe the duty of course to their employer or client; and also I think to any third person to whom they themselves show the accounts, so as to induce him to invest money or take some other action on them. But I do not think the duty can be extended still further to include strangers of whom they have heard nothing and to whom their employer without their knowledge may choose to show their accounts. Once the accountants have handed their accounts to their employer they are not, as a rule, responsible for what he does with them without their knowledge or consent ... The test of proximity in these cases is: did the accountants know that the accounts were required for submission to the plaintiff and use by him?"

All accountants and auditors, when carrying out their duties, must also exercise skill and care. The degree of skill and care, in relation to the depth of the investigation and the sorts of checks to be made, is not laid down in statute but rather has developed through decisions made by the judiciary.

The first case to establish the duty of care owed by auditors and accountants was *Re London and General Bank* (1895). In this case, the greater part of the capital of the bank, which was being wound up, had been advanced to four companies and a few special customers on securities which were insufficient and difficult to realise. The auditors drew attention to the situation in a confidential report to the directors, stressing its gravity, and ending by saying: "We cannot conclude without expressing our opinion unhesitatingly that no dividend should be paid this year." The Chairman, Mr Balfour, persuaded the auditors to strike this sentence out before the report was officially laid before the board of directors. The certificate, signed by the auditors and laid before the shareholders at the annual general meeting stated that "the value of the assets as shown on the balance sheet is dependent on realisation". It also said: "And on this point, we have reported specifically to the board." However, again, Mr Balfour persuaded them to withdraw this statement by promising to mention this in his speech to the shareholders, which he did without drawing special attention to it. The directors declared a dividend of 7%.

It was held by the Court of Appeal that the auditors had been guilty of misfeasance, and were liable to make good the amount of dividend paid. It is the duty of an auditor to consider and report to the shareholders, whether the balance sheet exhibits a correct view of the state of the company's affairs, and the true financial position at the time of the audit. In the course of his judgment, Lord Justice Lindley said:

> "An auditor ... is not an insurer; he does not guarantee that the books correctly show the true position of the company's affairs; he does not even guarantee that his balance sheet is accurate according to the books of the company ... but, he must be honest, i.e. he must not certify what he does not believe to be true, and he must use reasonable skill and care before he believes that what he certifies is true. What is reasonable care in any particular case must depend upon the circumstances of the case."

The principal case with regard to the duty of care owed by both accountants and auditors is that of *Hedley v. Byrne* (1964) (discussed above under Negligent Misstatement). As shown, this case established that a duty of care exists when one person making an inquiry trusts the other to exercise reasonable care and skill in giving advice, and the other person, in giving the advice, knows or ought to know that their advice is being relied upon.

The present position with regard to the duty of care owed by accountants and auditors was the subject of comprehensive analysis by the House of Lords in *Caparo Industries plc v. Dickman* (1990) (discussed above in the Special Relationship section). *Caparo* established that a duty of care is owed to existing shareholders, but not to potential investors, as an auditor cannot know that their advice is going to be relied upon.

However, in the case of *Morgan Crucible Co. Plc v. Hill Samuel Bank Ltd* (1991), the Court of Appeal held that a duty of care can exist if an auditor is aware of both user and use for which this advice is going to be relied upon. The facts of this case were that Morgan Crucible bid for First Castle Electronics and its bid was rejected by the board of First Castle. Hill Samuel were advisors to Morgan Crucible. Further advice was provided by Hill Samuel to Morgan Crucible and this advice referred to earlier financial statements, namely the company's most recently published reports and accounts. The advice forecast a 38% increase in pre-tax profits. Morgan Crucible therefore increased their bid after that and subsequently gained control of the company. However, the investment subsequently proved worthless and Morgan Crucible brought a claim against Hill Samuel for negligence. The court held that a duty of care did exist in this case. The distinction between this case and *Caparo* is that:

> "mere foreseeability that a potential bidder may rely on the audited accounts does not impose on the auditor a duty of care to the bidder, but if the auditor is expressly made aware that a particular identified bidder will rely on the audited accounts or other statements approved by the auditor, and intends that the bidder should so rely, the auditor will be under a duty of care to the bidder for the breach of which he may be liable." (*Galoo Ltd v. Bright Grahame Murray* (1994))

Defences in Tort

There are a number of general defences which may be raised to any tort action. A successful defence will absolve the defendant from wrongdoing.

Contributory Negligence

Prior to 1945, at common law, if a plaintiff was guilty of any negligence that contributed to a cause of an accident, he recovered nothing. However, the Law Reform (Miscellaneous Provisions) Act (Northern Ireland) 1948 now sets out the principle of 'contributory negligence'. Section 2(1) provides that the damages will be reduced according to his or her share of responsibility:

> "Where any person suffers damage as the result partly of his own fault and partly of the fault of any other person or persons, a claim in respect

of that damage shall not be defeated by reason of the fault of the person suffering the damage, that the damages recoverable in respect thereof shall be reduced to such an extent as the Court thinks just and equitable having regard to the Claimant's share and the responsibility for the damage ..."

For example, in *O'Connell v. Jackson* (1971), the defendant, a car driver, knocked the plaintiff off his moped, the accident being entirely the defendant's fault. The plaintiff suffered severe head injuries which would have been less serious if he had been wearing a crash helmet. It was held that the damages would be reduced by 15%.

Likewise, in *Froom v. Butcher* (1976), it was held that failure to wear a seat belt amounted to contributory negligence and so the plaintiff's damages were reduced by 20%.

Mistake

It is generally accepted that mistake is no defence to a tort action. However, there are exceptions to this rule but the outcome of the defence rests upon whether or not the defendant acted reasonably in making the mistake. For example, if a policeman, without warrant, arrests somebody who has not committed a crime but the policeman reasonably believes that they have, the plaintiff may have no redress against the policeman in tort if the policeman can prove that this belief was genuine.

Act of God

This defence applies to accidents or injuries which human foresight could not guard against or have avoided. For example, in the case of *Nichols v. Marsland* (1876) the defendant constructed a series of artificial pools by damming a natural stream. The pools were well constructed and adequate in all normal circumstances. However, they were destroyed by a storm of exceptional violence with resulting damage to the plaintiff's bridges. It was held that no one had been negligent and the accident was due entirely to an act of God.

Self-defence

A person may use reasonable force to defend himself, or his property, or another person against unlawful force, and this may be a defence in tort.

Statute Barred

A claim is said to be statute barred if it is not brought within the proper time limit. The limitation period for a plaintiff to bring a claim for personal injuries is three years from the date of accrual of the cause of the action (e.g. accident) or the date of knowledge (if later) of the injury. Actions must be commenced within this statutory limitation period or else the plaintiff will lose the right to sue. To defend a claim in this regard, the defendant should plead the Limitation (Northern Ireland) Order 1989 (1989 No. 1339 (N.I. 11)).

Volenti Non Fit Injuria

Volenti non fit injuria means literally that "there is no injury to one who consents". If a defendant can prove the existence of a voluntary agreement on the part of the plaintiff to agree to either consent to an 'intentional tort' or to voluntarily assume the risk attaching to the endeavour which caused him harm, this constitutes an absolute defence to liability.

Mitigation of Loss

If a plaintiff fails to take reasonable steps to minimise his injuries, he is deemed contributorily liable in respect of the amount by which such damage exceeds the damage that would otherwise have occurred.

Remedies

Damages may be classified in two main groups:
(a) general and special; and
(b) nominal, real or substantial, exemplary, contemptuous and aggravated.

General and Special Damages

General damages are damages awarded because a tort has been committed from which the law presumes loss or injury to follow, for example, the plaintiff's loss of the use of his private car after it has been damaged by the defendant's negligence.

Special damages are awarded for injury or loss arising from the tort which is of a kind that the law does not presume to follow from it, for example, loss of earnings, pain and suffering or hospital expenses. Special damages must be specially pleaded and quantified.

Nominal Damage

Nominal damages are a small sum of money awarded, not as compensation, but solely because the plaintiff has proved that a tort has been committed against him, e.g. in a case of trespass to land involving no physical damage to the land or other loss to the plaintiff. In *Constantine v. Imperial London*

Hotels Ltd (1944), a famous West Indian cricketer was refused admittance to the defendant's hotel without reasonable cause but suffered no special damage. It was held that the exclusion was tortious and he could confer nominal damages.

Real, Substantial or Ordinary Damages

These are the general, unliquidated damages awarded to compensate the successful plaintiff for the loss, injury or damage he has suffered and, as far as possible, to restore him to the condition he was in before the tort.

Exemplary Damages

Exemplary damages (sometimes called *vindictive* or *punitive* damages) represent an addition to what is awarded as real damages, to compensate the plaintiff for what the court considers deplorable or outrageous conduct by the defendant and (in effect) by way of punishment for it. In *Rooks v. Bernard* (1964), the House of Lords laid down that exemplary damages should be awarded only on the following types of cases:
1. where there is an oppressive, arbitrary or unconstitutional action by the servants of the Government;
2. where the defendant's conduct was calculated to gain a profit which might exceed the compensation payable to the plaintiff; or
3. where a statute expressly provides for exemplary damages.

Contemptuous Damages

These are awarded to unmeritorious plaintiffs who are nevertheless entitled to succeed. They are the court's expression of its displeasure at a frivolous, vexatious or vindictive action. A plaintiff awarded contemptuous damages is unlikely to be awarded costs.

Aggravated Damages

These are reciprocal to contemptuous damages in that they represent an additional sum awarded to the plaintiff because the defendant's conduct was, for example, wilful or malicious. Aggravated damages differ from exemplary damages in that aggravated damages represent merely additional compensation, whereas exemplary damages contain a punitive and deterrent element.

The Measure of Damages

The function of damages is that, theoretically, they should restore the successful plaintiff to his original condition (*restitutio in integrum*). In practice, however, this is often impossible, e.g. where the plaintiff has lost a limb and it is therefore better to regard damages merely as monetary compensation for the loss or injury suffered by the plaintiff. For the purposes of assessment, damages may be classified under the headings of:

(a) damage to property; and
(b) injuries to the person.

The actual sum arrived at will be a question of fact in each case.

Reference

- W.V.H. Rogers, *Winfield & Jolowicz on Tort* (Thomson Sweet & Maxwell, 18th Edition, 2010).

REVIEW QUESTIONS

(See Suggested Solutions at the end of this textbook.)

Question 2.1

Florence and Theodore have been operating a jewellery design business, Little Gems, in partnership for the past 15 years. Both Florence and Theodore are active partners in the business, and Florence's father, Ralph, is their silent partner. When the partnership was established, Ralph invested 75% of the venture capital; the balance was invested equally by Florence and Theodore.

Stella is a head of sales of Little Gems. Last month Stella approached the company's financial controller, Myles, to inform him that she was attending a sales conference in Milan and that she was intending to take numerous samples of Little Gems jewellery to the conference in order to solicit orders. She told Myles that the consignment of sample jewellery she was taking with her was valued at £500,000 and she asked him to arrange the appropriate insurance for this trip.

While in Milan there was a robbery of the conference centre's secure vault and the case with the Little Gems jewellery samples were one of the many stolen. Little Gems filed a claim for the stolen jewellery from their insurance company, but discovered that an error by the financial controller means that the amount insured was actually £50,000 and not £500,000. As a consequence of this loss, Little Gems is now operating at a loss and Florence and Theodore have decided to dissolve the partnership.

Requirement: Little Gems is considering suing their financial controller for negligence. Outline the factors that the court could take into consideration in determining whether there has been a breach of the standard of care and assess whether the financial controller could be liable for his negligence.

(Source: Chartered Accountants Ireland, CAP 1, Law for Accountants (NI), Summer 2010, Extract: Q4(a)(iii))

Question 2.2

Martin has been the auditor to Acme Enterprises Ltd for the past 15 years. In the past five years he has failed to attend the company's stock take, although he has continued to sign-off on the company's accounts. It has recently been discovered that the directors have been falsifying the stock figures to make the company appear more profitable and that Martin has been inadvertently signing off on these falsified accounts.

Requirement: Discuss the law in relation to negligence and determine whether Martin is liable for any loss sustained by the company.

(Source: Chartered Accountants Ireland, CAP 1, Law for Accountants (NI), Autumn 2008, Extract: Q3(c))

Question 2.3

Your firm has acquired a new client, BlueSky Ltd. You are part of the team on the first audit of Bluesky Ltd. While carrying out the audit, you note that Bluesky Ltd has made a provision for damages in relation to pending court proceedings. The office manager explains to you that last April, Denis, the store manager, was supervising the delivery of a number of new computers when a printer fell on him from an overhead shelf. As a consequence of this incident, Denis broke his arm in three different places and required surgery. Since the accident Denis has been unable to work.

Requirement: In the context of the law of negligence, discuss the concept of remoteness of damages. Your answer should include an assessment of whether the company is obliged to compensate Denis for his injuries.

(Source: Chartered Accountants Ireland, CAP 1, Law for Accountants (NI), Autumn 2012, Extract: Q2(c).)

Question 2.4

ABC employs a warehouse manager, Peter Murphy. Last week, an accident occurred in the warehouse when a chemical drum was overturned.

This resulted in a spillage all over the warehouse floor, as the lid of the drum was not properly sealed. Peter, who had been on the warehouse floor at the time of the spillage, incurred serious third-degree burns to both feet, as the liquid burnt through the soles of his shoes. At the time of the incident, Peter was not wearing his regulation work boots, as required by health and safety law.

ABC has recently been contacted by Peter's solicitor informing them that he intends to sue them in negligence for his injuries. ABC's solicitors have advised them that they should defend this claim on the grounds of 'contributory negligence'.

Requirement: Outline the nature of the defence of 'contributory negligence' and assess whether this defence can be successfully raised on this occasion.

(Source: Chartered Accountants Ireland, CAP 1, Law for Accountants (NI),
Summer 2013, Extract: Q1(b)(i))

Question 2.5

Six months ago, the Health Service Executive of Northern Ireland (HSENI) put its waste management contract out to tender and Premier Waste Disposal Limited (Premier) decided to put in a bid for this lucrative contract. As Premier had never been involved in the disposal of medical waste before, it hired an independent consultant, Matt, to advise them on the various costs that it would incur to safely dispose of this waste. Based on Matt's figures, Premier submitted its tender to the HSENI.

Premier's bid was accepted and it was awarded the contract. However, Premier's accountant has recently informed it that the costs relating to the disposal of this medical waste are significantly higher than Matt originally estimated. Consequently, this additional cost has reduced Premier's estimated profit on the contract by 23%. PREMIER is now considering suing Matt for negligence.

Requirement: Pursuant to the law on negligence, discuss the current test that the court will apply to determine whether Matt owed Premier a duty to take reasonable care.

(Source: Chartered Accountants Ireland, CAP 1, Law for Accountants (NI),
Autumn 2013, Extract: Q3(b).)

Question 2.6

Aunty Em's Catering School Ltd (Aunty Em) has been trading successfully since 1963. Since its incorporation, its founder and primary shareholder,

Emilia, has acted as the company's managing director. Emilia celebrated her 75th birthday last year and at that stage she decided to sell the business. She received an offer from the Dingle Catering School Ltd (Dingle) proposing to purchase all of the assets of Aunty Em for £2.5 million. Emilia accepted this offer and has been advised by her solicitor to effect a members' voluntary liquidation of Aunty Em in order to distribute the £2.5 million to the company's shareholders.

Prior to the sale of the business, Emilia had received two letters instituting legal action against Aunty Em, as follows:

1. The first letter was from a former student of the catering college claiming compensation arising from the theft of her purse and bag from her assigned locker, while she was attending a one-day course at the college. Emilia is denying that Aunty Em is liable for this loss, as a large notice, containing an exemption clause, is prominently displayed in the locker room. This notice states that Aunty Em is not liable for any loss, theft or damage to valuables left in storage lockers.
2. The second letter was from the solicitor of a former lecturer employed by Aunty Em, claiming compensation arising from injuries incurred as a result of negligence. The injuries arose when the lecturer was conducting a food demonstration, showing students how to caramelise the sugar on top of a crème brûlée. The flame from the blowtorch being used by the lecturer exploded, causing her serious burns. Upon inspection it was discovered that the explosion was the result of loose wiring in the blowtorch. This wiring problem had been brought to the kitchen manager's attention, but the lecturer was told to keep using the blowtorch, until a replacement was purchased.

Requirement: With regard to the second letter, discuss any TWO factors that the court will take into consideration in determining whether the instructions given by the kitchen manager are in breach of the required standard of care in respect of negligence actions AND assess the potential liability of the company in this situation.

(Source: Chartered Accountants Ireland, CAP 1, Law for Accountants (NI), Summer 2014, Extract: Q4(b)(ii).)

Chapter 3

THE LAW OF CONTRACT

The Nature of a Contract

A contract is an agreement, formed by the mutual consent of both parties, which is legally binding. In order for a contract to be binding, there are three essential elements in the formation of a contract:

(a) that an agreement is made as a result of an offer and acceptance;
(b) consideration must be provided by each of the parties, i.e. there must be some kind of exchange between the parties; and
(c) the parties must intend to create legal relations.

A contract that does not satisfy the above three elements is classed as either a voidable contract or an unenforceable contract.

A *void* contract is not a contract and has no legal effect. Where a contract is declared void, the effect is that there was no contract to begin with and, therefore, neither party can enforce the agreement. If property has been transferred between the parties, ownership of this property will not pass to the buyer and therefore he or she will not be able to sell it to anyone else. The original seller will therefore be able to recover the property from the person in possession.

If a contract is *voidable*, the innocent party can choose whether or not to make the contract binding, if at all. A voidable contract remains valid unless and until the innocent party chooses to terminate it.

An *unenforceable* contract is a valid contract and any goods or money transferred cannot be recovered, even from the other parties whom the contract is from. Nevertheless, if either party refuses to perform his or her part of the contract, the other party cannot compel him to do so. A contract will be unenforceable when the required written evidence of its terms is not available, for example the written evidence for a contract for the sale of land.

Capacity to Contract

Certain categories of persons are deemed, by law, incapable of making contracts. For example, sane and sober adults are perceived as having the capacity to enter into contracts. Minors and people with a mental disorder, on the other hand, are said to be incapable of entering into a contract. If a minor or someone with a mental disorder enters into a contract, this person is said to lack the capacity to enter into a contract and, therefore, the resulting contract is declared either void or voidable.

Minors

Minors are defined by the Age of Majority Act (Northern Ireland) 1969 as any person under the age of 18. The Act states that they have limited contractual capacity. Any contract made by an infant or minor is generally regarded as being void. There are, however, some types of contract that are binding on minors, or which are merely voidable.

Contracts Binding on Minors The only contracts that are binding on minors are:
- contracts for necessary goods and services; and
- contracts of service for the minor's benefit.

Contracts for necessary goods and services 'Necessaries' include not only the supply of necessary goods and services, but also contracts of service for the minor's benefit. Necessaries are defined by the Sale of Goods Act 1979 as "goods suitable to the condition of life of the minor or other person concerned and to his actual requirements at the time of sale and delivery". If a court is deciding whether or not a contract is one for necessaries, the test to apply is the subjective test. The court must establish whether or not the goods or services are capable of amounting to necessaries in law and then they consider whether they are in fact necessaries as far as the minor before them is concerned.

For example, in the case of *Nash v. Inman* (1908), a tailor supplied a Cambridge undergraduate with "11 fancy waistcoats at 2 guineas each". When the tailor sued for payment, it was claimed that the contract could not be enforced against the student, as he was a minor (at this time people were considered minors until the age of 21). The Court of Appeal held that, although the goods were suitable to the young man's "condition in life" (he was the son of an architect), they did not satisfy the second limb of the statutory definition. They could not be regarded as suitable to his actual requirements at the time because his father had given uncontradicted evidence that he already had enough clothes and had no need for anymore. Thus, the contract was not binding.

Contracts of service for a minor's benefit A contract of service, such as an apprenticeship contract or a training or education contract, is considered binding on an infant or minor as long as it is beneficial to him or her. For example, in *Clements v. London and Northwestern Railway Co.* (1894), a minor made an agreement under which he gave up his statutory right to personal injury benefit but gained rights under an insurance scheme to which his employers would contribute. It was held that the rights gained were more beneficial than those given up and so the contract was, on balance, for the minor's benefit and therefore binding.

Persons of Unsound Mind

Persons with a mental incapacity have limited capacity to enter into a contract, as do people who are drunk at the time of making a contract. Contracts made by someone in a drunken capacity or with a mental incapacity are said to be valid unless, at the time when the contract is made, that person is incapable of understanding the nature of the transaction and the other party knows this. In such circumstances, the contract is said to be voidable, i.e. the person suffering from mental disability or drunkenness can choose whether or not to terminate it.

However, if another party to a contract does not realise that the other party is incapable, either through drunkenness or mental disability, of understanding the nature of the contract he is entering into, the courts ignore the incapacity. For example, in *Hart v. O'Connor* (1985), the court held that the person of unsound mind was bound by his agreement to sell some land because, when the contract was made, the buyer did not realise that the seller had any mental incapacity.

Corporations

A corporate body is an artificial person, an entity distinct in law from those who own the corporation. While corporate bodies *do* have the capacity to enter into contracts, that contractual capacity is *more limited* than that enjoyed by natural persons. Essentially, there are three different types of corporation:
- registered companies;
- corporations established by statute; and
- chartered corporations.

Registered companies must state the objects for which they were formed and may only enter into contracts that further these objects. Statutory corporations are created by Acts of Parliament and may only enter into contracts that have been specified within the Act creating the corporation's existence. Finally, chartered companies are corporations set up by Royal Charter, which means that their rights are officially granted by the Crown.

Examples of chartered companies are universities and charities. Such corporations can only enter into contracts within the spirit of the charter.

Formalities of a Contract

As stated above, every contract has three essential elements:
1. offer and acceptance,
2. consideration, and
3. intention to create legal relations.

1. Offer and Acceptance

For a contract to be made, one party must make an offer and another party must accept it. Once acceptance has taken place, a contract will be deemed to be binding on both parties as negotiations are perceived to have crystallised into a binding contract.

Offer A person who makes the offer is known as the 'offeror' and the person to whom the offer is made is the "offeree". An offer is a definite promise to be bound on certain specific terms. In *Gunthing v. Lynne* (1831) it was stated that an offer cannot be vague. In this case, the offeror promised to pay a further sum for a horse if it was "lucky".

An offer can be made to various offerees, i.e. a particular person, a class of persons (groups) or to the public (*Carlill v. Carbolic Smoke Ball Co.* (1983)). In this case, the defendants were the manufacturers of smoke balls, which they claimed could prevent flu. The published advertisement stated that, if anyone used their smoke ball for a specified time, they would pay that person £100 if they still caught the flu. To prove they were serious about the claim, they had deposited £1,000 with their bankers.

The claimant bought and used the smoke ball but still ended up with the flu. She therefore claimed the £100, which the company refused to pay. They argued that their advertisement could not give rise to a contract since it was impossible to make a contract with the whole world and that, therefore, they were not legally bound to pay the money. This argument was rejected by the court, which held that the advertisement *did* constitute an offer to the world at large and this became a contract when it was accepted by Mrs Carlill using the smoke ball and getting flu. She was therefore entitled to the £100.

Invitation to Treat An offer should be distinguished from an invitation to treat. An *invitation to treat* is when one party invites another party to make an offer. An offer can be converted into a contract by acceptance, provided the other requirements of a valid contract are present. However, an invitation to treat cannot be accepted. The following are examples of invitations to treat:

1. Goods Displayed in Shops The prices of goods marked on display on shelves or in the windows of shops are generally regarded as invitations to treat and not as offers to sell goods at that price. For example, in *Fisher v. Bell* (1960), the defendant displayed flick knives in a shop window. He was convicted of the criminal offence of offering such knives for sale. On appeal, however, the court held that the display of an article with a price on it in a shop window was only an invitation to treat and not an offer and therefore the conviction was overturned.

   In the case of *Pharmaceutical Society of GB v. Boots Cash Chemists (Southern) Ltd* (1953), it was held that a customer makes an offer to buy when presenting the goods at the cash desk where the shopkeeper may reject or accept that offer. In this case, Boots were charged with an offence concerning the sale of certain medicines which could only be sold by or under the supervision of a qualified pharmacist. Two customers in a self-service shop selected the medicines, which were price-marked, from the open shelves and placed them in their shopping baskets. The shelves were not supervised by a pharmacist but a pharmacist had been instructed to supervise the transaction at the cash desk. The issue for the court was, therefore, whether the sale had taken place at the shelves or at the cash desk. The Court of Appeal decided that the shelf display was like an advertisement and was, therefore, merely an invitation to treat. The offer was made by the customer when medicines were placed in the basket and was accepted only when the goods were presented at the cash desk. Since the pharmacist was supervising at that point, no offence had been committed under statute.

2. Invitation for Tenders A 'tender' is an estimate that is made in response to a prior request. An invitation for tender does not thereby amount to an offer to employ the person quoting the lowest price. However, exceptions may occur were tenders have been solicited from selected persons and the invitation to tender sets out a prescribed clear procedure. For example, in the case of *Blackpool and Fried Aero Club v. Blackpool Council* (1990), the Council, who managed Blackpool Airport, intended to grant a concession to operate pleasure flights from the airport. It therefore sent invitations to tender to the plaintiff and six other parties. All of the invitees were known to the Council. The invitation stipulated that tenders received after the last date would not be considered. While the plaintiff posted their tender in good time in the town hall letterbox, it was not opened when it was supposed to be. Consequently, the plaintiff's tender arrived late and was excluded from consideration. The plaintiff sued in contract and negligence.

The contract claim was that, when inviting tenders, the Council promised that it would consider tenders that were received on time. The plaintiff's claim succeeded and the Court of Appeal held that it was possible to have exceptions to the rule that invitations to tender were not contractual offers. This would apply where tenders are invited from known and selected persons under a clear, prescribed procedure.

3. Request for Bids at Auction If an advertisement states that an auction will be held (without reserve), it means that the auctioneer must sell to the highest bidder, as demonstrated in the case of *Barry v. Heathcote Ball & Co.* (2000) in which the auctioneers included two new engine analysers, worth £14,000 each, for sale by auction without reserve. The plaintiff bid £200 for them. There was no other bid and the defendant withdrew the items from the sale. The plaintiff sued the auctioneers on the basis that he was the highest bidder. It was held that if the lots were auctioned without reserve, the auctioneer would be in breach of contract if he withdrew them. At the auction in dispute before the court, there was a collateral contract between the auctioneer and the highest bidder consisting of an offer by the auctioneer to sell to the highest bidder and acceptance of that offer when the bid was made.

Termination of an Offer An offer does not last forever. An offer ceases to exist when any one of the following circumstances arises:

1. Lapse of Time Where an offer states that it will remain open for a specific length of time, that offer lapses when the time is up. If no time is stipulated, the courts will decide what a reasonable time is. What constitutes reasonableness will depend on the circumstances. For example, in the case of *Ramsgate Victoria Hotel v. OV Montefiore* (1866) the defendant applied for shares in the plaintiff's company, paying a deposit into their bank. He did not hear anything further from them for five months, when he was informed that the shares had been allotted to him and he should pay the balance due on them. The plaintiff refused to do so arguing that five months was not a reasonable length of time for acceptance of an offer to buy shares. The court upheld his argument, agreeing that the delay was too long and that the offer had lapsed. It was held that there was no binding contract made between the parties.

2. Death The position as to what happens when one party dies during the offer process is not entirely clear. However, it would appear that, if the offeree knows that the offeror has died, the offer will lapse. The case of *Bradbury v. Morgan* (1862) would suggest, however, that if the offeree is unaware of the offeror's death, it probably will not.

3. Revocation The offeror is permitted to revoke or withdraw their offer before it has been accepted (*Payne v. Cave* (1789)). Revocation of an offer must be communicated to the offeree. However, revocation does not have to be communicated by the offeror – the communication can be made by a third party. In *Dickinson v. Dodds* (1876), the defendant offered to sell a house to the plaintiff, the offer "to be left open until Friday, 12 June 9.00 am". On 11 June, the defendant sold the house to a third party and the plaintiff heard about the sale through a fourth person. Before 9.00 am on 12 June, the plaintiff handed the defendant a letter in which he said he was accepting the offer. The Court of Appeal held that the offer had already been revoked by the communication from the fourth man, so there was no contract. On hearing the news from the fourth man, the plaintiff knew the defendant was no longer minded to sell the property to him.

Counter Offer A counter offer terminates the original offer. In *Hyde v. Rench* (1840), a defendant offered to sell his farm for £1,000 and the plaintiff responded by offering to buy it at £950, thereby making a counter offer. However, the defendant refused this offer and later the plaintiff tried to accept the offer of £1,000. The plaintiff sued for breach of contract but his action failed because his offer of £950 was held to be a counter offer thereby terminating the defendant's original offer of £1,000.

Rejection An offer lapses when the offeree rejects it. For example, if A offers to sell B her car and B says no, B cannot come back at a later stage insisting on accepting the offer.

Failure of a Precondition Some offers are made subject to certain conditions and, if such conditions are not in place, the offer may lapse. In *Financing Ltd v. Stimson* (1962), a defendant, who wished to purchase a car, signed a hire purchase form on 16 March. This was the offer. The form stated that the agreement would only become binding when the finance company signed the form. On 24 March, the car was stolen from the dealer's premises and it was recovered badly damaged. On 25 March, the finance company signed the form. It was held that the defendant was not bound to take the car. There was an implied condition in the finance company's offer that the car would be in substantially the same condition when the offer was accepted as when it was made.

Acceptance Acceptance of a contract may be in writing, oral (i.e. spoken) or it may be inferred from conduct. However, a court will only perceive conduct as indicating acceptance if it appears reasonable to infer that the offeree acted with the intention of accepting the offer.

For example, in *Brogden v. Metropolitan Rail Co.* (1877), the plaintiff supplied the railway company with coal for several years without any formal agreement.

The parties then decided to make things more official and so the company's agent sent the plaintiff a draft agreement which left a blank space for the plaintiff to insert the name of an arbitrator. After doing so and signing the document, the plaintiff returned it marked approved. The defendant's agent put the draft away in a desk drawer where it stayed for the next two years without any further steps being taken regarding it. The plaintiff continued to supply coal under the terms of the contract and the railway company to pay for it. Eventually, however, a dispute arose between them and the plaintiff denied that any binding contract existed.

The courts held that, by inserting the arbitrator's name, the plaintiff added a new term to the contract and therefore in returning it to the railway company he was offering to supply coal under the contract. The question arose as to when that offer was accepted. It was held by the House of Lords that an acceptance by conduct could be inferred from the parties' behaviour and a valid contract was completed either when the company first ordered coal after receiving the draft agreement from the plaintiff or, at the latest, when he supplied the first lot of coal.

Acceptance is not effective until communicated to and received by the offeror. Furthermore, acceptance must be communicated by the offeree or by someone with his ability. In *Powell v. Lee* (1908), the plaintiff applied for the post of headmaster of a school. He was called for interview and the interviewing panel, of which the defendant was a member, passed a resolution appointing him but did not make any arrangements to notify him. However, one of the panel members, without authority, informed the plaintiff that he had been successful. The defendant subsequently re-opened the matter and appointed another candidate. It was held that the plaintiff failed in his action for breach of contract since acceptance had not been properly communicated to him.

It has also been found that remaining silent cannot amount to an acceptance. In the case of *Felthouse v. Bindly* (1863), the plaintiff was engaged on negotiations to purchase his nephew's horse. Confusion arose as to the price so the plaintiff wrote to his nephew saying: "If I hear no more about him, I consider the horse mine at that price." The nephew, at this stage, was on the point of selling off some of his property in an auction. He did not reply to his uncle's letter, but he did tell the auctioneer to keep the horse out of the sale. The auctioneer forgot to do this and the horse was sold. It was held that there was no contract between the uncle and nephew. The court felt that the nephew's conduct in trying to keep the horse out of the sale did not necessarily imply that he intended to accept his uncle's offer and therefore it was not clear that his silence in response to the offer was intended to constitute acceptance.

'The Postal Rule' The general rule for acceptance by post is that it takes effect when letters are posted rather than when they are communicated.

The postal rule was laid down in *Adams v. Lindsell* (1818). In this case, the defendants wrote to the plaintiff, who processed wool, offering to sell them a quantity of sheep fleeces and stating that they required an answer "in course of post". The defendants did not address the letter correctly and therefore it did not reach the plaintiff until the evening of 5 September. The plaintiffs posted their acceptance on the same evening and it reached the defendants on 9 September. If the original letter had been correctly addressed, the defendants could have expected a reply by 7 September. That date came and went and the defendants had heard nothing from the plaintiffs, so on 8 September they sold the wool to a third party. The issue therefore arose as to whether or not a contract had been made before the sale to the third party on 8 September. It was held by the court that a contract was established as soon as the acceptance was posted so that the defendants were bound from the evening of 5 September. They had therefore breached the contract by selling the wool to a third party.

It should be noted that parties are free to exclude the postal rule by providing that the contract is not formed until the letter has arrived. This may be done by the offeror stipulating that acceptance should be "by notice in writing".

Consequences of the Postal Rule The postal rule has three practical consequences:
- A postal acceptance can take effect when it is posted, even if it gets lost in the post and never reaches the offeror. In *Household Fire Insurance v. Grant* (1879), the defendant applied for shares in the plaintiff company. The shares were allotted to him and his name was put on the register of shareholders. The company did write to say that the shares had been allotted to Grant but the letter was lost in the post and he never received it. Some time later, the company went into liquidation and the liquidator claimed from the defendant the balance owing on the price of the shares. It was held that the defendant was bound to pay the balance because the contract had been completed when the company's letter was posted.
- If an acceptance is posted after the offeree posts a revocation of the offer, but before that revocation has been received, acceptance will be binding (posted acceptance takes effect on posting, posted revocations on communication).
- The contract is completed at the time of posting, so it has priority over any other contract concerning the same subject matter which was made after the original acceptance was posted but before it had reached the offeror.

Exceptions to the Postal Rule:

- Offers requiring communication of acceptance – The postal rule can be avoided if the offeror makes it a term of their offer that acceptance will take effect only when it is communicated to them. In *Holwell Securities v. Hughes* (1974), the plaintiffs were offered freehold property by the defendants but a condition of the offer was that the acceptance had to be "by notice in writing". The plaintiffs accepted the offer and posted their acceptance. However, despite being properly addressed, it never reached the defendants. The court held that "notice" meant communication and therefore it was not appropriate to apply the postal rule.

- Instant methods of communication – The postal rule does not apply to instant methods of communication, i.e. when an acceptance is made by telephone or fax. In these cases, the acceptor will usually know instantly that they have not managed to communicate with the offeror and therefore will need to try again.

  For example, in the case of *Entores v. Miles Far East Corporation* (1955), the plaintiffs were a London company and the defendant was an American corporation with agents in Amsterdam. The plaintiff alleged that the defendant had broken its contract with them and wanted to sue in England. The question therefore arose as to whether the contract was formed as contracts are governed by the rules of the country in which they are formed. The plaintiff had telexed its offer from London to Amsterdam and the defendant telexed back its acceptance to London. It was held by the courts that because telex allows almost instant communication, the parties were in the same position as if they had negotiated in each other's presence or over the telephone and therefore the postal rules did not apply. As the acceptance had been received in London, the contract was deemed to have been made there and so the legal action could go ahead.

- This approach was given further approval by the House of Lords in *Brinkibon v. Stahag Stahl GmbH* (1983). The facts in this case were very similar to those of the *Entores* case, with the exception that the offer was made by telex from Vienna to London, and accepted by telex from London to Vienna. The House of Lords therefore held that the contract was made in Vienna.

- In both cases, the telex machines were in the offices of the parties and the messages were received inside normal working hours. In *Brinkibon*, the House of Lords said that a telex message sent outside working hours would not be considered instantaneous and so the time and place in which the contract was completed would be determined by the intentions of the parties, standard business practice and, if possible, by analysing where the risk should most fairly lie.

Whether or not the postal rule applies to e-mail is still uncertain and there is no case law, at present, on this point. E-mail, however, cannot be said to be an instantaneous form of communication because e-mails can be delayed in a system for hours or days. As to the present position, it could be said that the postal rule should probably apply to e-mail. However, as e-mail technology improves, delays are becoming less frequent and it is possible to request electronic confirmation of receipt.

2. Consideration

Consideration is said to be something that represents either some benefit to the person making a promise (the promisor) or some detriment to the person to whom the promise is made (the promisee) or both. In *Currie v. Misa* (1875), it was stated that consideration existed when there was:

> "some right, interest, profit or benefit accruing to the one party, or some forbearance, detriment, loss, or responsibility, given, suffered, or undertaken by the other".

Within the law of contract, an agreement is not usually binding unless it is supported by consideration. This means that each party must give something in return for what is gained from the other party.

Executory and Executed Consideration Consideration can be executory or executed, but it cannot be past. *Executed* consideration is the performance of an act in return for a promise and usually occurs in unilateral contracts. (Unilateral contracts arise where only one party assumes an obligation.) For example, Mr X promises to pay a reward of £100 to anyone who returns his lost dog. This is unilateral in the sense that Mr X is obliged to pay a reward to anyone who finds his dog but nobody is obliged to do so. If the dog is returned, the act of returning is both acceptance of the offer and executed consideration for the promise.

Consideration is said to be *executory* when the defendant makes a promise and the plaintiff offers a counter promise. For example, if Mr Y orders a car from Mr Z and promises to pay for it when it is delivered, the promise is *executory* because it is something to be done in the future. It is said to be bilateral as it usually involves executory rather than executed consideration.

Consideration Must Not be Past Consideration must be given in return for a promise or act of another person. An act that is classified as consideration cannot be performed before any promise of a reward is made, otherwise it is not valid consideration. Hence, if A looks after B's house while B is on holiday, and when B returns she promises to give A some money, A cannot enforce that promise because she did not look after the house in return for it. She had already looked after the house.

In *Roscorla v. Thomas* (1842), the plaintiff purchased a horse from the defendant. Once the sale was completed, the defendant promised that the horse was not vicious. However, this was incorrect. The plaintiff sued on this promise but the plaintiff failed because the consideration was deemed to be in the past. As the promise about the horse's condition was made after the sale, the consideration was past because it had not been given in return for the promise.

Exceptions to the Past Consideration Rule There are two exceptions to the rule that past consideration is no consideration:

- The first exception to the rule is the bill of exchange. Section 27 of the Bills of Exchange Act 1882 states that an "antecedent debt or liability" may be consideration for receipt of a bill of exchange.
- The second exception establishes that where the past consideration was made at the promisor's request, and it was understood that payment would be made, then the promisee can rely on this promise. This was illustrated in the case of *Lampleigh v. Braithwaite* (1615), in which the defendant killed a man and asked the plaintiff to obtain a pardon for him from the King. The plaintiff did so and the defendant then promised to pay him £100. However, Braithwaite broke this promise and Lampleigh sued him. Lampleigh succeeded in his action as the court decided that Braithwaite's request for a Royal pardon was regarded as containing an implied promise to pay.

Sufficiency and Adequacy of Consideration "Consideration must be sufficient, but it need not be adequate." This principle was espoused in the case of *Chappell & Co. Ltd v. Nestlé Co. Ltd* (1959). It is a rather confusing principle, but it effectively means that the courts will not question the adequacy of consideration, provided some consideration is given. Therefore, as long as some consideration is given, a court will not question whether it is proportionate in value to the thing given in return. For example, if A promises to sell an iPhone to B for £5, clearly this £5 will not be of much benefit to A but it is still a consideration.

In *Thomas v. Thomas* (1842), the plaintiff was a widow whose husband had stated that, if he died before his wife, she should be allowed to live in his house for the rest of her life, after which it was to pass to his sons. When the husband died, the executors agreed to convey the home to the widow in exchange for £1 per year rent and the house to be kept in good repair. The defendant later tried to evict the widow but she sued him for breach of contract claiming that her promise to pay £1 and keep up the repairs was sufficient consideration to make the owner's promise binding. The widow's case was upheld.

Similarly, in *Chappell & Co. Ltd v. Nestlé Co. Ltd* (1960), the defendant ran a special offer involving a recording of a song called "Walking Shoes". If customers sent in 1 shilling and 6 pence and three wrappers from Nestlé's bars of chocolate, they could get a copy of this record. However, the copyright holders of the recording brought an action against Nestlé claiming that royalties should be paid on the price of the record. It was held by the House of Lords that the wrappers did form part of the consideration and the fact that they were of no real worth to Nestlé was irrelevant.

Equitable Estoppel The rule of equitable estoppel is a way of making a promise binding, even if no consideration has been given. The rule can be expressed as follows: where a person promises that he will not insist upon a strict legal right, and the other party acts upon that promise, then the law will require that such a promise be honoured and that he be stopped from going back on that promise, even though it is not supported by consideration.

An example of this is found in the case of *Hickman v. Haynes* (1875). A buyer asked a man to deliver goods later than originally agreed and then refused to accept the goods when the delivery was made. The seller sued for breach of contract and the buyer responded by arguing that in fact the seller was in breach as he delivered the goods later than specified on the original contract. However, the court rejected this argument on the grounds that the late delivery was made at the buyer's request.

Likewise, in *Central London Property Trust v. High Trees House* (1947), the plaintiff leased a block of flats to the defendant. As a result of the war, the defendant was unable to sublet the flats and so the plaintiff agreed to accept half rent. However, after the war, the plaintiff claimed full rent for the post-war period and the claim succeeded. The court, in this case, considered whether the plaintiff would have succeeded if he had claimed the full rent back to the start of the war. However, Lord Denning said that he would not have been successful because he would have been estopped in equity from going back on his promise.

Lord Justice Birkett said that the doctrine of equitable estoppel is to act "as a shield and not a sword". Hence, it can only be used when a person who promises not to enforce his strict legal right goes back on this promise.

3. Intention to Create Legal Relations

Even where offer, acceptance and consideration are present, parties will not be bound to a contract unless it can be shown that they intended the contract to be legally binding. Intention can be expressed, or implied, from the circumstances, e.g. in the *Carlill* case an intention to enter into a contract was inferred from the deposit of money in the bank by the Carbolic Smoke Ball Company, meaning that their advert was treated as a serious offer.

Whether the parties intend to be legally bound depends on the circumstances. In deciding whether or not there were legal intentions, the courts will assess the parties' intentions objectively. In looking at whether or not legal intentions were present, contracts are often divided into two categories – domestic and social agreements, which *do not* imply legal relations, and commercial agreements, which *do* imply legal relations.

Social and Domestic Arrangements Agreements or arrangements among family or friends are presumed not to be legally binding. For example, in *Balfour v. Balfour* (1919) the defendant was a civil servant stationed in Ceylon who came to England with his wife and remained there until his leave was up. His wife, the plaintiff, remained in England on doctor's advice and the husband, before sailing, promised her £30 per month until he returned. When the marriage later ended in divorce, the wife sued for the promised maintenance. It was held that an informal agreement of an indefinite period made between husband and wife whose marriage was intact was not intended to be legally binding. The Court of Appeal stated:

> "One of the most usual forms of agreement which does not constitute a contract appears to be arrangements made between husband and wife. To my mind, these arrangements do not result in contracts at all, even if there is consideration."

In *Merritt v. Merritt* (1970), a husband left the family home, which was owned by him, to live with another woman. The spouses met in the husband's car, where the husband agreed to pay the wife £40 per month, out of which sum she would pay the mortgage on their house. The wife refused to leave the car until the husband signed a note agreeing to these terms and an undertaking to transfer the house into her sole name when the mortgage was paid off. The wife paid off the mortgage, but the husband refused to transfer the house to her. It was held that, in these circumstances, an intention to create legal relations could be inferred and the wife could sue her husband for breach of contract.

In *Simpkins v. Pays* (1955), A, her granddaughter and a paying boarder took part in weekly competitions organised by a Sunday newspaper. Entries were made in A's name and there were informal arrangements about postage, etc. On one particular week, they won £750. The paying boarder was denied a share by the other two entrants. It was held that there was a mutuality of agreement amongst the parties, amounting to a joint enterprise. It was not a "friendly adventure", as A had claimed, but a contract.

Commercial Agreements In commercial situations, there is a strong presumption that the parties intend to enter into a legally binding relationship in consequence of their dealings. This was seen in the case of *Edwards v. Skyways* (1964) where, in negotiations over redundancy terms with an employee, the employer undertook to make an ex gratia payment to him (an ex gratia payment is a payment made where there was no obligation to pay). It was held by the court that the denial of previous liability was not sufficient to rebut the presumption that the agreed terms were intended to be legally binding in their future operation.

In *Rose & Frank v. Crompton* (1924), the plaintiff entered into an agreement with the defendant whereby they were appointed the defendant's agents in the United States. The agreement stated that "this agreement is not entered into nor is this memorandum written as a formal or legal agreement and it shall not be subject to legal jurisdiction in the Courts of US or England". The court held that it would respect the intention of the parties that the agreement was not to be legally binding, even though it would be classified as a commercial agreement.

Privity of Contract

The doctrine of privity of contract states that only the parties to a contract incur rights and obligations under it. Hence, a person who is not a party to the contract, called a third party, can neither sue nor be sued on the contract.

The general rule of privity of contract was established in *Tweedle v. Atkinson* (1861). In this case, a groom's father agreed with the bride's father that they would both pay the groom an annual sum of money. One father died owing payments and so the son-in-law sued the deceased's estate for the money owing to him and his wife. However, it was held that consideration must move from the promisee to the promisor and therefore the groom was not privy to the contract.

A similar approach was taken in the case of *Beswick v. Beswick* (1968). A plaintiff's husband sold his business to his nephew in return for an annual allowance to be paid to himself and, after his death, to his widow. When the husband died, the nephew refused to make any further payments to the widow. While the husband had clearly intended the widow to benefit from the contract, the court held that a widow could not sue the nephew on her own behalf as she was not privy to the contract.

Exceptions to the Privity of Contract Rule

Over the years, a number of exceptions to the privity of contract rule have developed in order to meet the demands of other common law principles. The courts have played an important role in mitigating the harshness that may arise following a strict application of the rule. The most important exceptions can be listed as follows:

Assignment of Contractual Rights A's rights under a contract with B may be transferred to a third party in a transaction known as an assignment (i.e. sale). The privity of contract rule would prevent the third party from suing B on any outstanding obligations under the contract, but the law has overridden this hurdle in assignment situations.

Law of Agency A party to a contract can always act through an agent. This party is called the principal. The relationship existing between principal and agent need not itself take the form of a contract but a principal can sue and be sued on contracts made on his or her behalf by an agent. This is permitted even if the existence of the principal was not made known to the person with whom the agent agreed the contract. For example, in the case of *Crawford v. Curry* (1984), the plaintiff bought a bull at a sale organised by the Northern Ireland Charolais Club. When the bull proved impotent, the plaintiff was paid some compensation by the seller's insurance company, but the plaintiff wanted to sue the club for consequential losses. It was held that the club was not liable because, where an agent, in making the contract, discloses both the existence and the name of his or her principal, the agent is not as a general rule liable to the third party.

Executor or Administrator of a Deceased's Estate A person not originally privy to a particular contract can acquire the power to enforce the contract if they are legally appointed to administer the estate of the original party to the contract.

Where it is Foreseeable that the Damage Caused by Breach of Contract will Cause a Loss to a Third Party This is illustrated in the case of *Lyndon Gardens Trust Ltd v. Lenesta Sludge Disposals Ltd* (1994). In this case, the parties had entered into a contract for work to be carried out on property on the assumption that the work would subsequently be transferred to a third party. However, the defendants' substandard work amounted to a breach of contract and this became apparent only after the property had been transferred. As there had been no assignment of the original contract, under the privity of contract doctrine, the new owners would have no contractual rights against the defendants. The original owners also would have suffered only a nominal breach if they had sold it at no loss to themselves. The House of Lords, in this case, held that under the circumstances the original promisee should be able to claim full damages on behalf of the third party.

The Doctrine of Constructive Trust In a constructive trust situation, a party to a contract can create a contract specifically for the benefit of a third party. The promisee is considered as a trustee of a contractual promise for the benefit of the third party. The beneficiary cannot sue to enforce the contract without the promisee also being a party to the action. Increasingly, however, the courts have become reluctant to imply the existence of a trust in this way and will do so now only if it is very clear that there was an intention to create a trust in favour of a third party (*Re Schebsman* (1944)).

Specific Performance and Damages in Respect of a Third Party's Loss A party to a contract who has given consideration can obtain a Decree of Specific Performance of the promise in order to benefit a third party. This remedy, however, is discretionary and will be awarded only in limited circumstances. If a contracting party sues for damages in respect of loss suffered by a third party due to the promise or breach of contract, it is only in exceptional circumstances that he or she will obtain anything more than nominal damages. In the case of *Jackson v. Horizon Holidays Ltd* (1975), the plaintiff made a contract with the defendant for the provision of a holiday which, in the event, fell well below the standards described in the brochure. The plaintiff sued for his own disappointment and for that of his wife and children. It was held that the plaintiff could recover damages in both respects as the contract was also made for the benefit of his family.

Statutory Exceptions to the Privity of Contract Rule There are a number of statutory exceptions to the Privity of Contract Rule. For example, under the Road Traffic (Northern Ireland) Order 1981 (1981 No. 154 (N.I. 1)), the personal representatives of an insured person who has died have the right to be indemnified (i.e. compensated) under a motor insurance policy if that person is successfully sued by the victims of a car accident in which that person was involved. Likewise, under the Third Parties (Rights Against Insurers) Act (Northern Ireland) 1930, third parties are given direct rights against insurers of third-party risks in the event of the insured becoming insolvent. Furthermore, under the Law Reform (Husband and Wife) Act (Northern Ireland) 1964, a husband or wife can take out a policy of insurance expressly for the benefit of the other spouse or for their children. In *Collins v. Northern Ireland Housing Executive* (1994), a husband and wife leased a flat from the defendant under a tenancy agreement that was signed by the husband only and not the wife. The heating system provided by the defendant turned out to be unsatisfactory. It was held that the wife could not claim under the husband's contract because section 5 of the 1964 Act applied only were the contract was made expressly for the benefit of a spouse or child. In this case, no expressed benefit was conferred on the wife with the tenancy agreement signed by the husband.

Form of Contracts

It is often assumed that a contract must be in writing. However, there is no legal requirement to have a contract in writing and oral contracts can also be binding and enforceable. However, it can be very difficult to prove what was said orally and, therefore, it is always more advantageous to put a contract in writing.

The case of *Hadley v. Kemp* (1999) illustrates this point. Gary Kemp was a songwriter with the pop group Spandau Ballet. The other members of the group sued Mr Kemp for royalties received from the group's music. The other members claimed that there had been an oral agreement to share these royalties. However, they were unable to prove the existence of any oral agreement and therefore their action failed.

The advantage, therefore, in having a written agreement is that the existence and terms of the contract are then much easier to prove in the event of a later dispute. There are, however, a few particular types of contract which do not need to be put in a special form. The most important of these cases are as follows.

Deeds Under Seal

A conveyance or transfer of a legal estate and land or the grant of a lease for three or more years must be by deed. The Law Reform (Miscellaneous Provisions) (Northern Ireland) Order 2005 (2005 No. 1452 (N.I. 7)) states that you no longer have to affix a seal to the deed. If the document refers to itself as a deed and it is signed by the parties to be bound, this will suffice.

Contracts that Must be in Writing

Most contracts for the sale or disposition of an interest in land must, since the Law of Property (Miscellaneous Provisions) Act 1989, be in writing and they must also incorporate all the terms that have been expressly agreed in one document. The document must also be signed by each party or their representative. In addition, other contracts that need to be made in writing include: a transfer of shares in a limited company, bills of exchange and consumer credit contracts.

Contracts that Must be Evidenced in Writing

"Evidenced in writing" means that although the contract itself need not be a written one, there must be some written evidence of the transaction. An example of a contract which requires written evidence is that of a mortgage, i.e. when one party lends money in exchange for a security interest over goods belonging to another.

Electronic Contracts

The Electronic Communications (Northern Ireland) Act 2001 was passed to facilitate the development of electronic commerce. It provides for legal recognition of electronic signatures and it also facilitates the amendment of many existing pieces of legislation to allow for practical changes brought about by e-commerce.

The Terms of a Contract

Terms and Representations

In the formation of a contract there is a distinction between a *contract term* and a *contract representation*. This distinction is important because, if a term is broken or a representation is untrue, different remedies are available.

Whether a statement is a representation or a term is largely a question of the parties' intentions. If parties indicate that a particular statement is a term of the contract, the court will carry out that intention. If parties do not indicate whether or not a statement is a term or representation, the courts will look at the following questions for guidance. If the answer to any of the following questions is yes, a court will hold that the statement is more likely to be a term.

- **At what stage was the statement made during the negotiation of the contract? Was it made close to the moment that the contract was formed?** If yes, the courts will consider it more likely to be a term of the contract. The more time that elapses between the statement being made and the contract concluding, the less likely the courts will be to regard the statement as a term. For example, in *Routledge v. McKay* (1954) the parties had been discussing the sale of a motorbike. Both were private individuals without specialist knowledge of motorcycles. The defendant stated that the motorbike was a 1942 model and he based this on information from the registration book. However, the motorbike later turned out to be a 1930 model and the buyer claimed that the date of manufacture was the term of the contract. The buyer's claim failed because the interval between the statement being made and the contract concluding suggested the statement was not a term.

- **Is the statement important to the overall purpose of the contract?**
  If one party makes another party aware that they would not have entered into the contract but for the statement, such a statement is more likely to be viewed as a term.
- **Did the maker of the statement have specialist knowledge and skill?**
  If a statement is made by someone who has expert knowledge or skill that is relevant to the subject in hand, as opposed to an amateur making the statement with no special expertise in the matter, a court will be more willing to deem that statement a term. For example, in the case of *Oscar Chess v. Williams* (1957), the defendant, a private individual, wanted to trade in his Morris car and buy a new car. The defendants stated that his car was a 1948 model and, on this basis, the plaintiffs allowed £290 discount on the price of the new car. It was later discovered, however, that the car was a 1939 model and therefore only worth £175. The car dealer sued the defendant for the difference in price between the valuations. The Court of Appeal rejected the plaintiff's claim and stated that the seller was a private individual and he had innocently trusted the registration book, which stated that the car was a 1948 model.

Implied Terms

Terms implied into a contract are implied either by fact, by custom, by statute or by the courts.

Terms Implied in Fact These are terms which it is assumed both parties would have intended to include but were simply left out by mistake or because one or both parties thought them so obvious that they did not need to be specified. The test to establish whether or not these terms are implied is called the 'reasonable by-stander' test. In *The Moorcock* (1889) case, the defendants were wharf owners contracted to allow the plaintiff to unload their ship at the wharf. The ship grounded at ebb tide and was damaged by settling on a ridge of hard ground. The defendants were held to be in breach of the implied term that the wharf was safe.

Terms Implied by Local Custom or Trade Usage Terms can be implied into a contract by reference to customs prevailing in the trade, unless a contrary intention is shown. For example, in the case of *Hutton v. Warren* (1836), a farmer was leaving his tenancy and he claimed that he was entitled to a fair allowance for seed and labour expended on the land that he had been letting. The court decided that it was a term of the contract that the farmer had with the landlord that he should be paid money.

Terms Implied by Statute Certain statutes imply terms into contracts and these terms must be read into a contract regardless of the party's intentions. For example, under the Consumer Rights Act 2015, it is implied that goods sold to a consumer must correspond with their description, are of satisfactory quality and are fit for the purpose for which they are required.

Conditions and Warranties

A **condition** is a key term of a contract. If a condition is breached, an innocent party is entitled to regard the contract as repudiated. The innocent party can also seek damages. For example, in the case of *Bunge Corporation v. Tradax Export SA* (1981), a seller contracted to ship 5,000 tonnes of US soybean meal by the end of June 1975 and the buyer took responsibility for arranging for the ship to transport the goods. The buyer agreed to give "at least 15 consecutive days'" notice of probable readiness of the vessel. However, the buyer only gave notice on 17 June, thereby giving the seller only 13 days notice to load the ship rather than 15. The House of Lords held that the seller's obligation to ship the produce before the end of the month was a condition of the contract. The buyer could terminate if loading was not finished by 1 July. It follows that the buyer's obligation to give notice was a condition as, in a contract of this kind, it would be unfair to deprive sellers of their full period of notice.

Whereas a condition permits a contract to end or become discharged, a **warranty** is a less important term of a contract and only allows the innocent party to receive damages for breach. For example, in the case of *Hong Kong Fir Shipping Co. v. Kawasaki Kisen Kaisha Ltd* (1962), the plaintiffs owned a ship that was chartered to the defendant organisation. A term of the charter was that the ship be "in every way fitted for ordinary cargo service and also that the ship be seaworthy". However, the ship was inadequately staffed and had very old and unreliable machinery. As a result, a total of 20 weeks' delay was caused to the defendants, who subsequently repudiated the contract. When the plaintiffs sued for breach of contract, they argued that a condition had been broken. It was held, however, that the terms broken were warranties and not conditions and so the defendants were not entitled to repudiate the contract but were only entitled to damages.

Collateral Contracts

Collateral contracts occur when one person promises something to another by means of an oral agreement. This agreement is said to exist alongside the main contract. This can be seen in the case of *Shanklin Pier Ltd v. Detel*

Products Ltd (1951). In this case, the plaintiffs owned Shanklin Pier and wanted to have it repainted. They contacted the defendant in an effort to find out about the quality of the defendant's paints. They were informed that the paints lasted for between seven and 10 years. The plaintiffs subsequently entered into a contract to have the pier repainted and indicated to their painters that they wished them to use Detel paint. Once the painting was completed, the paint began to deteriorate after about three months. The court, in this case, found that there was a collateral contract between the plaintiffs and the defendants.

Exemption Clauses

Exemption clauses arise when one party to a contract seeks to avoid incurring liability for certain breaches of the contract. They can also arise when one party specifies that their liability for any breach will be limited. An exemption clause becomes a term of the contract by signature or by notice. The term "exemption clause" is commonly used to cover both limitation and exclusion clauses. However, it should be noted that, over the past 40 years, the law has endeavoured to control the use of exemption clauses, most recently in Part 2 of the Consumer Rights Act 2015.

Exemption clauses can be incorporated into contracts in three ways:

1. **Incorporation by Signature** If a person signs a document, at the time of making the contract, the contents of the contract automatically become terms of the contract. This rule applies regardless of whether or not the terms of the contract have been read or understood by the person signing the contract. This principle applied in the case of *L'Estrange v. Graucob* (1934). In this case, the terms of a hire purchase agreement for a vending machine were signed without having been read. In very small print, the agreement contained a statement which said, "any expressed or implied condition, statement or warranty, statutory or otherwise, is hereby excluded". The machine was later proven to be defective but the fact that the exclusion clause had been signed meant that the terms of the contract were binding.

   However, this rule will not be applied if it is found that misrepresentation has occurred. For example, in the case of *Curtis v. Chemical Cleaning and Dyeing Company Co.* (1951), the plaintiff took a wedding dress to the defendant company for dry cleaning. At the time, the plaintiff was asked to sign a document which exempted the cleaners from liability "for any damage howsoever arising". She queried this document at the time but was told that it simply meant that the cleaner would not accept liability for any sequins or beads in the dress. However, when the dress was returned, it was badly stained. The cleaners denied liability for the stain and relied on the exclusion clause. The Court of Appeal held that the defendants could not rely on the clause, even though the claimant had signed it, as the assistant had misrepresented the statement.

2. **Incorporation by Reasonable Notice** An exemption clause will apply only if reasonable steps are taken to bring the notice to someone's attention before the contract is made. For example, in the case of *Olley v. Marlborough Court* (1949), the plaintiff booked into the defendant's hotel. There was a notice in her room which stated that the hotel would not accept liability for any articles lost or stolen unless they were handed in for safe keeping. When the plaintiff left the room at a later stage, she left furs in the bedroom which were subsequently stolen. The court held that the exemption clause, in this instance, was not effective as the contract was completed at the reception desk. A notice in the bedroom came too late to be incorporated into the contract.

3. **Incorporation by Course of Dealing** If two parties have had previous dealings with each other and a number of contracts have been signed between them incorporating an exemption clause, the courts have found that these clauses may apply to subsequent transactions even if the usual steps to incorporate the clauses have not been taken.

In the case of *Hollier v. Rambler Motors* (1972), a plaintiff had repairs made to his car on a number of occasions over a period of five years. On each occasion that work was carried out to his car, the plaintiff signed a form disclaiming liability for any damage caused by fire to his car. On a particular day, he left his car at the garage but did not sign the usual form. A fire subsequently broke out at the garage and the plaintiff's car was damaged. However, the garage claimed that the disclaimer previously signed applied in this instance also. The court found that the garage was liable and said that there was insufficient evidence to show that the plaintiff knew of and agreed to the condition as a continuing term of his contract with the garage.

Contracts in Restraint of Trade

Within the area of business law, it is common for contracts to contain restraint of trade clauses. Such clauses are commonly found in employment contracts, but they are also found in commercial contracts whereby a vendor can restrict a buyer's liberty to compete with the vendor. In general, courts view such clauses as contrary to public policy and will render them void unless parties take steps to justify that they are reasonable and in the interest of their business. The question of what is reasonable is considered on a case-by-case basis, as the clause must go no further than is reasonable for the protection of the employer's business.

In an employment contract, it is not uncommon or illegal for an employer to restrict a former employee from working within a fixed geographical area or from working for a rival business of the former employer for a period of time after the employee's contract ceases. However, the restrictions must not be excessive. What is excessive depends on the nature of the work in question and the structure of the business.

For example, in the case of *Fitch v. Dewes* (1921), a solicitor's clerk entered into an agreement which prevented him from practising as a solicitor, once qualified, within seven miles of Tamworth Town Hall, for the rest of his life. It was held that, even though the restraint was unlimited in duration, it was still reasonable in the circumstances.

By contrast, in the case of *Wyatt v. Kreglinger and Fernau* (1933), the plaintiff worked for a wool company and was given a £200 annual pension on his retirement on the condition that he did not compete against his employers in the wool trade. It was held that the restraint was so wide as to be unreasonable and therefore void.

In the case of *Esso Petroleum v. Harper's Garage (Stourport)* (1968), Harper's garage agreed to take all petrol supplies from Esso for a period of 21 years. In effect, the garage had entered into a 'solus agreement', which is a contract whereby the retailer could sell or supply only Esso's products for a number of years. The court held that a solus agreement is acceptable so long as it has a limited time frame. A solus agreement for a 21-year period was unreasonable and therefore the court held it to be void.

In *Norbrook Laboratories Ltd v. Smith* (1987), an international manufacturer of pharmaceutical products employed the defendant, a chemist, who signed a confidentiality agreement promising not to take up any employment in which he might disclose confidential information within one year of the end of his employment with the plaintiff. The defendant announced his intention to take up work as a chemist for another international company and the plaintiff sought an injunction to prevent him doing so. It was held, by the Northern Ireland Court of Appeal, that the injunction should be granted as the agreement was reasonable in relation both to the parties and to the public. In arriving at this decision, the court considered the worldwide scope of the plaintiff's business, the competition the plaintiff faced and the fact that the defendant would be putting himself in a position to pass confidential information to the plaintiff's rivals.

Discharge of Contracts

When a contract is brought to an end, it is said to be discharged. Contracts can be discharged in a number of ways between two parties. These are as follows:
1. performance;
2. agreement;
3. breach; and
4. frustration.

1. Discharge by Performance

Discharge by performance is the most usual method of discharge. The general rule is that performance must exactly match the requirements laid down in the contract, otherwise known as 'entire performance'. In *Cutter v. Powell* (1795), a sailor contracted to serve on a ship travelling from Jamaica to Liverpool. He was to be paid 30 guineas for the voyage. This was to become payable when the ship arrived in Liverpool. He died during the journey. His widow later sued for his wages up until his death, but her claim was unsuccessful. The court held that the contract required entire performance and, as the husband had not completed the voyage, the plaintiff was not entitled to any money. There are a number of exceptions to the general rule requiring complete performance:

- **Divisible Contracts** This is where a contract may provide for performance by instalments, i.e. each contract is independent of the other and this would have overcome the harshness of the rule in *Cutter v. Powell*.
- **Partial Performance** This arises where a contract has partially been discharged. The party performing the act can claim the contract price but will remain liable for any deduction of the work which has not been completed. This principle can be seen in *Sumpter v. Hedges* (1898). In this case, a builder agreed to construct two houses and a stable on the defendant's land for £565. However, he abandoned the project after completing £333 worth of work so the defendant had to complete the building himself and did so using materials left behind by the builder. The builder claimed for the work that he had done and materials supplied. The claim for the work failed because the defendant was not choosing to accept poor performance and had to finish the job himself. He had no alternative but to complete the building, which would otherwise be useless. However, the builder was allowed to claim for the materials left behind as the defendant did not have to use these.
- **Prevention of Performance** This arises where one party is prevented from completing the performance by the other party. If this occurs, the

party prevented from performance can sue for breach of contract or on a *quantum meruit* basis. An example of this is in *Planche v. Coburn* (1831) where the plaintiff was contracted to write a book on costume and ancient armour for a fee of £100. After he had begun writing, the defendants decided to cease publishing a series of which the book was to form a part. The author, however, was able to recover £50 on a *quantum meruit* basis.

2. Discharge by Agreement

A contract can be discharged by agreement in the following ways:
- There may be a clause within the contract providing for discharge by imposing a condition precedent that is preventing the contract from coming into existence unless the condition is satisfied.
- The contract may impose a condition subsequent – a provision for termination by notice to the other party.
- A contract may be discharged by subsequent agreement, for which there must be some consideration, if the contract remains unperformed by both parties and each party provides consideration by agreeing to release the other from their obligation. However, if one party completely performed his obligations, his agreement to release the other from his obligations requires consideration, such as payment of a cancellation fee.
- The parties enter into a completely new contract, i.e. a *novation* contract.

3. Discharge by Breach

As stated previously, a breach of contract does not end the contract. Instead, the breach gives the innocent party the right to end the contract should they choose to do so. However, the injured party may want to treat the contract as still continuing and simply claim for loss or damages. There are two types of breach which can occur.

Anticipatory Breach An anticipatory breach occurs where a party declares in advance that they will not perform their obligations under the contract. The other party can sue for the breach straight away and it is not necessary to wait until the performance falls due. In *Frost v. Knight* (1872), the defendant promised to marry the plaintiff once his father had died. The defendant later broke off the engagement while his father was still alive. The plaintiff sued him for breach of promise, but the defendant argued that she had no claim as the time for performance had not yet arrived. The argument was rejected and the plaintiff's claim succeeded.

Repudiatory Breach A repudiatory breach occurs where one party does not fulfil their obligations under the contract. The difference between an anticipatory and repudiatory breach is that, in a repudiatory breach, performance of the contract has actually begun when one party breaches it.

4. Discharge by Frustration

This type of discharge arises where, as a result of unavoidable circumstances, the contractual obligations can no longer be performed. The general rule is that, if a person contracts to do something, he is not discharged if performance proves to be impossible. The case of *Paradine v. Jayne* (1647) stated that, when a party, by his own contract, creates a duty or charge upon himself, he is bound to make it good, notwithstanding any accident by inevitable necessity, because he could have provided against it by his contract. This rule was mitigated by the doctrine of frustration.

In the case of *Krell v. Henry* (1903), the defendant agreed to pay £75 for the hire of the plaintiff's flat in order to watch the King's coronation. However, the coronation was postponed due to the King's illness. It was held that the contract was frustrated because the sole purpose for which the contract had been made could not be fulfilled.

Likewise, in the case of *Taylor v. Caldwell* (1863), the defendant allowed the plaintiff to use the Surrey Gardens and Music Hall for four specified days at a cost of £100 per day. However, before the date of the first concert, a fire burnt down the music hall. It was held that the contract was frustrated and both parties were excused from further performance.

It is impossible to compile an exhaustive list of the situations in which a contract will be frustrated. However, examples are: the destruction or unavailability of something essential for contract performance, the death of either party to a contract, the unavailability of a party or the method of performance being impossible.

Remedies for Breach of Contract

If a contract is breached, the innocent party has the right to sue for breach of contract. Other remedies available are injunctions, specific performance, rescission and rectification. These remedies can be sought in addition to the remedy of damages or they can be sought separately.

Damages

Damages are the most important common law remedy. The remedy of damages aims to restore the party who has suffered loss to the same position he or she would have been in had the contract been performed. A party therefore sues for damages as compensation for the loss caused by breach.

Remoteness of Damage In determining whether a loss arising out of a breach of contract can be compensated for, a party must look at whether the damage is too remote. Damage is not too remote if it is "such as may fairly and reasonably be considered either arising naturally, i.e. according to the natural course of things from the breach itself, or such loss as may reasonably be supposed to have been in the contemplation of both parties at the time that they made the contract". In *Hadley v. Baxendale* (1854), the plaintiff owned a mill that ceased to operate because the main drive shaft had broken. He had contracted with the defendant to transport the broken shaft to the makers who would use it as a pattern for making a new one. However, as a result of the defendant's neglect, delivery was delayed and the mill was out of action for longer than was necessary. The defendant did not know that his delay would cause the mill to be out of action. The plaintiff claimed for loss of profits. The court held that the claim must fail. As the defendant did not know that the mill would be idle due to his neglect and as the loss was outside the natural course of events, it was held that damage was not a natural consequence of the delay in transport of a broken shaft.

In *Victoria Laundry (Windsor) v. Newman Industries* (1949), the defendant contracted to sell a boiler to the plaintiff for immediate use. The boiler was delivered six months late. During this time, the plaintiffs were offered a contract to dye soldiers' uniforms and had to turn it down. Claiming for breach of contract, the plaintiff claimed damages for:
1. normal loss of profits; and
2. loss of special profits which would have been earned on completion of the dyeing contracts.

It was held that the damages for loss of profits were recoverable but the claim for loss of special profits failed. These were considered to be special facts not reasonably foreseeable and not arising naturally according to the ordinary course of things.

Measure of Damages The *quantum* of damages is the amount of damages to be paid to the plaintiff. Damages can be assessed under the following headings:
- **Non-financial Loss** This loss was developed in the case of *Jarvis v. Swan Towers* (1973). The plaintiff took a two-week ski holiday in Switzerland based on a brochure description. The brochure stated that the owner of the accommodation had excellent English, that there was

a bar on the premises and regular entertainment. When the plaintiff arrived, the whole holiday was far inferior to the one described in the brochure – it lacked the advertised afternoon teas, the functioning bar or the English-speaking proprietor. The plaintiff sued for both financial loss and non-financial loss. He was awarded damages of £125 for non-financial loss to compensate him for his unenjoyable holiday.

- **Liquidated Damages** Such damages are damages that are capable of calculation and become payable in the event of a breach. In some contracts, parties include in the contract a genuine estimate of the loss likely to result from a breach of contract and they agree that this amount will be payable if the breach occurs. However, in some cases a clause of this kind may be construed as a penalty clause, which the courts refuse to enforce. For example, in the Northern Irish case of *United Dominions Trust Ltd v. Patterson* (1973), the plaintiff granted the defendant a loan of £900 repayable with interest in 36 monthly instalments. One clause of the agreement stated that, in the event of default of an instalment payment, the whole amount would immediately become due. The defendant had the option to pay the balance at any time with interest only to the date of payment. The defendant defaulted and the plaintiff claimed the whole amount, including interest, for the full period. It was held that, to the extent that the demand for the amount included interest beyond the date of actual payment, it was in the nature of a penalty. The defendant was free at any stage to pay the balance with interest only, up until the date of payment, as such a demand for the 36 months would exceed any loss brought about as a result of the default.
- **Unliquidated Damages** In the absence of any pre-estimated amount set by the parties, the courts must calculate unliquidated damages. In calculating unliquidated damages, the court will consider what kind of loss the plaintiff is entitled to recover for, in what matter the measure of damage is assessed and to what extent the plaintiff is expected to mitigate the loss that he or she has suffered.
- **Nominal Damages** Such damages are a token award given where there has been a contractual breach but little or actual loss.
- **Punitive Damages** Such damages are punitive in nature and are designed to punish the party who deliberately breaches the contract.

Mitigation of Loss All parties have a duty to reduce or mitigate their loss. This means that a plaintiff cannot sit back and let the damages build up. He or she must take all steps to recover any loss that ought to have been compensated for. For example, in the case of *Darbishire v. Warren* (1963), the plaintiff owned a car, which, although it was old, he maintained was in an excellent condition. It had a market value of about £85. The car was damaged by the defendant's negligence and the plaintiff was advised that it would cost him £192 to get it repaired. The plaintiff went ahead with the repairs and claimed the money spent from the defendant, less the money he had received from his insurance company. His claim failed because the court held that the expenditure during the repairs was not justified. The plaintiff should have mitigated his loss by buying a replacement vehicle on the open market.

Equitable Remedies

Specific performance, injunctions, rectification and rescission are called equitable remedies. The courts have a discretion as to whether or not to grant them in the particular circumstances of a case.

Specific Performance An order of 'specific performance' directs a party to perform his or her obligation under a contract. Specific performance will be awarded only where damages are an inadequate remedy and will not replace the goods. Specific performance will be awarded for the sale of land and the sale of unique goods. It will not be awarded for contracts for personal services, contracts to advance money, contracts which require the constant supervision of the court (e.g. most contracts to erect or repair buildings), contracts where one of the parties is an infant or minor and contracts that are neither fair nor equitable. For example, in *A. Nesbitt and Co. Ltd v. Rollo E. McClure* (1971), the defendant had been appointed liquidator of a textile company and had agreed to sell printing screens and a quantity of special cloth to the plaintiff. After this agreement, the defendant received an attractive offer for the whole business, including the entire factory and stock. When the plaintiff sought to have the agreement with the defendant specifically enforced, the defendant claimed that this would cause the defendant undue hardship in having to turn down the later offer. It was held that specific performance would be awarded to the plaintiff because for hardship to be used as a defence it must exist at the time of the contract which the plaintiff is seeking to enforce. That was not the case here as the attractive offer only came to light afterwards.

Injunction An injunction is a discretionary equitable remedy of the court which requires a party to stop or refrain from doing a particular act. Injunctions can be perpetual or they can be granted on a time-specific basis. Types of injunctions granted by the court include:
  • interim injunctions, which last only until the next sitting of the court;

- interlocutory injunctions, which last from the application until the court hearing months later;
- perpetual injunctions, which last forever; and
- mareva injunctions, which are forms of injunction that stop the defendant distributing his assets prior to a case coming to court.

Rectification   An order of rectification is made to fix a mistake in a document so that it reflects what the parties actually intended. In *Rooney and McParland v. Carlin* (1981), the plaintiff sought rectification of a written contract settling a previous claim. It was held by the Northern Ireland Court of Appeal that rectification would be refused since it could not have been the common intention of the parties' counsel to draw up a contract in the terms now being suggested by the plaintiff.

Rescission   The remedy of rescission aims to restore parties to the position they were in prior to a contract being performed. It operates in cases of misrepresentation, duress and undue influence where the contract is voidable.

Limitation Periods

The right to sue for breach of contract is subject to limits under the Limitation (Northern Ireland) Order 1989 (1989 No. 1339 (N.I. 11)). Legal proceedings cannot be brought after six years have elapsed from the date on which proceedings could first have been taken. On that basis, time begins to run against the plaintiff sooner than it would do for a claim in tort law and proceedings become available only when the plaintiff becomes aware of the loss or damage they have sustained. However, if the contract in question is under seal (i.e. in the form of a deed), then the legal proceedings can begin up to 12 years after the breach of contract occurred. With regard to persons who are suffering from a contractual incapacity (i.e. because they are mentally ill or not yet 18), time does not begin to run against them until their incapacity disappears.

References

- *Chitty on Contracts* (30th Edition, Thomson Sweet & Maxwell, 2009).
- Brice Dickson, "Contract Law" in Brice Dickson and Deborah McBride (eds), *Digest of Northern Ireland Law* (SLS Legal Publications (NI), 1995–1996).
- Catherine Elliott and Frances Quinn, *Contract Law* (3rd Edition, Longman, 2001).

REVIEW QUESTIONS

(See Suggested Solutions at the end of this textbook.)

Question 3.1

Shoreland Enterprises Ltd ('Shoreland'), is a furniture manufacturing company. Jacob, a Chartered Accountant, is one of Shoreland's employees who is about to be made redundant. When he received this news he began looking for another position. He recently applied for a job as an accountant with Candace Publications Ltd ('Candace'). After two interviews, he received an offer letter in the post from the company and replied by return of post accepting this position. The following day, however, he received a phone call from the company revoking the job offer as a consequence of a decline in their business.

Requirement: Outline the postal rule of acceptance and the rules regarding revocation of an offer, and advise Jacob as to whether an enforceable contract exists between him and Candace or whether the purported revocation by Candace was valid in the circumstances.

(Source: Chartered Accountants Ireland, CAP 1, Law for Accountants (NI), Summer 2010, Extract: Q1(b))

Question 3.2

Sheila works as a financial accountant for Power Alliance Consultancy Ltd ('PAC'). Last week she approached her manager and informed him that, although it was not part of her job, she had developed a new software program to simplify the operation of the company's payroll system. Sheila further informed him that she had already implemented the program with the assistance of the company's finance department and that the August payroll run had been successfully completed on the new system. Sheila's manager was so delighted with the new system that he promised Sheila a bonus of £5,000 for all of her hard work. However, the company's financial controller is refusing to pay the bonus on the basis that there is no consideration, as the benefit is past.

Requirement: Define consideration, and evaluate the concept of past consideration. In light of this evaluation, determine whether the promise of the £5,000 payment to Sheila is legally enforceable.

(Source: Chartered Accountants Ireland, CAP 1, Law for Accountants (NI), Autumn 2009, Extract: Q2(a))

Question 3.3

A client has come to you seeking advice in relation to the law of contract. Your client is a car dealer and has agreed to sell five vans to an engineering company. A contract has not yet been signed between the parties and no money has been exchanged.

Requirement: List and describe briefly the main elements of a contract and determine whether or not a valid contract was entered into between the parties.

(Source: Chartered Accountants Ireland, CAP 1, Law for Accountants (NI), Summer 2009, Extract: Q2(a))

Question 3.4

James, a trainee accountant and keen collector of antique books, is browsing at a local book fair when he comes across a stall selling rare books. When he reviews the collection he discovers a first edition copy of Luca Pacioli's book *Summa de Arithmetica* published in 1494, which contains a chapter on the first record of double-entry bookkeeping. The book is priced at £1,500. James thinks that £1,500 is too expensive and offers to buy the book for £1,000. The stall owner refuses to sell the book at that price but says that he will sell it for £1,300. James says that he will have to call his bank and see if he can extend his overdraft to purchase the book and, if he can, he will come back to the stall owner before 5.00 pm and accept his offer of £1,300.

At 4.45 pm he returns to the stall and attempts to buy the book for £1,300. Unfortunately, the owner of the stall informs him that he already sold the book 15 minutes earlier to another customer for the asking price of £1,500. James is furious to have missed out on the opportunity to purchase the book.

Requirement: Advise James as to whether he can sue the stall owner for breach of contract.

(Source: Chartered Accountants Ireland, CAP 1, Law for Accountants (NI), Summer 2008, Extract: Q2(a))

Question 3.5

(a) Adam has recently commenced employment with Downey Investment Advisors as a financial accountant. Adam has taken over the position of management accountant from Gabriel, whose contract with the company was terminated as a consequence of contractual frustration resulting from Gabriel's permanent incapacity.

Requirement: Define the concept of contractual frustration, and outline any other FOUR situations where the Court is likely to uphold a claim of frustration.

(b) As Adam has regular access to confidential company information and trade secrets in his employment, Downey Investment Advisors have included a restraint of trade clause in Adam's employment contract to the effect that should he leave their employment he is restrained from working for a competitor or setting up a business in competition with Downey Investment Advisors for a period of six months, and within a 50-kilometre radius of Downey's offices in Belfast and Omagh.

Requirement:
 (i) Assess the nature of a restraint of trade clause.
(ii) Outline the factors that a court will take into consideration in determining the validity of these clauses.
(iii) Determine whether the court would consider the clause in Adam's contract as valid or invalid.

(Source: Chartered Accountants Ireland, CAP 1, Law for Accountants (NI), Summer 2011, Extract: Q2(b) and (c).)

Question 3.6

ABC Ltd is a private company in Northern Ireland. ABC Ltd has encountered a problem with one of its suppliers. The supplier signed a contract with ABC Ltd for the supply of component parts at a price of £85 per unit, with the requirement that 200 units are delivered on a monthly basis. Last month, the supplier notified ABC Ltd that they would no longer be able to supply the components at the agreed price. ABC Ltd is outraged and is considering asking the Court for an 'Order for Specific Performance' of the contract.

Requirement: Explain the nature of an 'Order for Specific Performance', referring specifically to the various grounds when this Order will not be granted, and review the likelihood of the court granting ABC Ltd the Order in these circumstances.

(Source: Chartered Accountants Ireland, CAP 1, Law for Accountants (NI), Autumn 2011, Extract: Q4(b).)

Question 3.7

Purity plc, a public limited company, is a pharmaceutical company. Jim has worked for Purity for the last 10 years as a research scientist. Prior to joining the company, Jim signed a contract that contained a restraint of trade clause which stated that he was prohibited from working for a competitor of Purity within Northern Ireland for six months after the termination of his contract. He has recently resigned and is now taking up employment with Purity's main rival company.

Requirement:
  (i) Explain the nature of a restraint of trade clause, and give TWO examples of such clauses.
 (ii) Outline whether you consider the clause in Jim's contract is likely to be classified as valid or invalid, providing ONE reason for your answer.
(iii) On the assumption that the clause is valid, Purity are considering applying for an injunction to restrain Jim taking up employment. Explain the purpose of an injunction.

(Source: Chartered Accountants Ireland, CAP 1, Law for Accountants (NI), Summer 2012, Extract: Q4(b).)

Question 3.8

ABC Pharmaceuticals ('ABC') has had a contract with Rossmore Medical ('ROSSMORE') for the past three years for the supply of drugs to treat clinical depression. The contract term agreed between the parties was five years, but last month Rossmore contacted ABC to inform them that they would be cancelling the contract with immediate effect, as a Government Order recently enacted in the country in which Rossmore is located has put a ban on the importation of this drug.

ABC are considering suing ROSSMORE for breach of contract, but their solicitor has advised them that they are unlikely to be successful as the contract is frustrated.

Requirement:
  (i) Define 'frustration' and explain any THREE grounds upon which a contract can be deemed to be frustrated.
 (ii) State, with a reason, whether the contract between ABC and Rossmore is frustrated.

(Source: Chartered Accountants Ireland, CAP 1, Law for Accountants (NI), Summer 2013, Extract: Q1(a).)

Question 3.9

Last year Dylan Accounting College ('Dylan') experienced a 20% drop in student numbers and, in an attempt to stem this decline, Dylan called a meeting with all 20 of their lecturing staff to discuss what could be done to increase student numbers. Following this meeting, Dylan's CEO sent an email to all lecturers stating that they had decided to offer a £5,000 bonus to any lecturer who developed and marketed a new course that generated in excess of 50 student applications.

For the next nine months, one of the lecturers, Anne, devoted all of her free time to developing and marketing a course leading to the award of a Masters in Corporate Governance and Ethics. As a result of Anne's work, Dylan had secured applications from 72 students for entry onto the Masters programme.

In addition, Frank, the college's registrar (who is not part of the lecturing team), developed a Diploma in Advanced Auditing Practice. Two weeks ago, the marketing department informed Frank that, to date, they had received 53 applications for entry onto the Diploma course.

Last week, the CEO called a meeting with both Anne and Frank and informed them that Dylan did NOT intend to run either of their new proposed courses, as another new course had generated over 100 student applications and would generate more income than either Anne's or Frank's courses. When Anne and Frank queried whether or not they would be receiving the £5,000 bonus, the CEO told them that they were not entitled to it as they had no contract with Dylan. Anne and Frank believe that there is a contract and are considering suing Dylan for breach of contract.

Requirement: By discussing the law regarding 'offer and acceptance', assess whether a valid contract has been formed between:

  (i) Dylan Accounting College and Anne; and
  (ii) Dylan Accounting College and Frank.

(Source: Chartered Accountants Ireland, CAP 1, Law for Accountants (NI),
Autumn 2013, Extract: Q1(a).)

Question 3.10

Last year Bella was made redundant from her job. Following this redundancy, Bella decided to change her career path and pursue her lifetime ambition of opening a bakery. She signed a lease on commercial premises for a period of 12 months and then set about refitting these premises to become an operational bakery. Prior to opening the business, the bakery was inspected by the Fire Safety Authority for the purpose of obtaining a fire safety certificate. Unfortunately, the premises failed the inspection, due to a lack of fire-retardant ceiling tiles, an improper swing of the exit door and the fact the cooking ventilation system was not fire compliant and needed updating. Following this inspection, Bella contacted the landlord, Alliance

Realty ('Alliance'), requesting that they make the required alterations to the property as specified in the inspection report. Alliance is refusing to undertake the alterations as they consider the premises fire compliant. Bella is now considering terminating the lease with ALLIANCE and seeks your advice.

Requirement:
 (i) Discuss any FOUR methods by which a contract can be discharged.
(ii) Advise Bella of the most appropriate method of contractual discharge in the circumstances, commenting also on the legal consequences for Bella of this discharge.

(Source: Chartered Accountants Ireland, CAP 1, Law for Accountants (NI), Summer 2014, Extract: Q1(a).)

Question 3.11

Aunty Em's Catering School Ltd ('Aunty Em') has been trading successfully since 1963. Since its incorporation, its founder and primary shareholder, Emilia, has acted as the company's managing director. Emilia celebrated her 75th birthday last year and at that stage she decided to sell the business.

Prior to the sale of the business, Emilia had received a letter instituting legal action against Aunty Em. The letter was from a former student of the catering college claiming compensation arising from the theft of her purse and bag from her assigned locker, while she was attending a one-day course at the college. Emilia is denying that Aunty Em is liable for this loss, as a large notice, containing an exemption clause, is prominently displayed in the locker room. This notice states that Aunty Em is not liable for any loss, theft or damage to valuables left in storage lockers.

Requirement: Summarise the rules relating to incorporation of exemption clauses. In light of this summary, determine whether this clause excludes Aunty Em's Catering School Ltd in respect of this loss.

(Source: Chartered Accountants Ireland, CAP 1, Law for Accountants (NI), Summer 2014, Extract: Q4(b)(i).)

Question 3.12

(a) Anton and Aaron are two friends, both 16 years old. Both are avid computer programmers and have recently developed their own computer game called "Asteroid Fighters". Bridgewater Computer Gaming Ltd ('BCG') is a Belfast-based private company specialising in computer games. Anton and Aaron have approached the owners of BCG to purchase the rights to the game. BCG is keen to do so and have approached you to draft the contract for purchasing the rights to the game. However, you explain to BCG that Anton and Aaron have no contractual capacity to enter into a contract.

Requirement: In relation to the law of contract, explain the concept of contractual capacity and determine whether Anton and Aaron have the capacity to enter into a contract with BCG Ltd.

(b) BCG is expanding its business and wishes to purchase land in North Antrim from Mr Elis. BCG has agreed a purchase price of £100,000 with Mr Elis and it is the intention of BCG to build the company premises on the land. Contracts were signed between Mr Elis and BCG and a completion date finalised for the transfer of the land and monies to be exchanged. However, Mr Elis has been told he could have received twice the price for the land and has just phoned his solicitor to say that he no longer wishes to sell the land and is refusing to sign the transfer document.

Requirement: In relation to the law of contract, list and describe briefly the main elements of a contract and state with reasons, whether or not a valid contract was entered into between Mr Elis and BCG Ltd.

(Source: Chartered Accountants Ireland, CAP 1, Law for Accountants (NI), Autumn 2014, Extract: Q2(a) and (b).)

Question 3.13

Bill is the general manager of The River Spa, an exclusive hotel and spa in Dungannon. As part of his role, Bill is responsible for overseeing and managing all reservations made at the hotel. In order to improve the reservation service, Bill decided to upgrade the reservation's computer package to allow online reservations. He contacted a local computer company, Mid Ulster Computer Services ('MUCS'), in January 2015 and signed a contract with it. MUCS agreed to upgrade the computer system, by February 2015, to allow reservations to be made online. The River Spa agreed to pay a fee of £1,500 upon completion of the work and receipt of an invoice. The River Spa received an invoice in March 2015 but it remains unpaid.

By April 2015, Bill noticed that no reservations were being made online and he asked a friend of his, who works for ABC Computer Ltd, to check the reservation system. His friend tells him that the work he asked MUCS to carry out has not been carried out as there is no facility for making online reservations on the hotel website. The River Spa now plans to sue MUCS for breach of contract.

Requirement: In relation to the law of contract, state whether a valid contract was entered into between The River Spa and MUCS and comment whether The River Spa will be successful in suing MUCS for breach of contract.

(Source: Chartered Accountants Ireland, CAP 1, Law for Accountants (NI), Summer 2015, Extract: Q1(a).)

Question 3.14

Harrison has been employed as a business development manager with Providence Financial Analysts ('PFA') since 2009. PFA is based in Belfast city. Harrison agreed to sign a restraint of trade clause as part of his contract of employment. This clause restricts Harrison from setting up a business in direct competition to PFA within 30 miles of Belfast city for six months, following termination of his employment with PFA.

Two months ago PFA made Harrison redundant. Last week the managing partner of PFA heard that Harrison is establishing his own financial consultancy firm, located approximately three miles from their offices. PFA's solicitor sent Harrison a letter threatening legal action against him to enforce the restraint of trade clause.

Requirement:
(a) Define the meaning of a restraint of trade clause.
(b) List the THREE main factors that a court will take into consideration in determining the validity of a restraint of trade clause in an employment contract.
(c) Advise Harrison as to the validity of the restraint of trade clause, and assess whether PFA can prevent him from establishing his business.

Prior to receiving the letter from PFA's solicitors, Harrison had contracted with Redmound Construction ('Redmound') for the renovation of an office building that he had leased as a base for his business. Redmound commenced work on the renovation, but two weeks into the four-week project they stopped working, as they had won a contract to build a shopping centre. Redmound informed Harrison that they will not be able to complete the renovation and that they will be sending him a bill for the work that they have already done. Harrison is considering applying to the court for an Order of specific performance to force Redmound to complete the renovation project as agreed.

Requirement:
(d) List any THREE grounds upon which the court will refuse to grant an Order for specific performance.

(e) Assess the likelihood of Harrison obtaining this Order against Redmound.

(f) If Harrison is unsuccessful in obtaining this Order, advise him as to whether he is obliged to pay Redmound for the work they have already completed on this renovation.

(Source: Chartered Accountants Ireland, CAP 1, Law for Accountants (NI), Autumn 2015, Extract: Q1(a) to (f).)

Chapter 4

COMMERCIAL LAW

Introduction

This chapter examines the law relating to commercial contracts in Northern Ireland. There are many types of commercial contracts by which ownership and/or the possession of goods, services or digital content passes from one party to another. This includes contracts for the sale of goods, services or digital content and contracts for the supply of goods, services or digital content. This chapter will examine the Consumer Rights Act 2015 ('the Act') and will also look at the law relating to unfair terms in consumer contracts.

The Consumer Rights Act 2015

The Consumer Rights Act 2015 (the '2015 Act') came into force on 1 October 2015 and was the biggest shake-up of consumer rights law in a generation. The aim of the Act was to simplify, strengthen and modernise UK consumer law. Prior to the Act coming into force, there was "general agreement across business and consumer groups that existing UK consumer law was unnecessarily complex".

Before October 2015, the main pieces of consumer legislation governing consumer law were:
- the Sale of Goods Act 1979;
- the Supply of Goods and Services Act 1982;
- the Sale and Supply of Goods Act 1994; and
- the Unfair Contract Terms Act 1977.

With the introduction of the 2015 Act, key consumer rights are now consolidated into a single piece of legislation. These rights cover contracts for goods, services, digital content and unfair terms in consumer contracts.

The Act is split into three parts (which, in turn, as with all statutes, are divided into 'chapters'). 'Part 1' deals with consumer contracts for goods, digital content and services. 'Part 2' deals with unfair terms, while 'Part 3' contains miscellaneous provisions, including enforcement powers. This discussion will only focus on Part 1 and Part 2 of the Act.

Consumer Contracts for Goods, Digital Content and Services

Consumer Contracts (Chapters 1 and 2) According to the explanatory notes to the Act: "Part 1 is concerned with contracts between a trader and a consumer under which a trader agrees to supply goods, digital content or services (or any combination of these) to a consumer. It does not matter whether the contract is written or oral or implied by the conduct of the trader and consumer, or a combination of these. This means that, for the Part to have effect, there must be a contract and the contract must be for a trader to supply goods, digital content or services to a consumer." Hence, the rules of contract will always apply.

A consumer is defined as "an individual acting for purposes that are wholly or mainly outside that individual's trade, business, craft or profession". This new definition of a consumer is wider than existing definitions found in UK and EU law as it includes individuals entering into contracts for a mixture of business and personal reasons. The burden of proof in showing that an individual is not a consumer is on the trader.

A 'trader', which replaces the term 'seller', is defined as "a person acting for purposes relating to that person's trade, business, craft or profession, whether acting personally or through another person acting in the trader's name or on the trader's behalf". This definition includes government departments and public sector authorities.

Terms Implied into Contracts Terms implied into contracts between a trader and consumer by the 2015 Act include:

- **Satisfactory Quality (Section 9)** Section 9 of the Act states that goods should be of satisfactory quality, meaning that goods should "meet the standard that a reasonable person would regard satisfactory, taking into account any description of the goods, the price or other consideration for the goods (if relevant), and all the other relevant circumstances". Therefore, the test as to whether goods are of satisfactory quality is an objective one and depends on what is acceptable to a reasonable person. This means that although the goods may not be acceptable to the actual buyer, this will not be sufficient to justify a claim that the goods were not of satisfactory quality.

  Section 9 provides a (non-exhaustive) list of factors that can be relevant in determining the quality of goods, including:
  - fitness for all the purposes for which goods of the kind in question are commonly supplied;
  - appearance and finish;
  - freedom from minor defects;
  - safety; and
  - durability.

Case law that previously used to assist in cases dealing with the Sale of Goods Act 1979, the Supply of Goods and Services Act 1982 and the Sale and Supply of Goods Act 1994 is still applicable in this context. Hence, in the case of *Lutton v. Saville Tractors (Belfast) Limited* (1986), the court held that a second-hand car that developed a large number of defects within two months of being bought by the plaintiff was neither of merchantable quality nor reasonably fit for its purpose.

Similarly, in the case of *Shine v. General Guarantee Corp Limited* (1988), the defendant finance company purchased a car from a third party which was then let to the plaintiff through a hire-purchase agreement, having described the car as being in good condition. The plaintiff, however, subsequently learned that the car had been written-off by an insurance company. Accordingly, the plaintiff brought an action against the defendant alleging breach of the condition of 'merchantable quality' (similar to the 'satisfactory quality' of section 9 of the 2015 Act) implied by section 14(2) of the Sale of Goods Act 1979. The Court of Appeal held that the plaintiff had thought he was buying a second-hand enthusiast's car in good condition at a fair price when in fact he was buying it at a substantially overpriced amount. No one knowing its history would have bought it other than at a substantially reduced price. Consequently, there had been a breach of the implied condition of merchantable ('satisfactory') quality, for which the plaintiff was entitled to damages.

- **Goods Shall be Fit for a Particular Purpose (Section 10)** A second implied condition contained in section 10 is that goods must be reasonably fit for the purpose for which they are bought. This term applies only where the trader is acting in the course of business. Furthermore, the buyer must make known to the trader the purpose for which the goods are being bought. Once again, as is the case with satisfactory quality, the goods must not only be reasonably fit for their purpose at the time of sale, but they must remain so for a reasonable period of time afterwards. For example, if Mr X wanted to buy a piece of equipment to use for a specific purpose, he must tell the seller exactly what he needs the equipment for.

This was seen in the case of *Frost v. Aylesbury Dairy Company* (1905). The defendants were sellers of milk and supplied the plaintiff with a daily supply of milk for his household. The plaintiff's wife drank the milk and subsequently died from typhoid fever contracted from the milk supplied by the defendants. An action for damages for breach of the implied condition of fitness for consumption as food followed. The Court of Appeal decided that the defendants had taken great care to print in their account book comments on their skill and special knowledge in the matter of milk and there was evidence that the plaintiffs had relied on that skill. As there was no doubt of the purpose for which the milk was required, the defendants were in breach of the implied condition of fitness for purpose, notwithstanding the fact that the defect could not have been found by casual inspection.

Likewise, in *Heil v. Hedges* (1951) the plaintiff sued for breach of the implied condition of fitness for purpose as pork chops supplied by the defendants were infected with tapeworm. In this instance, the plaintiff's claim failed because the court decided that had the pork chops been cooked thoroughly, the tapeworm would have died and the plaintiff would have not come to any harm.

- **Goods Should Correspond with their Description (Section 11)** Section 11 of the Act deals with 'supplies by description', providing that there is an implied condition that goods should correspond with their description. Furthermore, if a supply is by sample (i.e. if a buyer has the opportunity to test the goods purchased in the shop beforehand) as well as by description, the goods must also correspond with the sample. The basic case in this area is *Beale v. Taylor* (1967). The seller of a car advertised it as a 1961 Triumph Herald 1200. A buyer came to see the car and noted that there was a metal disc in the rear of the car showing "1200". However, the buyer later discovered that while the rear half of the car was part of a 1961 Herald convertible, the front half was part of a much earlier model; two separate models of the Herald car had been welded together. In this case, the seller argued that it had not been a sale by description and tried to rely on the buyer's inspection of the car. The court held that the advertisement and the metal disc indicated that the car was a 1200; even though the buyer had inspected the car, the buyer had relied to some extent on the description, and therefore it was a sale by description.

Similarly, the case of *Godley v. Perry* (1960) concerned a catapult which when tested by the plaintiff worked well. On this basis, the plaintiff bought the catapult in a shop but, when he used it again, it backfired and damaged his eye. It was held by the court that the goods sold did not correspond to the sample, and the plaintiff was successful in his claim.

- **The Right to Sell (Section 17)** Under contract law, a seller must have an implied right to sell the goods at the time they are selling them, i.e. they must have legal title to the goods. This is perceived to be one of the most important terms of a contract for the supply of goods. For example, if goods are stolen, the person who has stolen the goods has no right to sell these goods. This was seen in the case of *Rowland v. Divall* (1923), in which the plaintiff bought a motorcar from the defendant and used it for several months. It later transpired that the defendant had no legal title to the car and the plaintiff was subsequently required to return the car to the true owner. As a result, the plaintiff was entitled to get the purchase money back because he did not receive what he had contracted for, i.e. the property and lawful possession of the car.

Contracts for the Supply of Services (Chapter 4) The statutory requirements for contracts for the supply of services to consumers are contained in Chapter 4 of the Act, which sets out a consumer's rights when a trader provides a service to them under contract. In effect, these are contractual rights and, if breached, it is therefore a breach of contract. While the law in this regard also applies to all service sectors, it is not applicable where a trader provides a service to another trader or where a consumer provides a service to a consumer or a trader. The Act also sets out that contracts of employment or apprenticeships are not covered.

The Act imposes the following statutory rights into contracts for the supply of services:
- that the trader will carry out the service with reasonable care and skill (section 49);
- that the service will be performed in line with information provided concerning the service (section 50);
- where the consideration (charge/fee) for the service is not dealt with by the contract or determined by the course of dealing between the parties, there is an implied term that the party contracting with the supplier will pay a reasonable charge (section 51); and
- where the time for the service to be carried out is not dealt with by the contract or determined by the course of dealing between the parties, there is an implied term that the trader will carry out the service within a reasonable time (section 52).

Unfair Terms in Consumer Contracts

Part 2 of the Consumer Rights Act 2015 clarified and consolidated existing consumer legislation on unfair terms. As stated earlier, prior to the 2015 Act, the law on unfair contract terms was contained in two separate pieces of legislation: the Unfair Contract Terms Act 1977 (UCTA 1977) and the Unfair Terms in Consumer Contracts Regulations 1999 (1999 No. 2083) (UTCCR 1999). In 2005, the Law Commission concluded that the law on unfair contract terms was particularly complex and made recommendations to reform it. As a result of this, Part 2 of the Act now consolidates the UCTA and UTCCR by removing conflicting overlapping provisions.

The primary purpose of Part 2 is to afford protection to consumers. Hence, under section 62, it requires consumer contracts to be fair. If the contracts are not fair, they will not bind the consumer. It should be noted that, according to section 67, if a term is deemed to be unfair, the court can still allow the contract to continue, but for the unfair term, if it is practical to do so. A term is said to be unfair if it "causes a significant imbalance in the parties' rights and obligations under the contract". To determine if this has happened, the 2015 Act states that account should be taken of the subject matter of the contract. Moreover, cognisance should also be paid to all the other circumstances existing when the term was agreed.

There are certain terms that are automatically unenforceable. For example, under section 65(1), a trader cannot "limit liability for death or personal injury resulting from negligence".

Finally, section 68 of the 2015 Act further states that terms in consumer contracts must be transparent. This means that they must be plainly expressed and in intelligible language.

The Grey List In order to establish whether or not a term is fair, the 2015 Act has devised what is called a 'grey list'. The purpose of this 'grey list' is to provide consumers with guidance on what is deemed to be an unfair term. This grey list, which is not exhaustive, essentially replicates the grey list in the previous Unfair Terms and Consumer Contracts Regulations 1999. These unfair terms include those that:

- exclude legal liability for death or injury;
- inappropriately exclude liability for total or part non-performance of the contract on the part of the trader;
- permit the trader to retain sums paid by the consumer where the consumer decides to end the contract but without providing the consumer the same opportunity if the trader decides to cancel the contract;
- require a consumer, who ultimately fails to honour their part of the contract, to pay a disproportionate high amount in compensation in comparison to what a trader has to pay if they ultimately fail to honour their part of the contract;
- make an agreement binding on the consumer but give the trader an option regarding performance of that contract;
- enable the trader to terminate a contract of indefinite duration without first giving reasonable notice;
- require the consumer to pay disproportionate amounts if they do not continue the contract, including where a consumer cancels a contract (a so-called 'termination fee');

- allow the trader to determine the subject matter of the contract after the contract has been agreed with the consumer (excluding indefinite contracts); and
- allow the trader to set, for the first time, the price under a contract (or the method for calculating the price) after that contract has been agreed with the consumer.

Note: the contract terms included on the grey list are not *automatically* unfair. The list is intended as a guide for the court, which must still apply the fairness test. The Act also gives the Secretary of State the power to amend the grey list by way of statutory instrument.

Remedies

One of the significant features of the Consumer Rights Act 2015 is the inclusion of sections that provide for buyers' remedies. The remedies are set out in sections 19–24 and are in addition to all common law remedies. Consumers now have statutory remedies of the short-term right to rejection, repair or replacement and price reduction if a service, e.g. car repairs, home improvements including building and decorating work, dry cleaning, etc., does not conform to the contract. The remedy available to a consumer depends on the breach involved. The following remedies are available if the breach relates to: satisfactory quality; fitness for purpose; goods to be as described; goods to match sample; or model and digital content supplied with goods to conform to contract.

1. the short-term right to reject the goods or service (sections 20 and 22);
2. the right to repair or replacement of the goods or service (section 23); and
3. the right to a price reduction or the final right to reject the goods (sections 20 and 24).

Manufacturer's Liability

Currently, there are three grounds on which a manufacturer can be held liable for losses suffered by a consumer. This can occur under:

- the provisions contained in a guarantee in relation to the goods;
- the tort of negligence; or
- the Consumer Protection (Northern Ireland) Order 1987 (1987 No. 2049 (N.I. 20)).

Guarantees

Often when goods are purchased, they are issued with a guarantee that offers protection in relation to the goods if they become faulty. This guarantee will provide that, if the goods turn out to be defective within a specified period of time, the manufacturer will repair them free of charge. It should be noted, however, that a manufacturer is not under any obligation to issue a guarantee and, if one is issued, a manufacturer is entitled to restrict most of his/her obligations to any desired extent. Furthermore, a guarantee will not offer compensation for personal injury or damage to property.

Negligence

As discussed in **Chapter 2**, the case of *Donoghue v. Stevenson* (1932) established that a manufacturer owes a duty to take reasonable care, in the manufacture of his product, towards those people who are likely to come into contact with it. If a manufacturer fails to do so and a person is injured, or his property is damaged, the manufacturer is liable. For example, in the case of *Grant v. Australian Knitting Mills Ltd* (1936), a pair of underpants contained an excess of sulphate and this caused personal injury to the wearer when wearing them. The manufacturer was held liable in negligence.

Consumer Protection (Northern Ireland) Order 1987

Under this Order, a producer of defective products shall be held liable for any damage caused by a defect in the product. Such a manufacturer is liable irrespective of whether or not he exercised reasonable care or skill in the manufacturing process. The 1987 Order also deals with providing the public with better protection from unsafe consumer goods.

Product Liability

In order to successfully bring a claim against a manufacturer for product liability, the plaintiff must show that the product contained a defect and that the plaintiff suffered damage. A plaintiff must also establish that the damage was caused by the product. The last hurdle for a plaintiff to overcome is that he or she must show that the defendant was a producer or importer of the product. Furthermore, it should be noted that the supplier can also be held liable in the event that he is unable to identify the producer or importer if he is requested to do so.

For the purposes of the Order, the producer includes anyone who is a manufacturer of a finished product, who makes themselves out to be a producer by putting their own brand or other distinguishing mark on the goods supplied to them by manufacturers, or someone who has imported the product into a Member State of the European Union.

Meaning of 'Defect'

Under the 1987 Order, a product is considered defective if it does not comply with the standard of reasonable safety that a person is reasonably entitled to expect of the product. In establishing what this standard is, all circumstances are taken into account. Certain factors, however, are highlighted within the Order and these include:
- the manner in which the product has been marketed;
- the purpose for which the product has been marketed;
- any instructions accompanying the product;
- the use to which the product could reasonably be expected to be put; and
- the time at which the product is made available for supply after being manufactured.

The standard of reasonable safety is an objective one. Indeed, the expectations of the consumer or the producer are not relevant. For example, in *A & Others v. National Blood Authority & Others* (2001), the defendant was held liable for damage caused to recipients of blood infected by Hepatitis C following blood transfusions. The court found that the danger was known in 1988 but the defendant did not introduce screening tests until 1991. Hence, blood and blood products contaminated with the virus were defective products under the Consumer Protection (Northern Ireland) Order 1987.

Loss and Damage

Establishing that a product is defective is the burden of the consumer. He or she is entitled to claim only in respect of damage to or loss of something other than the defective product itself. For example, if a laptop explodes as soon as it is switched on and only the laptop itself is ruined, a consumer is not entitled to sue under the Order. However, if a consumer is injured or the contents of the room are damaged, in addition to the damage to the laptop, a consumer can sue in respect of any personal injuries or property damage. This property must be the consumer's property and the consumer must have been using it for his own private purposes. Furthermore, the amount of compensation which the consumer is claiming must be at least £275.

Defences under the 1987 Order

There are a number of defences under the 1987 Order, which are as follows:
1. the defect in the product is an inevitable consequence of compliance with a requirement imposed by statute or a European Union obligation;
2. the person being sued did not supply the defective product to another person;

3. the product supplied was not supplied in the course of the supplier's business;
4. the product was not defective when it left the supplier's hands;
5. the state of scientific and technical knowledge at the relevant time was not such that the producer might be expected to have discovered the defect;
6. the defect constituted a defect in a product in which the product in question had been comprised and was wholly attributable to the design of the subsequent product; and
7. more than 10 years has elapsed since the product was first supplied.

The fifth defence stated above is called the 'development risks' defence or the 'state of the art' defence. This defence is available to a manufacturer who can show that, in the manufacturing process, despite the fact that he used the most modern and advanced scientific and technical knowledge available, this knowledge was not sufficient to enable him or her to discover the defect in the product. It is particularly relevant in the field of medicine and drugs due to the fact that new products are constantly being developed. A defect in a new drug has the potential to affect numerous users. Such users cannot be compensated if there was no way of knowing that the defect existed at the time of the product's initial circulation.

Enforcing Consumer Rights

A consumer has three avenues by which to enforce his or her rights. First, he or she may bring a claim using the small claims procedure of the County Court (the Small Claims Court) if he or she is claiming up to £3,000. However, if the consumer is claiming up to £30,000, he or she can initiate an action in the County Court. If a consumer is claiming £30,000 or more, they should issue an action in the High Court.

The Consumer Council for Northern Ireland

The Consumer Council of Northern Ireland was set up in 1985 and has a general duty to promote consumer interests. To this end, it has powers to carry out research, provide information and investigate matters of consumer concern.

It consists of a Chairperson, a Deputy Chairperson and eight other members. There is a supporting staff of 26 employees. The members represent a wide range of organisations and interests, such as the trade union movement, advice centres, local authorities and women's groups. These representatives make up a central body of consumer opinion, watching over consumer interests and speaking on the consumer's behalf to the Government. The Council liaises closely with the Consumer Council as well as with the consumer councils for Scotland and Wales. The Consumer Council regularly commissions and publishes reports on matters such as buying a home, private rented housing for students, and remedies for consumer complaints.

REVIEW QUESTIONS

(See Suggested Solutions at the end of this textbook.)

Question 4.1

(a) James, a trainee accountant, purchases an academic textbook for his accountancy course that was recommended by his college lecturer. When he gets home and is flicking through the book he is shocked to discover that several pages have been torn out and that other pages of text are blank. He takes the book back to the store the following day, but the store manager refuses to replace the book or refund the purchase price, and points instead to a notice on the wall behind the cash desk, which reads: "No returns on books".

Requirement: Advise James as to his legal options as a consumer, pursuant to the terms of the Sale of Goods Act 1979.

(b) In the context of consumer law, outline the requirements in order to bring a successful claim for a defective product.

> (Source: Chartered Accountants Ireland, CAP 1, Law for Accountants (NI), Summer 2008, Extract: Q2(b) and (c))

Question 4.2

REGAL has been contacted by the General Consumer Council for Northern Ireland regarding consumer complaints in relation to a recent advertising campaign. The campaign involved female models dressed as air stewards but wearing very short skirts and very low-cut tops. The General Consumer Council for Northern Ireland has informed REGAL that it will refer these complaints to the Advertising Standards Authority unless REGAL voluntarily withdraws the advertisement.

Requirement: The directors of REGAL are unaware of the functions of the General Consumer Council for Northern Ireland and have asked you to advise them of the functions of this body.

(Source: Chartered Accountants Ireland, CAP 1, Law for Accountants (NI), Autumn 2013, Extract: Q4(c))

Question 4.3

Marcus and Isabella run a furniture shop in County Antrim, called MI Ltd ('MI'), which stocks sofas, luxury chairs and dining furniture. Last year, the store stocked a number of glider chairs from a producer called Children's Supplies Limited. However, in recent months, an increasing number of customers are contacting MI complaining that they have fallen off the chairs and suffered injury. MI is now threatening legal action against the producer, Children's Supplies Ltd.

Requirement:
(a) In accordance with consumer law and the provisions of the Consumer Protection (Northern Ireland) Order 1987:
   (i) Define a defective product and producer.
   (ii) Outline any THREE defences that may be raised by a producer where such a defective product claim is made.

(Source: Chartered Accountants Ireland, CAP 1, Law for Accountants (NI), Autumn 2014, Extract: Q4(a)(i)(ii))

Question 4.4

The directors of Chancery Furniture Ltd ('CHANCERY') were anxious due to declining sales figures, and decided to import a range of reclining sofa chairs. They were able to purchase this furniture at a discounted price, but they decided to sell the furniture at a 25% mark up in order to boost sales. They were made aware, in advance of the purchase, that a number of the reclining sofa chairs were defective, but they failed to disclose this information to the public when selling the sofas. Two weekends ago, they put the sofas out for sale and by the end of the first day they had sold 20 sofa chairs.

However, last weekend, the directors were contacted by all 20 purchasers who informed them that the reclining sofa chairs were faulty and all of the purchasers had fallen off the chairs and had ended up in casualty. One purchaser suffered a broken hip; five purchasers suffered fractured arms; six purchasers suffered a fractured leg; and the remainder suffered minor sprains. As a result, all of the consumers are now threatening joint legal action against the directors for breach of the Consumer Protection (Northern Ireland) Order 1987.

CHANCERY has now contacted you for consumer advice.

Requirement:
(a) Explain to the directors the steps consumers must take to successfully bring a claim against CHANCERY.
(b) Explain the defences, if any, available to CHANCERY.

(Source: Chartered Accountants Ireland, CAP 1, Law for Accountants (NI), Autumn 2015, Extract: Q4(a) and (b))

CHAPTER 5

LANDLORD AND TENANT LAW

Introduction

The law relating to the relationship between landlord and tenant is one of the most important aspects of land law.[1] This relationship is governed by the Landlord and Tenant Law (Amendment) Act 1860, which is more commonly known as "Deasy's Act". The nature of the relationship between the landlord and a tenant is that of a contract between the parties, whereby in exchange for a periodic payment in the form of rent, paid by the tenant to the landlord, the tenant is permitted to use and enjoy land owned by the landlord. The relationship of the landlord and the tenant is therefore based on the express or implied contract of the parties.

Examples of a Landlord and Tenant Relationship

There are many instances in which the landlord and tenant relationship is met. The following instances may be identified:
- houses or flats let on periodic tenancies, for example student accommodation;
- shops and offices held for short terms, e.g. 10 or 15 years; and
- long leases, e.g. 10,000 years, of residential premises.

It is helpful to express the relationship of landlord and tenant diagrammatically. A landlord is the person who lets the property to the tenant, who then has the use of the property, for which he or she pays the landlord rent. The contract between the parties is the tenancy. Diagrammatically, the position may be shown as follows:

LANDLORD

TENANT

---

[1] JCW Wylie, *Irish Land Law* (3rd Edition, Butterworths, 1997).

Where the landlord and tenant record their agreement in writing, they are frequently referred to as '**lessor**' and '**lessee**', and the document containing their agreement is a '**lease**'.

Landlord and Sub-tenant

A *sub-tenancy* is a tenancy where the tenant is a landlord to someone else, the sub-tenant. There are now two tenancies in existence:

- that between the landlord and the tenant; and
- that between the tenant and the sub-tenant.

The tenant's own landlord is now the head landlord and the tenant is also the sub-landlord.

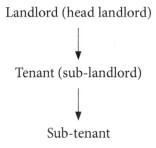

Landlord (head landlord)

Tenant (sub-landlord)

Sub-tenant

Advantages of the Landlord and Tenant Relationship

The landlord and tenant relationship has a number advantages which make it attractive to both parties. First, a tenant, while getting to enjoy the use of a particular piece of land, does not have to spend a large amount of capital outlay in purchasing premises he wants to occupy. He can defer his expenditure over the term of his occupation in the form of the rental income that he pays to the landlord.

Secondly, the payment of rent to a landlord provides a landlord with a regular income. Under usual business leases, it is common for a clause to be inserted permitting the income to be reviewed at regular intervals, thereby increasing it in line with market values.

The third advantage of a landlord and tenant relationship is that a landlord will have an asset, at the end of a lease, which will typically be worth more than it was at the beginning of the lease. This stems from the fact that the property is an appreciating asset.

One further advantage to the landlord and tenant relationship is that any obligations undertaken by the parties, for example repairs to the premises, can be enforced more easily under a lease agreement than in other instances.

Formalities of a Lease

Section 4 of Deasy's Act requires that leases for a fixed term of more than one year be *in writing*. Furthermore, section 4 also states that a lease for a period of one year or more must be signed by a landlord.

In order to bring the relationship of a landlord and tenant into existence, Deasy's Act further stipulates that both parties must have intended to create the relationship in addition to complying with the formalities. If both of these factors exist, a lease will exist. In the case of *Street v. Mountford* (1985), the House of Lords stated that the hallmarks of a tenancy are exclusive possession, payment of rent and a fixed term. In this case, the landlord gave his 'tenants' a furnished room in a property, which was defined as a 'licence'. All the relevant clauses in the agreement referred to a licence and specifically said that the agreement was not intended to give a tenancy. The tenants said that the agreement was a lease, but Mr Street applied for a declaration that it was only a licence. When the case got to the House of Lords, the court decided that the test of whether or not there was a tenancy was not based on the wording of the agreement, but on whether or not the agreement gave the occupier exclusive possession for either a fixed or periodic term at a rent. In this particular case, Mr Mountford had exclusive possession of the room at a rent and he was therefore a tenant.

Leases

Deasy's Act defines a lease as:

> "any instrument in writing, whether under seal or not, containing a contract of tenancy in respect of any lands, in consideration of a rent in return."

A lease therefore is a property interest giving a tenant exclusive possession of the land. There are a number of different types of lease and each will now be considered below:

1. **Fixed-term lease** – A fixed-term lease is, as the name implies, a lease where both the start and end dates are specified. Once the fixed term is up, the possession of the premises reverts back to the landlord. Sections 10 and 18 of Deasy's Act contain restrictions on a tenant's right to assign or sublet, whereby it is not lawful to do so without the written consent of the landlord or his agent.
2. **Tenancy at sufferance** – This occurs where the tenant continues to use the property after the end of the formal term of the agreement without a landlord's specific agreement.
3. **Periodic tenancy** – This lease continues indefinitely from one period to another until either the landlord or tenant terminates it by giving notice. The period is based upon how the rent is calculated (month to month or

year to year) rather than how it is paid, although there is a presumption that the frequency of payment of rent is based on the period by which it is calculated.

4. **Tenancy at will** – This arises where a person is in possession of land for an indefinite period of time, with the consent of the landowner and without the payment of rent (if rent is paid it will become a periodic tenancy). Under section 17 of the Statute of Limitation Act 1857, a tenancy at will is deemed to end after one year. Once the tenancy at will ends, the former tenant is regarded as being in adverse possession of the land, which means that after 12 years they may gain property rights over it (squatter's rights). The tenancy at will may be terminated by either party at any time.

5. **Tenancy by estoppel** – This arises where a lease was not properly executed, but the parties have acted as if a valid lease exists. In such circumstances, the parties are bound by the same rights and obligations as if a valid lease was in existence. The landlord cannot revoke the tenancy except in compliance with the terms of the agreement and general law. The landlord is said to be 'stopped' from repudiating the tenancy.

Licences

It is important to note the distinction between a lease and a license. The case of *Kelly v. Woolworth & Co. Ltd* (1922) confirmed that a licence is permission, given by the owner of the land to another person, to do something that would otherwise be trespass. A licence does not confer a property right on the holder but a lease attracts statutory protections that a licence would not. A key distinguishing factor between a lease and a licence is that of exclusive possession, as established in the case of *Street v. Mountford* (1985) (discussed above).

There are different types of licence. These include:

1. **A bare licence** – This is a simple, personal permission given to another to enter onto lands, e.g. a party invitation.

2. **A licence coupled with an interest** – This arises where a person has a right to do something on another's land, for example to maintain a boundary wall.

3. **A contractual licence** – This is a licence created by a contract, e.g. the right to enter the cinema once you have paid for your ticket. This is revocable only as per the contract.

Contents of a Lease

All leases should contain the following information:
- the names and addresses of the parties to the lease;
- the date of commencement of the term of the lease;

- recitals (if any), which explain the reason for the lease;
- consideration, if any (i.e. money paid upfront for the lease);
- a clear and exact description of the premises – in some cases this may amount to a simple house number;
- the length of the term being granted – often referred to as the *habendum;*
- exceptions and reservations to the landlord;
- the rent payable to the landlord, if the tenancy is a periodic tenancy;
- the notice period for termination and rules for timing and service of same;
- forfeiture clause – this is the term allowing forfeiture for non-payment of rent or for breach of the covenants;
- the lessee's covenants (see below);
- the lessor's covenants (see below); and
- any other business.

Covenants

Covenants are the additional promises made by both the landlord and the tenant and contained in the lease. It is noted that covenants are binding, both on the landlord and the tenant and on any future persons who may acquire interest in the land. Typical covenants that bind the tenant include covenants to:
- pay service charges;
- contribute towards insurance premiums or to keep the premises insured;
- keep the premises in good repair;
- pay the rent in full and on time;
- alienate, i.e. not to assign, sub-let or share the premises without the consent of the landlord;
- permit the landlord to enter at reasonable times for the purposes of inspection and repair;
- maintain furniture and fittings in good repair; and
- confine the use of the premises.

Covenants that bind a landlord include covenants to:
- allow the tenant the quiet enjoyment of the premises;
- pay all rates and taxes on the premises;
- repair and maintain the structure; and
- insure the premises.

Forfeiture

A landlord may be entitled to bring a lease to an end earlier than is stated in the tenancy agreement if a tenant breaches a covenant of the lease. If such a situation arises, this is known as forfeiture.

Examples of when forfeiture may arise include:
- if the tenant claimed that he was the legal owner of the property and issued legal proceedings; and
- if the tenant does not comply with the covenants in the lease and there is an expressed term of forfeiture.

In circumstances where the tenant does not comply with the covenants and there is no expressed term allowing for forfeiture, the courts will have to determine if the term is a condition or a warranty.

Landlord's Remedies for Non-payment of Rent

There are a number of remedies open to a landlord should a tenant fail to pay rent.

First, a landlord has the option of *suing for arrears*. This option is provided for under section 45 of Deasy's Act. Section 45 applies only where the rent is defined in the lease or the agreement for lease. If there is no defined rent, section 46 of Deasy's Act allows the landlord to "recover a reasonable sum for use and occupation".

Alternatively, a landlord can sue for *ejectment*. Usually, there will be a specific clause in the lease stating that if the rent remains unpaid for a certain period of time, the landlord has the right to forfeit the lease and remove the tenant from the premises. Almost all leases specify the period of arrears. If no period is specified within the lease for the length of arrears, section 52 of Deasy's Act states that rent must have been in arrears for one year or more. However, a landlord should bear in mind that forfeiture of any lease, unless the tenant leaves voluntarily, can be actioned only under a Court Order. The landlord cannot simply go to the property and throw the tenant into the street.

It is worth noting that an option that was previously available to a landlord if a tenant failed to pay rent was the 'right of distress'. If rent was in arrears, a landlord could seize or 'distrain' the tenant's possessions in place of the rent without resorting to court action. However, this right was abolished in Northern Ireland by the Judgments (Enforcement) Act (Northern Ireland) 1969. In Northern Ireland, the enforcement of any debt proceedings is now carried out by the Enforcement of Judgments Office. If a landlord were to act as though the right of distress was still in existence, he could find himself open to both civil and criminal penalties – the courts would take an extremely dim view of action of this nature.

Business Tenancies

The Business Tenancies (Northern Ireland) Order 1996 (1996 No. 725 (N.I. 5)) came into force on 1 April 1997. The main purpose of the legislation was to give business tenants in Northern Ireland a measure of security of tenure. This means that landlords can only recover their property from business tenants if they follow the procedure of the Order. If the strict termination rules are not followed, the business tenancy continues after its expiry date subject to the same terms and conditions as on the original lease and also with the same rent.

Scope of the 1996 Order

The 1996 Order only applies to business tenancies. These tenancies can either be for a fixed term or for a periodic tenancy. It should be noted that the Order does not apply to:
- licences,
- tenancies at will,
- tenancies at sufferance, or
- mortgage tenancies.

Furthermore, the property comprising the tenancy must be or include business premises. The fact that the premises includes other types of premises does not mean that the premises do not come within the ambit of the legislation. For example, if a shopkeeper uses the bottom part of a building as his business premises and lives on the top floor, the only part of those premises which will be protected by the legislation will be the part used as business premises.

The 1996 Order is also very specific in that it applies only to premises. While this can be the obvious shop or office, it should be noted that the scope of 'premises' is much wider than this and includes open space, for example, a car park or garden centre.

For the purposes of the Order, the premises must also be occupied and, further, must be occupied by the tenant. If a tenant is not in occupation, he cannot claim protection under the 1996 Order. Finally, the premises must be used for the purposes of the business. This does not necessarily mean the public space of the business. Premises, for the purposes of the Order, can also include a store or warehouse used as a retail shop or an area used for staff training.

Tenancies Excluded from the 1996 Order

It should be noted that there are several types of tenancies that are not afforded protection under the Business Tenancies (Northern Ireland)

Order 1996. These include a tenancy for a term not exceeding nine months, unless the tenant or their predecessor in the business of the tenant has been in occupation of the premises for a period exceeding 18 months. Also excluded from protection from the 1996 Order are:

- agricultural tenancies;
- protected residential tenancies;
- tenancies created by a mining lease;
- tenancies granted by the personal representatives of the deceased owner of land; or
- tenancies granted or made to be dependent on the continuance of the tenant in any office, employment or appointment.

Termination of Business Tenancies

A business tenancy can be brought to an end either by a landlord serving notice on a tenant or a tenant serving notice on a landlord. Business tenancies do not come to an end by natural expiration. If neither party serves notice on the other to end a business tenancy, the tenancy merely continues on with the same rent and on the same terms.

Landlord Serving Notice on a Tenant

A Notice to Determine is a notice served by a landlord on a tenant when the landlord wants to end the business tenancy. It cannot be served earlier than 12 months before the date specified for termination in the notice nor less than six months before it. There are standard forms that a landlord must complete in order to serve notice on a tenant. (In Northern Ireland, these are available from the Lands Tribunal.) Once a landlord serves notice, he can indicate to the tenant that he is agreeable to a new tenancy being commenced. As long as the tenant agrees to the new terms proposed by the landlord, the tenancy continues thereafter on the new terms. However, if a landlord does not agree to the granting of a new tenancy, he must specify on what grounds he opposes a new tenancy within the landlord's Notice to Determine. These grounds may be as follows:

1. the state of repair of the premises, resulting from the tenant's failure to comply with obligations in respect of the repair and maintenance of the holding;
2. the persistent delay by the tenant in paying rent;
3. other substantial breaches by the tenant of the tenant's obligations under the current tenancy;
4. alternative accommodation has been offered by the landlord (although this ground is rarely used);

5. where the tenancy has a sub-tenancy and the landlord could obtain a greater rent by letting the premises as a whole;
6. where the landlord intends to demolish the building structure, which comprises or forms the substantial part of the holding, and to undertake a substantial development on the holding or to carry out substantial works in construction on the holding or part thereof and the landlord cannot reasonably do so without obtaining possession of the holding; or
7. where the landlord intends to occupy the premises for his own purposes.

Tenant's Notice to Determine

If, at the end of the specified term of lease, a tenant *does not* wish to continue with the business tenancy, he should serve the standard Notice to Determine on the landlord under the Order stating that he does not wish the tenancy to continue. However, if a tenant *does* want to continue to occupy the business premises, he can choose to take no action and simply continue in occupation of the premises on the same terms as the original lease. Alternatively, a tenant can take steps, through the procedure of the Order, to establish the terms of a new tenancy. A tenant does this by serving a necessary notice for a request for a new tenancy. If a landlord does not oppose the granting of a new tenancy, the new tenancy terms are agreed and a new tenancy is established. However, if a landlord does oppose the granting of a new tenancy, he must specify the grounds on which he opposes it (as set out above).

Residential Tenancies

The Private Tenancies (Northern Ireland) Order 2006 (2006 No. 1459 (N.I. 10)) came into operation on 1 April 2007. It is the first piece of legislation in Northern Ireland that deals exclusively with the regulation of privately rented dwelling houses in Northern Ireland. (The Order does not apply to business lettings, which are dealt with in the Business Tenancies (Northern Ireland) Order 1996, as discussed above.)

For the first time, with the introduction of the 2006 Order, landlords have been under a number of obligations to tenants. It should be noted that tenancies that began before 1 April 2007 do not have to have a written tenancy agreement unless the tenancy is for a fixed term of over one year and one day. However, the landlord of a tenancy that began after 1 April 2007 must provide confirmation of the terms of the tenancy agreement within 28 days of the start of the tenancy. This document is known as a *statement of tenancy terms* and must provide written details on a number of issues. Failure to provide such a written statement is an offence punishable, on conviction, by a fine of up to £2,500.

The Unfair Terms in Consumer Contract Regulations 1999 (1999 No. 2083) (as discussed in **Chapter 4**) apply to tenancy agreements and, if a term is found to be unfair, it is not enforceable. The Office of Fair Trading publishes guidance on what is and what is not considered unfair.

Landlord's Obligations Imposed by the Private Tenancies (Northern Ireland) Order 2006

Under the 2006 Order, a landlord is legally obliged to provide a rent book to all tenants, regardless of when the tenancy commenced. Even if the rent is paid by electronic means, a rent book must still be provided. The rent book must provide a range of information, including the name and address of the landlord, the amount of rent and rates to be charged, the amount of any deposit and the circumstances when this can be withheld. The rent book must be held by the tenant, but it is up to the tenant to make it available to the landlord for updating.

Under the 2006 Order, a landlord must also ensure that a fitness inspection of the property is conducted by the local district council. A number of properties are exempt from this requirement and these include:

- properties where a renovation grant was paid by the Housing Executive within the past 10 years;
- properties in which a HMO (Houses in Multiple Occupation) grant was paid by the Housing Executive within the past 10 years;
- properties that are currently registered as HMO with the Housing Executive; and
- properties in which a regulated rent certificate was issued by the district council within the past 10 years.

Landlords are under a further obligation, by virtue of the 2006 Order, to keep the structure and exterior of the dwelling house in good repair and to keep the interior of the dwelling house and fittings, fixtures or furnishings which the landlord has provided, and installations for the supply and use of water, gas and electricity, sanitation, heating and water in good working order. These default repairing obligations apply to any private tenancy granted on or after 1 April 2007, subject to any express terms that may be in the tenancy agreement itself. The standard of repair applied is determined having regard to the age, character and prospective life of the property. The landlord does not have to repair unless he has actual knowledge of the need for the works. Furthermore, the landlord is not required, under the Order, to rebuild or reinstate the dwelling house in the case of destruction or damage by fire, flood or other inevitable accident.

Finally, it should be noted that landlords have an obligation to comply with regulations separate from the Private Tenancies (Northern Ireland) Order 2006 dealing with health and safety issues, including such obligations of the landlord as ensuring that gas appliances and pipework are well maintained and safe to use. A safety check must be undertaken on appliances once a year and a copy of safety records must be issued to the tenant.

Tenant's Obligations Imposed by the Private Tenancies (Northern Ireland) Order 2006

The obligations imposed upon a tenant under the 2006 Order are not as onerous. These include obligations to:
1. take proper care of the dwelling house as a good tenant;
2. make good any damage that is done to the property;
3. keep the interior of the dwelling house in reasonable decorative order; and
4. allow the landlord or anyone authorised by them to inspect the state of repair or to carry out the repairs which the landlord is legally obliged to do at a reasonable time and with reasonable notice.

Commercial Leases

A commercial lease is a lease that applies to business property. Short-term commercial leases run for a period of less than five years, whereas long-term leases tend to run for 2,025 years.

Full Repairing and Insuring Lease

A full repairing and insuring lease (FRI lease) usually runs for a term of 20 years, in open-market rent, subject to an upward-only rent review every five years. In the case of an FRI lease, the tenant is responsible for all repairs, insurance and outgoings on the building.

Common Terms in Commercial Leases

There are a number of terms that are commonly found in all commercial leases. These are set out below.

Rent Review Clauses One of the most important aspects of a commercial lease is that of rent. Having established the amount of rent payable in a commercial lease, it is prudent to consider whether it is appropriate to review the amount of this rent during the term of a lease. Having decided in principle that the rent should be reviewed, there are various matters that should be agreed between the parties. The first is that of the frequency of reviews. A balance must be struck here. Obviously, if reviews are too infrequent, the landlord may not get a proper return on his investment. However, if reviews are too frequent, expense and uncertainty will result and this will not be acceptable to the tenant. A typical period between reviews is around five years. Secondly, rent review clauses should also consider the mechanics of the rent review. It is common to find a provision stating that new rents should be agreed between the parties and, failing agreement, should be fixed by a valuer. In some leases, the valuer is to be agreed between the parties but, in other cases, the valuer is to be appointed by the Royal Institute of Chartered Surveyors.

Service Charge Clauses If any common area is used by a tenant, there will need to be a service charge arrangement. This will usually be contained in the lease and provide for a sum of money to be paid each year by the tenant into a communal fund for the upkeep of the common areas. The clause should also provide for increases in the service charge (usually either by a specific percentage or in line with the consumer price index). The lease should be clear on what services are provided and covered by the charge, for example, gardening or waste removal. If the landlord carries out a service that is not listed, he may not be able to recover the expenditure from the service charge funds. The amount to be paid is usually eliminated in the first year and after that is based on actual expenditure.

Alienation (assignment and subletting) This is the legal term used for assignment or subletting by the tenant of the lease to a third party.

Insurance Clause This will provide that the landlord will seek and maintain an insurance policy but that he will recover the insurance premiums from the tenant. It will generally also provide that the insurance policy may not be ended without the tenant being informed and it is often included in the service charge.

REVIEW QUESTIONS

(See Suggested Solutions at the end of this textbook.)

Question 5.1

Your client mentions to you that he has recently purchased a house that he is keen to lease out. He seeks your advice on what information should be contained in a lease.

Requirement:

(1) Advise your client on ANY FIVE pieces of information/contract terms typically contained within a lease.

(2) Explain briefly ANY SIX of the typical covenants of the tenant to the landlord and any FOUR covenants of the landlord to the tenant.

(Source: Chartered Accountants Ireland, CAP 1 Law (NI), Summer 2009, Extract: Q2(b))

Question 5.2

Explain the significance of a rent review clause in a commercial lease.

(Source: Chartered Accountants Ireland, CAP 1, Law for Accountants (NI), Summer 2011, Extract: Q4(c))

Question 5.3

Six months ago, the Health Service Executive of Northern Ireland (HSENI) put its waste management contract out to tender and Premier decided to put in a bid for this lucrative contract. Premier's bid was accepted and it was awarded the contract. As a consequence of obtaining the HSENI contract, Premier has decided to lease a new business premises.

Requirement: Outline for Premier any FOUR terms normally included in a commercial lease.

(Source: Chartered Accountants Ireland, CAP 1, Law for Accountants (NI), Autumn 2013, Extract: Q3(c))

Question 5.4

Marcus and Isabella run a furniture shop in County Antrim, called MI Ltd ('MI'). During their first few years of trading, Marcus and Isabella operated MI out of the garage of their home. However, due to MI's continued expansion, Marcus and Isabella are now considering taking on a commercial lease of a store for the business.

Requirement: List and explain any THREE terms normally included within a commercial lease.

(Source: Chartered Accountants Ireland, CAP 1, Law for Accountants (NI), Autumn 2014, Extract: Q4(b))

CHAPTER 6

PLANNING AND DEVELOPMENT LAW

Introduction

The purpose of the planning system in Northern Ireland is to regulate the development and use of land in the public interest. Planning legislation in Northern Ireland was first introduced in 1931, but it was not until 1944, with the passing of the Planning (Interim Development) Act Northern Ireland, that an effective development control system was put in place.

In 1970, the Macrory Report on the review of local government in Northern Ireland proposed that planning should become a central government responsibility. As a result, the Town and Country Planning Service was established in 1973 and the responsibilities of the local planning authorities passed to the Ministry of Development. Until April 2015, responsibility for local panning rested with the Department of Environment for Northern Ireland (DOE). However, in April 2015, most planning powers held by the Planning Service within the DOE were devolved to the 11 new amalgamated super councils set up in Northern Ireland. The 11 super councils were set up as a result of local government reform. The DOE retains a handful of existing applications and will deal with any new regionally strategic development applications in the future, but these are expected to be few and far between (e.g. major roads and railways, major energy projects, etc.).

Development of Land

The development and use of land in Northern Ireland is controlled by the following key pieces of legislation:
- the Planning Act (Northern Ireland) 2011;
- the Planning (Uses Classes) Order (Northern Ireland) 2015 (2015 No. 40); and
- the Planning (General Development Procedure) Order (Northern Ireland) 2015 (2015 No. 72).

Under the Planning Act (Northern Ireland) 2011, planning permission is required for the carrying out of any development of land, unless the need to obtain planning permission is specifically excluded or permission is granted automatically. Development, for the purposes of the 2011 Act, is defined as "the carrying out of building, engineering, mining or other operations in, on, over or under land, or the making of any material change in the use of any buildings or other land" (section 23). That said, the 2011 Act does specify several classes of permitted development that can be carried out without the need to obtain express planning permission. For example, a listed building can be altered with a listed building consent. Permitted development rights are mainly applied to minor, non-contentious developments that are generally considered not to be subject to the planning application process.

According to the www.planningni.gov.uk (Planning Portal) website:

> "A new hierarchy of development has been introduced which categorises planning applications as local, major and regionally significant with councils responsible for determining all local and major applications. Each council will establish a planning committee to consider and decide these applications; however, not all applications will come before the planning committee for decision. The council will publish a Scheme of Delegation that will set out which applications will be dealt with by the Planning Committee and which will be delegated to officers. The applications likely to come before the committee for decision include large developments, contentious applications and those that receive a number of objections."

The Planning (Uses Classes) Order (Northern Ireland) 2015 places a number of the most common land uses into 12 groups (classes) that do not require planning permission. These classes include shops, residential institutions, dwelling houses, etc. It stipulates that any change in use between activities within the same group is not 'development' and therefore planning permission is not required. For example, planning permission is not required to change the use of a building from a hostel to a guesthouse.

Making an Application for Planning Permission

A person who wants to carry out work to land must make an application for planning permission. Any application for planning permission must be accompanied by a Certificate of Ownership, which states an applicant's legal interest in the land. If the individual or person does not own the land to which the application relates, they are legally required to give notice of the making of the planning application to the owner of the land. (See www.planningni. gov.uk, "Explanatory Notes on Applying for Planning Permission, Approval of Reserved Matters and Other Types of Planning Consent".)

An application for planning must be made on a Form P1 and can be found on the Planning Portal website. This form should be used for making an application for most types of planning permission, including:

- outline planning permission;
- full planning permission;
- reserved matters application;
- renewal of planning permission; and
- application for mineral workings.

The P1 form provides information on certain supplementary forms that may be required with an application also. It should be noted that the form P1 should not be used for householder development.

The most common application made by householders is a full application. To assist applicants when making applications, the Planning Portal website helpfully sets out the statutory minimum information that should be included within an application form. This includes:

- A written description of the development. This should include a postal address for the land to be developed.
- The name and address of the applicant.
- A plan sufficient to identify the site and the surrounding locality. Ideally, this should be an Ordnance Survey-based site location plan.
- A certificate of ownership (section 42 of the 2011 Act). The purpose of this certificate is to inform all concerned who is in actual possession of the application site.

When making an application, the application should be accompanied by three additional copies of the application forms/plans and the appropriate application fee.

Proposal of Application Notice

If an application is for a major or regionally significant development, a 'proposal of application notice' should be submitted at least 12 weeks prior to submitting a planning application for the proposal. The proposal of application notice should set out how the applicant will engage and seek the views of the community on the proposed development.

Any application made for planning will naturally incur a fee, the amount of which will vary depending on the type of development. Details of the relevant fees are provided on the Planning Portal website and additional guidance is available in the form of a fee calculator.

Making a Decision

In deciding whether or not to grant an application, proposals are assessed in relation to relevant planning policy and all other material considerations. Either the council or the DOE can make one of three decisions. They can:

- grant permission unconditionally;
- grant permission subject to certain conditions (reserved matters); or
- refuse permission.

If an application is approved, the work can begin. However, if it is rejected, an appeal can be made to the Planning Appeals Commission. The Commission is an independent body and appeals may only be made by or on behalf of the person who made the application. There is no third right of appeal and an appeal must be made within four months of the date of the refusal of planning permission.

A full planning permission is usually only valid for five years after it has been granted. After five years, it can no longer be relied upon and a fresh application will have to be made. That said, the works will only have to be started within that period – they do not have to be completed. In the case of outline permission, approval of the reserved matters must be resolved within three years and work must have begun within five years of the outlined permission or two years of final approval, whichever is the later.

Building without Planning Permission

If a premises is erected without planning permission, or if any condition of the planning permission is breached, the relevant council has the power to issue an enforcement notice outlining the procedure to be followed to remedy the breach.

The relevant council has four years from the date the works are carried out to issue an enforcement notice. This four-year time limit applies only if the breach relates to an operational development or if there has been a change of use to a single dwelling.

REVIEW QUESTION

(See Suggested Solutions at the end of this textbook.)

Question 6.1

Michael and Joseph are brothers who were left land, in equal shares, by their father in his will. They are considering building a restaurant on this land.

Requirement: Identify any FOUR steps involved in the application process for planning permission and name any ONE consequence of proceeding without planning permission.

(Source: Chartered Accountants Ireland, CAP 1, Law for Accountants (NI), Summer 2012, Extract: Q3(b)(i))

Chapter 7

EMPLOYMENT LAW

Background

In the last 30 years, employment law has developed into one of the most complex areas of law but this was not always the case. Until the end of the 19th Century, employment law consisted of little more than the recognition of rights and obligations agreed between the employer and employee.

The early 20th Century saw a number of Acts passed relevant to the employee, but it was not until the 1960s, following the publication of the *Donovan Report*, that Parliament began to regulate closely the employment relationship. The Contracts of Employment Act 1963 decreed the provision by the employer to each employee of a written statement of contractual terms. The Redundancy Payments Act 1965 provided a statutory right to compensation in certain circumstances. In Northern Ireland, these Acts were combined in the Contracts of Employment and Redundancy Payments Act (Northern Ireland) 1965. The main piece of legislation governing the regulation of employment in Northern Ireland is the Employment Rights (Northern Ireland) Order 1996 (1996 No. 1919 (NI 16)).

Distinction between a Contract for Service and a Contract of Employment

The Meaning of 'Employee'

The definition of the term '**employee**' is of critical importance to employment law and to anyone concerned with the rights of individuals at work. At the outset, an *employee* has to be distinguished from a *self-employed person*. An employee works under a contract of employment, while a self-employed person works under a contract for service.

As we shall see below, this distinction is important, as the legal rights enjoyed by employees and the self-employed can be quite different. Also, two people working side by side in an office doing exactly the same work could have quite different employment status: one could be a core employee employed directly by the employer; the other a worker supplied by an agency. The example originally cited in the case law to illustrate the difference is the contrast between the legal status of a chauffeur and a taxi-driver. Their day-to-day work may be similar, but one is an employee, the other self-employed (per Lord Denning in *Stevenson, Jordan & Harrison Ltd v. Macdonald* (1952)).

The Significance of the Distinction between Employee and Self-Employed

There are a number of reasons why it is important to make the distinction between an employee and a self-employed person. First, some employment protection measures apply only to 'employees'. Under the Employment Rights (Northern Ireland) Order 1996 (the '1996 Order'), employees are afforded the right not to be unfairly dismissed, the right to receive written particulars of employment, minimum periods of notice, statutory redundancy pay, maternity and parental leave and time off for dependents. This point is illustrated in the case of *Costain Building v. Smith* (2000). In this case, a technically self-employed contractor was appointed as a trade union safety representative on a construction site. He had been placed as a temporary worker with the company through an employment agency. After a number of health and safety failings were raised, he was dismissed by the agency at the request of the company. He complained that he had been unfairly dismissed for carrying out his duties as a safety representative. His case failed because he was unable to show that he was an employee. The statutory protection against dismissal was only enjoyed by employee safety representatives.

Secondly, self-employed people are taxed under Schedule D for income tax purposes, rather than under Schedule E, which is applied to employed earners. This allows the self-employed to offset business expenses against income for tax purposes. In the case of *Hall v. Lorrimer* (1994), a vision mixer decided to become freelance. He was used by a large number of companies for a short period each, working on their premises and using their equipment. The Inland Revenue took the view that this was a series of short employment contracts, while he argued that he was now self-employed and entitled to offset over £9,000 expenses against his income tax bill for the year. His argument succeeded.

Another distinction between a self-employed person and an employee relates to the National Insurance payable. National Insurance Contributions are payable by an employer in respect of employees (who earn more than the lower earnings limit) but not in respect of the self-employed. The administration of the employee's own contribution must also be undertaken by the employer. This normally means that employees' contributions are deducted from their wages at source.

Employers are also vicariously liable for torts (legal wrongs) committed by their employees during the course of employment, but not for the actions of the self-employed, sometimes referred to as independent contractors. In *Hawley v. Luminar Leisure Ltd* (2006), Mr Hawley was assaulted outside a nightclub by a doorman and suffered permanent brain damage. The doorman was not employed directly by the nightclub, but had been supplied by another company, ASE Security Services Ltd, to whom the nightclub had subcontracted door duties. The Court of Appeal upheld the finding of the High Court that the nightclub exercised sufficient practical control over the doorman to make it the "temporary deemed employer" for the purposes of vicarious liability.

An employer will owe a number of so-called common law duties to employees but not necessarily to self-employed people. These include the duty of care as shown in *Lane v. Shire Roofing* (1995). Damages in excess of £100,000 were awarded following a work-related accident. The claimant was held to be an employee. The award would not have been made if he had been found to be self-employed.

The common law has developed a number of tests for distinguishing those who have a contract of employment from those who are self-employed contractors. The tests are not mutually exclusive but have developed gradually over the years. As the courts have been faced with an increasingly complex workplace and a greater variety of work situations, the tests have grown in sophistication.

Tests for Distinguishing a Contract of Employment from a Contract for Service

The Control Test This test was developed during the 19th Century. The determining factor was said to be the degree of control exercised by the employer. Could the employer tell the worker not only **what** to do, but also **how** to do it? Did he or she control the manner of performance? In the case of *Walker v. Crystal Palace Football Club* (1910), a professional footballer was held to have a contract of employment with the club. He was expected to play exclusively for Crystal Palace; the club dictated his training regime; they decided in which games he should play; they laid down strategy and tactics on the field. The club had argued that he was not an employee because they lacked a sufficient degree of control over how he played – he was hired to display his own talents and skills. This argument was dismissed – he was still subject to follow the directions of his master.

The test is now regarded as somewhat limited in its scope, though control remains one significant factor among many.

The Organisation (or Integration) Test Organisations can involve complex employment relationships, particularly where highly skilled individuals are carrying out work which, except in the most general sense, cannot be subject to any close control by an employer. A test suggested first by Lord Denning in the 1950s requires us to ask, "Is the individual integrated into the organisational structure?" If so, he or she is more likely to be an employee. The less degree of integration there is, the greater the likelihood of self-employment. This test was approved in *Whittaker v. Ministry of Pensions* (1967). Whittaker was a trapeze artiste in a circus, but she also sold programmes and ice-creams during the interval. When she fell and injured herself, she claimed she was entitled to industrial injury benefit. The court held that she was an employee. It was held that she was an integral part of the organisation and therefore entitled as an employee.

The Economic Reality Test It is possible for a worker to be closely integrated into an organisation and to be closely controlled, and yet to remain a self-employed worker rather than an employee. This question was asked in *Market Investigations v. Ministry of Social Security* (1968). The issue was whether part-time market researchers employed to carry out specific and time-limited assignments were employed under a contract of service or a contract for services. The court ruled that further tests were necessary and stated that the crux of the matter was whether the individual "was in business on her own account as an interviewer". It was concluded that she was employed by the company on a series of contracts of service. She was not in business on her own account, even though she could work for other employers. In practice she did not; nor did she provide her own tools or equipment, or risk her own capital. The court pointed out that there is no exhaustive list of factors to be taken into account in determining the status of the individual. The test builds upon the control and integration tests, but considers other matters such as investment in the business or economic risk.

The Multiple Factor Test This test, established around the same time, is a further recognition that there is no one factor that can establish whether a contract of service exists or not. In different situations, different factors can assume greater or lesser importance. All relevant factors must be taken into account. In *Ready Mixed Concrete v. Ministry of Pensions* (1967), the company, with the workers' agreement, decided to change the basis of employment from a contract of service to self-employment. New contracts were drawn up and, throughout the contract, the employees were referred to as self-employed. Under the new terms, the employees were to purchase their own lorries, but with financial assistance from the firm. They were to paint the lorries in company colours and use them exclusively for company business. The employees had to maintain the lorries, and had to wear company uniforms. They had to obey the orders of the company's servants.

They could delegate a driving job to someone else; they were paid for the jobs actually done subject to an annual retainer. They were responsible for their own income tax and National Insurance and the firm paid no employer's National Insurance Contribution in respect of the men. It was this last feature that led the Ministry to challenge the arrangement. Were the workers indeed self-employed, or had the basis of employment remained the contract of service? The House of Lords ruled by a majority of one that the employees were now self-employed. This actual decision on the facts has been the subject of criticism, but there is no doubt that the new multiple test put forward in the judgments has many advantages. It expressly states that all relevant factors must be taken into account, including control, integration and the degree of entrepreneurship. There must be a balancing of all the multiple factors. The case, however, gives little guidance on the weight that should be attached to the various factors. One of the important factors in the decision itself was the possibility of the workers engaging substitute drivers. This "absence of a duty personally to perform the work" was felt to be critical.

Other Factors

Recent case law has also highlighted a number of other factors that a court will look at in deciding whether or not someone is employed or self-employed. These are set out below.

No Right to Arrange for a Substitute More recent cases have suggested that the right to arrange for a substitute is not necessarily inconsistent with a contract of employment. In *McFarlane v. Glasgow City Council* (2001), the question was whether a contract that provided for gym instructors working in Council leisure centres was a contract of employment or not. The instructors were permitted to arrange for a replacement from the register maintained by the Council if they were unable to work a particular shift. The EAT held that this did not prevent the contract being a contract of employment. It was enough that the dominant obligation was to do the work personally.

A Mutual Obligation to Provide Work and to Accept the Work There must be 'a mutual obligation' between the parties. In *O'Kelly v. Trust House Forte plc* (1983) a 'regular casual' made a claim for unfair dismissal. Although he had worked for the hotel at functions for many years, the work was seasonal and irregular. There was no mutual obligation to provide or to accept work. It was said by the Court of Appeal to be custom and practice in the industry that casual workers were not to be considered employees working under a contract of employment. There was no right to claim unfair dismissal.

This idea of 'mutuality of obligation' means that casual workers are unlikely ever to be employees.

In *Carmichael v. National Power* (2000), the same factor proved crucial to the decision that tour guides were not employees and were not therefore entitled to a written statement of their terms and conditions of employment under section 1 of the 1996 Order. The court accepted that they worked on a casual "as and when required" basis. An important issue in the case was that there was no requirement for the employer to provide work and for the individual to carry out that work. Indeed the court heard that there were a number of occasions when the applicants had declined offers of work. There was an "irreducible minimum of mutual obligation" that was necessary to create a contract of service. There needed to be an obligation to provide work and an obligation to perform that work in return for a wage or some form of remuneration. Part-time home workers, for example, who had been provided with work, and had performed it over a number of years, could be held to have created this mutual obligation. When the mutual obligation is missing on either side, then a contract of service will not come into existence.

In the case of *James v. Greenwich Borough Council* (2007), one of a series of cases raising the status of agency workers, it was stressed that one of the key features of a genuine agency relationship is the fact that the end user (the client employer) cannot insist on the agency providing any particular individual worker. Only where the arrangement has changed so that the agency worker can show that he or she is working pursuant to mutual obligations with the end user (which are incompatible with the agency relationship) will a contract of employment come into being.

A local case provides a final illustration of the issues. The case of *Major v. Help the Aged* (2004) was decided on a pre-hearing review by a Chairman of the Industrial Tribunal sitting alone. The sole issue was whether the claimant was an employee for the purposes of Article 3 of the 1996 Order and thus entitled to bring a claim of unfair dismissal, or whether she was self-employed. Factors that led to the conclusion that she was self-employed included the following:
- the claimant was an intelligent and capable individual who signed, annually, a document that described itself as a contract for services;
- substantial expenses (in excess of £10,000) were offset against income tax each year;
- the absence of holiday pay;
- the absence of sick pay;
- no pension arrangements were in existence;
- there was no disciplinary code of procedures in respect of her;

- the absence of any substantial degree of day-to-day control or supervision;
- there was no evidence that she was integrated into the management structure; and
- income fluctuated from month to month.

The tribunal concluded that the claimant intended to be self-employed and derived substantial financial benefit from that status. She was not an employee and was not entitled to bring an unfair dismissal claim.

Contracts of Employment

The contract of employment between the employer and employee remains the primary source of rights and obligations between the employer and employee. The terms of the contract are legally enforceable obligations that establish the basic rights and duties of the employer and the employee or supplier of services. Statutory regulation often supplements, qualifies and occasionally replaces those rights and obligations. However, a proper analysis of the employment relationship should always include an examination of the contract of employment.

An employment contract is subject to the same basic principles that apply to all contracts. Consequently, the following have to be present:
1. an offer;
2. an acceptance of that offer;
3. consideration (something of benefit to pass between the parties);
4. intention to create a legal relationship;
5. certainty (i.e. the terms of the contract must be sufficiently clear and certain for the courts to construe); and
6. legality: illegal contracts of employment will not be enforced by the courts (*Vole v. Fred Stacey* (1974)).

Once all of these elements are present, the contract will come into being. An employment contract will consist of a variety of terms and conditions that set out the rights and obligations of the parties.

Sources of Contract Terms

Express Terms These are terms specifically agreed between the employer and employee. As employment contracts range from basic statements through to complex and lengthy documents, the longer and more detailed a contract, the greater the scope for argument on interpretation or allegation of breach. The courts are regularly called upon to decide what terms were actually agreed and what the parties actually meant by the words they used. The interpretation of an express clause is a question of law that can be appealed to a higher court. In *T & K Home Improvements v. Skilton* (2000), the court was called upon to consider whether the contractual term that an employee could be dismissed "with immediate effect" for failing to miss his performance targets excluded his contractual right to three months' notice. The contract had to be read as a whole, against the background of its formation, and considering what the parties would reasonably have understood the term to mean. In order to deprive the employee of his right to notice or pay in lieu, there had to be a clear and specific provision to that effect. Any ambiguity was to be construed against the company. The Court of Appeal held that the employee was entitled to full notice.

Express terms can also be agreed verbally. Hence, when an employer accepts a job offer based on a verbal guaranteed minimum commission of £10,000 per annum, this will be an enforceable express term of the contract.

Statutory Written Statement There is a statutory right to a written statement of main terms and conditions of employment under Article 33 of the Employment Rights (Northern Ireland) Order 1996. This should be provided within two months of starting employment. The statement must contain the following information:
- names of employer and employee;
- date of commencement of employment and relationship with previous employer (if any);
- date the statement is issued;
- scale or rate of remuneration;
- intervals at which remuneration is paid;
- terms and conditions relating to hours of work;
- holiday entitlement;
- sickness notification rules and procedures;
- details of pensions and pension schemes;
- length of notice that employee must give and is entitled to receive;
- job title or description;
- date of expiry of a fixed-term contract;
- place of work;
- collective agreements; and
- disciplinary rules and grievance procedures.

The written statement is not necessarily the same as the contract of employment, but rather is evidence as to what the main terms are. It is open to either party to argue that the written particulars do not accurately reflect the terms of the contract.

Collective Agreements These are agreements between employers and trade unions that are concerned with terms and conditions of employment. They may be written or oral but are not usually legally enforceable. However, they may acquire the status of legally binding contract terms if they are incorporated into a contract term. This can be done either expressly or by implication.

Staff Handbooks Most companies today issue employees with a work rulebook or staff handbook. The form of the rulebook is not that of a written contract, but rather a document containing instructions and information. The contents of these documents vary, but they often include a mixture of statements about the employer's policies, the employer's expectations from employees, explanations of procedures and the authority structure of the firm. In the absence of a contractual term expressly incorporating the provisions of a staff handbook, it is difficult to predict whether courts will regard the contents of a staff handbook as having contractual status. The test is whether the parties intended the contracts to have contractual force.

Custom and Practice The increasing formalisation of the contract of employment has led to a corresponding decrease in the importance of custom and practice as a source of terms. However, it may still provide a source of regulation of terms and conditions within a particular industry, locality or individual firm. In *Sagar v. Ridehalgh* (1931), custom and practice was the basis for deducting wages on account of poor quality work. It was held to be a long-standing custom in the Lancashire cotton industry. Custom and practice will not be allowed to override written contract terms. Very clear evidence is required to establish a custom. It must be long-established, certain in its scope, reasonable and not contrary to law or to the written terms of the contract. In *Pellow v. Pendragon* (1999) it was argued that there was a custom that employees with more than 20 years' service were entitled to enhanced redundancy payments. The details of the enhancements were set out in a management manual that was not published to the workforce. The court ruled that management had not committed itself either expressly or by implication through custom and practice to any contractual obligation to make the payments.

Implied Terms The law of contract recognises implied terms in a variety of situations: because they are necessary to give business efficacy to an agreement; because they are customary in the trade; or because the term is so obvious that the courts assume the parties must have intended it. Employment contracts are no different. Terms will be implied into the contract of employment where necessary to ensure it makes sense, or where such a term is common practice, or because the employer and employee must have intended it.

Due to the importance of establishing a contractual term in order to found a claim of constructive dismissal (discussed in the section on Constructive Dismissal below), implied terms are particularly relevant in constructive dismissal cases.

A set of implied terms exist for both an employee and employer and can be summarised as follows:

The Implied Duties of the Employee

To be Ready and Willing to Work This is the primary responsibility of every employee. In the case of *Beveridge v. KLM (UK) Ltd* (2000), an employee on long-term sickness sought to return to work. She produced a report from her GP which declared her fit to do so. However, her employer refused to take her back until the Occupational Health Unit in the firm declared her fit. The unit was unable to see her for six weeks, during which time she received no wages. The court held that she was entitled to wages during this period as she was ready and willing to work.

If an employee attends work, but not for all the hours prescribed in the contract, the employer has an option either to refuse any of the work offered and thereby avoid any payment, or to accept the work offered and reduce pay on a *pro rata* basis. In *Miles v. Wakefield M.D.C.* (1987), a registrar of births, marriages and deaths refused to work on Saturday mornings. The House of Lords held that the employer was entitled to deduct 3/37ths of his salary. The court pointed out that the employer could also refuse to pay any wages at all, since the employer is entitled to refuse partial performance of the contract. The employer must make it clear to the employee that the refusal to perform some aspect of the job is regarded by the employer as a fundamental breach (of the contractual term to be ready and willing to work).

To Take Reasonable Care and Skill Employees must take reasonable care when performing their duties. In principle, an employee who causes loss to his employer by failing to take reasonable care could be sued by the employer (*Janata Bank v. Ahmed* (1981)). This duty also requires an employee to be reasonably competent.

To Obey Lawful and Reasonable Orders An employee is under an implied obligation to carry out the employer's reasonable and lawful orders. A failure to do so will place the employee in breach of contract and is usually listed as a disciplinary offence in the employer's contract (although a first offence is unlikely to justify a dismissal). An order is lawful if it falls within the employee's job description and does not break the law; for example, an instruction to a lorry driver to drive at 100 mph would be an unlawful order, and the driver could not be justifiably disciplined for refusing to follow it. A further example is the case of *Morrish v. Henlys (Folkestone) Ltd* (1973), where an employee was dismissed for refusing to falsify the accounts in his work. The refusal to obey this order, which was clearly illegal, was held not to be a breach of contract, and so the dismissal was both wrongful and unfair.

Whether an instruction is reasonable will depend on all the circumstances: the classic case involves an instruction to an employee to visit Turkey where he had been sentenced to be executed (*Ottoman Bank v. Chakarian* (1930)). Unsurprisingly, this was held to be an unreasonable instruction. In other words, the employer will be subject to the implied obligation of trust and confidence when giving instructions: an employer is likely to be in breach of the obligation in so far as he demands of the employee an impossible, criminal or ludicrous act.

To Act Co-operatively and with Good Faith   This is an important duty and is wide ranging in its application. This has been described by Lord Wolff in *Attorney General v. Blake* (2000) as follows:

> "The employee must act in good faith; he must not make a profit out of his trust; he must not place himself in a position where his duty and his interest may conflict; he may not act for his own benefit or the benefit of a third party without the informed consent of his employer."

This duty requires more from the employee than mere obedience to rules and orders. It includes a general obligation to co-operate with the employer and not to act in a way that is contrary to the interests of the employer. It incorporates obligations of good faith and loyalty. Neither party should act in a way calculated or likely to destroy or seriously damage the relationship of trust and confidence. The duty embraces such activities as the employee taking bribes and making secret profits or working for a rival of the employer during spare time (*Symbian Ltd v. Christensen* (2001)). In this case the court held that the implied duty of fidelity on its own would not prevent an employee working for a competitor, during a period of "garden leave" (i.e. a period of notice where the employee remains on full pay, is not obliged to work but is not allowed to work for anyone else). The only way that an employer could enforce this was through the use of an express term in the contract (known as a restrictive covenant). Such clauses were a restraint of trade and would only be enforced if they were reasonable; could be justified by reference to a legitimate business interest; and necessary to prevent harm to the employer. It seems that during a period of "garden leave" the contract only exists in a skeleton form with scaled-down duties applying.

The duty of good faith also includes a duty of confidentiality from the employee to the employer. Employers should unambiguously express the information that they require to be kept confidential and make it clear that the obligation of confidence persists after the employment relationship has ended. Such information might include customer lists or trade secrets. If the clause is sufficiently precise, injunctive relief will be granted to prevent employees from misusing this confidential information during, or after, their employment.

To Not Enter into Competition during Employment An implied term also prevents employees from setting up in competition with the employer, or for working for a competitor (even outside working hours, if such employment truly competes with the employer), whilst the employment subsists. Often contracts include restrictive covenants which define the geographic areas of the type of work in which the employee is prohibited from competing. Note that the law distinguishes between actual competition (which an employee cannot engage in) and steps taken in anticipation of competition, i.e. preparing to compete (which the law does not imply a term to prevent).

The Implied Duties of the Employer

The Duty of Trust and Confidence In *Malik v. BCCI SA* (1998), the House of Lords ruled that there is an implied term that the employer will not conduct business in such a fraudulent or dishonest way as to cause damage to the employee's reputation and place him or her at a severe disadvantage in the labour market. The House of Lords confirmed the existence of the implied term of mutual respect and confidence and awarded damages for loss of reputation, and the "stigma" caused by the manner of the employee's treatment in this case.

The Duty to Pay Wages This is a fundamental obligation, which is normally a matter of express agreement. The wages payable are the employee's normal net wages. An employer cannot avoid paying wages by asserting that no wages were ever agreed. In the absence of express agreement, the law requires a reasonable wage to be paid.

The Duty to Indemnify the Employee against Reasonable Expenses Necessarily Incurred The parties frequently have express agreement on matters like travelling or subsistence expenses. If there is none, the employer must pay a reasonable sum.

The Duty to Take Care of the Employee's Safety and Health at Work This is another very important common law duty, which essentially covers three distinct aspects:
- to provide safe plant, appliances and place of work;
- to provide a safe system of work; and
- to provide reasonably competent fellow employees.

The duty exists alongside the key health and safety statutes, and is often used as the basis for a damages claim by an employee injured in the workplace. Every employer must exercise reasonable care for the safety of every individual employee. The common law demands that he acts as "an ordinary, prudent employer would act in the same circumstances". He must guard against all reasonably foreseeable risks. Increasingly, work place stress claims are becoming more prevalent in this area.

The first successful action for work-related stress was *Walker v. Northumberland County Council* (1995), where a senior social services officer with responsibility for four teams of social workers suffered a work-related mental breakdown. Three months later he returned to work, but despite assurances that he would receive additional staff, none materialised. The situation continued to deteriorate, and six months after returning to work, Walker suffered a second mental breakdown, which proved to be so severe that he was forced to give up work permanently. He brought an action for compensation.

It was held that, while the first breakdown was not reasonably foreseeable, the second was. A reasonable employer would have foreseen that, if Walker were once again to be exposed to a workload of the sort which had brought about the first breakdown, there was a reasonably foreseeable risk that he would suffer a second breakdown which would probably bring his career to an end. They should have provided him with substantial backup. Damages of £200,000 were awarded.

A further significant decision in this area is the House of Lords case of *Barber v. Somerset County Council* (2004), where four appeals from different County Courts were heard together. The Court of Appeal took the opportunity to lay down guidelines for dealing with occupational stress claims and these were subsequently approved in the House of Lords. What is important is whether harm, as a result of the pressures in the workplace, is reasonably foreseeable with respect to the individual concerned. The test is the same whatever the employment. It is not the job itself which causes harm, but the interaction between the individual and the job. There needs to be an indication to the employer that steps need to be taken to protect an employee from harm. Factors which are relevant include:

- The nature of the job and the workload. Is the workload greater than the normal level for the job? Is the work particularly demanding for the employee? Are there signs of stress amongst others doing the same job? Is there a high level of absenteeism?
- The next stage is to consider whether there are signs of impending harm for the particular individual employee involved. Are there frequent or prolonged absences? Has the employee or his or her doctor warned about the risk of harm?
- Once harm is assessed as being foreseeable, the next issue is what the employer ought to do about it. The actions that are reasonable will depend upon the size of the organisation and its resources, but might include a reallocation of duties, a transfer of the individual to a less onerous post, a period of leave or the engagement of more staff to help.
- It is also necessary to show causation – that the employer's failure to take action was at least partly responsible for the harm.

The ruling emphasises the importance of employers taking proactive steps to address any situation where they have been put on notice that an employee's working conditions are subjecting him or her to the risk of significant mental ill health.

Stress can also result from workplace bullying, as well as from overwork or other pressures. The case of *Green v. DB Services Ltd* (2006) reinforces the fact that protection from harassment legislation can now be used as an alternative route for legal redress in bullying cases. Damages of £852,000 were awarded to a well-paid employee who suffered severe ill health as a result of workplace bullying. The relevant legislation in Northern Ireland is the Protection from Harassment (Northern Ireland) Order 1997 (1997 No. 1180 (N.I. 9)), which provides both civil and criminal remedies.

The Duty to Provide Work Generally, it is said that there is no obligation on an employer to provide work. This was seen in the case of *Collier v. Sunday Referee* (1940), where Asquith J stated:

> "Provided I pay my cook her wages regularly she cannot complain if I choose to take any, or all, of my meals out."

There are exceptions of course, that is, situations where there is a duty to provide work, because failure to do so will lead to a reduction in actual or potential earnings. More recently the courts have been willing to imply a right to work where an employee needs to exercise his or her skills to avoid them becoming obsolete or defunct. With the growth of computer technology, this implied right is becoming increasingly important to a growing number of employees such as computer technicians. In *William Hill v. Tucker* (1998) the court considered that such skills had to be exercised frequently and implied a right to work in the absence of any express term to the contrary.

The Duty to Exercise Reasonable Care and Skill in the Giving of a Reference There is no general common law duty to provide a reference, although there may be a specific statutory duty as was seen in *Spring v. Guardian Assurance plc* (1994). In this case, Spring had worked for Guardian Assurance, but was dismissed when they discovered that he was planning to go to work for a competitor. Spring then applied for a job with Scottish Amicable who, like Guardian Assurance, were members of LAUTRO. Under LAUTRO's Code of Conduct, Scottish Amicable were bound to request a reference from Guardian Assurance before appointing Spring, and the Code also required Guardian Assurance to provide one. The reference supplied stated that Spring "was a man of little or no integrity and could not be regarded as honest". It also said that he ignored the concept of 'best advice' and promoted those policies that would bring him the highest commission. Upon receiving the reference, Scottish Amicable refused to appoint Spring and so did a number of other companies to whom he applied. The trial judge found as a fact that Spring had never been guilty of dishonesty nor a lack of integrity, though perhaps of incompetence and inexperience. It was held by the House of Lords that an employer who gave a reference about a former employee owed that employee a duty to take reasonable care in the preparation of the reference and would be liable to him in negligence if he failed to do so and the employee thereby suffered damage.

It should also be noted that failure to provide a reference can amount to victimisation under anti-discrimination legislation, as in *Coote v. Granada* (2000). Mrs Coote was originally sacked for becoming pregnant and settled her case for £11,000. When she asked for a reference, Granada refused and she brought a second case to tribunal. This was referred to the European Court of Justice on the question of whether the sex discrimination legislation protects former employees or only those currently in employment. The ECJ ruled that former employees were protected and, when the case was re-heard by the tribunal, agreed damages of £195,000 were awarded. New statutory provisions, expressly outlawing post-employment discrimination, were introduced during the course of 2003. These apply to cases of race, sex, religious or political and sexual orientation discrimination.

On refusal to give a reference, the case of *Chief Constable of West Yorkshire v. Khan* (2001) is also relevant. Khan complained of race discrimination consisting of the failure to support him for promotion. He subsequently applied for a post with another police force. The Chief Constable was requested to provide observations on Khan's suitability, in line with normal practice. Ordinarily, the request would have been met, but the Chief Constable declined on the grounds that Khan had an outstanding tribunal application and the Chief Constable did not wish to prejudice his own position before the tribunal. This course of action was upheld in the House of Lords, which took the view that employers ought to be able to take steps to preserve their position in pending discrimination proceedings without laying themselves open to a charge of discrimination. The action is taken, not because the claimant is being victimised, but because the employer, currently and temporarily, genuinely needs to preserve his position.

Terminating the Employment Contract

A Contract of Employment may be terminated in several ways: by mutual agreement, by frustration, by expiry, by dismissal by the employer, by notice given by the employee or by acceptance of a fundamental repudiatory breach of contract by the employer or employee. The death of either party terminates the contract of employment unless the contract implies otherwise.

When an employment contract is terminated, an employer potentially faces two distinct but linked claims – *wrongful* and *unfair* dismissal.

Wrongful Dismissal

Wrongful dismissal relates to the contractual right of an employer to terminate a contract. For example, all contracts will be subject to certain amounts of notice of termination by both parties. If the employer fails to give the appropriate amount of notice under the contract then the employee may sue for breach of contract. The amount of any award would normally be limited to the amount that would have been earned during the notice period had the employee been allowed to work out his or her notice.

There may be occasions when the amount of compensation sought is much higher than the amount an employee would normally associate with a statutory notice period. Statutory notice periods under the Employment Rights (Northern Ireland) Order 1996 range from one week's notice after the employee has been employed one month or more, to a maximum of 12 weeks' notice after 12 years' service. However, employees engaged on fixed-term contracts that contain no other termination or notice clause may be able to sue for the entire amount remaining under the fixed-term contract. Football managers' contracts are usually fixed term and it is common for managers to seek compensation based on what they could have earned (under a two-to-three-year period) had they not been sacked partway through a season.

In *Morrish v. NTL Group* (2007), the Court of Session (the Court of Appeal in Scotland) said that, if employers wish to terminate a contract of employment with payment in lieu of notice, they must have an express right to do so and such a term should not be implied into the contract.

Employers might also find themselves sued for damages for wrongful dismissal where the employer fails to follow particular procedures that pertain to particular contracts. For example, a manager who dismisses without authority to do so or an employer in the public sector who fails to follow the full rules under a complicated disciplinary procedure and reduces time limits for holding meetings might find themselves sued for an amount equivalent to the money that would have been earned had the contract not been terminated early.

In certain circumstances employees may seek injunctions against employers to stop a dismissal from taking effect and may ask the courts to order the employer to start again or rule that an original decision was 'ultra vires', i.e. outside the powers of the body that made the decision.

Until 1994, all breach of contract claims arising out of employment had to be pursued through the civil courts rather than a tribunal. This meant that, prior to that date, employees who had been dismissed summarily would have to take a County Court action for damages for the employer's failure to give notice and a separate claim for unfair dismissal to the Industrial Tribunal. However, in 1994, the Industrial Tribunal in Northern Ireland was given the authority to hear some breach of contract claims, meaning that only one linked claim need be brought in a tribunal in many cases.

The maximum award that a tribunal may give in a breach of contract claim is £25,000 and this figure has remained static since 1994. Higher paid employees, or those who have perhaps lost out on a large bonus as a result of a contractual breach by the employer, may continue to lodge separate tribunal and civil court claims.

Unfair Dismissal

An employer who dismisses an employee without good reason or without following a fair procedure leaves themselves open to a claim for unfair dismissal. When such a claim is brought, the employer has to establish the reason for the dismissal. The Industrial Tribunal then has to consider whether the dismissal was fair in all the circumstances. If the dismissal is held to be unfair, the employer can be ordered to re-engage, reinstate or to pay compensation to the ex-employee. The parties to the claim are known as the claimant (employee) and the respondent (employer).

A claim for unfair dismissal must be made to the tribunal within three months, beginning with the effective date of termination. Under Article 145 of the Employment Rights (Northern Ireland) Order 1996, tribunals have the discretion to extend the time limit if the claimant can show that it was not reasonably practicable to put the claim in on time and that the claim has been submitted within a reasonable time of its becoming practicable to present the claim.

There are various qualifying conditions in relation to unfair dismissal, e.g. the claimant must be an 'employee' and not a 'worker', the employee must normally have worked continuously for one year for his or her former employer when their employer terminated his or her legal contract of employment; and the employee must have been within the proper age limit. Most importantly, however, it is vital that the employee can show that a dismissal occurred.

Dismissals in Law An employee who wishes to claim unfair dismissal must show first that he or she has been dismissed within the meaning of Article 127 of the Employment Rights (Northern Ireland) Order 1996. Under this provision, a dismissal can occur through the termination of the employment contract by the employer with or without notice. A dismissal can also occur through the expiry of a fixed-term contract without its being renewed on the same terms, or a constructive dismissal can take place. This is when an employee resigns in circumstances in which he or she is entitled to terminate the contract without notice by reason of the employer's conduct.

The Fairness of the Dismissal The test to determine whether a dismissal is fair is two-fold:
- The employer must show the reason for the dismissal and that the reason is one of the five potentially fair reasons set out in Article 130 of the Employment Rights (Northern Ireland) Order 1996.
- If, and only if, the employer is successful at this first stage, the tribunal must then consider whether the employer acted reasonably and it must be satisfied that, in all the circumstances, the employer was justified in dismissing for that reason.

The five potentially fair reasons for dismissal as set out in Article 130 are:
1. a reason related to the capability or qualification of the employee for performing work of the kind he or she was employed by the employer to do;
2. a reason related to the conduct of the employee;
3. that the employee was redundant;

4. that the employee could not continue to work in the position he or she held without contravention of a duty or restriction imposed by or under an enactment; and

5. "some other substantial reason for dismissal" of a kind such as to justify the dismissal of an employee holding the position that that employee held.

A dismissal will be automatically unfair if the dismissal is:
- related to an employee's membership of, and/or activity in, an independent trade union, or non-membership of a trade union;
- for a reason connected with health and safety;
- for asserting a statutory right;
- for maternity-related reasons; or
- in contravention of the Transfer of Undertakings (Protection of Employment) Regulations 2006 (2006 No. 246).

Constructive Dismissal

A constructive dismissal arises when:
- the employer's conduct entitles the employee to terminate the contract without providing notice; and
- the employee terminates the contract on account of the employer's conduct.

In the majority of cases, the employee must be continuously employed for a minimum period of one year to pursue a complaint of unfair constructive dismissal. However, the one-year rule will not apply where the employee terminates the contract on account of the conduct of the employer that constitutes an automatically unfair reason for dismissal. For example, if an employer disciplines an employee who is a health and safety representative and the principal reason for the disciplinary action is that the employee was performing the functions of a representative, the employee could leave and claim unfair constructive dismissal. The employee will not be required to have completed a one-year period of continuous service. Other rights might also apply in relation to constructive dismissal situations. For example, in *Horkulak v. Cantor Fitzgerald International* (2003) a city trader who was bullied and sworn at by his manager resigned and claimed that the employer had fundamentally breached the trust and confidence required for a contract to operate. Instead of claiming unfair dismissal, which would have netted the trader £50,000+, the employee took a breach of contract claim to the High Court and was awarded £912,000, although that sum was reduced slightly on appeal. In the case of *Thorpe v. Poat* (2005) two housekeepers resigned during their probation period because the employers did not provide them with a safe and hygienic workplace (the parties argued over the owners allowing their dogs to defecate freely). The employees did not have unfair dismissal rights but claimed damages for the probation period.

Burden of Proof The burden of proof in establishing that a constructive dismissal took place, rather than a resignation, rests with the employee. In other words, the employee must establish, on the balance of probabilities, that the employer's conduct justified the employee abandoning the contract. Often the employer will try to show that the employee merely resigned and that no dismissal took place. Of course, if the employer fails to convince the tribunal that this was the case, it will then be extremely difficult for the employer to proceed to show that the employee was actually dismissed for a fair reason, that a fair procedure was adopted and the dismissal was reasonable in all the circumstances.

Breach of Contract The statutory definition of the circumstances constituting a constructive dismissal does not explain what sort of behaviour on the employer's part will entitle the employee to terminate the contract. However, two categories of conduct that may justify an employee treating his or herself as constructively dismissed can be extracted from case law:
1. a breach of a fundamental term of the employment contract; or
2. a series of actions, which when considered cumulatively, constitute a repudiation of the contract by the employer, or the 'last straw' doctrine.

- *Fundamental Breach* The ruling of the Court of Appeal in England in the leading case of *Western Excavating (ECC) Ltd v. Sharp* (1978), is helpful. The crux of the decision in that case is that the employer must be in breach of the contract of employment for there to be a constructive dismissal; it is not sufficient that the employer acted unreasonably. The court focused on the wording of the legislation, stipulating that the employee must be "entitled" to terminate the contract. This was interpreted as meaning "entitled according to the law of contract". According to Lord Denning, "An employee is entitled to treat himself as constructively dismissed if the employer is guilty of conduct which is a significant breach going to the root of the contract of employment; or which shows that the employer no longer intends to be bound by one or more of the essential terms of the contract. The employee in those circumstances is entitled to leave without notice or to give notice, but the conduct in either case must be sufficiently serious to entitle him to leave at once."

- *The 'Last Straw' Doctrine* There appears to be one exception to the requirement that the employer is guilty of a fundamental breach. Conduct amounting to a repudiation of the contract by the employer can be a series of small incidents over a period of time. This is often referred to as the 'last straw' doctrine. In the case of *Garner v. Grange Furnishing Ltd* (1977), the Employment Appeals Tribunal held that where the conduct of the employer was making it impossible for the employee to go on working that amounted to a repudiation of the contract. In the case of *Lewis v. Motorworld Garages Ltd* (1985), the employee had resigned following a series of incidents including demotion, and no pay increases. The Court of Appeal ruled that an employee is entitled to add one breach of the contract to other actions to assess whether, when the employer's actions are taken cumulatively, there has been a repudiation of the contract by the employer. This will often include the phenomenon of 'squeezing' an employee out of his or her job by a subtle but steady campaign of changes, which has the effect of unsettling the employee.

Remedies for an Unfair Dismissal

Three remedies are available for unfair dismissal: reinstatement, reengagement and compensation. Although the legislation gives primary emphasis on securing the reinstatement or reengagement of the dismissed employee, there is in fact no legal right for an employee to get his or her job back. Few awards of reinstatement or reengagement are made.

Reinstatement This takes effect as if an employee has never been dismissed. This therefore involves full restoration of pay and other benefits, seniority and pension rights, etc.

Re-engagement This occurs in situations where the tribunal thinks that reinstatement is not practicable. It allows the employer to offer the employee a different but comparable job or another suitable job.

Compensation Compensation is generally the type of award made by the Industrial Tribunal, particularly were the employer and employee consider that reinstatement or reengagement would be unworkable. There are two elements to a compensatory payment. The first is the basic award, which aims to compensate the employee for the loss of his or her job and is calculated in the same way as a redundancy award. The basic award is:

- half a week's pay for each year of employment between the ages of 18 and 21;

- one week's pay for each year of employment between the ages of 22 and 40; and
- one-and-a-half weeks' pay for each year of employment between the ages of 41 and normal retirement age for men and women.

The weekly pay figure is limited to a maximum of £475 per week (from 1 April 2015 but subject to amendment each year) and the maximum amount of years that will be considered is 20. Therefore, the absolute maximum that can be awarded under the basic award is:

$$20 \text{ years} \times £475 \times 1.5 = £14,250$$

The second part of the compensatory award compensates the employee for any loss sustained until the date of the tribunal hearing and any future loss. This award is not capped.

Under the compensatory award, the maximum an employee can be awarded is £65,300. This award is intended to compensate the employee for financial loss relating to the dismissal.

Redundancy

As stated above, redundancy is a potential fair reason for dismissal of an employee. Redundancy is defined as:

"a dismissal which is wholly or mainly due to the fact that the business in which the employee works has or will cease to exist; the business has or will cease to exist in the place in which the employee works; or the requirements of the business for employees to carry out work of the particular kind carried out by the employee either generally, or the place where the employee works, have ceased or diminished or are expected to cease or diminish." (1996 Order, Article 174)

Employees with at least two years' continuous employment have the right to receive a statutory redundancy payment if they are made redundant. An employee will forfeit the right to a statutory redundancy payment if they have unreasonably refused an offer of suitable alternative employment by the employer.

Although redundancy is a potentially fair reason for dismissal, the procedure adopted in selecting employees for redundancy must also be fair. An employer should ensure that: a fair process is used to select employees for redundancy; consultation is carried out with employees before making a final decision on redundancy; alternatives to redundancy are considered as well as whether there is any suitable alternative employment available for employees within the workplace, and they must make sure it is offered if available.

If an employer wishes to make 20 or more employees redundant, a collective redundancy process must be followed. Consultation must be carried out with representatives of the affected employees and the representatives must be trade union representatives. Consultation should begin no later than 90 days before the first dismissal is planned. There is also an obligation to notify the Secretary of State where the employer is proposing to dismiss as redundant 20 or more employees at the same establishment. The consultation should discuss ways of avoiding redundancies or reducing the number and mitigating the consequences of the dismissals and it must be taken with a view to reaching agreement with the representatives. Employees can complain to an Industrial Tribunal in relation to a breach of the statutory rules governing the election of employee representatives and if they believe that the appropriate consultation has not taken place.

Disciplinary and Grievance Procedures

There are two very good reasons for having disciplinary and grievance procedures. First, April 2005 saw the introduction of the statutory minimum dispute resolution procedures to Northern Ireland. These legal provisions were contained in the:
- Employment (Northern Ireland) Order 2003 (2003 No. 2902); and
- Employment (Northern Ireland) Order 2003 (Dispute Resolution) Regulations (2004) (2004 No. 521).

Since then, both employers and employees have been required to follow specific procedures when dealing with dismissal (and other types of disciplinary sanction) or where the employee has a complaint that could result in a tribunal claim (grievance) against their employer.

A second reason for having grievance and disciplinary procedures is that it is considered to be an integral part of good management practice. Procedures promote fairness, consistency and order; set acceptable standards of conduct and performance at the workplace; provide a recognised and fair method for dealing with alleged failures to observe the rules; help to ensure that the standards are observed and provide a mechanism for dealing quickly and fairly with employees' grievances. In addition, research also shows that employers with robust procedures can expect fewer successful tribunal claims against them, particularly relating to unfair dismissal. There is a good business case to be made for having such procedures.

The aim of the dispute resolution procedures, referred to above, was to encourage good management and early discussion of workplace issues. The intention was that by setting out clear policies and processes for dealing with workplace issues, this would promote fairness, consistency and order. Additionally, it was hoped that both employers and employees would be fully aware of the mechanisms to resolve potential issues quickly. Thus, the clear premise of the introduction of the statutory procedures was to bring about a wholesale change in the way employers and employees dealt with workplace issues. It was also expected that when both employers and employees followed robust, minimum procedures it would lead to a decrease in tribunal claims against them, particularly in relation to unfair dismissal.

However, this proved not to be the case. A plethora of cases were brought to test various strands of the procedures and in Great Britain (GB) this led to the abandonment of the procedures altogether. A review of the procedures carried out by Michael Gibbons (known as *The Gibbons Review*) in March 2007 found that they had had a number of unintended outcomes, i.e.:
- there was increased complexity and confusion;
- parties became focused on the process rather than on resolution;
- too much formality was brought to internal procedures at an early stage; and
- an unnecessarily high administrative burden for employer and employee.

The Gibbons Review also made a series of recommendations which included repealing the dispute resolution procedures and providing clear and simple guidelines for parties on grievances, discipline and dismissal in the workplace.

Code of Practice on Disciplinary and Grievance Procedures

In GB, *The Gibbons Review* recommendations have been largely implemented following consultation with the Department for Business Innovation and Skills (DBIS). In Northern Ireland, the Department for Employment and Learning (DELNI) conducted a consultation which concluded that stakeholders here wished to retain the statutory procedures for discipline and dismissal matters, while workplace grievances should be addressed on the basis of the Labour Relations Agency (LRA) Code of Practice on Disciplinary and Grievance Procedures (the 'Code'). Since then, in April 2011, the existing statutory workplace grievance procedures under the Employment (Northern Ireland) Order 2003 have been repealed with an LRA Code of Practice on Disciplinary and Grievance Procedures.

Accordingly, while employers in Northern Ireland no longer have to follow the statutory grievance procedure, it is still recommended that employers follow the grievance procedures as set out in the LRA Code of Practice. The aim of carrying out this course of action is that most grievances will be settled informally and, if this fails, that the employee should raise their grievance formally with management using the organisation's formal grievance procedure. Failure to adhere to the LRA Code of Practice does not of itself make a person or an organisation liable to proceedings; however, industrial tribunals will take the Code into account when considering relevant cases. Indeed, the LRA Code of Practice states the following:

> "Employers and employees should be aware that failure to follow any aspect of the statutory dismissal and disciplinary procedure will result in any industrial award being adjusted to reflect this failure."

Furthermore, with regard to "grievances, an industrial tribunal can take account of any unreasonable failure to follow the grievance aspects of the Code and may financially penalise the employer or the employee." Failure to follow the grievance procedure may mean that an industrial tribunal can adjust any award by a percentage of up to, or down by, 50% to reflect the provisions of the Code not being reasonably followed.

The LRA Code of Practice on Disciplinary and Grievance Procedures states that when dealing with disciplines, there are three main steps to be followed:

> **Step 1:** Write to the employee notifying him/her of the allegations against him/her, and invite him/her to a meeting to discuss the matter;
>
> **Step 2:** Inform the employee of the basis of the allegation before holding the meeting to discuss this – at which the employee has the right to be accompanied – and notify the employee of the decision;
>
> **Step 3:** If the employee wishes to appeal, hold an appeal meeting at which the employee has the right to be accompanied – and inform the employee of the final decision."

It should be remembered that these procedures are additional to, rather than a substitute for, the existing law on unfair dismissal, which requires that:

- the employer must have a potentially fair reason for dismissal; and
- the employer has acted reasonably.

The Code confirms the following as core principles of reasonable behaviour:

- "Use procedures primarily to help and encourage employees to improve/modify behaviour rather than just as a way of imposing a punishment.
- Inform employees of the complaint against them in advance of a meeting, and provide them with an opportunity to state their case before decisions are reached.
- Allow employees to be accompanied at disciplinary meetings.

- Make sure that disciplinary action is not taken until the facts of the case have been established and that the action is reasonable in the circumstances.
- Never dismiss employees for a first disciplinary offence, unless it is a case of gross misconduct.
- Give employees a written explanation for any disciplinary action taken and make sure they know what improvement is expected and how it will be monitored.
- Give employees an opportunity to appeal if they are unhappy with the decision or outcome.
- Deal with issues reasonably and without unnecessary delay.
- Act consistently."

Modified Dismissal Procedure

There may be some very rare cases of gross misconduct dismissals (but not other dismissals) to which a modified procedure can be applied. However, these situations have proven to be very exceptional and it is advisable to seek legal advice or more detailed information from the Labour Relations Agency before using it.

The 'modified dismissal procedure' is intended for use in the following very limited circumstances, all of which are rightly described by DELNI as being 'exceptional':
1. the employer dismissed the employee by reason of his or her conduct without notice;
2. the dismissal occurred at the time the employer became aware of the conduct or immediately thereafter;
3. the employer was entitled, in the circumstance, to dismiss the employee by reason of their conduct without notice or any payment in lieu of notice; and
4. it was reasonable for the employer, in the circumstance, to dismiss the employee before enquiring into the circumstance in which the conduct took place.

(See Code of Practice on Disciplinary and Grievance Procedures, Annex B.)

When carrying out a modified dismissal procedure, there are two steps:
- **Step 1: The Letter** The employer must set down in writing the nature of the alleged misconduct that has led to the dismissal, the evidence for this decision and the right to appeal against the decision, and send a copy of this to the employee.
- **Step 2: The Appeal** If the employee wishes to appeal, he or she must inform the employer. The employer must invite the employee to attend a hearing to appeal against the employer's decision, and the final decision must be communicated to the employee.

There are a number of special circumstances when the statutory or modified dismissal procedure does not have to be followed. These are as follows:

Dismissal then Re-engagement in Certain Circumstances Where the employer seeks to dismiss all employees of a description or in a category to which the employee belongs and offers to re-engage all those employees either before or on the termination of their contracts.

Where the Collective Redundancy Consultation Duty Applies There is no need to use the dismissal and disciplinary procedures when an employer wishes to make 20 or more employees at the same establishment redundant within a 90-day period. Where 19 or fewer employees are to be made redundant, the statutory procedure will have to be completed in respect of each of them.

Industrial Action Dismissals If, at the time of the employee's dismissal, he/she is taking part in an unofficial strike or other unofficial industrial action, or an official strike or industrial action that is not 'protected industrial action' (i.e. properly balloted, etc.) The exception to this is where one or more participants have not been dismissed or one or more participants have been offered re-engagement within three months and the complainant has not.

The Dismissal is an Unfair Dismissal for Taking Protected Industrial Action In short, the procedures do not apply to the majority of dismissals for, or whilst, taking part in industrial action.

Where the Employer's Business Suddenly and Unexpectedly Ceases to Function Because of an unforeseen event, it becomes impracticable to employ any employees. Examples could include flood damage or where the business premises has burnt down or has been bomb damaged.

Where the Employee Cannot Continue to Work in the Position which he or she held without Contravening a Duty or Restriction Imposed under any Statutory Provision DEL guidance gives as examples where it would be unlawful to employ someone with certain medical conditions in a number of industries or where a valid driving licence is an essential qualification for a certain position.

The Importance of Disciplinary Procedures and Rules

Disciplinary rules set standards of conduct for the workplace. Disciplinary procedures help to ensure that the standards are adhered to and provide a fair method of dealing with alleged failures to observe the rules. The law surrounding procedures of disciplinary offences has arisen largely in the area of unfair dismissal. An employee has a statutory right not to be unfairly dismissed.

This means that the employer must have a defined 'fair' reason for the dismissal, and also that the employer must follow a fair procedure. It is at this second stage of an unfair dismissal action that disciplinary procedures and their observance or non-observance become important.

In the past, employers who failed to follow agreed disciplinary procedures may also have been in breach of contract and liable to the employee for the claim in common law damages. More recently, doubt has been cast upon this by Lord Hoffman's dictum in *Johnson v. Unisys* (2001). In this case the House of Lords held that no contractual term had been breached when the claimant was dismissed in contravention of his employer's disciplinary procedure. Lord Hoffman said that, since the whole procedure was designed to ensure that the employee was not unfairly dismissed and had been framed with regard to the ACAS Code, it was impossible to believe that Parliament, when it provided that the statement of particulars must contain a note of applicable disciplinary rules, intended that the inclusion of those rules would create a common law remedy in damages.

Disciplinary Procedures in Operation

In cases of misconduct, an employer who decides to proceed to a formal disciplinary hearing is expected to follow the rules of natural justice. In non-legal terms this simply means the notion of 'fair play'. As Kilner Brown put it:

> "Although domestic tribunals are not expected to apply and follow the strict procedures appropriate to judicial tribunals they must in these days avoid a fundamental breach of natural justice. This is essential where a man's job is at stake" (*Haddow & Ors v. Inner London Education Authority* (1979)).

In *Polkey v. A.E. Daton Services Ltd* (1988), the House of Lords said that a serious breach of the rules of natural justice will make a dismissal unfair, except in exceptional circumstances.

The rules of natural justice are commonly considered to contain three elements:
1. an opportunity for employees to state a case;
2. the right of an employee to know the case against him or her; and
3. the avoidance of bias.

1. The Opportunity to State a Case This normally involves the holding of a hearing, the purpose of which should be twofold:
- to allow the employer to find out whether or not the misconduct has been committed; and
- to give an employee a chance to explain the conduct or any mitigating circumstances.

The second of these two components is seen as one of the most essential procedural safeguards and should be present whatever the circumstances. Where it is absent, the employee is likely to succeed in a claim for unfair dismissal. The case of *Lambie v. Tyne and Wear* (EAT, unreported) illustrates well why a chance to explain is essential. In this case, the applicant was dismissed after he was discovered drunk on his way home from work. He was not asked for an explanation. It was held that the applicant had taken medication for toothache. The tribunal considered he had been unfairly dismissed finding the employer's failure to interview him "deplorable and incomprehensible".

There is no set time as to the point of the disciplinary process at which the employee should be given the chance to state his or her case. However, where the decision to dismiss is taken by a person who has not heard the employee's account directly, a claim is more likely to succeed. A case in point is *Budgen & Co. v. Thomas* (1976). In this case, the applicant, a supermarket cashier, admitted breaching till procedures to a security officer. The matter was reported to the manageress who gave the security officer permission to dismiss without first hearing from the employee. It was held that the dismissal was unfair. The applicant had had no opportunity to explain to the person responsible for the dismissal.

2. The Right to Know the Case Against You The rules of natural justice require that the employee must know the case he or she has to meet at the disciplinary hearing. The allegation must be specific. In *Moorby v. Summer Products* (EAT, unreported), a broad allegation of theft was put to the employee without date, time, place or any other details of the matter. The EAT stated, "if you make a blanket allegation, you are only going to be met by a blanket defence".

The evidence against an employee, including any witness statements, should be made available at the start of the hearing or preferably before. The following case resulted in a successful claim for unfair dismissal due to the employer's failure to put the evidence properly before the employee. In *British Railways Board v. Hamment* (EAT, unreported), the applicant was dismissed for issuing vouchers fraudulently. Central to the case against the applicant was the report of a handwriting expert who had been retained by the employer. The report was not made available to either the applicant or his trade union representative. It was held that the failure to release the report to the applicant meant that the employers had failed to act fairly and had breached a rule of natural justice.

3. Avoidance of Bias It is a fundamental tenet of many legal systems that you cannot be a judge in your own case. This means that the person conducting the disciplinary hearing should not have a direct interest in the outcome of proceedings and should not appear biased or partial.

One element of this rule is that the person dismissing should not form an opinion on the employee's case before the disciplinary hearing. In the case of *Carey v. Solaglas Ltd* (EAT, unreported), a dismissal was considered unfair because it transpired that a letter of dismissal had been drafted prior to the disciplinary hearing taking place.

To avoid the appearance of bias, the employer should separate the following three processes:
1. investigation,
2. decision-making,
3. appeal.

In the case of *Moyes v. Hylton Castle Working Men's Club EAT* (1986), two club officials who witnessed the alleged misconduct also sat on a committee that investigated the incidents and then acted as both witnesses and judges at the full disciplinary hearing. The tribunal held that the rules of natural justice had been breached and that the dismissal was unfair.

It has regularly been acknowledged that a requirement of absolutely no bias cannot always be applied at work. For example, the three terms stated above cannot always be separated in small organisations with few employees. In such cases the overriding consideration appears to be that the "disciplinary tribunal acted fairly and justly" (*Haddow & Others v. ILEA* (1979)).

Coming to a Decision

Most disciplinary panels will adjourn the hearing in order to consider the case in full before coming to a decision. In coming to a decision, it is usually important to take into account a range of factors. These normally include:
(a) length of service;
(b) disciplinary record;
(c) similar offences;
(d) employee's personal circumstances;
(e) seriousness of the breach or failing;
(f) breach of rule, inadvertent or wilful;
(g) appropriate level of sanction – dismissal should not generally occur for a first offence;
(h) consistency in application of the rule (i.e. have previous breaches been ignored?); and
(i) consistency in treatment of employees (i.e. have employees who behaved in a similar manner been disciplined in the same way?).

Dealing with Grievances

A grievance is an issue raised by an employee and brought to the attention of the manager. It usually involves a concern about the working environment, workplace relationships, new working practices, organisational change or equal opportunities. For example, if an employee thinks she is being unfairly treated at work by a fellow employee who is bullying her, this treatment becomes a grievance for the employee in question which she should bring to the attention of her line manager in accordance with the company's grievance procedure.

A grievance procedure can be important as it provides a mechanism for resolving employees' problems and concerns at work and ensures that issues are dealt with speedily, before major problems develop. Grievance procedures should be simple, set down in writing, operate within quick time limits and address the issue confidentially. They should be communicated to all relevant employees, supervisors and managers. The statutory right to be accompanied applies where a worker is required or invited to attend a grievance hearing and reasonably requests to be accompanied at the hearing.

The process for raising a grievance is as follows:
- **Step 1:** Set out the grievance in writing and send it to the employer.
- **Step 2:** Hold a meeting with the employee to discuss the grievance and decide on appropriate action.
- **Step 3:** Allow the employee to appeal against the decision if they feel it has not been satisfactorily resolved.

It should be noted that the employee has a statutory right to be accompanied at the meeting and the appeal meeting.

Many routine complaints and grievances can be best dealt with informally. Notes of informal meetings should be kept. Where informal resolution by a line manager is not possible, then a formal procedure should provide for a multi-stage resolution of grievances. The first stage would usually involve the employee putting the complaint in writing and sending it to their line manager. The manager should arrange a formal hearing, at which the employee has a right to be accompanied. The manager should respond within a specified time (e.g. five days) in writing. If the matter is not resolved then the employee should be permitted to raise the matter in writing with a more senior manager. A similar procedure should be followed at this stage. Finally, where the matter has still not been resolved, stage three should allow the employee to raise her grievance with the chief executive, managing director or similar officer.

Sometimes an employee may raise a grievance about the conduct of a manager during the course of a disciplinary process. It may be appropriate to suspend the disciplinary procedure for a short while until the grievance can be resolved. Consideration might be given to bringing in a different manager to deal with the disciplinary case.

The importance of having a right to raise a grievance has been emphasised by the courts on a number of occasions. An employer will be in breach of contract in the event that a grievance procedure set out in the contract is not followed. Furthermore, there is now an increasing body of case law that indicates that tribunals will, in certain circumstances, imply terms into a contract that require an employer to deal promptly and adequately with legitimate grievances raised by an employee.

In the case of *W. A. Goold (Pearmak) Ltd v. McConnell & Anor* (1995), two employees worked as salesmen and were paid on the basis of salary plus commission. In 1992, new charges and sales methods resulted in a substantial drop in their take-home pay, a matter of some concern to them. There was no established procedure for dealing with such matters and the employees had never received a written statement of terms and conditions of employment specifying a method of pursuing a grievance. The employees resigned and claimed constructive dismissal.

The Employment Appeals Tribunal suggested that in each contract of employment there was an implied term requiring the employer to take grievances seriously. In this case, the EAT upheld the tribunal's decision that there was an implied term in the contract of employment that the employers would "reasonably and promptly afford a reasonable opportunity to their employees to obtain redress of any grievance they may have". The EAT went on to state that they were of a view that, when Parliament introduced the requirement that details of a grievance procedure must be given to employees in their written statement of terms and conditions, "Parliament must have considered that good industrial relations requires employers to provide their employees with a method of dealing with grievances in an adequate and prompt manner."

Grievance procedures are especially important in the area of discrimination law and under the Public Interest Disclosure (Northern Ireland) Order 1998. Under this piece of legislation, workers who honestly and reasonably raise issues of health and safety, criminal acts, miscarriage of justice, etc., are legally protected from "suffering a detriment", which would include being disciplined or dismissed. Such action against "whistleblowing" employees will be more difficult to justify where there are no grievance procedures in place that allow individuals to formally bring certain matters to the attention of appropriate personnel.

In the area of discrimination, the case of *Drummond v. Copygraphic plc* (EAT Case No. 70669/95) illustrates that a failure to take an individual's grievance seriously may in itself amount to discrimination. In this case, the claimant claimed that he had suffered racial discrimination on grounds of his colour. He alleged that he was frequently picked on and treated in a different way to his white colleagues. He put in a grievance which was never dealt with and he was subsequently dismissed in breach of procedures. It was held that, in the absence of any possible explanation for not dealing promptly with the grievance, the tribunal were prepared to infer discrimination.

Industrial Tribunals in Northern Ireland

Employment disputes arising in Northern Ireland are dealt with by the Industrial Tribunals (called Employment Tribunals in England). Disputes relating to religious and political discrimination in employment law in Northern Ireland are dealt with by the Fair Employment Tribunal.

The Industrial Tribunal in Northern Ireland was constituted under the Industrial Tribunals (Northern Ireland) Order 1996 (1996 No. 1921 (N.I. 18)). The rules of procedure governing conduct up to and during the hearing are now contained in the Industrial Tribunals (Constitution and Rules of Procedure) Regulations (Northern Ireland) 2005 (2005 No. 150). The headquarters of the Office of the Industrial Tribunals and the Fair Employment Tribunal are at Killymeal House, Belfast, but the Industrial Tribunal also sits in five different venues in County Court rooms in Londonderry, Strabane, Omagh, Limavady and Enniskillen.

Unlike the County Courts, the Industrial Tribunal is not chaired by judges but by a legally qualified Chairperson and two lay members. One lay member is from a panel appointed after consultation with organisations representative of employers, and the other lay member is from a panel appointed after consultation with organisations representative of employees. Tribunal hearings are conducted in public. However, tribunals may sit in private, in certain cases, if, in their opinion, evidence on matters is to be given that would be against the interests of national security if heard in public. The tribunal may also sit in private where evidence may consist of information that could not be disclosed without a breach of a statutory prohibition or which has been communicated or obtained by a witness in confidence or which, if publicly disclosed, could substantially damage a witness's undertaking for commercial reasons.

The 2005 rules, which govern proceedings, set out in detail the way in which tribunals must be conducted. There are strict rules of evidence and Chairmen are required to take notes of proceedings. From that point of view, tribunal cases generally proceed at a slow pace. It is not unusual to find discrimination cases taking one or two weeks to reach a conclusion and often unfair dismissal cases last for two or more days depending on the number of witnesses called. However, the decisions issued by tribunals are often detailed because the 2005 rules require this. A written decision from a tribunal must include certain detailed information. It must include the issues that the tribunal or Chairman has identified as being relevant to the claim. If some issues were not determined by the tribunal, the decision must state what those issues were and why they were not determined. The decision must contain finding of fact relevant to the issues which have been determined and the decision must also contain a concise statement of the applicable law. Furthermore, the decision must state how the relevant findings of fact and applicable law have been applied in order to determine the issues. In addition, where the decision includes an award of compensation or a determination that one party may make a payment to the other, the decision must contain a table showing how the amount or sum has been calculated.

Challenging a Tribunal's Decision

A tribunal's decision may be challenged either by a review to the tribunal itself, a judicial review to the High Court or by an appeal to the Court of Appeal by way of a case stated on a point of law. As we saw in **Chapter 1**, a decision from the Court of Appeal can be appealed to the House of Lords. Unlike Great Britain, there is no Employment Appeals Tribunal in Northern Ireland. However, very few tribunal decisions are appealed in Northern Ireland and most of those that are tend to be discrimination cases where awards are unlimited.

Enforcing Tribunal Decisions

If an Industrial Tribunal makes an award of money to one of the parties and that party proves unwilling to pay, the award may be enforced through an application first to a County Court and then, if necessary, to the Enforcement of Judgments Office. The Enforcement of Judgments Office (EJO) is essentially a centralised unit for enforcing judgments of the courts.

The Fair Employment Tribunal

The Fair Employment Tribunal (FET) was set up by the Fair Employment (Northern Ireland) Act 1989 to adjudicate upon individual complaints of discrimination on grounds of religious belief or political opinion. The relevant legislation in this area is now consolidated in the Fair Employment and Treatment (Northern Ireland) Order 1998 (1998 No. 3162 (N.I. 21)) ('FETO 1998').

Equality Law in Northern Ireland

The Equality Commission for Northern Ireland

The Equality Commission for Northern Ireland is an independent public body established under section 73 of the Northern Ireland Act 1998. It came into being on 1 October 1999. The Equality Commission's functions derive from those previously exercised by the Fair Employment Commission for Northern Ireland, the Equal Opportunities Commission for Northern Ireland, the Commission for Racial Equality for Northern Ireland and the Northern Ireland Disability Council. The Equality Commission has established four directorates to take over the work of those pre-existing bodies.

In addition, the Equality Commission is also charged with enforcing the statutory duties placed on public authorities in Northern Ireland to promote equality of opportunity and good relations. Section 75 of the Northern Ireland Act 1998 obliges designated public authorities in Northern Ireland to have due regard to the need to promote equality of opportunity between persons of different religious belief, political opinion, racial group, age, marital status, sexual orientation, men and women generally, persons with a disability and persons without, and persons with dependents and persons without. Likewise, section 75 obliges such authorities to have regard to the desirability of promoting good relations between these persons of different religious belief, political opinion or racial group. Public authorities covered by section 75 have to produce an equality scheme demonstrating how they are complying with their duties. This needs to be submitted to, and approved by, the Equality Commission. If the Equality Commission does not feel able to approve it, the scheme is referred to the Secretary of State for Northern Ireland, who has the powers to make the authority create a revised scheme or to make a scheme himself for the authority. To gain approval from the Equality Commission, the scheme has to address a number of points. In particular, it has to state the authority's arrangements for assessing the likely impact (as regards equality of opportunity) of policies proposed to be adopted by the authority, and for monitoring any adverse impact of policies that are adopted.

Anti-Discrimination Laws in Northern Ireland

There is no general prohibition against discrimination in the workplace. Legislation is in place that protects actual or potential employees in Northern Ireland against discrimination if they have a disability and on the grounds of their race, religious belief or political opinion, sex, pregnancy, sexual orientation, gender reassignment, marital status or age.

The main legislation currently relevant to discrimination in Northern Ireland includes:

- Sex Discrimination (Northern Ireland) Order 1976 (1976 No. 1042 (N.I. 15)), as amended;
- Equal Pay (Northern Ireland) Act 1970;
- Disability Discrimination Act 1995;
- Race Relations (Northern Ireland) Order 1997 (1997 No. 869 (N.I. 6));
- Fair Employment and Treatment (Northern Ireland) Order 1998;
- Employment Equality (Sexual Orientation) Regulations (Northern Ireland) 2003 (2003 No. 497); and
- Employment Equality (Age) Regulations (Northern Ireland) 2006 (2006 No. 261).

Codes of Practice

The Equality Commission has issued publications and codes of practice to provide guidance and set standards for equality on employment law. Some of the publications available include: *Fair Employment in Northern Ireland Code of Practice; Code of Practice for Employers for the Elimination of Racial Discrimination and the Promotion of Equality Opportunity in Employment; A Code Of Practice: Removing Bias from Recruitment and Selection; Code of Practice On Equal Pay; Disability Code of Practice – Employment and Occupation.*

Failure to observe any provision of a code of practice does not of itself render a person liable for discrimination. However, in a discrimination case, a code of practice is admissible in evidence and a tribunal must take into account any provision of the relevant code of practice that appears to be relevant to any question arising in proceedings.

For instance, in *Montague v. Templeton Robinson* (2005), the FET suggested that the Fair Employment Code of Practice 1989 is a useful document for both would-be claimants and employers. The FET stated that it is important that employers should read it, particularly paragraph 5.2.2, which sets out nine policies that should be adopted to promote equality of opportunity.

Types of Discrimination

Discrimination legislation now has common definitions across different jurisdictions, but there are specific differences and nuances that are worth knowing. There are four types of discrimination:

- direct discrimination;
- indirect discrimination;
- victimisation; and
- harassment.

Direct discrimination occurs when someone is treated less favourably than others are treated or would be treated. Indirect discrimination in employment exists where a provision, criteria or practice is applied equally to everyone but which has the effect of putting people of a particular sector at a disadvantage compared to others. Victimisation means treating someone less favourably than others because they have brought proceedings under particular equality legislation, or they have given evidence or information in connection with proceedings brought under a particular piece of legislation. Harassment is the fourth type of discrimination and is defined as unwanted conduct which has the purpose or effect of violating a person's dignity or creating an intimidating, hostile, degrading, humiliating or offensive environment for a person.

Awards under Discrimination Legislation

The Industrial Tribunal, when looking at the award of compensation in a discrimination case, will aim to put the claimant in the position they would have been in had the discrimination not occurred. The tribunal will also seek to establish whether the loss was caused by the discrimination. *Vento v. The Chief Constable of West Yorkshire Police (2)*(2003) and *Da'Bell v. National Society For Prevention of Cruelty to Children* (2009) are the leading cases on awards in discrimination cases. The latter states that the top band should normally be between £18,000 and £30,000. This range applies to the most serious cases where there has been a lengthy campaign of discriminatory harassment on grounds of sex or race. Only in the most exceptional cases should an award of compensation for injury to feelings exceed £30,000.

The middle band of £6,000 and £18,000 should be used for serious cases that do not merit an award in the highest band. Finally, awards between £500 and £6,000 are appropriate for less serious cases. In general, awards of less than £500 are to be avoided, as they risk being regarded as so low as not to be a proper recognition of injury to feelings. In the case of *Miles v. Gilbank* (2006), the Employment Appeals Tribunal, in England, and subsequently the Court of Appeal, upheld a tribunal's award of £25,000 for injury to feelings in a pregnancy discrimination case were Mrs Gilbank was subjected to "a catalogue of behaviour towards her on the part of the First Respondent and the other managers which goes beyond malicious and amounts to downright vicious..." The award was challenged before the Employment Tribunal as manifestly excessive. However, the EAT pointed out that:

> "Vento is now three years old. Whilst we do not have raging inflation, we nevertheless do have quiet inflation which devalues monitory values."

The Court of Appeal upheld the decision stating "there would be cases where the amount of the award could exceed even its [the *Vento*] guidelines."

Equal Pay

The Equal Pay Act (Northern Ireland) 1970 implies into all contract of employment an equality clause which operates when an employee is employed either on like work, work rated as equivalent or work of equal value to that performed by a member of the opposite sex in the same employment. The effect of this is to modify any term in a woman's contract which is less favourable than that in a man's and to include in a woman's contract any benefit in a man's contract not otherwise included in hers and vice versa.

Health and Safety at Work

Health and safety standards in employment are regulated by both judge-made common law and by a wide range of legislation. In common law, employers have a general duty to take reasonable care for the safety and health of their employees. Therefore, a person who is injured at work because of an employer's negligence can sue for damages in the ordinary courts.

In addition to specific health and safety provisions granting protection in particular types of work, such as factories and offices, all employees receive health and safety protection under the Health and Safety at Work (Northern Ireland) Order 1978 (1978 No. 1039 (NI 9)) (the 1978 Order). While defining the duties of employers and employees, the 1978 Order provides additional enforcement procedures and gives rights to trade unions to enable them to help secure safer working conditions for their members. The general purposes of the 1978 Order, as set out in Article 3, are to:
1. secure the health, safety and welfare of people at work;
2. protect other people from risks to health and safety caused by work activities (visitors, neighbours, etc); and
3. control the keeping and use of explosive or highly inflammable or otherwise dangerous substances.

Employer's Duties

The general duties of employers are set out in Article 4 of the 1978 Order, which provides that every employer will ensure, as far as is practicable, the safety, health and welfare at work of employees. Specifically, an employer must:
1. Take measures to safeguard the health, safety and welfare of employees. Whatever the work process, it must be carried out in a manner which is safe and which will not adversely affect the health of employees, either now or in the future.
2. Provide and maintain work systems which are safe and without risk to health. Plant and machinery must also be maintained to appropriate

standards of safety. This involves planning the work processes, assessing the risks involved and putting in place measures to deal with the risks identified.

3. Make provision for the safe use, handling, storage and transport of articles or substances used at work.
4. Provide to employees information, instruction, training and supervision in order to ensure their health and safety at work.
5. Ensure the workplace is maintained in a condition that is safe and without risk to health, and that all means of access and egress are similarly kept safe.

Employee's Duties

The duties of employees while at work are set out at Articles 8 and 9 of the 1978 Order:

1. Employees must take reasonable care for their own health and safety. They must also have regard for the health and safety of other people who may be affected by their actions or what they neglect to do.
2. Employees are obliged to cooperate with their employer, so far as is necessary, to make it possible for the employer to carry out its health and safety responsibilities.
3. Employees must not intentionally interfere with or misuse anything provided in the interests of health, safety and welfare or any piece of equipment especially provided to make a job safer.

In addition, there are various regulations concerned with health and safety at work, including the:

- Management of Health and Safety at Work Regulations (Northern Ireland) 2000 (2000 No. 388);
- Workplace (Health, Safety and Welfare) Regulations (Northern Ireland) 1993 (1993 No. 37);
- Health and Safety (Display Screen Equipment) Regulations (Northern Ireland) 1992;
- Provision and use of Work Equipment Regulations (Northern Ireland) 1999 (1999 No. 305);
- Manual Handling Operations Regulations (Northern Ireland) 1992; and
- Personal Protective Equipment at Work Regulations (Northern Ireland) 1993 (1993 No. 20).

Written Safety Policy

An employer must prepare and, when appropriate, revise a written statement of general policy with respect to the health and safety at work of his or her employees and bring it, and any revisions, to the notice of the employees.

Risk Assessment

The Management of Health and Safety at Work Regulations (Northern Ireland) 2000 require an employer to undertake a suitable and significant assessment of the risks to:

1. the health and safety to which employees are exposed whilst they are at work; and
2. the health and safety of persons not in employment arising out of or in connection with the conduct of the employer's undertaking.

A self-employed person is required to undertake a similar exercise. A risk assessment is to be reviewed if it is considered that it is no longer valid or if there has been a significant change in the matters to which it relates. Where the employer employs five or more employees, he or she must record the significant findings of the assessment and any group of employees identified by it as being especially at risk. The regulations require the employer to make and give effect to such arrangements as are appropriate for the effective planning, organisation, control, monitoring and review of the preventive and protective measures. In addition, an employer must ensure that the employees are provided with appropriate health surveillance and that employees receive information concerning matters such as risks to health and safety, preventive and protective measures, and procedures to be followed in the event of serious and imminent danger. Finally, an employer must appoint one or more competent persons to assist in undertaking the measures needed to comply with the statutory obligations.

Safety Representatives and Safety Committees

The Safety Representatives and Safety Committee Regulations (Northern Ireland) 1979 (1979 No. 437) require employers to accept safety representatives appointed by recognised trade unions and to consult with them. An employer must establish a safety committee within three months if two or more safety representatives request it. After a request, an employer must consult safety representatives and representatives of recognised trade unions regarding the committee's membership and activities. The powers and duties of a safety representative are set out in the 1979 regulations. These are elaborated upon in two accompanying codes of practice on safety representatives and safety committees and in guidance notes.

To enable them to carry out their functions, safety representatives are entitled to such time off work with pay as is necessary and to undergo such training as may be reasonable in the circumstances. If an employer refuses to give a safety representative time off work or refuses to pay for time off work, the safety representative can complain to an Industrial Tribunal. If the Industrial

Tribunal upholds the complaint, it must make a declaration to that effect and may make an award of compensation to be paid by the employer.

Enforcement

Enforcement of the health and safety legislation is vested in various government departments. The main enforcing body is the Health Service Executive of Northern Ireland (HSENI). Failure by an employer to comply with safety legislation is normally a criminal offence. For breaches of duties imposed by the order, or by regulations made under it, Article 31 imposes a range of penalties. On summary conviction in a magistrate's court, usually in the case of less serious offences, penalties are by way of fines only. On conviction on indictment, the penalty is up to two years' imprisonment and/or an unlimited fine.

Common Law Liability

An employer is under a duty in the law of tort to take reasonable care towards employees in the course of their employment. (See The Implied Duties of the Employer, above.)A tort is a civil wrong usually remedied by an award of damages. This duty requires the provision of a safe system of work. Examples of this are a duty to provide:
1. reasonably competent fellow employees;
2. safe plant and appliances, equipment, tools and machinery; and
3. a safe system of work, training and supervision, protective clothing, etc.

Generally, the more dangerous the process, the greater is the need to ensure it is safe. If an employee wishes to sue an employer for not providing a safe place of work, they can bring a claim for negligence in either the County Court or the High Court. In order to successfully bring such a claim, they must show that:
1. the employer owed him a duty of care;
2. there was a breach of that duty; and
3. loss and damage resulted from the breach.

Corporate Manslaughter and Corporate Homicide

Under the Corporate Manslaughter and Corporate Homicide Act 2007, the offence, called 'corporate manslaughter' in England, Wales and Northern Ireland, and 'corporate homicide' in Scotland, came in to force on 6 April 2008.

The 2007 Act applies only to organisations. It replaces the common law offence of manslaughter by gross negligence for companies and other organisations and is designed to ensure that the application of the common law offence is restricted to individuals in the future. The Act is intended to complement, rather than replace, existing health and safety offences, for which organisations may still be prosecuted as an alternative to, or in addition to, the new offence under the Act.

Under the previous, common law, before a company could be convicted of manslaughter, proof was required that a 'directing mind' (that is, an individual at the very top of the company, who could be said to embody the company in his actions and decisions) was personally guilty of manslaughter. This was known as the 'identification principle': if there was insufficient evidence to convict an individual, the prosecution of the company failed.

In contrast now to the identification principle, under the 2007 Act, the court looks at management systems and practices across the organisation. It is concerned with how an activity is managed and the adequacy of those arrangements.

What Constitutes an Offence? An organisation will be guilty of the offence of corporate manslaughter if the way in which its activities are managed or organised:

- causes a person's death;
- amounts to a gross breach of a relevant duty of care owed to that person.

An organisation cannot be convicted of corporate manslaughter unless the prosecution can prove that a substantial element of the breach lies in the way an organisation's senior management managed or organised activities.

A 'gross breach' means conduct falling far below what can reasonably be expected from the organisation in the circumstances. Corporate manslaughter is triable in the Crown Court in Northern Ireland. If convicted, the penalty is an unlimited fine, remedial orders and publicity orders.

In 2012, a pig farm company in Co. Armagh (JMW Farms) was fined £187,500 after it pleaded guilty to corporate manslaughter over the death of one its employees on 15 November 2010. The employee, Mr Robert Wilson, was tragically killed when he was struck by a metal bin which fell from the raised forks of a forklift truck and he suffered fatal crush injuries. The joint investigation by the Health and Safety Executive of Northern Ireland and the Police Service of Northern Ireland found that it was not possible to insert the lifting forks into the sleeves of the bin. The forks were too large and incorrectly spaced, causing the bin to fall. JMW Farms pleaded guilty to the offence under the 2007 Act. They were also ordered to pay £13,000 in costs.

Miscellaneous Matters

The Right to Request Flexible Working

The right to request flexible working was first introduced in Northern Ireland in 2002, by the Employment (Northern Ireland) Order 2002 (2002 No. 2836 (NI 2)). It was one of a number of measures introduced by the then Labour Government to promote work–life balance. Article 15 of the Employment (Northern Ireland) Order 2002 does not as such introduce a 'right to work part-time' as claimed by sections of the media. Rather, it means that employers have a statutory duty to seriously consider requests for flexible working. Initially, such a request could be made by an employee with six months' continuous employment with the employer and whose child is below the age of six years. For the parents of disabled children, the cut-off age is 18. Parents must have responsibility for the child's upbringing and be making the request to enable them to care for the child.

In April 2007 the right was extended to the carers of adult dependants. The provisions are contained in the Flexible Working (Eligibility, Complaints and Remedies) (Amendment) Regulations (Northern Ireland) 2007 (2007 No. 53).

In order to qualify for the extended right to care for a person aged over 18, an employee needs to meet the following conditions:
"(a) has been continuously employed for a period of not less than 26 weeks; and
 (b) is or expects to be caring for a person in need of care who is either—
   (i)   married to or the partner or civil partner of the employee;
   (ii) a relative of the employee; or
   (iii) living at the same address as the employee."

The term 'relative' covers any of the following:
- parent, guardian, step-parent, parent-in-law, son, daughter, step-son, step-daughter, brother, sister, step-brother, step-sister, brother-in-law, sister-in-law, uncle, aunt, grandparent; and
- adoptive relationships, and relationships such as half-brother and half-sister.

Examples of flexible working include annualised hours, compressed hours, flexi-time, home-working, job-sharing, shift-working and staggered hours.

In order to make a request for flexible working, the following steps need to be taken:
- Employees should make the request in writing, setting out the detail of the working pattern they want.
- There should be a meeting within four weeks to consider the request – employees would have a right to be accompanied at this meeting.

- The employer should write within two weeks of the meeting, giving their decision – either agreeing to the request, setting out a compromise, or rejecting the request. Details of the appeal procedure should be provided.

An employee who is dissatisfied with the decision should complain, through the internal grievance procedure, followed by arbitration or access to a tribunal.

If rejecting the request, the employer can put forward a 'good business case' to justify their decision. Examples of these would include:
- the burden of additional costs;
- inability to meet customer demand;
- inability to organise work within available staffing;
- detrimental impact on quality or performance; and
- inability to find extra staff.

These measures were intended to promote dialogue between the employer and employee. Requests are meant to be non-confrontational and acceded to by the employer wherever accommodation is possible. The intention is that staff will be more contented in the workplace, resulting in greater loyalty and commitment and thus higher productivity. In addition, employers will secure advantages in terms of retention of valuable staff, with savings in recruitment costs and lower absenteeism rates. The proposals are therefore seen as entirely compatible with business efficiency.

In Northern Ireland, the Flexible Working (Eligibility, Complaints and Remedies) (Amendment) Regulations (Northern Ireland) 2010 (2010 No. 221) came into effect in July 2010 and essentially amended and extended the existing right to request flexible working to parents of children under the age of 17 rather than under the age of six. In 2015, the Work and Families (Northern Ireland) Act 2015 came into effect and amended the right to request flexible working to all employees who have 26 weeks' continuous service, regardless of their child's age.

The National Minimum Wage

The right of every worker in the United Kingdom to a statutory minimum rate of pay was established for the first time by the National Minimum Wage Act 1998. The Act is supplemented by the National Minimum Wage Regulations 1999 (1999 No. 584). The right came into effect on 1 April 1999 and is often hailed as one of the principal achievements of the Labour Government of the 1990s and early 2000s.

Who is Covered? Entitlement to the minimum wage is extended to 'workers' as defined in section 54 of the Act. Agency workers are expressly covered by section 34. To determine who the employer is in these circumstances, the duty to pay the national minimum wage falls on the person who is responsible for paying or actually pays the worker. The Act also applies to homeworkers, unless they are genuinely self-employed. In October 2004, entitlement for young people aged 16 or 17 was introduced for the first time. There are special rules for apprentices and some workers are excluded, such as share fishermen, voluntary workers, family members working for the family business and prisoners working under prison rules.

The Rates The rates for the national minimum wage at the time of writing (effective from 1 October 2015 and subject to an annual increase) are as follows:
- main (adult) rate for workers aged 21 and over – £6.70 per hour;
- development rate for workers aged 18–20 (inclusive) – £5.30 per hour;
- rate for 16-and 17-year-olds – £3.87 per hour; and
- apprentice rate – £3.30.

The national minimum wage rate applies to 16-year-olds who are no longer of compulsory school age. In Northern Ireland, a person reaches this age immediately after 30 June of the school year in which their 16th birthday occurs. The rate does not apply to 16- and 17-year-old apprentices.

Leave Entitlement

In addition to introducing the right to request flexible working, the Labour Government of the late 1990s and early 2000s also introduced a number of other family-friendly rights as part of their efforts to deal with work–life balance. These are discussed in the following:

Annual Leave The right to annual leave is governed by two things: the employee's contract and Regulation 13 of the Working Time Regulations (Northern Ireland) 1998 (1998 No. 386). This Regulation introduced, for the first time, a statutory entitlement (for workers) to paid annual holidays. From 23 November 1999, employees were entitled to four weeks' paid annual leave. From 1 October 2007 this rose to 4.8 weeks, and it rose again in April 2009 to 5.6 weeks.

Maternity Leave and Related Matters The right to take maternity leave was originally introduced in 1976 and has been amended many times over the intervening years. The basis of the current scheme of maternity leave provisions was provided for in Article 14 of the Employment (Northern Ireland) Order 2002. New, enhanced rights were introduced by the Work and Families (Northern Ireland) Order 2006 (2006 No. 1947) and these apply from 1 April 2007.

There are two main types of maternity leave, ordinary maternity leave (OML) and additional maternity leave (AML), although the differences between them are gradually disappearing. Neither type of maternity leave now requires a woman to have a qualifying period of service with her employer.

- **Ordinary Maternity Leave** The basic right to maternity leave is known as 'ordinary maternity leave' and lasts for 26 weeks. All female employees are entitled to OML, which is normally paid at 90% of the normal week's wages for the first six weeks, followed by 20 weeks at £139.58 per week (or 90% of normal wages if this is less than £139.58 per week) and is called 'statutory maternity pay' (SMP). OML may begin on any date from the beginning of the 11th week before the expected week of confinement (EWC). However, if the pregnant employee is absent from work for a reason connected with her pregnancy or childbirth in the four weeks leading up to the EWC, the employer is entitled to trigger the commencement of her maternity leave. If childbirth actually takes place before maternity leave is due to commence, then leave will commence on the date of childbirth.
- **Additional Maternity Leave** The qualifying service previously required (employee to have been continuously employed for 26 weeks at the 15th week before the EWC) for the second type of leave – 'additional maternity leave' – has now been removed. AML runs immediately from the end of ordinary maternity leave and is available for a further 26 weeks. Statutory maternity pay (SMP) is available for the first 13 weeks of AML. The remaining 13 weeks' leave is usually unpaid, although a woman may have contractual rights to pay.

Employees are required to take a minimum of two weeks' (four weeks' for those who work in factories) maternity leave immediately following the birth. This is known as 'compulsory maternity leave'. Other than this, an employee can largely choose when to start her maternity leave. This can usually be any date from the beginning of the 11th week before the week the baby is due up until the day of the birth. An employee who is absent from work due to illness will normally be able to take sick leave until she starts maternity leave on the date notified to her employer. However, if the illness is related to her pregnancy, the maternity leave period starts automatically on the day after the first day of absence following the beginning of the fourth week before the expected week of childbirth. All pregnant employees are entitled to paid time off for antenatal care.

Notification Requirements Before taking maternity leave, an employee should inform her employer no later than the end of the 15th week before the week the baby is due (or as soon as is reasonably practicable) that:
1. she is pregnant;
2. when the expected week of childbirth is; and
3. when she wants her maternity leave to start.

The employer may require medical certification from a GP or midwife to confirm the EWC. The employer should respond within 28 days of the notification, setting out the employee's rights to take leave, her expected return-to-work date and her responsibilities for notifying the employer of any changes to her plans. The employee can change the date she starts her maternity leave as long as she gives 28 days' notice to her employer

During Maternity Leave The employer may make contact with an employee (and vice-versa) during her maternity leave, once the extent and manner of the contact is not unreasonable, to discuss a range of issues, e.g. her plans for returning to work, or to keep her informed of important workplace developments. The employee should be informed of any relevant promotion opportunities or job vacancies that arise during maternity leave.

'Keeping in Touch' Days 'Keeping in touch' days are intended to help an employee keep in touch with her workplace while she is off on maternity leave, and help ease an employee's return to work after her time off on maternity leave. The employee can do up to 10 days' work during maternity leave, without affecting her maternity rights. Her SMP will not be stopped for the week in which the work occurs, as was previously the case. There are no restrictions on when 'keeping in touch' (KIT) days can be used: it is entirely a matter for the employee and her employer to agree how and when the KIT days are used during the maternity pay period. It is important to note, however, that employers are not obliged to offer work and employees are not required to accept it. An employee will be protected from suffering a detriment or dismissal for accepting or for refusing to accept offers of work from her employer.

The Work and Families (Northern Ireland) Order 2006 does not require employers to pay employees for the work done on these days and many employees will be in receipt of maternity pay as noted above. However, the maternity regulations do specify that any work done on any one day constitutes a day's work. Therefore, an employee attending work for even a few hours would have completed a day's work. This gives rise to several questions. If an employee works a KIT day but she is no longer receiving maternity pay, how much should she be paid and will she be entitled to receive employment-related benefits, such as pension contributions, for those KIT days worked? Failing to do so could result in a claim for breach of contract, breach of Equal Pay legislation or even a breach of the National Minimum Wage legislation.

It is important that the employee and her employer agree in advance what work is to be done and how much she will be paid for it.

Returning to Work If an employee returns to work at the end of her full 52 weeks of maternity leave and has not told her employer that she wishes to come back at any other time, she does not need to provide any further notice.

The employee can change the dates of her return to work as long as she gives eight weeks' notice to her employer.

If the employee decides not to return to work at the end of her maternity leave, she is entitled to continue to receive her full amount of statutory maternity leave and pay. She must give the employer at least her contractual notice, which is defined in her contract of employment, or, where there is none, the statutory notice.

Rights during Maternity Leave From 5 October 2008, an employee can benefit from her normal terms and conditions of employment, apart from pay, throughout her maternity leave. Before this change in the law, entitlement existed only during 'paid maternity leave', with more limited terms and conditions during the final 13 weeks of additional maternity leave. Throughout the duration of her maternity leave, an employee will continue to be entitled to such things as:

- any benefits calculated by reference to length of service or seniority;
- pension entitlements, including membership of an occupational pension scheme and employer's contributions (there are detailed rules about what happens to pension contributions during maternity leave);
- statutory and contractual holiday entitlements; and
- company car, mobile telephone, gym subscription, etc.

Following the ruling in *Gillespie v. Northern Health and Social Services Board* (1996), an employee on maternity leave is entitled to receive the benefit of any pay rise awarded while she is absent from work. The European Court of Justice held in the case of *Alabaster v. Barclay's Bank* (2005) that any pay rise awarded between the beginning of the reference period (the eight-week period that ends 15 weeks before the EWC) and the end of maternity leave must be included when the amount of maternity pay (contractual or SMP) is calculated.

One particularly thorny issue is whether bonuses must be paid during maternity leave. Discretionary bonuses must be paid during compulsory maternity leave – to fail to pay these will amount to unlawful sex discrimination by virtue of the Sex Discrimination Order 1976 (Amendment) Regulations (Northern Ireland) 2008 (2008 No. 159). However, the answer is not so clear-cut in other situations. Much depends upon exactly what the bonus is for, how it is calculated, how it is paid and precisely what the contract states. Specific legal advice should always be sought where this is an issue.

Paid Paternity Leave The right to paid paternity leave was introduced by Articles 4 and 5 of the Employment (Northern Ireland) Order 2002. Eligible employees (those who have a service qualification of 26 weeks and who earn above the lower earnings limit for Northern Ireland) can take up to two weeks' paid leave to care for their new baby and support the mother. This is paid by the employer at a rate of £139.58. Leave must be taken within eight weeks of the child's birth and must be taken as a block of either one week or two consecutive weeks. Statutory paternity pay is paid at the same rate and on the same basis as statutory maternity pay.

Paid Adoption Leave Articles 3 and 6 of the 2002 Order introduced rights to pay and time off work for adoptive parents. Again, there is a 26-week service qualification. A couple must choose who is to get the adoption leave and the statutory adoption pay (SAP). The provisions mirror closely the rights to maternity leave and pay, with SAP being paid for a maximum of 39 weeks, while a further 13 weeks' unpaid leave may be taken. Similar notification requirements apply.

Parental Leave The right to parental leave was introduced in Northern Ireland in December 1999 by the provisions of Article 9 of the Employment Rights (Northern Ireland) Order 1996 and the Maternity and Parental Leave etc. Regulations (Northern Ireland) 1999 (1999 No. 471), which were amended by the Maternity and Parental Leave etc. (Amendment No. 2) Regulations (Northern Ireland) 2002 (2002 No. 135). Together, these give effect to the Parental Leave Directive 96/34/EC, which contains a framework agreement granting men and women workers an individual right to parental leave on grounds of the birth or adoption of a child and to enable them to take care of the child.

The Regulations specify a number of criteria:
- entitlement to parental leave is restricted to employees;
- the employee must normally have one year's continuous employment with the same employer; and
- the employee must have responsibility for a child, which means they must either be named on the birth certificate or named in a parental responsibility order or agreement made and recorded in accordance with the Children (Northern Ireland) Order 1995 (1995 No. 755 (N.I. 2)).

Parents who satisfy the above criteria are entitled to a total of 18 weeks' unpaid parental leave to look after the child or to make arrangements for the child's welfare until the child reaches 18 years of age. In the case of the parent of a disabled child (a child in respect of whom disability living allowance (DLA) is payable) the entitlement is 18 weeks' parental leave, to be taken up to the child's 18th birthday. Entitlement arises in respect of each individual child and cannot be transferred from one child to another. The 18 weeks' entitlement applies as a total amount per employee, rather than 18 weeks with each particular employer. There is no requirement to keep records of employees' parental leave. The question of passing on records between employers is not addressed by the regulations.

All employees are also entitled to take a reasonable amount of (unpaid) time off work to deal with an emergency or unexpected situation involving a dependant.

Shared Parental Leave Shared parental leave (SPL) and statutory shared parental pay (ShPP) is available for eligible employees whose baby is due on or after 5 April 2015 or who have a child placed with them for adoption on or after that date. The legislation governing this leave is the Shared Parental Leave Regulations (Northern Ireland) 2015 (2015 No. 95), which came into force on 15 March 2015. Both maternity leave/pay and paternity leave/pay are, and remain, free-standing rights owned by an individual mother or father. They form part of a menu of different rights. SPL is different as it involves a conscious decision by the mother to curtail her maternity leave/pay and instead share some of it with her partner. The aim of SPL is to give parents flexibility in the childcare arrangements for their child in his/her first year.

As the mother must take two weeks maternity leave at time of birth (four weeks if working in a factory), the maximum amount of leave that can be shared is 50 weeks, and the maximum amount of statutory maternity pay/allowance that can be shared is 37 weeks.

Reference

- Special thanks to Legal Island and Pat Maxwell, Senior Law Lecturers, University of Ulster, for permissions.

REVIEW QUESTIONS

(See Suggested Solutions at the end of this textbook.)

Question 7.1

Shoreland Enterprises Ltd ('Shoreland'), a furniture manufacturing company, has recently been experiencing cash-flow problems as a consequence of the failure by their customers to pay invoices on time. To overcome this crisis, Shoreland has decided to make 20% of their workforce redundant. The company does not have a Human Resource Department.

Requirement: Advise Shoreland in relation to the following matters:
(i) The legal definition of redundancy.
(ii) The steps Shoreland should follow to ensure the redundancy procedure they follow is fair.

(Source: Chartered Accountants Ireland, CAP 1, Summer 2010, Extract: Q1(a))

Question 7.2

Dermot has been employed as a cost accountant with an electronics company for the past ten years. Last week he was called to a meeting with the company's head of operations and informed that, due to the economic downturn, he was being made redundant. Dermot feels that his selection for redundancy has been unfair. He believes that the real reason for his selection is that he recently sued the company for injuries arising from an occupational accident.

Requirement: Advise Dermot on the grounds upon which a dismissal is automatically deemed unfair and, if his dismissal is as a result of a genuine redundancy, how much compensation he will be entitled to in respect of the loss of his job.

(Source: Chartered Accountants Ireland, CAP 1, Autumn 2009, Extract: Q3(a))

Question 7.3

(a) XYZ Ltd employed its own in-house company accountant, Mr Barnes, 18 months ago. Last month, it was discovered that Mr Barnes was completing fraudulent overtime claims and he was dismissed for gross misconduct. Mr Barnes has now initiated a claim in the Industrial Tribunal for unfair dismissal.

Requirement: Outline to XYZ Ltd the law relating to lawful and unfair dismissal in Northern Ireland.

(b) XYZ Ltd is now recruiting for a new company accountant and, once selected, would like to issue him or her with an employment contract. The company is keen to update all their existing employment contracts.

Requirement:

(1) Outline the express terms of an employment contract.
(2) Outline an employee's and employer's implied duties in an employment contract.

(Source: Chartered Accountants Ireland, CAP 1, Summer 2009,
Extract: Q4(a) and (b))

Question 7.4

ABC Accounting Services ('ABC') has contracted with IT Solutions Ltd. ('IT Solutions') for the past six years in relation to the implementation and servicing of its accountancy software systems. ABC has now decided to terminate the contract with IT Solutions and to employ its own in-house IT expert.

Requirement: Outline to ABC the typical express terms of an employment contract.

(Source: Chartered Accountants Ireland, CAP 1, Autumn 2008, Extract: Q4(b))

Question 7.5

Peter has been employed as an accountant with a pharmaceutical research company for the last 12 years. His contract describes him as an 'independent contractor' and he receives payment at an hourly rate following the submission of monthly invoices, without the deduction of tax and social insurance.

The research company provides Peter with his own office, which is equipped with a computer, phone, fax and Internet access. His normal hours of work are 9 am to 5 pm Monday to Friday. During his 12 years' employment, the research company has paid for Peter to undertake training and professional courses, he has regularly attended company social events, and he is a member of the company's pension and medical insurance scheme.

Peter's contract requires him to obey all reasonable instructions, to comply with the company's employment policies, to sign a confidentiality agreement and to refrain from working for a competitor whilst in the employment of the company.

The company, who have recently been experiencing financial difficulties, called Peter to a meeting yesterday and informed him that they were terminating his contract with immediate effect. Peter asked whether he was entitled to any redundancy for the loss of his job, but the company informed him that redundancy only applies to employees and not independent contractors.

Requirement: Advise Peter on the main tests that can be used to distinguish between a person employed under a contract of service and a contract for services, and in this scenario advise Peter whether, on the basis of the circumstances described, the Court would view him as an employee or a contractor for the purpose of redundancy.

(Source: Chartered Accountants Ireland, CAP 1, Summer 2008, Extract: Q4(a))

Question 7.6

Adam has recently commenced employment with Downey Investment Advisors as a financial accountant. This is Adam's first job as a qualified financial accountant and in this regard he seeks your advice on the following employment law matters.

Requirement:

(a) List any FOUR duties owed by an employer to an employee.
(b) List the FOUR main sources of terms in employment contracts.

(Source: Chartered Accountants Ireland, CAP 1, Law for Accountants (NI),
Summer 2011, Extract: Q2(a)(i) and (ii))

Question 7.7

Mr Sharp, a client, says he has heard that employees who bring claims for unfair dismissal can, if successful, have a number of remedies available to them.

Requirement: Advise Mr Sharp of the THREE main remedies available to an employee bringing a claim for unfair dismissal.

(Source: Chartered Accountants Ireland, CAP 1, Law for Accountants (NI),
Autumn 2011, Extract: Q3(e))

Question 7.8

Sarah has worked at a university since 2000 as a clinical demonstrator within the biology department. On commencement of her employment, Sarah's contract stated that she was being employed under a 'contract for services'. Since her appointment, she has worked for 12 weeks in the first semester, eight weeks in the second semester and four weeks in the third semester. Before each semester commenced, she was always told the start and end time for classes. She was also given a teaching syllabus, told what was required in each class and had set hours each week. Sarah was also required to write an exam paper and, after correction of exam papers, she was required to be present at the exam board, where results were being reviewed and validated.

In September 2011, Sarah was told that the university would no longer be requiring her services and not to return for the next semester. Sarah is now considering suing the university for unfair dismissal, but she has been told, by a colleague, that she does not have a contract of employment but instead works under a contract for services and she cannot bring such a claim.

Requirement:

(a) Outline any TWO prerequisite requirements to bring a claim for unfair dismissal.
(b) Identify and explain any TWO tests that an Industrial Tribunal will look at to establish whether or not someone is an employee for the purposes of an unfair dismissal claim.
(c) State whether you consider that Sarah is likely to be classified as an employee or as a contractor, providing reasons for your answer.

(Source: Chartered Accountants Ireland, CAP 1, Law for Accountants (NI),
Summer 2012, Extract: Q2(a), (b) and (c))

Question 7.9

Fiona has worked for Cruise Publications Ltd since 2000 as an accounts assistant. Twelve months ago, Cruise Publications Limited was taken over by another company, Parkway Publications Ltd. Since this takeover, Fiona has been experiencing problems with her new manager who wants her to change certain aspects of her employment contract. To date Fiona has refused to make any alterations to her contract.

Last week Fiona was called to a meeting with her manager and told that she was being given a final written warning arising from her missing a deadline to return completed accounts to the company's head office last month. Fiona believes that the real reason for the warning is that the company wants to get rid of her because she has refused to change the terms of her employment contract. Based on these events, Fiona is now considering resigning from her position and claiming constructive dismissal.

Requirement:

(a) Outline and explain the THREE principles of natural justice that employers should follow when subjecting employees to disciplinary actions.
(b) Define the term 'constructive dismissal'.
(c) List any TWO prerequisites to bring a claim for constructive dismissal.
(d) Assess whether the actions of Fiona's employer are likely to be classified as a constructive dismissal.

(Source: Chartered Accountants Ireland, CAP 1, Law for Accountants (NI),
Autumn 2012, Extract: Q3(a)(i)–(iv))

Question 7.10

ABC employs a warehouse manager, Peter Murphy. Last week, an accident occurred in the warehouse when a chemical drum was overturned.

This resulted in a spillage all over the warehouse floor, as the lid of the drum was not properly sealed. Peter, who was on the warehouse floor at the time of the spillage, incurred serious third-degree burns to both feet as the liquid burnt through the soles of his shoes. At the time of the incident, Peter was not wearing his regulation work boots as required by health and safety law.

Requirement: List any TWO sanctions that can be imposed upon an employer where they fail to comply with health and safety legislation.

(Source: Chartered Accountants Ireland, CAP 1, Law for Accountants (NI), Summer 2013, Extract: Q1(b)(ii))

Question 7.11

Lola, Freddie and Kate are the sole directors/shareholders of Cherry Cottage Limited ('Cherry'), a private company providing self-catering holidays on the island of Ireland. Recently, Lola had been disagreeing with Freddie and Kate as to the future direction of Cherry and, as a consequence, she resigned as company director. Following Lola's resignation as director of Cherry, she incorporated a rival company, Indigo Holidays Limited ('Indigo'). Lola and Edward (Cherry's current sales manager) are the sole directors/shareholders of Indigo. Cherry intends on dismissing Edward for breach of his employment contract, which states that he cannot work for any direct competitor of Cherry while still in their employment.

Requirement: List any TWO grounds that may constitute a **fair** dismissal under the terms of the Employment Rights (Northern Ireland) Order 1996. Advise Cherry on the procedure they should follow to effect a fair dismissal of Edward.

(Source: Chartered Accountants Ireland, CAP 1, Law for Accountants (NI), Summer 2013, Extract: Q3(c))

Question 7.12

Last month, one of the employees of Regal Airways Limited ('Regal') was injured when he was hit by a bus that was shuttling passengers out to a plane. Regal discovered that the employee had only commenced employment the week before the incident and was not wearing any high-visibility clothing as the airline had none in stock in his size and was awaiting a delivery. Regal's human resources manager has advised the directors that it is likely that they will be prosecuted for breach of their duties as an employer.

Requirement: Write a memo to the board of directors of Regal advising them on any THREE duties an employer owes to an employee pursuant to the Health and Safety at Work (Northern Ireland) Order 1978. Comment also on whether Regal breached its duty to the injured employee.

(Source: Chartered Accountants Ireland, CAP 1, Law for Accountants (NI),
Autumn 2013, Extract: Q4(b))

Question 7.13

Porter was an executive director and de facto managing director of Cupcake and Coffee Ltd ('Cupcake'), a nationwide coffeehouse chain, since the company's incorporation in 2001. Last month at an extraordinary general meeting of the company, a resolution was passed removing Porter as a company director. The rationale for this decision was that the company discovered that Porter had lodged a number of cheques payable to Cupcake into his personal bank account. It was also noted that Porter had entered into a number of profitable leases with Cupcake, using a company that, on paper, was owned by his brother to disguise his true identity. Since his removal, Porter has contacted Cupcake seeking redundancy for the termination of his appointment, based on his 13 years of service. To date Cupcake has refused to pay any statutory redundancy to Porter, claiming that he is not entitled to this payment.

Requirement:

(a) Define the meaning of the term 'redundancy'.
(b) Outline any TWO eligibility requirements to obtain a statutory redundancy payment.
(c) Assess whether Porter is entitled to a redundancy payment in these circumstances.

(Source: Chartered Accountants Ireland, CAP 1, Law for Accountants (NI),
Summer 2014, Extract: Q3(a))

Question 7.14

James Holmes Snr died in October 2013. Under the terms of his will, he bequeathed his printing business ('Printshop') equally to his two sons, Robert and Matthew Holmes. At the date of his death, James Holmes Snr employed 12 staff within Printshop. No member of staff has ever been given a contract of employment. You advise the brothers that they are obliged to issue each member of staff with a written statement of particulars under the Employment Rights (Northern Ireland) Order 1996.

Requirement: List any FIVE items that should be contained within a contract of employment under the provisions of this legislation.

(Source: Chartered Accountants Ireland, CAP 1, Law for Accountants (NI), Autumn 2014, Extract: Q3(b))

Chapter 8

DATA PROTECTION

Introduction

The Data Protection Act 1998 (the Act) came into force on 1 March 2000, replacing the earlier Data Protection Act 1984. The purpose of the Act was to establish a framework of rights and duties for both individuals and businesses in relation to personal data. The Act considers the needs of organisations and how they should collect and use personal data for business and other purposes, but it also takes account of the rights of individuals and the need for privacy regarding their personal details.

The Act itself is very complex. However, there are eight key principles that are fundamental to the Act. These principles state that all personal data should be:
1. fairly and lawfully processed;
2. processed for limited purposes;
3. adequate, relevant and not excessive;
4. accurate;
5. not kept for longer than is necessary;
6. processed in line with an individual's rights;
7. secure; and
8. not transferred to other countries without adequate protection.

The Data Protection Act 1998 also uses a number of definitions throughout its text which are key to understanding how the Act applies. For example, the general effect of the Act is to give individuals ('data subjects'), including employees, rights of 'subject access'. Individuals are also permitted to have access to information held about them which is defined in the Act as 'personal data'. Moreover, the Act also gives individuals the right to have this information corrected or deleted if appropriate. An employer, and indeed any organisation, for the purposes of the Act, is known as a 'data controller'. A request to access personal data is called a 'data subject access request'.

Definition of Key Terms in the Data Protection Act 1998

'Personal Data'

'Personal data' is defined under the Act as "data relating to a living individual who is or can be identified from the data or from the data in conjunction with other information that is in, or is likely to come into, the possession of the data controller". Over the years, this definition has left businesses wondering exactly what this entails. In short, there is no clear-cut definition of what constitutes 'personal data'. Perhaps the most straightforward way to think of data is that if information can be used to identify an individual, then it most likely can be classified as personal data.

'Data Subject'

'Data subject' means an "individual who is the subject of personal data". A data subject must be a living individual. Thus organisations, such as companies and other unincorporated bodies of persons, cannot be data subjects.

Under the Act, the data subject might not be a United Kingdom or national resident. Provided that the data controller (see below) is subject to the Act, rights with regard to personal data are available to every data subject, whatever their nationality or residence.

'Data Controller'

'Data Controller' means a person who (either alone, jointly or in common with other persons) determines the purposes for which and the manner in which any personal data are, or are to be, processed. A data controller can be a 'person' recognised in law, which means that it can be an individual, organisation or other corporate or non-incorporated body. Data controllers are usually organisations, but a data controller can also be an individual.

'Data Processor'

The Act defines 'data processor' as follows: "'Data processor', in relation to personal data, means any person (other than an employee of the data controller) who processes the data on behalf of the Data Controller." An example would be when a utility company engages a company that operates call centres to provide many customer service functions on its behalf. The call centre staff have access to the utilities company's customer records for the purpose of providing those services, but may use the information they contain only for specific purposes and in accordance with strict contractual arrangements. The utility company remains the data controller;

the company that operates the call centre is a data processor. (Source: Information Commissioner's Office: www.ico.org.uk.)

The Act imposed specific obligations on data controllers when the processing of personal data is carried out on their behalf by data processors. The data controller retains full responsibility for the data processor and so the definition of data controller has an impact in this context.

'Data Subject Access Requests'

An individual's right to make a data subject access request (DSAR) to find out what information a data controller holds about them is a central tenet of the Data Protection Act 1998. The English courts have adopted a particularly restrictive interpretation of the scope of the 1998 Act. In *Durant v. Financial Services Authority* (2003), the Court of Appeal considered the meaning of 'personal data' in the context of a DSAR. In brief, the court decided that for data to be 'personal' it should be information that affects the person's privacy, and for information to affect privacy, it needs to be "biographical in a significant sense" and have the individual as its focus. The court also held that manual files were covered only if they were highly structured and sophisticated.

Since *Durant*, commentators have taken the view that manual personnel files are outside the scope of the Act and that only limited data held in a computer will be personal (and therefore disclosable) in the sense that it is significantly biographical. This decision has therefore placed significant limitations on the scope of personal information that an employee will be able to recover through a DSAR.

The Eight Principles of the Data Protection Act

As stated above, there are eight key principles that form the basis of the Data Protection Act 1998:

1. Personal Data Must be Processed Fairly and Legally

Processing means collecting, storing, retrieving or organising data. Accordingly, personal data can be processed fairly and legally only if the individual concerned (i.e. the data subject) gives their permission or the processing is necessary for legal or contractual reasons. In order for processing to be fair, the data subject should know who is processing data about them and why. The first principle therefore upholds that the individual should not be misled as to why data is needed about them. In order to be processed legally, data should not lead to any form of discrimination.

2. Personal Data Must only be Processed for Limited Purposes and in an Appropriate Way

This principle states that there must be a valid reason why an organisation is collecting personal data about a data subject. Information that is collected for one reason should be used for that reason and not for any other unrelated purpose. For example, names and addresses held for a particular purpose should not be given to a mail order company without permission.

3. Personal Data Must be Relevant and not Excessive for the Purpose

This principle states that only data necessary for the purpose stated should be collected. Information which is to be used at a later date should not be collected at that time.

4. Personal Data Must be Accurate and Up-to-date

An individual from an organisation who is collecting and using information must take all reasonable steps to check for accuracy. Information which is susceptible to change over time should be monitored to ensure it is kept up to date if it continues to be processed. This principle also establishes that personal comments about an individual can be recorded only if they are relevant, objective and up to date.

5. Personal Data Processed for any Purpose Should be Kept no Longer than is Necessary to Fulfil that Purpose

This principle establishes that information which is out of date or redundant should be destroyed in a confidential manner and on a regular basis. For example, application forms from unsuccessful job applicants should be destroyed after a few months unless otherwise stated in the company's policy.

6. Personal Data Must be Processed in Accordance with the Rights of the Individual

This principle establishes that the rights of access by an individual to information held about them should be considered, as well as the right to prevent processing likely to cause damage or distress.

7. Personal Data Must be Kept Securely

This principle establishes that an organisation should ensure that all information kept about an individual should be secure and protected against unauthorised or unlawful processing, destruction or damage.

8. Personal Data can only be Transferred to Countries that have Suitable Data Controls

This principle establishes that personal data will only be transferred to a country or a territory outside of the European Economic Area which has an equivalent or adequate level of control.

Who Does the Data Protection Act Apply to?

The Data Protection Act 1998 applies not to a particular of group of people or organisations but rather to a particular activity – that of processing personal data. Hence, if anyone processes personal data, they must comply with the Act. In particular, they must handle personal data in accordance with the eight data protection principles (discussed above). On that basis, the scope of the Act is extremely wide. It can apply to any number of situations that involve an individual's personal details.

Anyone who processes personal data must notify the Information Commissioner (see below under The Role of the Information Commissioner's Office) that they do so. If they fail to do this, it is a criminal offence. The Information Commissioner maintains a register of all organisations that process personal data. This register is available for public inspection at any time. It is a central tenet of the Act that the public should know who is processing personal data about them.

The Act lists a number of exempt organisations who do not need to notify the Information Commissioner if they process personal data. These include organisations that process personal data for staff administration only (including pay roll), advertising, marketing and public relations and accounts and records, some not-for-profit organisations, organisations that process personal data for maintaining a public register only, organisations that do not process personal information on computer, and individuals who process personal data for domestic purposes only.

Information Covered by Direct Subject Access Requests

An employee (the subject) making a DSAR is entitled to be informed by their employer (data controller) whether personal data is being processed

about them and, if so, to be given a description of the data, which should cover:
- the purposes for which the personal data is processed;
- the recipients to whom the data may be disclosed;
- the information which comprises personal data; and
- any information available to the employer on the source of the data.

Making a Direct Subject Access Request

A DSAR must be made **by a data subject** in writing (section 7(2) of the Data Protection Act 1998). Before complying with the DSAR, employers are entitled to request a fee of £10 and such information as may reasonably be necessary to satisfy themselves as to the identity of the individual making the DSAR in order to locate the information sought. If the employee concerned is still working for the employer, there is unlikely to be any uncertainty about their identity – though the employers still make sure that the request is from the employee and not, for example, from an inquisitive colleague. DSARs may be expressed as general requests for all information held on an individual employee, and a request for any of the information within the scope of section 7(1) (a–c) is treated as a request for all the information.

Responding to a Direct Subject Access Request

An employer must comply with the DSAR promptly and, in any case, within 40 days of the receipt of a request or, if later, within 40 days of receipt of:
- the £10 fee;
- evidence to confirm the identity of the individual; and
- any information necessary to locate the information sought.

If the employee concerned has previously made a similar request, the employer will only be obliged to respond if a reasonable interval of time has elapsed in the interim. Whether a further response should be provided will depend upon the circumstances, for example, whether the nature of the data is likely to have changed and the employee's reason for making the request.

Finding and Retrieving Information

The Act explicitly states that extensive efforts to find and retrieve relevant information should be made. The Code of Practice on subject access requests, released by the Information Commissioner's Office, states that as it is difficult to truly erase all electronic records, a data subject may be entitled to personal data that an employer does not have ready access to as long as it still holds the data and in time and with technical expertise can retrieve it. Employers should have procedures in place to find and retrieve personal data that has been electronically archived or backed up.

Health Records

In addition, an employer is not required to disclose health records in response to a DSAR where disclosure would be likely to cause serious harm to the physical or mental health of the employee or any other person. Employers should consult an appropriate health professional before making an assessment about either disclosing or withholding records.

Remedies for Non-Compliance

The main remedies open to individuals if they suspect their employer (or former employer) has breached the DSAR rules are:
- A statutory request can be sent to the Information Commissioner (considered below) asking him to determine whether or not it is likely that the DSAR has been carried out lawfully. The Commissioner is under a duty to make an assessment in such manner as he considers appropriate. The Commissioner can serve a notice on an employer requiring the employer to give him information.
- They can apply to court alleging breach of the DSAR rules and seeking an Order for Compliance. The court has power to inspect relevant information but, unless finding in the individual's favour, cannot order disclosure to the data subject.
- They can make a claim for damages against the employer and, if the employee concerned can show that they have suffered damage, a claim for compensation for distress.

An employer will have a defence to a claim for damages under section 13 of the Act if the employer can prove that it had taken such steps as were reasonable in the circumstances to comply with the DSAR rules.

If the DSAR uncovers data that is inaccurate or if it defies other breaches of the Act, there are two potential statutory remedies open to an aggrieved employee:
- a limited right to prevent processing likely to cause damage and distress; and
- a right to obtain the rectification of inaccurate data.

Summary of Employer's Actions on Receipt of a Data Subject Access Request (DSAR)

1. Provide the employee with a written acknowledgement of receipt of the DSAR and indicate a likely timescale for a response (within the 40-day time limit).
2. Consider whether the DSAR provides sufficient information with which to identify the employee and the relevant data. If it does not, contact the employee to request clarification. Request a fee of up to £10 if required.
3. Appoint a manager with responsibility for overseeing the collation of relevant data and the preparation of a response to the employee. This could be the data protection manager, personnel manager or the line manager of the employee making the request.
4. Provide the heads of departments which might hold information on the employee with an explanation of the types of data which are required. These include databases, word-processing systems, e-mails, CCTV records, telephone records for landline and mobile phones, internet logs, automated payroll systems, and records of automated door entry systems such as swipe cards.
5. Inform all staff involved of the timescale within which the data needs to be collated and instruct them not to delete any relevant data unless it would have been deleted in the ordinary course of events.
6. After collating data, consider whether to seek consent from any third parties which might be identifiable from the data being disclosed. Notify the employee if this is likely to lead to a delay in the provision of a response.
7. Consider whether any data is exempt from disclosure.
8. Provide a written response and consider including an explanation of the types of data provided and whether and for what reasons any data has been withheld.

The Role of the Information Commissioner's Office

The Information Commissioner is the United Kingdom's independent authority on data protection. The role of the Information Commissioner's Office (ICO) is to uphold information rights in the public interest and promote openness between public bodies and data privacy for individuals. Its role is also to oversee and enforce the Data Protection Act 1998. Specifically, the Act makes the Information Commissioner responsible for promoting good practice in handling personal data and giving advice and guidance on data protection. The Act also makes the Commissioner responsible for keeping a register of organisations that are required to notify the Commissioner about their information-processing activities. The Commissioner also helps to resolve disputes by deciding whether it is likely or not that an organisation has complied with the Act when processing personal data. Finally, the Commissioner can take action to enforce compliance with the Act, where appropriate, and bring prosecutions for offences committed under the Act.

Information Commissioner's Office Powers to Enforce

The ICO encourages individuals concerned about the use of their personal data to contact the relevant data controller in the first instance. If the data controller fails to respond appropriately (or at all) to complaints or requests, the data subject may then make a complaint to the ICO or, in certain circumstances, go directly to the courts to enforce his or her rights.

In particular, an individual has a right, where he or she "believes himself to be directly affected by the processing of personal data", to make a request to the ICO for an assessment on whether the processing complies with the DPA (section 42). On receiving such a request, the ICO is obliged to carry out the assessment (which may include serving an information notice on the data controller requiring it to provide information to assist the ICO in making the assessment), and to notify the person making the request whether an assessment has been made and of any view formed or action taken as a result.

Where it finds a breach of the DPA, the ICO may serve data controllers with:
- information notices, requiring data controllers to provide information about their processing operations (unless the information is self-incriminating or the subject of legal privilege);
- special information notices;
- enforcement notices, requiring data controllers to comply with the data protection principles.

Additionally, under certain circumstances, the ICO may (with a warrant from the court) exercise powers of entry, inspection and seizure of documents and equipment.

Inspection Powers and Powers to Impose Fines

It should be noted that from 6 April 2010, the ICO can issue civil penalties of up to £500,000 on data controllers. In order to exercise this right, the ICO must prove that there has been a serious violation of data protection principles.

They must further prove that the violation was likely to cause substantial damage or stress. Lastly, they must show that the violation was deliberate.

In 2013, Sony Computer Entertainment Europe Limited ('Sony') were served a fine of £250,000 from the ICO for breaching the seventh data protection principle, which provides that "appropriate technical and organisational measures shall be taken against unauthorised or unlawful processing of personal data and against accidental loss or destruction of, or damage to, personal data."

The facts of this case were that customers of Sony had to create an account to access the Sony PlayStation network platform. In April 2011, the network platform was hacked. Consequently, the personal information of millions of customers was hacked. Such information included their names, addresses, email addresses, dates of birth, account passwords and payment card details. The ICO investigated the matter and concluded that the attack took place due to a vulnerability within Sony's software. Consequently, they concluded that the attack could have been prevented if the software had been up to date and therefore Sony were in breach of the seventh data protection principle.

Actions for Damage or Distress

Individuals are entitled to compensation from data controllers for damage caused by any breach of the DPA (section 13(1)). This might arise, for example, if an employer discloses an employee's medical record to a third party, which results in the employee being refused credit. Compensation is also available, in certain cases, where the individual suffers distress as a result of the breach (section 13(2)). Compensation can only be awarded by the courts and not by the Commissioner. To date, very few claims for compensation have been made by individual data subjects.

REVIEW QUESTIONS

(See Suggested Solutions at the end of this textbook.)

Question 8.1

Thomas and his brother Patrick have decided to establish a restaurant business ... Thomas and Patrick seek your advice in relation to the obligations imposed upon them in the management of their employees' data.

Requirement: Explain to them the main rules on data processing under the Data Processing Act 1998.

(Source: Chartered Accountants Ireland, CAP 1, Autumn 2008, Extract: Q2(c))

Question 8.2

MS Printing Services, an expanding client of your firm, has asked your partner to permit you to go on secondment to their business for a year as their company accountant. Prior to starting your secondment, MS Printing Services make you aware that in your role as company accountant you will be responsible for dealing with all data protection queries that are lodged by employees.

Requirement: Write a memo to your client explaining any FOUR rules on data processing.

(Source: Chartered Accountants Ireland, CAP 1, Law for Accountants (NI), Autumn 2012, Extract: Q4(b))

Question 8.3

Lola, Freddie and Kate are the sole directors/shareholders of Cherry Cottage Limited ('Cherry'), a private company providing self-catering holidays on the island of Ireland. Recently, Lola has been disagreeing with Freddie and Kate as to the future direction of Cherry, and as a consequence, she has decided to resign as company director. Following Lola's resignation as director of Cherry, she incorporated a rival company, Indigo Holidays Limited ('Indigo'). Lola and Edward (Cherry's current sales manager) are the sole directors/shareholders of Indigo. Freddie and Kate have now discovered that prior to Lola's resignation she made a copy of Cherry's client list and has been soliciting contracts from Cherry's clients. One of Cherry's clients has contacted Freddie and Kate threatening to report them to the Information Commissioner for breach of the Data Protection Act – as his personal information is being used by Indigo for marketing purposes.

Requirement: Outline any THREE obligations imposed upon data controllers pursuant to the terms of the Data Protection Act 1998 and determine whether Cherry is in breach of the Data Protection Act 1998.

(Source: Chartered Accountants Ireland, CAP 1, Law for Accountants (NI), Summer 2013, Extract: Q3(b))

Question 8.4

Golfing Mania Ltd is a family-run golf shop business based in Newcastle. Golf Mania was established in 1985 by Mr O'Connor Senior. Mr O'Connor Senior tells you that one of his employees, a shop assistant, Joe, has been off on long-term sick leave. Joe has worked for the company since 1990. Joe has now submitted a Data Subject Access Request under the Data Protection Act for all of his personnel records, but Mr O'Connor Senior is unsure what to do with it and he asks your advice.

Requirement:
(a) State the EIGHT principles of the Data Protection Act.
(b) Outline the procedure to make a Data Subject Access Request.

(Source: Chartered Accountants Ireland, CAP 1, Law for Accountants (NI),
Summer 2015, Extract: Q4(c)(i) and (ii))

Chapter 9

THE LAW OF AGENCY

Introduction

An **agent** is a person who represents another person or company in a legal capacity such that they are able to bind their principal in a legal relationship provided they act within the scope of their agency. The **principal** is the proper party to sue or be sued rather than the agent. Agency agreements need not be in writing.

Categories of Agent

There are several types of agent, but all fall into one of three categories:
1. general agent
2. special agents
3. universal agents

A *general agent* has authority to perform any of the duties that are normally within the scope of the business entrusted to him, e.g. a solicitor.

The authority of a *special agent* is limited to the performance of a specific act, such as buying a particular car.

A *universal agent* is appointed by a 'power of attorney'. This type of agent has unlimited authority and would perform any acts that the principal could have performed.

Appointment of an Agent

An agent may be created by:
1. express agreement
2. implication
3. necessity
4. ratification.

By Express Appointment

An agent can be appointed either verbally or in writing, unless he is authorised to execute a deed. In this case, the appointment must be in writing.

By Implication

Agency by implication occurs when a contract can be implied from the conduct of the parties or the relationship between the parties even though no formal agreement exists between them. Hence, if a person, by his words or conduct, represents another as having authority to make contracts on his behalf, he would be bound by those contracts as if he had expressly authorised them. For example, in *Pickering v. Busk* (1812), a broker was employed by a merchant to buy hemp. After he had completed the purchase, the broker retained the hemp at his work at the request of the merchant. He then sold the goods. The purchaser was held to have obtained a good title to the goods because the broker was apparently an agent to sell and the merchant was stopped by his conduct from denying the agency.

By Necessity

An agency by necessity arises when a principal is bound to a contract made on his behalf without his authority. In order for this contract to be valid, three conditions must be satisfied:

1. The action by the agent must have been taken out of necessity. This is seen in the case of *Prager v. Blatspiel* (1924). In this case, the agent bought skins as agent for the principal but was unable to send them to the principal because of prevailing war conditions. Since the agent was also unable to communicate with the principal, he sold the skins before the end of the war. In this case, it was held that the agent was not an agent by necessity because he could have stored the skins until the end of the war. The court found that there was no emergency for the agent to sell the skins.
2. The second condition that must be satisfied, for an agency by necessity to have been formed, is that it must be impossible to get instructions from the principal. For example, in *Springer v. Great Western Railway* (1921), a consignment of fruit was found by the carrier to be going bad. The carrier sold the consignment locally instead of delivering it to its destination. The court held that the carrier was not an agent by necessity because he could have obtained new instructions from the owner of the fruit. The agent was therefore found liable in damages to the owner.
3. Finally, the third condition that must be satisfied for an agency by necessity to arise is that the agent must have acted in good faith. This is seen in the case of *Great Northern Railway v. Swaffield* (1874). In this case, a horse was sent by rail and, on its arrival at its destination, there was no one to collect it. The plaintiff incurred the expense of stabling the horse for the

night and it was held, by the court, that the plaintiff was an agent by necessity in this instance as he had implied authority to incur the expense in question.

By Ratification

An agency by ratification occurs if an agent makes a contract on behalf of the principal but, at the time of making the contract, the agent has no authority from the principal. The contract may be later ratified by the principal. For example, in *Kelner v. Baxter* (1866), the plaintiff sold wine to the defendant who purported to act as agent for a company which was about to be formed. When it was formed, the company attempted to ratify the contract made by the defendant. The court held that the company could not do so since it was not in existence when the contract was made. The defendant was therefore personally liable to pay for the wine.

In order for an agency by ratification to be valid, the following conditions must be met:
1. The agent must have named his principal and specifically informed the third party that they were contracting as agent at the time of the contract. This was seen in the case of *Keighly, Maxstead & Co v. Durant* (1901). In this case, the agent bought corn without disclosing that he was buying for the principal at a price higher than he had been authorised to do. The principal later attempted to ratify the contract but he failed to pay the agreed price. The defendant sued the plaintiff for the price promised by the agent. The court held that there was no contract as the agent had no authority to enter into the contract at that price.
2. The principal must, at the time the contract was made, have had contractual capacity to meet the contract and also have been in existence.
3. At the time of ratification, the principal either must have had full knowledge of the material facts or else must have the intention to ratify what ever may be the facts.

A void contract or a forgery cannot be ratified. In the case of *Brook v. Hook* (1871), a man forged his uncle's signature on a promissory note. When a third party came into possession of the note and discovered the forgery, he intended to bring proceedings against the forger. The uncle then attempted to ratify his nephew's act by signing the note, but later he refused to honour it. It was held that the ratification was ineffective and the promissory note was therefore void. The principal must ratify a contract within the time period fixed under the purported contract or, if no time period has been fixed, within a reasonable period of time.

The Authority of an Agent

There are three circumstances in which a party will be treated as being the principal's agent:
- where there is express authority;
- where there is **implied authority**; and
- where there is **apparent** (also called **ostensible**) **authority** or **agency by estoppel**.

Express Authority

Express authority is the most straightforward type of authority and means that the agent has been specifically asked to make the contract in question.

Implied Authority

Implied authority arises where the agent is asked to do something which by implication requires the contract to be made. An example might be where a driver is asked to take a car from London to Edinburgh, which would probably imply that the driver should buy petrol on the way, on behalf of the principal, so that in the contract for the petrol the driver would merely be the agent.

Apparent Authority

Apparent authority can cause more problems. It arises where the principal's past behaviour gives the other party to the contract reason to believe that the agent has authority to contract on the principal's behalf. For example, such a situation could arise where a firm employs an agent whose duties include buying stationery, and the agent usually orders the goods from a particular supplier and has the bill sent to the firm. The employee later leaves the company but the stationery supplier is not told. If the employee then collects an order as usual, the firm may be liable for the price even though the employee no longer has authority to buy for them.

Apparent authority cannot be created solely by the behaviour of the supposed agent. The fact that A claims to have authority to make a contract with B as the agent of C does not in itself make C liable on the contract as the principal. This would only be so if C had given B good reason to believe that A had such authority. If this is the case, C is liable, even though A is lying or mistaken.

Branch of Authority

Where an agent is covered by any of the three types of authority, the principal will be bound by any contract made that falls within that authority, as they are treated as having privity of contract. In *Waugh v. Clifford* (1982), a firm of solicitors was employed to pursue certain litigation. In such circumstances, solicitors generally have the implied authority to negotiate a compromise with the other party and so reach a settlement but, in this case, their client had specified that they were not to settle without reference to him. The other party to the litigation was unaware of this instruction, so assumed that the solicitors had the usual authority. The solicitors did in fact settle with the other side but their client claimed that he was not bound by this because they were acting outside their authority. Although the Court of Appeal recognised that the solicitors' implied authority had been terminated, it was held that they still had apparent authority and therefore their client was bound.

Where an agent makes a contract that lies outside the authority granted by the principal, or where the agent has no authority at all, the principal may nevertheless choose to ratify the contract, so long as the agent was purporting to act on the principal's behalf at the time the contract was made, and the principal had the capacity to make the contract at that time. Once a contract is ratified by the principal, it becomes binding on the principal.

In some cases, an agent may act for a principal without disclosing the principal's identity, or even the fact that there is a principal. Northern Irish law nevertheless holds that it is the principal with whom the contract is made, so that it is effectively possible to make a contract with someone without even knowing whether they exist.

While the principal remains undisclosed, the agent is personally liable on the contract; once the principal is disclosed, if a claim arises, the other party to the contract can choose whether to sue the principal or the agent.

There is one important limitation in the creation of an agency situation where the principal is undisclosed. If the contract is such that it was reasonable to infer that the agent could only have been contracting on their own behalf, there will be no agency, and the purported agent will in fact be liable on the contract. The most common example of this situation is where a service contracted for is one which relies on personal skill, such as painting a picture.

Agent's Duties to Principal

Once a contract is formed between an agent and a principal, a number of duties exist between the two parties. First, an agent must carry out his principal's lawful instructions. In the case of *Turpin v. Belton* (1843), an insurance broker, in return for a fee, agreed to effect insurance on the principal's ship. However, the agent failed to do this and the ship was lost. The broker was held liable to the principal.

An agent must also exercise reasonable care and skill in the performance of his duties for a principal. The degree of skill expected depends on the circumstances. However, the more experienced and skilled the professional person is, the more that is expected of them.

The agency must also act in good faith and for the benefit of his principal. He must be careful not to let his own interests conflict with his duty to his principal. For example, in *Armstrong v. Jackson* (1917), the plaintiff employed the defendant, a stockbroker, to buy shares for him. The defendant sold his own shares to the plaintiff. It was held by the court that the plaintiff could rescind the contract. The agent's interest as seller was to sell at the highest possible price whereas his duty as agent was to buy at the lowest possible price. This was clearly perceived to be a conflict of interest.

An agent must not abuse his position to make a secret profit or to secure a benefit for himself. In the case of *Lucifero v. Castel* (1887), an agent was appointed to purchase a yacht for his principal. However, he bought the yacht for himself and then sold it to his principal at a profit. The court held that the agent had to pay his profit to the principal.

An agent must not misuse confidential information regarding his principal's affairs. If a principal fears that an agent will destroy or dispose of confidential information, the principal may apply for an '*Anton Piller*' injunction authorising the principal's representative to enter the agent's premises to remove the confidential information. An *Anton Piller* injunction is an *ex parte* injunction, i.e. it is granted on the application of the principal without the agent being represented. It derives its name from the case *Anton Piller KG v. Manufacturing Processes* (1976), which was the first case in which such an injunction was granted.

Furthermore, an agent must not allow his own financial affairs to overlap with those of his principal.

Principal's Duties to Agent

The principal also owes duties to an agent. First, the principal must pay the agent the commission or remuneration that was agreed between the parties at the outset of the contract. If nothing has been agreed between the parties, the agent is entitled to what is customary in the particular business or to what is reasonable. A principal must indemnify an agent for losses and liabilities incurred by the agent in the course of the agency. In the case of *Adamson v. Jarvis* (1827), an auctioneer sold goods on behalf of his principal, being unaware that the principal had no right to sell. The auctioneer was held liable to the true owner. Similarly, in *Read v. Anderson* (1884), an agent was employed to bet on a horse. The horse lost and the agent paid the bet. It was held that he was entitled to an indemnity from the principal, since, if he had not paid, the agent would have been recorded as a defaulter.

Specialist Agents

Particular rules apply to particular types of agents such as auctioneers, estate agents, *del credere* agents and mercantile agent. (*Del credere* agents are agents who undertake to sell goods only to purchasers who are solvent.) For example, the Commercial Agent (Council Directive) Regulations (Norther Ireland) 1993 (1993 No. 483) apply to independent commercial agents who have continuing authority to negotiate the sale or purchase of goods. (They do not apply to agents who are employees, company directors or partners.) As a result of these Regulations, the agent and principal are each under a duty to the other to act dutifully and in good faith. Various other specific duties are also involved, such as the agent's authority to provide the principal with all necessary information available to the agent. The agent also has a general right to seek remuneration for work done.

Effects of Contracts Made by Agents

The effects of a contract entered into by an agent depend on the parties' intentions. If the intention of either party is not clear, the following factors are considered:

Whether or Not the Identity of the Principal is Disclosed

An agent generally incurs neither rights nor liabilities. Usually, an agent will disclose the identity of a principal to a third party and the agent will not be liable under contract to the third party. However, in the following exceptional cases, the agent may be personally liable:
1. if he signs his own name to a deed in which his principal is not named;
2. if he signs a negotiable instrument in his own name without adding words indicating that he is signing as agent;
3. if the custom of a particular trade makes him liable; or
4. if he agrees to be liable.

If the agent names the principal, the agent generally incurs neither rights nor liabilities and only the principal can sue and be sued.

Whether or Not the Existence of the Principal is Disclosed

If the agent does not disclose the existence of the principal when the agent enters into a contract on his own behalf, the doctrine of *undisclosed principal* applies.

The agent may sue and be sued on the contract and the undisclosed principal may also sue on the contract. For example, in the case of *Humble v. Hunter* (1842), an agent entered into a charter party and signed it as owner. It was held that the word "owner" was incompatible with an agency relationship. Evidence was not admissible to show that the owner was the principal. The principal could not therefore sue on the contract.

Whether or Not the Principal Exists

If the principal does not exist when an agent enters into a contract with a third party, the contract is enforceable against the agent only by the third party.

Termination of Agency

The agency may be terminated either by the acts of the parties, by operation of law or by completion of the agency agreement.

By Acts of the Parties

The parties may at any time agree to terminate the agency. Furthermore, a principal may revoke the agent's authority at any time.

By Operation of Law

An agency may be terminated by either the death or insanity of either the principal or the agent, on the bankruptcy of the principal, or if the subject matter or operation of the agency agreement is frustrated or becomes illegal.

By Completion of the Agency Agreement

An agency contract may also be terminated if the period fixed for the agreement comes to an end or the purpose for which the agreement was created was accomplished.

Reference

- G.H.L. Fridman, *The Law of Agency* (7th Edition, Butterworths, 1996).

REVIEW QUESTIONS

(See Suggested Solutions at the end of this textbook.)

Question 9.1

Edward is an executive director of Giselle Ltd ('Giselle'), an accessories manufacturing company, and is employed under a contract of service. Fairways Fabric has been a supplier to Giselle for the past five years. Two months ago Edward ordered a large quantity of fabric from Fairways Fabric and billed it to the company's account. However, there is no record of this order arriving at the company. Upon examination, the company discovers that this order was sent to a different delivery address, which is in fact Edward's home address. The company undertakes an investigation of this incident and discovers that Edward has been using the company account to order goods to establish a rival accessories manufacturing business from his home. Upon making this discovery, Giselle removes Edward as a director and is refusing to pay for the fabric supplied by Fairways Fabrics.

Requirement: Through an examination on the law of agency, assess whether Edward has the authority to bind Giselle to this contract and whether Giselle is legally obliged to pay Fairways Fabrics for the supply of the fabric.

(Source: Chartered Accountants Ireland, CAP 1, Summer 2010, Extract: Q3(a))

Question 9.2

Rose, Hyacinth and Petunia are the sole shareholders and directors of Daffodils and Dandelions Ltd, a company that specialises in providing floral displays for corporate clients. Rose has been delegated the position of managing director of the company by the board.

Daffodils and Dandelions Ltd has been trading successfully for the past eight years and, recently, the directors have been considering moving the business to larger premises. Last week they looked at a vacant store in Belfast's city-centre. They all agreed that the store was an ideal location, but both Hyacinth and Petunia considered the cost of the lease excessive and decided to keep looking for a more cost-effective solution.

Rose was very disappointed with Hyacinth and Petunia's decision, and after two weeks of viewing other premises, and having found nothing suitable, she signed a lease with the proprietors of the city-centre store on behalf of the company, without consulting with her co-directors.

When Hyacinth and Petunia discover that Rose has ignored their wishes and signed the lease, they are extremely annoyed. They are considering removing Rose as a company director and replacing her with Lilly. They also inform the city-centre store proprietor that they are challenging the validity of the lease on the basis that Rose did not have the authority to create this contract.

Requirement: Applying the law of agency, assess whether Rose had the capacity to sign the lease agreement and its validity.

> (Source: Chartered Accountants Ireland, CAP 1, Law for Accountants (NI),
> Summer 2011, Extract: Q4(b))

Question 9.3

MS Printing Services, an expanding client of your firm, has asked your partner to permit you to go on secondment to their business for a year as their company accountant. MS Printing Services has had an agency agreement with Harlow Publishers for the last four years. Prior to starting your secondment, the manager of MS Printing Services has contacted you and informed you that they wish to terminate their agency agreement with Harlow Publishers, and requests your advice on the various methods by which a contract of agency can be terminated.

Requirement: Write a memo to manager of MS Printing Services outlining any THREE methods by which a contract of agency can be terminated. Your answer should also advise him on the most appropriate method of termination in the circumstances.

> (Source: Chartered Accountants Ireland, CAP 1, Law for Accountants (NI),
> Autumn 2012, Extract: Q4(c))

Question 9.4

Porter was an executive director and de facto managing director of Cupcake and Coffee Ltd ('Cupcake'), a nationwide coffeehouse chain, since the company's incorporation in 2001. Last month at an extraordinary general meeting of the company, a resolution was passed removing Porter as a company director. The rationale for this decision is that the company discovered that Porter had lodged a number of cheques payable to Cupcake into his personal bank account. It was also noted that Porter had entered into a number of profitable leases with Cupcake, using a company that, on paper, was owned by his brother, to disguise his true identity.

Prior to his removal, Porter entered into a contract with the Aromatic Coffee Company ('Aromatic') to purchase a large consignment of Italian coffee beans on behalf of Cupcake for £3,000. These coffee beans were delivered to an address specified by Porter, but Cupcake has since discovered that this was the address of a restaurant owned by Porter's wife. Cupcake is refusing to pay Aromatic for the coffee beans supplied on foot of this contract, arguing that Porter had no authority to create this contract.

Requirement: Examine whether Cupcake and Coffee Ltd is legally obliged to pay the £3,000 due to the Aromatic Coffee Company; your answer should include a review of the law in relation to agency by estoppel (also known as ostensible or apparent authority).

(Source: Chartered Accountants Ireland, CAP 1, Law for Accountants (NI), Summer 2014, Extract: Q3(b))

CHAPTER 10

SOLE TRADERS AND PARTNERSHIPS

Introduction

This chapter examines the law relating to sole traders and partnerships. Operating a business as a sole trader offers, as we shall see, great flexibility as there is little legislation governing sole trader status. On the other hand, there are a number of legal requirements to be complied with in running a partnership. These requirements are set out in the Partnership Act 1890.

SOLE TRADERS

'**Sole trader**' is a term used to describe an individual who carries on a business or profession without partners. The term 'sole practitioner' is often used when describing a professional person (e.g. an accountant or solicitor). However, the term 'sole trader' is often used to describe a sole proprietor of a business.

Operating a business as a sole trader is very easy and offers great flexibility as there are very few formalities to be complied with. From a legal perspective, there are two main obligations that a sole trader must ensure compliance with:

1. A sole trader must register with HMRC. In doing so, the sole trader establishes that he or she is liable to pay their own tax. This also permits the sole trader to be issued with a VAT number.
2. A sole trader must ensure that they are careful when choosing a business name for their enterprise. The Company, Limited Liability Partnership and Business (Names and Trading Disclosures) Regulations 2015 (2015 No. 17) set out a number of restrictions that apply when choosing a business name. For example, no name should be used for a business if it would constitute an offence, is offensive, or if it includes a sensitive word or expression or signs or symbols which are not permitted under the 2015 Regulations. A full list of such words is included within the 2015 Regulations.

Advantages of Operating as a Sole Trader

The lack of statutory legal formalities to be complied with in operating a business as a sole trader provides a sole trader with a number of advantages. First, it ensures that the sole trader has a degree of flexibility in setting up the business: he or she is not subject to the registration or filing requirements which a company must comply with (these are examined further in **Chapter 11**). Secondly, the sole trader has an automatic say in the running of the business as he or she has no shareholders or partners to consult when making decisions. Thirdly, there are no formalities for ending the business of a sole trader; a sole trader may cease trading at any time.

Disadvantages of Operating as a Sole Trader

However, this degree of flexibility in operating as a sole trader also carries with it a number of disadvantages: a sole trader has unlimited personal liability, which means that he or she is personally liable for all the debts of the business. If the business of a sole trader fails, he or she is subject to the laws of bankruptcy.

Raising capital as a sole trader can also be difficult. A sole trader cannot issue shares and so he or she has to rely totally on their own funds, any borrowing which they get from banks as well as the profits generated by the business.

Sole trader businesses can also be difficult to sell. If a sole trader wishes to cease trading, they must sell each individual asset and this includes the client list, premises and goodwill.

PARTNERSHIPS

The law relating to partnerships is still governed by an Act of Parliament from the 19th Century: the Partnership Act 1890 (the 1890 Act).

Section 1 of the 1890 Act states that a **partnership** is "the relation which subsists between persons carrying on a business in common with a view of profit". This definition can be divided into six component requirements – every word and phrase in the definition is important.

Each of the component parts will now be considered separately:
- "relation"
- "which subsists between persons"
- "carrying on"
- "business"

- "in common"
- "with a view of profit"

"relation"

It is evident from section 1(1) of the 1890 Act that a partnership is a legal relationship between two or more parties and this relationship is based on contract. Each partner within a partnership has the authority to make agreements for and on behalf of his fellow partners.

"which subsists between persons"

The 1890 Act states that the partnership must subsist between "persons". This means that every person is entitled to form a partnership. However, there are a number of exceptions to this rule. Minors are young people under the age of 18 and therefore are persons for the purposes of the Partnership Act. However, it should be noted that a minor cannot be personally liable for debts of the partnership that are incurred when he or she is a minor. That said, a minor can be liable for debts incurred after he or she reaches the age of 21, unless the minor has repudiated the partnership contract before the debt was incurred.

Furthermore, persons of unsound mind can avoid a contract of partnership if they can prove that they either did not understand the nature of the contract or that the other partners were aware of this at the time. A person of unsound mind is fully liable for all the debts and liabilities of the partnership for as long as he remains a partner in the firm (partnership). However, if the other partners, at the time, knew that he did not understand the nature of the transactions involved, he or she is not liable for those debts and liabilities.

"carrying on"

In order for a partnership to exist, the third requirement of a partnership is that the parties to the relationship are 'carrying on' a business (the term 'business' is examined in the next section). This naturally implies that business has actually commenced. Hence, an agreement to enter into a partnership is not 'carrying on' business. In the case of *Macken v. Revenue Commissioners* (1962), an oral agreement to enter into a partnership was reached between a father and his two children in September 1953. This oral agreement dealt with matters such as the proportions in which profits, losses, assets and liabilities were to be shared. In addition, the trading name of the firm was also dealt with. The High Court held that the partnership did not come into existence until April 1954, as the parties only commenced carrying on business at that point, as opposed to September 1953 when the oral agreement was reached.

The English case of *Kahn v. Miah* (1998) reaffirmed this position. In this case, a chef, a manager and an investor all agreed to set up an Indian restaurant. The premises were purchased and a joint bank account was opened. All three individuals were described as partners for the purposes of the bank account. Before the business commenced, there was a disagreement amongst the three individuals. The Court of Appeal decided that there was no partnership in existence since there was nothing for the manager to manage nor was there any role for the chef. Only some preparatory work in setting up the business was already taking place.

"business"

The 1890 Act states that a business can include every trade, occupation or profession. Indeed, the Act itself states that a joint ownership of land or other property does not create a partnership in that property. For example, in the case of *French v. Styring* (1857), there was an agreement between two individuals who owned a race horse whereby they agreed to share the horse's winnings and expenses equally. This was held not to be a partnership for the purposes of the 1890 Act on the basis that the ownership of a horse was not a business.

"in common"

The next requirement, under the definition of partnership, is that all parties to the contract must be acting in common. This requirement "goes to the very heart of the question of whether a partnership exists and most cases of doubt about the existence of a partnership revolve around this issue".[1]

For example, the case of *Re Hall* (1864) involved a business which satisfied the other five conditions for the definition of the partnership. However, the requirement that the parties be carrying on business in common was not satisfied. This case involved an alleged partnership between Hall and Mallinson in a wholesale woollen business at 9 William Street, Dublin. It had been agreed that Mallinson was to manage the business for a year. At the end of this year, he could not decide whether he wanted to become a partner in the business. However, Mallinson never exercised this right. Hall subsequently went into bankruptcy and the creditors sought to have monies, owed by Hall to Mallinson, incorporated with their debts. Their basis for doing so was that Mallinson had been in partnership with Hall. The court ruled, however, that no partnership existed. They gave the following grounds for doing so:
1. Mallinson was simply managing Hall's business for a year.
2. Mallinson did not, in his own name, deal with any customer of the business as he would have done if he had been a partner.

---

[1] Michael Twomey, *Partnership Law* (Butterworths, 2000), p.40.

3. The name of the firm had not been changed.
4. He did not sign any bills, letters or other formal documents on behalf of the enterprise.

"with a view of profit"

The final requirement for the existence of a partnership is that the relationship between the parties is one in which there is a view to profit. The case of *MacCarthaigh v. Daly* (1985) considered the situation whereby a partnership does not have a view to profit. The case dealt with a solicitor in Cork who had entered into a limited partnership with six other limited partners and a general partner. Agreements for the leasing of equipment to the Metropole Hotel produced a substantial loss for the partnership. The solicitor, Mr Daly, wanted to use his share of the losses of the partnership to reduce his individual income tax as a solicitor. In this case, Mr Justice O'Hanlon stated that:

> "I would have some reservations, however, in coming to a conclusion that the arrangement entered into between them should properly be regarded as a partnership at all since The Partnership Act, 1890, which was largely declaratory of the common law, commenced by defining a partnership in section 1 of the Act as 'the relation which subsists between persons carrying on a business in common with a view of profit ...' it was fairly conceded in the course of the hearing before the appeal commissioner that an important reason behind this claim was to achieve a tax benefit for the participants."

From this judgment, it was clear that the judge did not believe that the arrangement constituted a partnership because of the absence of the "view of profit". Indeed, this case serves as a warning to persons who are involved in business ventures which use partnerships for their tax benefits.[2]

Clauses in a Partnership Agreement

The usual terms found within a partnership agreement are listed below. These terms form the basis of the contract between partners. It should be noted that this list is not exhaustive and partners can include other terms within the agreement. The usual terms are:

- the names of the partners;
- the name and location of the firm;
- the date of formation of the partnership and its duration;
- the nature of the business;

---

[2] Twomey (2000), *op. cit.*, p.39.

- the firm's capital and sharing of profits and losses;
- the assets of the partnership;
- the powers and duties of partners;
- any arbitration procedures;
- requirements for the administration and expulsion of partners, the effective death, retirement or bankruptcy of a partner; and
- requirements for ending of the partnership.

Not every partner will want every aspect of the relationship covered in the partnership agreement. Indeed, each partnership agreement should be considered on its own merits. For this reason, legal advice should always be sought before preparing a partnership agreement. Furthermore, partners should review the adequacy of their partnership agreement periodically to ensure it meets their needs.

Fiduciary Duties of Partners

The Duty of Good Faith

The courts have recognised a number of instances whereby partners owe a fiduciary duty of good faith to each other. The first case to recognise that partners owe such a duty was *Meagher v. Meagher* (1961). In this case, three brothers, who were partners in a firm, had no written partnership agreement. The firm bought and renovated houses for resale. When one of the brothers died, there arose the issue of whether his share of the partnership assets should be taken as one-third of the value of the houses owned by the firm as at the date of death, or should be taken as the value of those houses when they were realised by the firm, which was a number of years later. This involved a substantial difference in the value of the deceased partner's share, depending on the date on which the value was taken. The deceased's personal representatives claimed that they should be entitled to the increase in the value of his share in the partnership's assets. The court held in their favour and said that the deceased partner's estate was entitled to share the increase in value of the partnership assets. The court said that:

> "the claim made in this case is that the representatives of the deceased have no right to take the benefit of a general rise in prices occurring between the dissolution and sale, but that the whole advantage of such rise should go to the surviving partner. This appears to be contrary to the principles of equity and the provisions of the partnership act. Surviving partners stand in a fiduciary relationship to the representatives of the deceased partner ... a person in a fiduciary position cannot make a profit out of his trusteeship by appropriating to himself the rise in value of assets which he holds as trustee."

The 1890 Act also lays down four statutory elements of partners' fiduciary duties. These are as to:

1. render true accounts and full information to each other (section 28);
2. account for private profits (section 29);
3. not to compete (section 30); and
4. share post-dissolution profits (section 42).

Duty to Render True Accounts

All partners must render true accounts and full information to each other regarding the partnership. This is seen in the case of *Ferguson v. Mackay* (1985). In this case, a solicitor was retiring from his firm and he was negotiating the terms of his retirement package with the other partners in the firm. Before the terms were finalised, the remaining partners failed to disclose that three conveyancing instructions had been received by the firm. These transactions were of a substantial amount. The retiring partner, after he retired from the firm, later discovered these substantial transactions. He brought a case against them alleging that the partners had failed in their duty of disclosure. The court held that his partners had breached their fiduciary duty to give him full information and granted damages to the retiring partner for this breach.

The Duty to Account for Private Profits

Section 29 of the Partnership Act 1890 stipulates that all partners must account for all monies used by the business. This principle was established in the case of *Bentley v. Craven* (1853). In this case, the defendant was a partner in a sugar refinery business. He bought sugar independently and on his own account and later sold it to the partnership at a profit. He did not declare his interest to the other partners in the business. The court held, in this case, that the partnership was entitled to recover the profit from the defendant.

The Duty not to Compete

This duty, laid down by section 30 of the 1890 Act, provides that every partner who competes with a partnership business without the consent of the other partners will be held liable to account to the partnership any profits which arise in the course of that business. It was noted in the case of *Lough v. Lynam* (1854) that one of the primary reasons a partner is discouraged from competing with a firm is because he will be able to use this position as a partner to commit a fraud on his co-partners, "by siphoning off business opportunities from the firm for his own benefit".[3]

In *Lough v. Lynam* the court said that:

> "if two persons make such an agreement as the petitioner and respondent did here, the fact of either of them entering into other contracts of the same kind, without the knowledge and consent of his partner, gives the direct motive for the commission of fraud on his first partner and one can easily see how a fraud might be accomplished."

In this case, the parties had agreed to enter a partnership. This partnership dealt with the supply of meat to British troops based in Ireland. However, Lynam entered into a similar partnership with a third person and was able to share in the profits of similar contracts. Lough found out about these contracts and brought an action to the court seeking an amount of the profits of these contracts that Lynam had with third parties. The court held that such conduct by Lynam was a breach of his duty of good faith to his partner and ordered that an amount of those contracts be taken.

The Duty to Share Post-dissolution Profits

The final fiduciary duty, under the 1890 Act, is the duty of partners to share in post-dissolution profits. This was considered in the case of *Williams v. Harris* (1980). In this case, a partnership agreement stated that the share of a retiring partner shall "as and from the time of his death or ceasing to be a partner ... be purchased and belong to the remaining partners". In this case, the retiring partners did not receive the purchase price for their share until two years after the retirement. This delay was brought about by having the valuation fixed by arbitration. As a result, they sought interest for the two-year period at the rate of 5% under section 42 of the 1890 Act. The court rejected the claim for interest under section 42. Their basis for doing so was that the terms of the partnership agreement constituted an agreement that was contrary to the terms of section 42(1); thus, they were prevented from applying for the interest.

Relationship of Partners to Third Parties

Under section 5 of the 1890 Act, "Every partner is an agent of the firm and his other partners for the purpose of the business of the partnership".

---

[3] Twomey (2000), *op. cit.*, p.360.

As such, partnership law is therefore an extension of the law of agency in that the act of every partner will subsequently bind other partners. This was established in the case of *Mercantile Credit v. Garrett* (1962). In this case, both A & B were partners in a firm that let garages and repaired cars. As part of the partnership agreement, it was stated that the buying and selling of cars was expressly excluded. Without B's knowledge, A sold a car to a finance company for £700, paying the proceeds into the partnership account. It was held that B was liable to repay the £700 to the finance company. The prohibition on buying and selling in the partnership agreement did not entitle B (or the firm) to avoid liability since A's conduct was of the kind normally undertaken by persons trading as a garage, i.e. A apparently had authority to sell cars.

Relationship of Partners to Each Other

At all times, the rights and duties of partners to each other depend on the terms of the partnership agreement made between the partners. In the absence of an agreement between the partners, section 24 of the 1890 Act provides that all partners are entitled to share equally in the profits made by the business and must contribute equally to the losses. Section 24 further states that the firm must indemnify every partner in respect of payments made and liabilities incurred by the partner, both in the ordinary and proper conduct of the business of the firm, and about anything necessarily done for the preservation of the business or property of the firm.

Retirement of Partners

Most partnership agreements should provide for the retirement of the partners. In the absence of a retirement clause, retirement will automatically dissolve a partnership under the terms of section 26(1) of the Partnership Act 1890.

Retirement and Insolvency

If a partner wishes to retire, under the terms of his partnership agreement his right to do so is not affected if the firm from which he wishes to retire is insolvent. That said, he is still bound by the obligations of the firm that were incurred while he was a partner.

It should also be noted that, if a retiring partner holds himself out to an outsider as a member of the firm from which he has retired, and has not given notice that he has retired, the retiring partner still binds the firm. Under section 26(2) a partner must give notice of this intention to retire, in writing, to all other partners.

In addition, notice should also be given to all customers of the firm in order to prevent continuing liability of the firm.

Dissolution of a Partnership

The Partnership Act 1890 stipulates three ways by which a partnership can be brought to an end. These are by:
- agreement of the parties (section 32);
- operation of law (section 33 and 34); and
- order of a court (section 35).

By Agreement of the Parties

Under section 32 of the 1890 Act, a partnership is permitted to be dissolved at any time by the consent of all of the parties.

By Operation of Law

A partnership is dissolved, by operation of law, in one of the following ways:
- upon the expiry of a fixed term;
- on the completion of a single venture or undertaking;
- by one party giving notice to another;
- by the death or bankruptcy of a partner;
- by the agreement of all partners; or
- by the happening of an event that would make the partnership agreement become frustrated.

By the Order of a Court

A court can dissolve a partnership:
- if a partner becomes permanently incapacitated;
- if a partner becomes a patient under the Mental Health (Northern Ireland) Order 1986 (1986 No. 595 (N.I. 4)), as amended;
- if a partner has been found guilty of any conduct which is potentially prejudicial to the business of the firm;
- if a partner wilfully and persistently breaches the partnership agreement;
- if the partnership is carried on at a loss; or
- if it is just and equitable in all the circumstances for a court to dissolve the partnership.

Expulsion of a Partner

Under the 1890 Act, there is no right to expel a partner. This fact is expressly provided for by section 25 of the Act, which states, "No majority of the partners can expel any partner unless a power to do so has been conferred by express agreement between the partners". If an express right is given to expel a partner, this right is interpreted very strictly.

Next Steps After Partnership Dissolution

Once a partnership is dissolved, it ceases to be a going concern. As a result, the next steps in the partnership are to wind up the business, and this involves collecting and valuing the assets, paying off debts and distributing any surplus to the former partners.

Profits Made after Dissolution

Any profits generated by partnership dealings dealt with after the firm dissolves must be kept. This is because the winding-up period can sometimes be protracted. Generally, profits that were made after dissolution are shared between partners in the normal, profit-sharing ratio.

However, if dissolution occurs as a result of the death of a partner or if a partner ceases to be a member of the firm, the courts have the discretion to pay the outgoing partner his share of post-dissolution profits.

If, however, continuing partners have an option to acquire a former partner's share of the assets, then, so long as the terms of the option are complied with, a former partner's right to a share of the profits is negated.

Distribution of Assets and Adjustment of Accounts

Upon dissolution, partnership accounts must be prepared and they should incorporate any final adjustments required to reflect the rights and obligations of individual partners. If there is a partnership agreement, it will need to be considered closely at this stage. However, subject to any such agreement, the 1890 Act provides as follows:

1. Losses should be dealt with first. These should be met as far as possible out of profits, then out of capital and finally, if necessary, by partners individually in the proportion in which they were previously entitled to share profits.
2. The firm's assets, including sums contributed by the partners to make up losses or deficiencies of capital, will be applied as follows:
   - the debts and liabilities of the firm to outsiders will be paid;
   - each partner will be paid proportionally what is due from the firm to him in respect of the capital he put in; and
   - anything that is left will be divided among the partners according to their profit-sharing ratio.

Limited Partnerships

Limited partnerships were established by the Limited Partnership Act 1907. They allow for the protection of some partners within a firm (partnership).

Under such a partnership, the firm must have at least one general partner and one limited partner. The general partner is liable for all the debts of the partnership, as though he were an ordinary partner under the Partnership Act 1890, whereas a limited partner is liable only to the extent of his capital contribution.

A limited partnership must register the following information with the Registrar of Companies:
- the firm's name;
- the place and nature of business; and
- the full name of each partner.

Limited Liability Partnerships

Limited liability partnerships were established in 2000 as a new legal business form. They share many of the features of normal partnerships but provide more organisational flexibility than normal partnerships. They also share with limited companies the benefits of reduced liability. They are especially attractive to professional partnerships such as accountancy practices, law firms and graphic design partnerships.

A limited liability partnership offers reduced personal responsibility for business debts. Unlike a normal partnership, the limited liability partnership itself is responsible for any debts that it runs up, not the individual partners.

For tax purposes, a limited liability partnership is treated as a business run by the partners rather than as a limited company. Partners in a limited liability partnership are liable to pay National Insurance Contributions (NICs) on their share of the partnership profits in the same way as self-employed people. The limited liability partnership itself will not be liable to corporation tax.

References

- Michael Twomey, *Partnership Law* (Butterworths, 2000)
- Roderick I'Anson Banks, *Lindley and Banks on Partnership* (18th Edition, Sweet & Maxwell, 2002)

REVIEW QUESTIONS

(See Suggested Solutions at the end of this textbook.)

Question 10.1

Florence and Theodore have been operating a jewellery design business, Little Gems, in partnership for the past 15 years. Both Florence and Theodore are active partners in the business, and Florence's father, Ralph, is their silent partner. When the partnership was established, Ralph invested 75% of the venture capital, while the balance was invested equally by Florence and Theodore.

Stella is head of sales of Little Gems. Last month Stella approached the company's financial controller, Myles, to inform him that she was attending a sales conference in Milan and that she was intending to take numerous samples of Little Gems jewellery to the conference in order to solicit orders. She told Myles that the consignment of sample jewellery she was taking with her was valued at £500,000 and she asked him to arrange the appropriate insurance for this trip.

While in Milan there was a robbery of the conference centre's secure vault and the case with the Little Gems jewellery samples was one of the many items stolen. Little Gems has filed a claim for the stolen jewellery from their insurance company, but have discovered that an error by the financial controller means that the amount insured was actually £50,000 and not £500,000. As a consequence of this loss, Little Gems is now operating at a loss and Florence and Theodore have decided to dissolve the partnership.

Requirement: List any FOUR methods that can be used to affect the dissolution of a partnership.

(Source: Chartered Accountants Ireland, CAP 1, Summer 2010, Extract: Q4(a)(i))

Question 10.2

Thomas and his brother Patrick have decided to establish a restaurant business. They have decided to establish themselves in the form of a partnership and have asked you to draft a partnership agreement.

Requirement:

(a) Outline the nature and purpose of a deed of partnership and discuss the prudent terms that should be included in such an agreement.
(b) Outline the statutory duties owed between the partners, pursuant to the Partnership Act 1890.

(c) Explain to Thomas and Patrick FIVE other methods, provided for in the Partnership Act 1890, by which the partnership may be brought to an end in the event that their partnership agreement does not provide one.

(Source: Chartered Accountants Ireland, CAP 1, Autumn 2008,
Extract: Q2(a)(b) and (d))

Question 10.3

Bertie has been a client of your firm for 20 years. He has always operated as a sole trader. Bertie attends your offices with his son and daughter to discuss a future business plan for the business. One option that they are considering is to make the business a partnership.

Requirement:
(a) Advise Bertie on the main benefits and disadvantages of continuing to trade as a sole trader.
(b) In the event that they decide to operate as a partnership, outline four terms that should usually be included in a partnership agreement.
(c) Bertie also indicates to you that he has heard of the term 'limited liability partnership' but he is not sure what it is. Explain what a 'limited liability partnership' is and the steps necessary to incorporate a limited liability partnership.
(d) Bertie also seeks your advice on how a partnership can be terminated. Identify the three main provisions within the Partnership Act 1890 governing the termination of a partnership.

(Source: Chartered Accountants Ireland, CAP 1, Law for Accountants (NI),
Autumn 2011, Extract: Q2)

Question 10.4

James Holmes Snr died in October 2013. Under the terms of his will, he bequeathed his printing business, 'Printshop', equally to his two sons, Robert and Matthew Holmes. James Holmes Snr set up Printshop in 1960 and, up until the date of his death, he had always operated the business as a sole trader. Robert and Matthew have now taken legal advice and have decided to continue running Printshop but they wish to establish it as a partnership.

Requirement: Outline the purpose of a 'deed of partnership' and list FOUR items normally contained within a partnership agreement.

(Source: Chartered Accountants Ireland, CAP 1, Law for Accountants (NI),
Autumn 2014, Extract: Q3(a))

Question 10.5

Maddox Consultancy Solutions ('Maddox') was established as a business partnership in 2000. Maddox has two managing partners, Tom and Martin, as well as eight ordinary partners. Tom has just discovered that Martin has been misappropriating partnership funds for his own personal purposes and, following a meeting with the other partners, a decision has been taken to dissolve Maddox. They have contacted you for advice regarding this matter.

Requirement: Draft a **memo** to the partners of Maddox outlining the following:
(a) the various methods by which a partnership can be dissolved and comment on the most appropriate method of dissolution in this situation;
(b) the priority of debts payable on the dissolution of a partnership.

(Source: Chartered Accountants Ireland, CAP 1, Law for Accountants (NI),
Autumn 2015, Extract: Q3(a)(i) and (ii))

Chapter 11

COMPANY FORMATION

Introduction to Company Law

The Companies Act 2006 (hereinafter CA 2006) received Royal Assent on 8 November 2006. The largest Act ever passed by Parliament, the CA 2006 was the first major overhaul of company legislation in 20 years and its purpose was to consolidate all existing company legislation into one complete Act.

Prior to the CA 2006, companies in Northern Ireland were governed by the Companies (Northern Ireland) Order 1986 (1986 No. 1032 (N.I. 6)). Major changes to Northern Ireland law were made by the 2006 Act. These included, to name but a few:

- the codification of directors' duties (see **Chapter 13**);
- permitting a private company to reduce its own capital without court approval; and
- allowing a private company to provide financial assistance for the purchase of its own shares (see **Chapter 15**).

Having been introduced in four key stages since 2006, with the last stage in October 2009, all provisions of the 2006 Act are now fully operative in Northern Ireland. This chapter and the next four chapters will now consider the law relating to companies as it is stated in the Companies Act 2006.

Advantages of Company Status

In the previous chapter, we looked at the law relating to sole traders and partnerships. Trading as a company or a sole trader or partnership presents a number of advantages, depending on the choice made. Where the respective balance lies will depend on the particular individuals involved.[1]

A Company is a Legal Entity

The key advantage, in trading as a company, is that a company is a legal entity with perpetual succession. It can own property, make contracts and sue or be sued. In essence, it has a separate legal entity from the members of the company.

---

[1] Gerard McCormick, "Company Law" in Brice Dickson and Deborah McBride (eds.), *Digest of Northern Ireland Law* (SLS Legal Publications (NI), 1995–1996).

The company can also be liable for torts committed by the company as a separate legal person. It will also be vicariously liable for torts committed by any of its directors or employees acting other than in the scope of their employment. In all these matters, it must be emphasised that the shareholders themselves are not liable. The **veil of incorporation** protects them (this concept is discussed later in this chapter). Liability is clearly that of the company alone.

A partnership, on the other hand, is not a separate legal person. Both sole traders and partners own all the assets and the property of the firm, and are liable in any contracts made.

The Formal Registration Procedure

A company is created under the registration procedure set down in the Companies Act 2006. Disclosure provisions imposed by company legislation are rigorous. As a result, it is relatively easy to find out all kinds of information about a company. This often leads to other businesses having greater confidence in dealing with a company rather than a partnership where the affairs of the business are much more private.

In contrast, a partnership is created through the express or implied agreement of the partners. A special form of agreement is required and, in the absence of an agreement, the Partnership Act 1890 applies to the partnership.

Liability of Members

A member of a company cannot bind the company by his or her acts. The general rule is that members of a company are not liable for the debts and obligations incurred on the company's behalf. A company is a separate legal person that acts through its agents, usually its directors, and is responsible for their acts. The extent of the company's liability will depend, first, on whether or not it has the capacity to enter into the contract in question and, secondly, on whether the directors, who act as agents of the company, have sufficient authority to enter into the contract on the company's behalf. The capacity of the company will depend on whether or not the acts in question are expressly or impliedly permitted by the company's objects clause. All other acts are **ultra vires** (a concept which we will discuss later in the chapter) of the company and void. In a partnership, however, a partner is an agent of the firm and the firm consequently will be bound by the acts of the partner.

Limited Liability

Clearly the most important advantage of the corporate form is the privilege of limited liability which it bestows on its members. It is important to remember, however, that, at least in its initial stages, most of the external finance of the business will come from a bank or other institutional lenders who will usually insist on the promoters providing personal guarantees. This has the effect of removing the protection of the limited liability in relation to the liabilities in question. Nevertheless, the members will continue to be protected from claims from trade creditors and the Revenue if things go wrong and the company becomes insolvent. In contrast, in a partnership, the partners will be fully liable for all the liabilities of the business. The same applies to the sole trader.

Furthermore, the liability of shareholders to contribute to the assets of a company, in order to help meet its liabilities, is severely limited. They will be required to contribute only when the company is being wound up and is unable to pay its debts and the expenses of the winding up from its own assets. In that case, each shareholder is liable to contribute a sufficient amount to enable the company to meet its obligations but only to the extent of the amount that remains unpaid on its shares. Usually, no further liability is imposed even when the assets of the company are wholly inadequate to meet the large claims of creditors.

Raising Finance

The ability of the company to give a floating charge (as discussed in **Chapter 14**) as security for its debts gives the company a distinct advantage over the sole trader or partnership as this type of security device is not available to either of them. A further advantage lies in the company's potential to 'go public' and raise much-needed equity capital in times of expansion by offering its shares for sale to the public.

Expansion

The two advantages of limited liability and easier means of raising finance make the company an ideal framework for a business expansion. Furthermore, the separation of ownership from management makes it easier for the company to raise external investment capital. This is particularly so for public companies which are able to offer their shares to the public through one of the established markets. Moreover, while a company must have at least two members, there is no upper limit on the membership of a company. By contrast, a partnership cannot consist of more than 20 persons, while a sole trader can consist of only one person.

Perpetual Succession

The concept of a separate corporate personality allows the company to continue to exist until steps are taken to wind it up. The company's ownership of property and liability for contracts are not affected, therefore, by the debt, bankruptcy or retirement of any of its members. In contrast, a sole trader or a partnership has no legal existence apart from that of the members. Changes in membership may bring about termination of the business and, with that, the complicated issues as to the distribution of the assets and the responsibility for obligations under existing contracts.

Disadvantages of Company Status

There are many legal controls and formalities that must be complied with in a limited company. This routine administration can be both burdensome and costly. Furthermore, the owner's disclosure provisions force much of the company's internal business into the public domain. In contrast, the sole trader and partnership enjoy the twin privileges of informality and privacy.

In making the choice, limited liability and the greater ability to raise finance will weigh heavily on the side of the company and, unless privacy is of fundamental importance, it is unlikely that the less burdensome administration and disclosure requirements involved in a partnership will be seen as sufficient advantages to make the partnership far more attractive. The deciding factor may well be the set-up in relation to taxation. Whether or not the company forum will bestow a tax advantage on a new business depends, to a large extent, on the size of the business and the financial position of the owners. All these matters should be considered very carefully before making the choice.

Types of Companies

There are a number of different types of companies. The categories can be listed as follows:
- chartered companies
- statutory companies
- companies limited and unlimited
- companies limited by shares and companies limited by guarantee
- public companies and private companies.

Each of these shall now be considered in detail.

Chartered Companies

A chartered company is formed by grant of a charter by the Crown operating under either prerogative or special statutory powers. The procedure for the formation of a chartered company is for promoters (see the Promoters section later in this chapter) to petition the Privy Council for the grant of a charter. Such a petition is addressed to the Lord President.

Charters are used to incorporate learned societies, professional bodies such as Chartered Accountants Ireland, the BBC, public schools, colleges and/or universities, e.g. Queen's University Belfast.

Statutory Companies

Statutory companies are formed by a special Act of Parliament. This method of company formation was formerly used for public utilities, such as electricity, gas, water and railways, because these undertakings need special powers, for example to complete the compulsory purchase of land.

Unlimited Liability Company

In such a company, the members are not liable to creditors of the company directly. In the event, however, that the company becomes insolvent, members' liability is to the company as a separate person. The main reason for having an unlimited company is that the company is exempt from the many disclosure requirements to the Registrar of Companies (these requirements will be discussed later in the chapter under Formation and Registration of a Company).

Limited Companies

The vast majority of companies are limited companies. In a limited company, the liability of the members, if the company is wound up, is limited to a fixed amount agreed with the company when they became members. If a company is applying for registration of a limited company, they must make a choice between liability limited by shares or liability limited by guarantee. The vast majority of limited companies are limited by shares.

Company Limited by Shares The issuing of shares in a company occurs if a company raises capital in exchange for part ownership of the company. The liability of the members is limited to the amount, if any, unpaid on the shares respectively held by the shareholders.

Company Limited by Guarantee In this type of company, membership is by subscription. Members sign an undertaking to contribute a specified sum towards payment of the company's debts in the event that the company becomes insolvent. This type of company is unsuitable for business activity and is usually formed for non-commercial purposes.

The advantages of both of the above types of company are that there is limited liability for investors, there is a separate legal personality for the company and there is a clear demarcation of ownership and control.

Private Companies and Public Companies

The vast majority of companies in Northern Ireland are private companies limited by shares. Private limited company shares cannot be offered to the public and the shares of a private company cannot be listed. In contrast, a public company's shares can be offered to the public and they can be listed. A public company must end with the words 'Public Limited Company' or the abbreviation "plc". Obviously, the principal reason for forming a public limited company lies in the benefit of obtaining capital from the public due to the fact that shares are listed. The minimum nominal value requirement for members to contribute in a public company is £50,000. By contrast, there is no minimum nominal value for authorised share capital in a private company.

Changing from a Public Company to a Private Company

A public company can re-register as a private limited company under CA 2006 (sections 97–101). This occurs, for example, if a public company is bought over or becomes a subsidiary of another company. In order for this change to take place, the members of the company must adopt a special resolution requiring a 75% majority.

In some instances, minority shareholders may not approve the change from public to private status, particularly if their shares lose their status. As a result of this, there is a provision within CA 2006 for the dissenting minority to object to re-registration as a private company. Holders of 5% or more of the nominal value of the public company's issued share capital can apply to court for the cancellation of the special resolution to request re-registration. However, they can do so only on the provision that they did not consent to or vote in favour of the resolution. Such an application has to be made within 28 days of the passing of the resolution. A court has the power to either cancel or confirm the resolution, once it hears the section 98 application. In addition, the court may make any order in such terms and conditions as it thinks fit: it has the power to adjourn proceedings to enable an arrangement to be made that is satisfactory for the minority shareholders' interest in the company, or it can give any other directions or Orders that it deems appropriate. The court can also provide for the purchase by the company of the shares of any members.

Changing from a Private Company Limited by Shares to a Public Company

A private company limited by shares can also re-register as a public company under sections 90–96 of CA 2006. This is the most common form of re-registration. The main reason for adopting such an action is when a private company wants to obtain more capital for growth by inviting the public to subscribe for its shares.

As is the case with a public company re-registering as a private company, a private company must also gain a special resolution with a 75% majority in order to re-register as a public company. Furthermore, on the day that the special resolution is adopted, a company must have allotted shares with a nominal value equal at least to the authorised minimum (£50,000). A private company re-registered as a public company does not need a trading certificate. An application to re-register a private company as a public company must be accompanied by a balance sheet of the company. This balance sheet must be for a date no more than seven months before the date of the application and it must also be accompanied by an auditor's unqualified report on the balance sheet.

Formation and Registration of a Company

Application for registration of a company is made by filing certain documents at the Companies House. The documents are as follows:
1. Memorandum of Association;
2. Articles of Association;
3. application for registration;
4. statement of capital and initial shareholdings;
5. statement of the company's proposed officers;
6. statement of compliance;
7. register of people with significant control (PSC) from June 2016; and
8. fee.

Memorandum of Association

The Memorandum of Association of a company that was registered before 1 October 2009 is a very different document from a Memorandum of Association of a company registered after 1 October 2009. A pre-2006 Memorandum was an extremely detailed document; it has been simplified considerably by the 2006 Act and came into force in October 2009. A Memorandum of Association under the 2006 Act simply has to state that the subscribers to the company (there need only be one) wish to form a company under CA 2006. The intention is that the Memorandum should be instantly recognisable as such and that it should not contain extra information. If it does, the application for registration is likely to be rejected by the Registrar of Companies.

Furthermore, the Memorandum must state that the subscribers agree to become members of the company upon its formation and, in the case of a company having shared capital, agree to take at least one share each. A Memorandum must be in a prescribed form.

The Companies (Registration) Regulations 2008 (2008 No. 3014) prescribe the form of Memorandum for a company having a share capital and for a company not having a share capital (these are set out in Schedules 1 and 2 of the Regulations). The Memorandum must state the name of each subscriber and their individual authentication.

The Memorandum is essentially a 'snapshot' of part of the company's constitution at the point of registration and will have no continuing relevance. It cannot be amended or updated during the life of the company.

Articles of Association

The Articles of Association set out the internal regulations of a company. The Articles will be the main constitutional document of a company. In effect, the Articles are a set of rules about how the company is managed and what rights will attach to members' shares; the Articles are a statutory contract between all the members and the company. If the terms are broken, members can sue to enforce their rights under the Articles.

The Articles contain rules about: how directors' meetings and shareholders' meetings are to be called and held, how many votes a director has at a board meeting, how many votes a shareholder has at a shareholders' meeting, what rights to income attach to shares and any other rights conferred on the shareholder.

From 1 October 2009, a company has the choice of adopting New Model Articles which are provided for by CA 2006. These model Articles are widely used by small companies as they are tried and tested and cut down the costs on drafting separate Articles of Association. Prior to 1 October 2009, companies adopting standard Articles of Association used the provisions of what were called Table A Articles. The New Model Articles, under CA 2006, are simpler and more user friendly for private companies.

Alternatively, a company can choose to adopt a new set of Articles which exclude the New Model Articles in their entirety. In practice, many large companies will have their own Articles as they may need to include complex provisions.

The third option open to a company is to adopt the New Model Articles as a basis for their Articles but make them subject to certain amendments. For a private company, this offers the benefit of a tried and tested document which can be tailored to suit their client's needs.

Changing the Articles The Articles may be altered by special resolution (section 21 CA 2006), subject to certain rules in charities legislation on the ability to change the constitution.

Section 25 CA 2006 retains the principle that a member is not bound by any alterations made to the Articles subsequent to him becoming a member, if the alteration has the effect of increasing his liability to the company or requires him to take more shares. A member may give his written consent to the alteration and is then bound by it.

The company must send a copy of any amended Articles to the Registrar of Companies within 15 days after the amendment takes effect (section 26 CA 2006). Failure to comply amounts to an offence committed by the company and every defaulting officer, punishable by a fine.

Section 27 gives the Registrar a means of ensuring that companies comply with the obligation set out in section 26 without having to resort to criminal proceedings. The Registrar may give notice to the company requiring it to rectify the breach within 28 days. Where the company complies with the notice, the company will avoid prosecution for its initial failure to comply. If the company does not comply, it will be liable to a civil penalty of £200, recoverable by the Registrar as a debt, in addition to any criminal penalty that may be imposed (e.g. under section 26).

Application for Registration

An application for registration, under CA 2006, must state:
- the proposed company name;
- where the company's registered office is situated;
- whether the liability of the members of the company is to be limited and, if so, whether it is to be limited by shares or by guarantee; and
- whether the company is to be a private or a public company.

Once these details are registered, these are the details that will appear on its certificate of incorporation, which is subsequently issued to a company.

Statement of Capital and Initial Shareholdings

Any application to register a company must contain a statement of capital and initial shareholdings. However, if a company is not to have a share capital, the statement is not required. A statement of capital and initial shareholdings must state what shares the company will issue when it is registered and who will own them.

Statement of the Company's Proposed Officers

Under section 9 CA 2006, any application for registration of a company should also contain a statement of the company's proposed officers. This statement should contain the particulars of each proposed director of the company together with their residential addresses. The particulars of the secretary must also be stated. Finally, a consent by each person named to act in the relevant capacity must also be included. When registration is complete, all the persons named in the statement take up office as from the date of incorporation.

Statement of Compliance

Any application for registration of a company must also be accompanied by a statement of compliance. This document states that the requirements of CA 2006 have been complied with.

Register of People with Significant Control (PSC Register)

From 1 June 2016, companies are now required to maintain a PSC register on incorporation and it should be updated when the company files a confirmation statement (see the related section in **Chapter 12** for further details).

Fee

Finally, the fee for the non-electronic registration of a company is £40, whereas the fee for electronic registration is £12.

Registration and Certificate of Incorporation

If the Registrar is satisfied that the requirements for registration and the purpose for which the incorporators are associated is lawful, the registrar will register the document submitted and will issue a **Certificate of Incorporation**. This states that the company is incorporated and gives its name and registered number, the date of incorporation, states whether it is limited and, if so, how, whether it is public or private, and in which jurisdiction its registered office is situated. Section 15(4) CA 2006 declares that the Certificate is conclusive evidence that the requirements of the Act, as to registration, have been complied with and that the company is duly registered under the Act. The effect of incorporation is that:

> "the subscribers to the Memorandum, together with such other persons as may from time to time become members of the company, are a body corporate by the name stated in the Certificate of Incorporation".

Further, the subscribers to the Memorandum become the holders of the shares specified in the statement of capital and the directors and secretary (if any) named in the statement of proposed officers are appointed to their offices.

In the case of a public company, there is a further legal obstacle to its beginning trading. It needs to obtain a further certificate from the Registrar (a Certificate of Trading) certifying that the amount of its allotted share capital is not less than the required minimum. Without it, the public company must not do business or exercise any borrowing powers unless it is re-registered as a private company. The Certificate of Trading is conclusive evidence that the company is entitled to do business and exercise any borrowing powers.

Lawful Purpose of Formation

It is a requirement of the Companies Act 2006 that a company should not be formed for an unlawful purpose. Companies House is permitted to refuse the registration of a company which it perceives is being formed for an unlawful purpose. Before CA 2006 came into force, Companies House had a better opportunity to establish whether the purpose for which a company was being formed was unlawful or not. This was because every company was required to state an object clause in the old-style Memorandum of Association. However, under CA 2006, a statement of objects must now be included in the Articles of Association but the statement is completely optional.

If Companies House refuses to register a company, it should be noted that its decision can be subject to judicial review. This was seen in the case of *R. v. Registrar of Joint Stock Companies, ex Parte More* (1931). In this case, the Registrar of Companies refused to register a company because it stated that its main object was to sell lottery tickets in Great Britain that emanated from what was then the Irish Free State. The promoters of the company sought a judicial review of the decision. The Court of Appeal held that selling such tickets in England would have been an offence under statutes then in force, although the Registrar was right to refuse to register the company as it was not formed for "a lawful purpose".

Company Names

When the name of a company is being chosen, a number of factors have to be taken into consideration. First, a limited company must indicate whether it is a public or private company. Furthermore, it should be noted that the Secretary of State has the power to prescribe what characters can be used in company names. Permitted characters include the Latin alphabet, Arabic numerals, punctuation marks and some signs and symbols. In addition, a company cannot be registered by a name that would be a criminal offence. Similarly, there are provisions that prevent companies being registered with similar names. This is because the goodwill and reputation attached to an existing business's name can be damaged by a new company using the same or a similar name. This is known as the tort of passing off and can be restrained by an injunction. For example, in the case of *Hendriks v. Montagu* (1881), the Universal Life Assurance Society obtained an injunction to prevent Montagu and his associates registering a company with the name Universe Life Assurance Association Limited.

Restricted Words and Expressions

Two sets of Regulations took effect on 31 January 2015 which have brought about further restrictions to business names and trading disclosures. These Regulations are:

- The Company, Limited Liability Partnership and Business Names (Sensitive Words and Expressions) Regulations 2014 (2014 No. 3140) (the '2014 Regulations'); and
- The Company, Limited Liability Partnership and Business (Names and Trading Disclosures) Regulations 2015 (2015 No. 17) (the '2015 Regulations').

In short, under the 2014 Regulations, 26 words will no longer be considered sensitive. These include:

- Authority
- Data protection
- European
- Group
- Holding
- International
- Register
- United Kingdom.

The 2015 Regulations extend the list of permitted characters that can be used for a company name.

Promoters

When someone has an idea for a business organisation or venture, he or she will usually go about engaging the support of others to help invest in the venture. This individual is often given the title of the 'promoter' of a company. However, the term 'promoter' has never been given a legal definition, despite being a term used frequently both in decisions of the courts and statutes, and even the Companies Act 2006 failed to define the term. Who constitutes a promoter, therefore, in any particular case, is a question of fact. Cockburn C.J., in *Twycross v. Grant* (1877), called a promoter "one who undertakes to form a company with reference to a given project, and to set it going, and who takes the necessary steps to accomplish that purpose". Moreover, Bowen J. in *Whaley Bridge Calico Printing Co. v. Green* (1880), said:

> "The term promoter is a term not of law, but of business, usually summing up in a single word a number of business operations familiar to the commercial world by which a company is generally brought into existence."

Hence, a promoter can be said to be any person involved in the planning, incorporation or initial running of a company, other than persons involved in a purely professional capacity. Accordingly, accountants, solicitors, etc. employed in their professional capacity to establish a company will not be considered to be promoters. The typical steps that a promoter would take include taking the procedural measures necessary to form a company, inviting other persons to become directors and seeking out investors for a company.

Duties of Promoters

A promoter stands in a fiduciary relationship with the company that he is promoting. On that basis, a promoter is not entitled to make a profit from establishing the company unless he has made full disclosure of that profit to the company and the company consents to the retention of the profit.

The main difficulty, however, lies in deciding how to effect the duty of disclosure – the company, when being promoted, is still an artificial entity. The first case on the subject, *Erlanger v. New Sombrero Phosphate Co.* (1878), suggested that it was the promoter's duty to ensure that the company had an independent board of directors and to make full disclosure to it. In this case, Lord Cairns said that the promoters of a company:

> "... stand ... undoubtedly in a fiduciary position. They have in their hands the creation and moulding of the company; they have the power of defining how, and when, and in what shape, and under what supervision, it shall start into existence and begin to act as a trading corporation ... I do not say that the owner of property may not promote and form a joint stock company and then sell his property to it, but I do say that if he does, he must take care that he sells it to the company through the medium of a Board of Directors who can and do exercise an independent and intelligent judgment on the transaction".

This view was, however, considered too strict and the boards of private companies, for example, are unlikely to be entirely independent of the promoter of the company. That said, nor can a promoter escape liability with partial disclosure to just a few people. This was emphasised in the case of *Gluckstein v. Barns* (1900). In this case, the promoters formed a syndicate for the purpose of buying and reselling an exhibition centre in London. They bought the property for £140,000 and then agreed to sell it to a company for £180,000. They disclosed the profit of £40,000 to the public, who were invited to subscribe for shares in the company, but did not disclose an additional profit of £20,000, which they were making on the sale of debentures they had purchased from the company that originally owned the property. It was held that there was only a partial and not a full disclosure and, accordingly, the contract could be set aside.

Pre-incorporation Contracts

It should be noted that, if a person attempts to make a contract on behalf of a company before the formation of the company, the contract is not binding on the company. This is so even if the company received the benefit of the contract. The person who purports to act on behalf of the company is personally liable on the contract unless there is some provision to the contrary. In addition, a company is unable to sue a third party on the agreement and the company cannot ratify the agreement even after its incorporation.

This is illustrated in the case of *Monogram Ltd v. Lane* (1981), which concerned the proposal to form a company, FM Limited, to run a pop group. Lane made a contract with Monogram Limited "for and on behalf of FM Limited". However, FM Limited never actually incorporated. It was therefore held that Lane was personally liable for money advanced to FM Limited by Monogram Limited. The Court of Appeal held that the fact that Lane had signed for and on behalf of FM Limited made no difference to his personal liability. They ruled that the pre-incorporation contract must expressly provide for his or her exclusion in these circumstances. To give effect to the words "subject to any agreement to the contrary", the words used would need to amount to an express exclusion of liability.

Promoters can, therefore, avoid liability for pre-incorporation contracts in a number of ways:
- by avoiding entering the contract until the company has been incorporated;
- by entering into an agreement 'subject to contract' with the effect that there is no binding agreement until the company itself enters into one; and
- where the promoters become the first directors of the company, they can ensure that the company does in fact enter into the pre-arranged contract.

Corporate Personality and the '*Salomon Veil*'

As mentioned above, once a company is formed, it has a separate legal personality, which means it can sue and be sued in its own right and also enter into contracts. It is also the subject of legal rights.

The famous case of *Salomon v. Salomon & Co.* (1897) illustrates this point. Salomon carried on business as a leather merchant and boot manufacturer. In 1892, he formed a limited company to take over the business. The Memorandum of Association was signed by Salomon, his wife, his daughter and four of his sons. Each subscribed for one share. The company paid £39,000 to Salomon for the business and the mode of payment was to give Salomon £10,000 in debentures, secured by a floating charge on the company's assets, £20,000 in shares of £1 each and the balance in cash. Less than one year later, the company ran into difficulties and a liquidator was appointed. If Salomon's debenture was valid, he was, as a secured creditor, entitled to be paid before the unsecured trade creditors. The assets were sufficient to pay off the debentures, but the true creditors would receive nothing. The unsecured creditors claimed all the remaining assets on the ground that the company was a mere alias or agent for Salomon. It was held by the court that the company was a separate existing person. The debentures were perfectly valid and Salomon was entitled to the remaining assets and payment of the secured debentures held by him.

This point was also illustrated in the case of *Macaura v. Northern Assurance Co. Ltd* (1925). Macaura was the owner of a timber estate in County Tyrone and he formed an estate company and sold the timber to it for £42,000. The purchase money was paid by the issue to Macaura and his nominees for £42,000 fully paid in shares of £1 each. No other shares were issued. He also financed the company and was an unsecured creditor for £19,000. Macaura effected an insurance policy on the timber, in his own name and not in that of the company or as agent for the company, and on 23 February 1922 most of the timber was destroyed by fire. Macaura claimed under his policies but he was held not to have an insurable interest. He could only be insured either as a creditor or as a shareholder of the company, as neither a simple creditor nor a shareholder has an insurable interest in a particular asset which the company holds, since the company is an independent entity.

A similar situation arose in *Lee (Catherine) v. Lee's Air Farming Ltd* (1954). Mrs Catherine Lee's husband formed the respondent company, which carried on the business of crop spraying from the air. In March 1956, Mr Lee was killed while piloting an aircraft during the course of top-soil dressing. Mrs Lee claimed compensation from the company, as the employer of her husband, under the New Zealand Workers Compensation Act 1922.

Since Mr Lee owned 2,999 of the company's 3,000 £1 shares, and since he was governing director, the question arose, for the court, as to whether the relationship of employer and employee could exist between the company and him. One of his first acts, as governing director of the company, had been to appoint himself the only pilot of the company at a salary arranged for himself. It was held that Mrs Lee was entitled to compensation because her husband was employed by the company in the sense required by the Act of 1922 and the decision in *Salomon v. Salomon & Co.* was applied.

Lifting the 'Salomon Veil'

The "veil of incorporation" is a metaphorical term given to separate a company from its members. The veil of incorporation gives members of the company protection in that they are not generally liable for the debts of that company. Hence, the corporate personality is the veil and it acts as a screen between the company and the members.

That said, there are a number of situations where the law is prepared to lift the veil of incorporation to go behind the corporate personality to the individual members. Such scenarios are referred to as examples of 'lifting the corporate veil' that is disregarding a company's separate legal personality and fixing its members with the legal consequences of the Companies Acts, including where "special circumstances exist indicating that [the corporate veil] is a mere façade concealing the true facts" (*Woolfson v. Strathclyde Regional Council* (1978) *per* Lord Keith of Kinkel). This can be done either by statute or by the judiciary. Each of these situations is considered below.

Lifting the Veil by Statute The corporate veil can be lifted by statute. In *Dimbleby & Sons Ltd v. National Union of Journalists* (1984), Lord Diplock said:

> "The corporate veil in the case of companies incorporated under the Companies Act is drawn by statute and it can be pierced by some other statute if such other statute so provides; but, in view of its raison d'etre and its consistent recognition by the Courts in *Salomon v. Salomon & Co Limited* (1897), one would expect that any parliamentary intention to pierce the corporate veil would be expressed in clear and unequivocal language. I do not wholly exclude the possibility that even in the absence of express words stating that in specified circumstances one company, although separately incorporated, is to be treated as sharing the same legal personality of another, a purposive construction of the statute may nevertheless lead inexorably to the conclusion that such must have been the intention of Parliament."

This is seen in the Inheritance Tax Act 1984, which states that, for the purposes of relief from inheritance tax for agricultural property, occupation of such property by a company controlled by an individual can count as occupation by the individual.

Furthermore, Article 178 of the Insolvency (Northern Ireland) Order 1989 states that the corporate veil may be lifted in a case of wrongful trading and also in a case of fraudulent trading. If, in the course of winding up, it appears that the business has carried on with intent to defraud creditors, the persons responsible may be made personally liable to make such contributions to the company's assets as the court thinks proper. The Order further states that a director may be personally liable for the company's assets. Before making the Order, the court will have to be satisfied that the director knew or ought to have concluded that there was no reasonable prospect of avoiding insolvent liquidation and that he failed to take every step to minimise the creditors' loss.

The Veil Lifted by the Judiciary   The corporate veil can also be lifted by the judiciary. In this category, the courts have discretion as to whether to lift the veil or not. Case law has established a number of situations whereby the courts have used their discretion to lift the corporate veil:

- *If the Company is a Sham*   For example, if the company is being used to enable a person evade his legal obligations. In the case of *Gilford Motor Co. v. Horn* (1933), an employee promised that, after the termination of his employment, he would not solicit his former employer's customers. Soon after the termination of his employment, he formed a company which sent out circulars to the customers of his former employer. The court lifted the veil of incorporation, granting an injunction which prevented both the former employee and his company from distributing the circulars even though the company was not a party to the covenant. The Court of Appeal stated that "the company was 'a mere cloak or sham' ... a mere device for enabling [H] to continue to commit breaches of [the covenant]".

- In the case of *Jones v. Littman* (1962), Littman contracted to sell his house to Jones. When he changed his mind, he formed a company and conveyed the house to it and then argued that the house was no longer his property to sell. It was held by the courts that the company was a device or sham formed solely to avoid the sale. The defendant was ordered to perform the contract.

- *Evasion of Liability including Tax Liabilities*   The veil of incorporation can also be lifted where directors themselves ignore the separate legal personality of two companies and transfer assets from one to the other in disregard of their duties in order to avoid an existing liability. In *Re H. and Others* (1996), the court was asked to rule that various companies within a group, together with the minority shareholders, should be treated as one entity in order to restrain assets prior to trial. The order was granted. The court thought that there was evidence that the companies had been used for the fraudulent evasion of excise duty.

- Likewise, a court may lift the veil of incorporation where it is being used to conceal the nationality of the company. In *Unit Construction Co. Ltd v. Bullock* (1960), three companies were wholly owned by a UK company but were registered in Kenya. Although the companies' constitutions required board meetings to be held in Kenya, all three were in fact managed entirely by the holding company. It was held that the companies were resident in the UK and therefore liable to UK tax. The Kenyan connection was a sham, the question being not whether they ought to have been managed, but where they were managed.

- *In the Time of War* A company is not permitted to trade with the enemy in a time of war. However, courts may lift the corporate veil if it is suspected that a company is controlled by the enemy. In the case of *Re FG Films Ltd* (1953), an English company was formed by an American company to make a film which would obtain certain marketing and other advantages by being called a British film. Staff and finance were in America and there were neither premises nor employees in England; the film itself was produced in India. It was held that the British company was the American company's agent and so the company did not qualify as being British. Effectively, the corporate entity of the British company was swept away and it was exposed as a sham company.

- *Quasi Partnership* Sometimes the courts will look at the reality behind a small company which functions on the basis of mutual trust and confidence between the members, recognising that, in fact, it is more akin to a partnership. Courts are willing in such cases to treat the said relationship between the directors as being that of partners, and rule that it would be unfair to allow the company to continue with only some of its original members. This is illustrated by the case of *Ebrahimi v. Westbourne Galleries Ltd* (1973). In this case, the majority shareholders in a company had the authority to dismiss Mr Ebrahimi from his position as a full-time working director of the company. The dismissal deprived Mr Ebrahimi of an income because the company profits were distributed as directors' fees and not as share dividends. However, the company had been formed on the basis that Mr Ebrahimi would be a full-time working director. The House of Lords found that the exercise of the legal right to dismiss Mr Ebrahimi breached the mutual understanding on which the company was formed and so was unjust and inequitable. The House of Lords affirmed that the company should be wound up on this ground.

- *Lifting the Veil in Group Situations* The courts have shown a reluctance to lift the veil on a group of companies where one company holds shares and controls another. In *Adam v. Cape Industries plc* (1991), the Court of Appeal refused to lift the veil of incorporation, holding a UK company liable for the acts of its subsidiaries abroad, even though it could be shown that the UK parent company had deliberately distanced itself from its subsidiaries in light of ongoing litigation. The court stated that the fact that one company controls the action of another does not make it 'at one' with that other – the Solomon principles must be upheld. In their judgment in *Adam v. Cape Industries plc* (1990), the Court of Appeal laid out three reasons for identifying companies as one and lifting the veil of incorporation. These can be summarised as follows: first, the subsidiary is acting as an agent for the holding company; secondly, the group is to be treated as a single economical entity because of statutory provision and, finally, the corporate structure is being used as a sham to conceal the truth.

In *Ben Hashem v. Al Shayif* (2008), Munby J. reviewed the authorities on the corporate veil, summarising the principles as follows:

1. Ownership and control of a company are not of themselves sufficient to justify piercing the veil. Control may be a necessary but it is not a sufficient condition.
2. The court cannot pierce the corporate veil, even where there is no unconnected third party involved, merely because it is thought to be necessary in the interests of justice.
3. The corporate veil can be pierced only if there is some "impropriety".
4. The court cannot, on the other hand, pierce the corporate veil merely because the company is involved in some impropriety. The impropriety must be linked to the use of the company structure to avoid or conceal liability.
5. It follows from all this that if the court is to pierce the veil it is necessary to show both control of the company by the wrongdoer(s) and impropriety, that is (mis)use of the company by them as a device or façade to conceal their wrongdoing. In this connection, the motive of the wrongdoer(s) may be highly relevant.
6. Finally, and flowing from all this, a company can be a façade even though it was not originally incorporated with any deceptive intent. The question is whether it is being used as a façade at the time of the relevant transaction(s). And the court will pierce the veil only so far as is necessary to provide a remedy for the particular wrong that those controlling the company have done. In other words, the fact that the court pierces the veil for one purpose does not mean that it will necessarily be pierced for all purposes.

In *VTB Capital plc v. Nutritek International Corp and Others* (2012), the Court of Appeal endorsed the restatement of principles set out in *Hashem v. Shayif*, although clarifying Munby J.'s final principle as to the requirement of necessity: "a piercing of the veil will not be available only if there is no other remedy available against the wrongdoers for the wrong they have committed". Further, expanding Munby J.'s fourth principle, the court confirmed that it is not sufficient for veil-piercing purposes merely to show that the company is involved in wrongdoing: "the relevant wrongdoing must be in the nature of an independent wrong that involves the fraudulent or dishonest misuse of the corporate personality of the company for the purpose of concealing the true facts".

The Doctrine of *Ultra Vires*

Until 30 September 2009, every company had to state its objects in the old Memorandum of Association style and every company was restricted to pursuing its stated objects. The effect of this was that, if a company's objects were restricted by its Articles, a company could not go beyond these powers. If a company did exercise powers outside of its objects, the company was said to be acting '*ultra vires*', or beyond the power of the company, and the acts were therefore void. This old position was established in the case of *Ashbury Carriage Co v. Riche* (1875) and has been referred to as the *Ashbury* rule. It could not be ratified by the shareholders of the company even if they were unanimously in favour of so doing.

This *ultra vires* doctrine was the cause of great hardship and injustice to innocent third parties dealing with the company. Accordingly, in an effort to protect third parties dealing with a company, an attempt to reform the *ultra vires* doctrine was made by section 9 of the European Communities Act 1972. This later became Article 45 of the Companies Northern Ireland Order 1986 and it has now been repealed by the Companies Act 2006. The present position with regard to *ultra vires* contracts is as follows:

- From 1 October 2009, the objects clause of any existing company became a provision of its Articles, which can be deleted by special resolution. Companies are now permitted to have an objects clause that simply states that the company aims to carry on business as a general commercial company. This has greatly cut down the likelihood of transactions being found to be *ultra vires*. Furthermore, a person dealing with a company is not bound to inquire as to any limitations on the powers of the directors to bind the company or to authorise others to do so (section 40(2)(b) of CA 2006).

- A director who enters into a transaction outside of the company's restricted objects must replace the money expended on the transaction unless the members ratify the transaction. In *Samuel Sherman plc* (1991), a director was disqualified from acting as a director for five years when he invested money in loss-making activities outside the restricted objects of the company.

Injunction to Stop Ultra Vires *Acts*

It should be noted that members can apply to court for an injunction restraining directors from entering into an *ultra vires* contract. Members can also apply to the court for compensation by the directors of the company if a third party seeks to enforce an *ultra vires* contract.

In the case of *Simpson v. Westminster Palace Hotel Co.* (1860), a company had been incorporated to build and operate an extremely large hotel. The directors decided that they would lease part of the hotel to the civil service for the first three years, in an effort to ensure income. However, a member of the company applied for an injunction to prevent this happening, stating that this was outside the objects of the company. The House of Lords denied the injunction and said that the proposed lease did not take the company outside the business of running a hotel.

References

- Gerard McCormick, "Company Law" in Brice Dickson and Deborah McBride (eds.), *Digest of Northern Ireland Law* (SLS Legal Publications (NI) 1995–1996).
- Derek French, Stephen Mayson and Christopher Ryan, *Mayson, French and Ryan on Company Law* (26th Edition, Oxford University Press, 2009–2010).
- Paul L. Davies, *Gower and Davies' Principles of Modern Company Law* (8th Edition, Thomson, Sweet & Maxwell, 2008).
- Gary Bagnell, Denis Boyd, Norma Davison, Eithne Harkness, Sheena McCormick, David Moore and Richard Steele, *Legal Aspects of Business Start-Up* (SLS Legal Publications (NI) 1992).

REVIEW QUESTIONS

(See Suggested Solutions at the end of this textbook.)

Question 11.1

Edward is an executive director of Giselle Ltd ("Giselle"), an accessories manufacturing company, and is employed under a contract of service. Fairways Fabric has been a supplier to Giselle for the past five years. Two months ago Edward ordered a large quantity of fabric from Fairways Fabric and billed it to the company's account. However, there is no record of this order arriving at the company. Upon examination, the company discovers that this order was sent to a different delivery address, which is in fact Edward's home address. The company undertakes an investigation of this incident and discovers that Edward has been using the company account to order goods to establish a rival accessories manufacturing business from his home. Upon making this discovery Giselle removes Edward as a director and is refusing to pay for the fabric supplied by Fairways Fabrics.

Giselle has now decided to alter its Articles of Association to state that any contract created by a company officer in excess of £10,000 must be sanctioned by a meeting of the Board of Directors.

Requirement: Outline the procedure necessary to effect this proposed alteration.

(Source: Chartered Accountants Ireland, CAP 1, Summer 2010, Extract: Q3(d))

Question 11.2

You have been approached by your manager who has indicated that he will be taking you along to a presentation which he will be giving to an audit client. The presentation is entitled "The Challenges Facing Directors in the 21st Century". In order to assist him in preparing for this presentation, your manager has asked you to draft a memo for him.

As part of his presentation, your manager has also indicated that he intends to discuss 'The Veil of Incorporation' and how it can be lifted by the courts.

Requirement: Outline in your memo the various circumstances when 'The Veil of Incorporation' can be lifted by the courts.

(Source: Chartered Accountants Ireland, CAP 1, Summer 2009, Extract: Q1(b))

Question 11.3

An engineering firm contacts your office for advice. They have operated their business in the form of a partnership for the last 10 years, and are considering converting it into a public limited company.

Requirement:

(a) Advise them on the main advantage and main disadvantage of operating as a limited company as opposed to a partnership.
(b) Outline the steps necessary to establish and trade as a public limited company.

> (Source: Chartered Accountants Ireland, CAP 1, Autumn 2008,
> Extract: Q1(a) and (b))

Question 11.4

You have been approached by a potential client, Mr Sharp, who has arranged an appointment with you to discuss a range of issues in relation to the setting up of a private limited company. In advance of the meeting, he has emailed you to let you know the issues he would like to discuss. You have promised the senior partner in your firm that you will draft a memo to him informing him of the issues that Mr Sharp wishes to discuss at the meeting. In memo format, provide your senior partner with the following information.

Requirement

(a) Advise your client on the role of a 'promoter' in the process of company formation.
(b) Under the company's registration process, advise your client of any of the FIVE main documents which should be filed at Companies House.

> (Source: Chartered Accountants Ireland, CAP 1, Law for Accountants (NI),
> Autumn 2011, Extract: Q3(a) and (c))

Question 11.5

Amelia has recently been made redundant and is considering using some of her redundancy payment to establish a company as a party planner. She has been discussing her plans with a number of her friends and colleagues, and has recently been contacted by a former work colleague to plan a party to celebrate her 40th wedding anniversary. Amelia is keen to take on this contract but is concerned that she will be exposing herself to liability if she creates a contract prior to the incorporation of her company, as she considers herself to be a promoter of the yet-to-be incorporated company.

Requirement:

(a) Explain the role of a promoter.

(b) Define a pre-incorporation contract and explain whether the company or the promoter is liable in respect of a pre-incorporation contract.

(c) State any ONE method by which a promoter can avoid liability for a pre-incorporation contract.

(Source: Chartered Accountants Ireland, CAP 1, Law for Accountants (NI), Summer 2012, Extract: Q3(a)(i)–(iii))

Question 11.6

Purity plc ('Purity'), a public limited company, is a pharmaceutical company. The directors of the company are of the opinion that the company should be re-registered as a private limited company and are seeking to put a proposal before the shareholders at an extraordinary general meeting to effect this alteration.

Requirement:

(a) Identify any TWO differences between the characteristics of a public limited company and a private limited company.

(b) State the type of resolution required by the company to effect this alteration in business form.

(c) Outline the procedure that a minority shareholder should follow in order to object to the privatisation.

(Source: Chartered Accountants Ireland, CAP 1, Law for Accountants (NI), Summer 2012, Extract: Q4(a)(i)–(iii))

Question 11.7

The Joe Glass Partnership operates a successful recycling business based in Belfast. The partnership has recently become a client of your firm. You have been brought along by the firm's senior partner to a meeting with Joe Glass. Joe explains to you that, every year, he prepares a business plan for the partnership. One of his goals for the next financial year is to expand the business into a public limited company, but he is unsure of the advantages and disadvantages in changing his corporate form.

Requirement: Outline any THREE advantages and any THREE disadvantages of operating as a company as opposed to a partnership.

(Source: Chartered Accountants Ireland, CAP 1, Law for Accountants (NI), Autumn 2012, Extract: Q1(a))

Question 11.8

MS Printing Services, an expanding client of your firm, has decided to change its status from that of partnership to that of a private limited company. The client asked your partner to permit you to go on secondment to their business for a year as their company accountant. Prior to starting your secondment, you are tasked with ensuring that the company has a proper Memorandum of Association and Articles of Association.

Requirement:
(a) Advise MS Printing Services as to the nature of a Memorandum of Association and Articles of Association, commenting (briefly) on the content of each.
(b) Explain how the Articles of Association can be altered.

(Source: Chartered Accountants Ireland, CAP 1, Law for Accountants (NI), Autumn 2012, Extract: Q4(a)(i) and (ii))

Question 11.9

Peacock Books Limited ('Peacock') is a private limited company, owned and managed by James and John, the sole directors and shareholders of the company. Peacock has been experiencing a downturn in its business in recent years.

In April 2013, HMRC made an application to the High Court for the compulsory liquidation of Peacock on the grounds that it cannot pay its debts. The Court granted this application and Robert Barry was appointed as the insolvency practitioner to manage the liquidation.

Following a review, Robert Barry, the insolvency practitioner, has become suspicious of a number of transactions involving the transfer of stock between Peacock and Bastian. These transactions occurred in the six months prior to Peacock going into liquidation and were substantially less than market value. Following a Companies House search, Robert Barry has discovered that Bastian is a wholly-owned subsidiary of Peacock, and Robert Barry is considering asking the Court to lift 'the veil of incorporation' in order that the assets of Bastian be used to repay the liabilities of Peacock.

Requirement: Discuss any THREE circumstances in which 'the veil of incorporation' can be lifted at the absolute discretion of the Court, and determine the potential success or otherwise of Robert Barry's legal action against Bastian.

(Source: Chartered Accountants Ireland, CAP 1, Law for Accountants (NI), Summer 2013, Extract: Q2(b))

Question 11.10

(a) Jane Matthews has just won a sum of £10 million in the weekly lottery. Jane wants to invest this money and set up a business baking and selling cakes. She is now taking advice from your firm on setting up the business as a company. Jane is unsure of the different types of company that can be set up.

Requirement: Explain to Jane any FOUR different types of company that can be set up.

(b) Jane wants to call her business 'Jane's Little Cupcake Café Limited'. However, further down the street from where Jane proposes to set up her business is another café called 'John's Little Cupcake Café'. John has threatened to bring an injunction against Jane if she calls her business 'Jane's Little Cupcake Café Limited'.

Requirement:
(i) Explain the factors that should be taken into account when choosing a company name.
(ii) Comment whether John will be successful in his action for an injunction.

(c) You explain to Jane that every business must have a set of Articles of Association with an objects clause defining the powers of the company. Jane tells you that she wants the business to only bake and sell cakes and asks you to draft an objects clause accordingly. However, within Jane's 10-year business plan, she states that she would like the company to expand into selling clothing, household items and other handmade craft items. You explain to Jane that if she wants to expand the business and do so, she will have to amend the objects clause; otherwise her actions will be *ultra vires*.

Requirement:
(i) Explain the concept of '*ultra vires*'.
(ii) Discuss the validity, or otherwise, of any *ultra vires* actions carried out by the company.

(Source: Chartered Accountants Ireland, CAP 1, Law for Accountants (NI), Autumn 2014, Extract: Q1(a)–(c))

Question 11.11

Maddox Consultancy Solutions ('Maddox') was established as a business partnership in 2000. Maddox has two managing partners, Tom and Martin, as well as eight ordinary partners. Tom has just discovered that Martin has been misappropriating partnership funds for his own personal purposes and, following a meeting with the other partners, a decision has been taken to dissolve Maddox.

Following the partnership's dissolution, Tom and the eight ordinary partners of Maddox have decided to establish a company, as they have been advised that a company has a separate legal personality. However, they are unsure as to what this means and whether they should establish a public or private limited company.

Requirement:
(a) Explain the meaning of the term 'separate legal personality' AND comment on any TWO consequences of a company having a separate legal personality.
(b) In tabular format, outline any THREE differences between public and private limited companies.

(Source: Chartered Accountants Ireland, CAP 1, Law for Accountants (NI), Autumn 2015, Extract: Q3(b) and (c))

CHAPTER 12

COMPANY MANAGEMENT

Introduction

In this chapter, we will examine how a company is managed. Under the Companies Act 2006 (CA 2006), companies are required to keep a number of accounting records, each of which will be discussed in detail in this chapter. Because auditors are responsible for ensuring that the financial statements of a company give a true and fair view of the company, the role of auditors, their appointment to a company, their duties and their removal are therefore also examined in this chapter. The chapter then concludes with a look at the various types of meetings held by a company. Directors are responsible for running a company and the different types of directors and their duties, as set out in CA 2006, are discussed separately in the following chapter, **Chapter 13**.

COMPANY ACCOUNTS, RETURNS, REGISTERS AND REPORTS

The Annual Return

An annual return contains general information about a company's directors (corporate or individual), the details of the Company Secretary (where one has been appointed), registered office address, shareholders and share capital, and the type of company it is.

Every company must deliver an annual return to the Registrar of Companies (Companies House) at least once every 12 months (section 854(1) of CA 2006). The company's director(s) and the Company Secretary (where applicable), are responsible for ensuring that they deliver the annual return to Companies House within 28 days after the anniversary of incorporation of a company or of the anniversary of the '*made up date*' of the last annual return. The made up date is the date at which all the information in an annual return must be correct. The made up date is usually the anniversary of the incorporation of the company or the made up date of the previous annual return registered at Companies House.

If you do not deliver the company's annual return, it may be assumed by Companies House that the company is no longer carrying on business or in operation. Consequently, steps may be taken to strike it from the Register. It is a criminal offence not to deliver the company's annual return within 28 days of the made up date and Companies House may prosecute the company and its officers.

From April 2016, section 92 of the Small Business, Enterprise and Employment Act 2015 will replace Part 24 of the Companies Act 2006, removing the requirement to file an annual return. Instead, all companies will be subject to a new requirement to deliver to Companies House a confirmation statement stating that the company has delivered all the information it was required to provide in the period to which the confirmation statement relates (new section 853A(1) CA 2006).

The confirmation statement must be provided within 14 days of the end of the relevant review period. The review period means the period of 12 months beginning with the day of the company's incorporation and each period of 12 months beginning with the day after the end of the previous review period (new sections 853A(3)–(5)). This means that a confirmation statement must be provided in every 12-month period. However, subject to this requirement, the company can choose to provide a confirmation statement at any point prior to the due date (in which case the next 12-month period will run from the day after the confirmation date, being the date specified in the statement).

The duties to deliver information that are subject to the confirmation statement include:
1. details of a change of registered office;
2. details of company registers relating to directors, company secretaries (if appropriate) and people with significant control;
3. any obligations that arise as a result of a decision by a company to keep any of its registers on the central register; and
4. details of where a company keeps company records if it uses a single alternative inspection location.

(new section 853B CA 2006.)

Accounting Reference Dates

A financial year is usually a 12-month period for which to prepare accounts. Every company must prepare accounts that report on the performance and activities of the company during the financial year (section 94 of CA 2006). This starts on the day after the previous financial year ended or, in the case of a new company, on the day of incorporation.

Financial years are determined by reference to an accounting period. The accounting reference period ends on the accounting reference date or on a date up to seven days either side of it, if this is more convenient (section 390 of CA 2006). For all new companies, the legislation sets the first accounting reference date as the first anniversary of the last day in the month in which the company was incorporated. The subsequent accounting reference dates will automatically be on the same day each year. For example, if the company was incorporated on 6 April 2008, its first accounting reference date would be 30 April 2009 and 30 April for every year thereafter.

An accounting reference date can be changed so as to extend or shorten the period. To do this, you must notify Companies House of a change of accounting reference date. You must submit an acceptable change of accounting reference date before the expiry deadline of the accounts for the period that you wish to change for. In other words, if accounts for a particular reference period become overdue, it is too late to change the accounting reference date.

Private companies have nine months and public companies have six months to submit their accounts after the end of each accounting reference period.

Companies may change an accounting reference date by shortening an accounting reference period as often as they like and by as many months as they choose. However, there are certain restrictions on extending accounting reference periods. Unless a company is in administration, you may not extend a period so that it lasts more than 18 months from the start of the accounting reference period. Furthermore, you may not extend it more than once in five years unless you have approval from the Secretary of State for Northern Ireland, the company is in administration, or the company is aligning its accounting reference period with that of a subsidiary company or parent company.

Accounting Records

Every company, whether they are trading or not, must keep accounting records (section 386 of CA 2006). Accounting records must in particular contain:
- entries showing all monies received and expended by the company; and
- a record of the assets and liabilities of the company.

Also, where the company's business involves dealing in goods, the records must contain:
1. statements of stock held by the company at the end of each financial year;
2. all statements of stock takings from which you have taken or prepared any statements of stock; and
3. a statement of all goods sold and purchased, other than by ordinary retail trade. This should list the goods, buyers and sellers.

The accounting records held must be sufficient to enable directors to ensure that any accounts required to be prepared comply with the requirements of CA 2006. The case of *R. v. Bennett* (1985) dealt with a similar provision that was contained in the New Zealand companies legislation. It was decided by the New Zealand Court of Appeal that the obligation stating that accounting records be 'kept' was not merely an obligation to retain and store records; the obligation extended to creating records so that they complied with the requirements of the provision (section). Furthermore, the case also stated that dealings between a company and its members are transactions of the company that must be included in its accounting records.

A company must keep its accounting records at its registered office address or a place that directors think suitable. The records must be open to inspection by the company's officers at all times. If the company holds the records at a place outside the UK, it must send accounts and returns at least every six months and keep them in the UK. Private companies must keep accounting records for three years from the date they were made, and public companies must keep them for six years (section 388(4) of CA 2006). An officer of the company will be guilty of an offence if he does not take reasonable steps to ensure that a company complies with these requirements (sections 389(3) and (4) of CA 2006).

The directors of every company must prepare accounts for each financial year. These are called *individual accounts*. The parent company must also prepare group accounts.

Generally, accounts must include:
- profit and loss account (or income and expenditure account if the company is not trading for profit);
- a balance sheet signed by a director;
- notes to the accounts; and
- group accounts (if appropriate).

In addition, accounts must generally be accompanied by:
- a directors' report (as discussed below) (with a business review if the company does not qualify as small); and
- an auditor's report (unless the company is exempted from audit).

Every company must send a copy of its annual accounts for each financial year to:
- every member of the company;
- every holder of the company's debentures; and
- every person who is entitled to receive notice of general meetings.

A public company must lay its accounts before its members at its annual general meeting. (There is no longer a statutory requirement for private companies to lay their accounts before members at a general meeting.)

The Directors' Report

The directors of a company are under an obligation to prepare a directors' report for each financial year (section 415(1) of CA 2006). If the company in question is a parent company, the directors prepare group accounts and therefore the directors' report must be a group directors' report (section 415(2)).

The directors' report will contain, among other things: the names of all persons who were directors of the company during the financial year; a corporate government statement; a statement outlining the principal activities of the company or group in the course of the year and the amount which should be paid by way of dividends for the year, together with a business review (where applicable). Furthermore, the directors of a quota company must prepare, for each financial year, a directors' remuneration report. This report must be approved by the board of directors and signed on behalf of the board by a director or the secretary of the company.

Register of People with Significant Control (PSC Register)

Part 21A of the CA 2006 came into effect from 1 April 2016. This new Part requires companies to keep and maintain a register of "persons with significant control" (PSCs) over a company. This register will become known as the PSC register and should be filed on incorporation of the company. It should be subsequently updated when the company files a confirmation statement. CA 2006 defines PSCs as "individuals" or "legal entities" meeting the following criteria:
- individuals holding, directly or indirectly, more than 25% of the shares in the company – if the company does not have a share capital, an individual holding a right to share in more than 25% of the entity's capital or profits;
- individuals holding, directly or indirectly, more than 25% of the voting rights in the company;
- individuals holding the right, directly or indirectly, to appoint or remove a majority of the board of directors of the company;

- individuals holding the right to exercise, or who actually exercise, significant influence or control of over the company; and
- trustees of a trust or the members of a firm (as defined in section 1173(1) CA 2006) that are not legal persons and in turn meet one or more of the other conditions specified above, having the right to exercise or actually exercising significant influence or control over the activities of that trust or firm.

Information to be included in the PSC Register (New Section 790K)

The PSC register must include the required particulars of each person with significant control over the company who is a registrable person, in each case within the meaning of Part 21A CA 2006. The company must also note the required particulars of any relevant legal entity in its PSC register (section 790M(5) CA 2006).

The required particulars are:
- **Individuals** Name, service address, country or state of usual residence, nationality, date of birth, usual residential address and if restrictions on using or disclosing any of the individual's PSC particulars are in force under regulations under section 790ZG, that fact.
- **Entities treated as individuals** In the case of entities to be treated as individuals for the purposes of Part 21A, its name, principal office, legal form and law by which it is governed.
- **Registrable relevant legal entities** In the case of a relevant legal entity, its corporate or firm name, registered or principal office, legal form of the entity and law by which it is governed, register of companies in which it is entered and registration number (if applicable). The scope of information required follows that currently held on corporate directors under section 164 CA 2006.
- **Date and nature of control** In all cases, the PSC register must also contain details of the date on which a person became a registrable person or registrable relevant legal entity and the nature of his, her or its control.

The required particulars of an individual must not be included in the PSC register unless they have been confirmed (section 790M(3)). This requirement does not apply to relevant legal entities. For this purpose, particulars are confirmed if they have been provided or confirmed to the company by the person or with the person's knowledge, or if they were included in the statement of initial significant control on formation of the company (section 790M(9)).

Company Secretary and Auditors

Company Secretary

A Company Secretary is employed to ensure that a company carries out its statutory obligations under the Companies Act 2006. Traditionally, every company had to have a Company Secretary. However, section 270 of CA 2006 now grants an exception to this rule for private companies. Public companies must still have a Company Secretary and failure to have one is an offence under section 271 of CA 2006.

A Company Secretary performs many of the administrative duties imposed upon companies, most of which are determined by the directors of the company. However, CA 2006 does not specifically set out any duties that must be performed by a Company Secretary. As was stated by the court in *Re Maidstone Buildings Provisions Ltd* (1971):

> "So far as the position of a Secretary as such is concerned, it is established beyond all question that a Secretary, while merely performing the duties appropriate to the office of secretary, is not concerned in the management of the company. Equally, I think he is not concerned in carrying on the business of the company. On the other hand, it is equally well established, indeed it is obvious, that a person who holds the office of secretary may, in some other capacity, be concerned in the management of the company's business."

However, it is not unusual to find a Company Secretary performing such duties as establishing and maintaining the company's statutory registers; filing accurate returns with the Registrar on time; organising and minuting company and board meetings; ensuring that accounting records meet the statutory requirements; ensuring that annual accounts are prepared and filed in accordance with statutory requirements; monitoring statutory requirements of the company and signing company documents as may be required by law. This is not an exhaustive list and a Company Secretary may perform many tasks in addition to this.

Directors must take all reasonable steps to ensure that the Company Secretary is the person who appears to them to have the requisite knowledge and experience and who:
1. already holds office as Secretary, Assistant Secretary or Deputy Secretary of the company;
2. for at least three out of the five years immediately preceding his or her appointment, held office as Secretary of a public company;
3. is a barrister, advocate or a solicitor;

4. is a member of one of the list of qualifying bodies such as Chartered Accountants Ireland or the Institute of Chartered Secretaries and Administrators; or
5. is a person who, by virtue of having held any other position or by being a member of any other body, appears to the directors to be capable of discharging the function of Secretary.

Auditor

An auditor is a person who makes an independent report to a company's members as to whether the company has prepared its financial statements in accordance with the Companies Act 2006 and the applicable financial reporting framework. The report must also state whether a company's accounts give a *true and fair view* of its affairs at the end of the year. An auditor must be appointed for each financial year (section 485(1) of CA 2006). The rules are different for public and private companies.

For public companies, the directors appoint the first auditor of the company. The auditor then holds office until the end of the first meeting of the company at which the directors lay their accounts before the members. At that meeting, the members of the company can re-appoint the auditor or appoint a different auditor to hold office from the end of that meeting until the end of the next meeting at which the directors lay accounts.

For private companies, the directors appoint the first auditor of the company. The members then appoint or re-appoint an auditor each year at a meeting of the company's members, or through a written resolution, within 28 days of the directors sending the accounts to the members. If they do not do so for a particular year, however, the appointed auditor is deemed to be reappointed unless a new appointment is made.

Failure to Appoint an Auditor A company must notify the Secretary of State, within one week of the end of the time during which an appointment must be made, that an auditor for a financial year has not been appointed (section 486(2) of CA 2006 for private companies, section 490(2) for public companies).

Qualifications of Auditors Under Directive 2006/43/EC, individuals carrying out an audit of a company must have a minimum standard of general education and they must also have passed an examination of professional competence and undergone at least three years' practical training. Auditors must also take part in continuing professional development (CPD) courses.

The rules relating to the appointment of an auditor are implemented by the Companies Act 2006, Schedule 10, paragraph 6. These rules state that a recognised supervisory body must have rules to the effect that a person is not eligible for appointment as a statutory auditor unless:

(a) in the case of an individual, he or she holds an appropriate qualification or has been approved by an EEA competent authority outside the UK;
(b) in the case of a firm:
  (i) the individuals responsible for statutory audit work on behalf of the firm are eligible for appointment as statutory auditors; and
  (ii) the firm is controlled by qualified persons.

Registration   Directive 2006/43/EC also requires EU Member States to create a public register of statutory auditors in audited firms. This list had to be fully operational by 29 June 2009. It has to be in electronic form and it must be electronically accessible to the public. If a person's name does not appear on this register, yet he describes himself as a registered auditor, he or she has committed an offence.

Ineligibility Due to Lack of Independence   Under sections 1214(1), (2) and (3) of CA 2006 a person is ineligible for appointment as auditor of a company if:

(a) he is an officer or employee of the company (section 1214(1));
(b) he is a partner or employee of such a person or of a partnership of which such a person is a partner (section 1214(2)); or
(c) he is ineligible by virtue of (a) or (b) for appointment as auditor of any associated undertaking of the company (section 1214(3)).

If a person is ineligible to act as an auditor, yet does so, he or she commits an offence. However, it is a defence for a person to state that he did not know and had no reason to believe that he was not eligible for appointment.

Auditor's Remuneration   Remuneration for a company's auditor should be fixed by the members of the company by ordinary resolution, or in such a manner as the members may, by ordinary resolution, determine (section 492(1) of CA 2006). The remuneration of a company's auditor, who is appointed by directors, must also be fixed by the directors (section 492(2)). If the Secretary of State appoints an auditor, he or she fixes the remuneration (section 496(3)). An auditor's remuneration should be disclosed in a note to the accounts (section 494).

Contents of an Auditor's Report   A company's auditor is required to report on the accounts for a financial year of the company. The case of *Re Allen, Craig & Co. (London) Ltd* (1934) stated that it is sufficient if an auditor delivers the report to the Company Secretary. They are not required to personally deliver it to all members of the company. An auditor's report should contain an introduction identifying the accounts that were the subject of the audit. The introduction should describe the scope of the audit, identifying the auditing standards used and the financial reporting framework used in the preparation of the accounts. The report should state clearly whether, in the auditor's opinion, the accounts have been prepared in accordance with CA 2006. The report must also state whether or not, in the opinion of the auditors, the report gives a true and fair view of the company's or, in the case of group accounts, the group's financial affairs. The report should further state as to whether the directors' report is consistent with the accounts. If auditors are of the opinion that the company has not kept adequate accounting records, a statement to that effect should be given and, if the company has not provided the auditors with all the information they need to complete the report, a statement to that effect should also be given.

The auditor's report must also be either unqualified or qualified and include a reference to any matters to which the auditors wish to draw attention by way of emphasis without qualifying the report. The auditors will qualify the report where either there has been a limitation on the scope of the auditors' work or where there is a material disagreement between the company and the auditors about the accounts.

Audit Exemption A substantial set of audit exemptions were introduced 10 years ago, to the point that more than 95% of registered companies were exempt from audit of their annual accounts. This situation has now been reversed and the current provisions regarding audit exemptions are now set out in sections 477 to 479 of CA 2006.

In order to qualify for the exemption from audit in a particular financial year, the company has to meet two conditions:
1. It must meet the criteria for being classified as a *small company* for the purposes of the accounting rules of CA 2006. This means meeting two out of three criteria relating to the size of the company's balance sheet, turnover and workforce over a period of two years. These figures are not more than:
   • £6.5 million for turnover,
   • £3.26 million for balance sheet total, and
   • 50 for employees.
2. The company must meet the specified turnover and balance sheet tests in the financial year in which it claims audit exemption.

A company that qualifies as *small* only through reliance on the employee numbers criterion (i.e. 50 employees) will not be exempt from audit, since by definition it does not meet one or other of the turnover or balance sheet criteria in that year, and so it fails the second condition. In other words, the audit exemption rules require compliance with the turnover and balance sheet criteria.

Removal of Auditors   As in the case of directors, a company may, by ordinary resolution, passed at a meeting at any time, remove an auditor from office. However, the auditor, unlike a director, may not be removed prior to the expiration of the term of office other than by resolution of the shareholders. In this way, the auditor is given some protection against management pressure. If management wish to remove an auditor prematurely, they must do so by means of a proposal to the shareholders.

Hence, not only has special notice (28 days) of a resolution to remove an auditor to be given to the company, but notice of the proposed resolution has to be given to the auditor. The auditor is entitled to make written representations which, if received in time, have to be sent to the members with the notice of the meeting, and which, if not received in time, have to be read out at the meeting. If the resolution is passed, the auditor still retains the right to attend the general meeting at which the term of the office would otherwise have expired or at which the vacancy created by the removal is to be filled. Nor does removal deprive the auditor of any right to compensation or damages, arising, for example, under the contract between auditor and company, in respect of the termination of the appointment as auditor or any appointment terminating with that of auditor.

Resignation of the Auditor   A breakdown in the relationship between auditor and management is more likely to reveal itself in the resignation, rather than the removal, of the auditor. Few auditors would want to retain office if relations with the management of the company had become seriously strained. The Companies Act 2006 contains two sets of provisions designed to achieve this objective, which require notice to be given to the company, on the one hand, and the regulatory authorities on the other.

Although CA 2006 provides that an auditor may resign by depositing a notice in writing to that effect to the company's registered office, the notice is not effective unless it is accompanied by the required statement. In the case of an unquoted company, what is required is a statement of any circumstances connected with the resignation which the auditor considers should be brought to the attention of the members or creditors, or a statement of reason, if that is what the auditor considers is the case. In the case of a quoted company, this statement applies in all cases, i.e. the statement must be given of the circumstances connected with the resignation.

Failure to Re-appoint an Auditor Finally, a management that has fallen out with its auditors may simply wait until the end of the term of office and replace them. As we have seen, in the case of a public company, this is an annual opportunity, since the term of office of the auditor runs, usually, from one accounts meeting to the next, and in the case of a private company, the deemed re-appointment mechanism can be brought to an end by appointing substitute auditors during the annual period for re-appointing them. Moreover, since a change of auditors, for good reasons, is not an uncommon event, failure to re-appoint may not be suspicious.

The auditor's relationship with the shareholders is underlined by the provision that requires him or her to be sent all notices and other communications relating to general meetings, to attend them and to be heard on any part of the business that effects or concerns the auditor (section 502(2) of CA 2006). In the case of a private company, which takes its decision by written resolution, the right becomes a simple right to receive the communications relating to their written resolutions, but there is no general right to make representations to the shareholders before they decide.

COMPANY MEETINGS AND RESOLUTIONS

Introduction

A company is managed by the directors through meetings. Meetings provide the opportunity for both directors and board members to act collectively and make decisions. There are three main types of meetings:
- the annual general meeting;
- extraordinary general meetings; and
- general and class meetings

Annual General Meetings

Under the Companies Act 2006, only public companies must hold annual general meetings (AGMs). Rather oddly, the law, whilst requiring the holding of AGMs by public companies, does not prescribe the business which has to be transacted at the AGM and in particular does not say that the annual directors' report and the accounts must be laid before the attendees of the AGM or that the directors due for re-election must be considered then.

However, it is normal for these matters to be dealt with at the AGMs as the shareholders have the opportunity to question the directors generally on the company's business and financial position. This has arisen as a result of practice, rather than of law, a practice which is encouraged by the *UK Corporate Governance Code* (see **Chapter 18**), applying to list the companies, which states that "boards should use the AGM to communicate with private investors and encourage their participation". That said, the business of a particular AGM may go far beyond these matters – indeed, there seems to be no limit to the business which may be transacted at an AGM, assuming only that it is business properly to be put before the shareholders.

Business of an Annual General Meeting

The following matters would usually be considered at an AGM of a public company:

1. the directors lay before the company the annual accounts and reports for the most recent financial year of the company;
2. the auditor's term of office ends at the end of the meeting and the auditor can be reappointed or a new auditor appointed instead;
3. the accounts for the financial year must be accompanied by a directors' report, which will contain a directors' recommendation of the dividend to be paid to shareholders, and a resolution will be proposed that the amount recommended be paid as a dividend;
4. in companies whose Articles require directors to retire by rotation, some directors will retire at each AGM and will have to be re-elected or replaced; and
5. the New Model Articles for public companies state that a person appointed to be a director by the other directors must retire at the AGM following appointment, which means he cannot continue in office unless re-appointed by the members (see **Chapter 11**).

Extraordinary General Meetings

Prior to the Companies Act 2006, meetings that were not AGMs or ordinary meetings were called extraordinary general meetings (EGMs). However, the phrase 'extraordinary general meeting' does not appear in CA 2006; that said, it is used by many people when they refer to general meetings.

Directors are required to convene an EGM at the request of the company's members/shareholders. Under section 303 of CA 2006, the Act provides that the directors must convene a meeting on the requisition of holders of not less than one-tenth of the paid-up capital carrying voting rights.

However, that fraction is reduced to one-twentieth in the case of a private company which has not held a meeting convened by the members under their statutory powers within the previous 12 months. This is the substitute for the previously available right, prior to 2006, of any member to insist on the holding of an AGM in a private company. The request must state the general nature of the business to be dealt with at the meeting. It may include the textual resolution intended to be moved at the meeting. This is because first, it makes their intentions clear and secondly, if what is proposed is a special resolution, notice of it has to be taken to the shareholders (or members).

If the directors fail to convene a meeting within 21 days of the making of the requisition, the shareholders making the requisition may, if representing more than half of the total voting rights of all, themselves convene the meeting, and their reasonable expenses must be paid by the company and recovered from fees or remuneration payable to the defaulting directors. If the directors are required under section 303 to call a meeting and do not do so, in accordance with section 304, the members may themselves call a general meeting, not more than three months after the date on which the directors become subject to the requirement to call a meeting. Furthermore, under Table A (Article 41, if it is adopted), if no quorum is present, the meeting is adjourned.

Under section 306 of CA 2006, the court may either, of its own motion or, on the application of a director or member, order that a general meeting be called, held and conducted in any matter that the court thinks fit and may give instructions for that purpose, including fixing a quorum of one.

An auditor who gives a Statement of Circumstances for his resignation, or other loss of office, in his written notice, may also call a meeting to receive and consider his explanation. In addition, the records of general meetings are required to be kept for a period of 10 years from the date of the relevant meeting under CA 2006, rather than for an indefinite period (as was the case under the Companies Order 1986).

Class Meetings

In addition to general meetings, it may be necessary to convene separate meetings of classes of members or debenture holders (for example, to consider variation of rights) or of creditors (for example, in connection with re-construction or in a winding up). This usually occurs when there is a variation of class rights. In general, class meetings are likely to be held at the same time as general meetings.

Information to Include on Company Website Relating to a General Meeting

Traded companies must ensure that the following information relating to a general meeting is made available on a website (section 311A CA 2006):
- The matters set out in the notice of the meeting (section 311A(1)(a)).
- The total numbers of shares in the company and of each class in respect of which members are entitled to exercise voting rights at the meeting (section 311A(1)(b), CA 2006). The totals must be given as at the latest practicable time before the first date on which notice of the meeting is given (section 311A(6)).
- The totals of the voting rights that shareholders are entitled to exercise at the meeting in respect of the shares of each class (section 311A(1)(c)). The totals must be given as at the latest practicable time before the first date on which notice of the meeting is given (section 311A(6)).
- Shareholders' statements, shareholders' resolutions and shareholders' matters of business received by the company after the first date on which notice of the meeting is given (section 311A(1)(d)).

Under section 311A(4) CA 2006, the information must:
- Be made available on or before the first date on which notice of the meeting is given in the case of information stating matters set out in the notice of the meeting and the total numbers of shares and voting rights.
- In the case of information regarding any shareholders' statements, shareholders' resolutions or shareholders' matters of business, be made available as soon as reasonably practicable.
- Be kept available throughout the period of two years beginning with the date on which it is first made available on the website. Failure to make information available throughout the entire two-year period specified is disregarded provided the information was made available for part of that period and the failure is wholly attributable to circumstances that it would not be reasonable to have expected the company to prevent or avoid (section 311A(5)).

The website must be maintained by or on behalf of the company and identify the company (section 311A(2) CA 2006). Access to the information on the website, and the ability to obtain a hard copy of that information, must not be conditional on payment of a fee or restricted in any way (section 311A(3)).

Where a traded company fails to comply with section 311A, the validity of the meeting or of anything done at the meeting is not affected (section 311A(7)), but an offence is committed by every officer of the company who is in default and is liable to be fined (section 311A(8) to (9) of CA 2006).

Notice of Meetings

Prior to 1948, the length of notice of meetings and how and to whom notice should be given depended primarily on the company's Articles of Association. The only statutory regulation that could not be varied was the 21 days' notice which was required for a meeting at which a special resolution was to be proposed. However, section 307 of CA 2006 now provides that any provisions of a company's Articles shall be void in so far as they allow for the calling of a meeting by fewer than 21 days' notice in the case of an AGM or 14 days' notice in the case of general meetings. The company's Articles may provide for longer notice but they cannot validly provide for shorter notice (section 307 of CA 2006).

It should be noted that the minimum periods of notice required are clear days (section 307 of CA 2006). This means the day on which the notice is given and the day of the meeting are excluded (section 360). In addition, notice of a general meeting can be given in one of the following forms: electronic form, on a website, or partly by one of these means and partly by another.

Special Notice

In certain circumstances, a 'special notice' has to be given, the principal examples being when it is proposed to remove a director or to remove or not to re-appoint the auditors. Hence, a special notice is not notice of a meeting given by the company but notice given to the company of the intention to move a resolution at the meeting. Under section 312, where any provision of the Act requires special notice of a resolution, the resolution is ineffective unless notice of the intention to move it has been given to the company at least 28 days before the meeting. The company must then give notice, in the normal sense, of the resolution, with the notice of the meeting or, if that is not practicable, either by newspaper advertisement or by any other method allowed by the Articles, at least 14 days before the meeting.

Special notice is required for resolutions to:
1. dismiss a director under section 168 of CA 2006 by ordinary resolution of a general meeting (section 168(2));
2. appoint a person to fill the vacancy caused by the dismissal of the director under section 168 at the same meeting (section 168(2));
3. dismiss an auditor (section 511(1) CA 2006); or
4. appoint an auditor as the person other than a retiring auditor (section 515 CA 2006).

The Contents of the Notice of the Meeting and Circulars

Statute now lays down some basic requirements in relation to the contents of the notice of meetings. The notice of the meeting must give:

- the date of the meeting;
- the time of the meeting;
- the place of the meeting;
- a statement of the general nature of the business to be transacted at the meeting; and
- any other matters required by the company's Articles (section 311 of CA 2006).

Obviously, the statement of the general nature of the business to be transacted at the meeting is the crucial requirement as the members are entitled to be put in receipt of sufficient information about the business of the meeting to determine whether or not to attend it. In practice, the notice of a meeting will be of a formal nature but, if anything other than ordinary business is to be transacted, it will be accompanied by a circular explaining the reasons for the proposals and giving the opinion of the board. In deciding whether the nature of the business has been adequately described, the notice and circular can be read together. However, the circular must not misrepresent the facts. For example, in the case of *Margate v. Mercantile Holdings* (1980) it was held that each shareholder should have clear and precise advance notice of the substance of any special resolution which it is intended to propose, so that he may decide whether he should attend the meeting or is content to absent himself and leave the decision to those who do attend. If it were open to the members who did attend to propose and vote on a special resolution differing in substance, even slightly, from the resolution of which notice was given, there would be a risk of unfair prejudice to those members who, after due consideration, had deliberately absented themselves.

Having prescribed the basic content of the notice, CA 2006 also specifies to whom it should be given, thus giving statutory form to something previously contained in the Model Articles. Those entitled to receive notice of the meeting are every member of the company (whether entitled to vote or not) and every director (section 310 of CA 2006). Members include those entitled to a share on the death or bankruptcy of a member, if the company has been notified of their entitlement.

Resolutions

It is important that company law allows for changes in companies: directors may be dismissed and replaced; capital structure may be altered; a company may change its name, its objects, its Articles of Association and so on.[1] The decision to make changes on many matters in connection with the company can be taken by the company's members only. Such decisions are known as 'resolutions'.

Ordinary Resolution

This is a resolution passed by a simple majority of those voting. Such a resolution is used for all decisions required under CA 2006 unless it specifies that a special resolution is needed. That said, a company's Articles can specify that a greater majority, up to and including unanimity, is required.

Special Resolution

This is a resolution that is passed by a 75% majority. A special resolution is required before any important constitutional changes can be undertaken and, as a result of legislation passed in the 1980s, the number of such cases has greatly increased. In the case of the special resolution, the notice of the meeting must specify the intention to propose the resolution as a special resolution.

When CA 2006 requires a decision to be taken by a resolution of the members, without specifying whether it is to be ordinary or special, an ordinary resolution is sufficient. That said, the Articles may require a larger majority or unanimity.

Examples of decisions requiring special resolution include decisions to:
- amend the company's Articles of Association;
- re-register from private to public or public to private;
- approve a substantial property transaction with a director;
- approve compensation to a director or shadow director of the company for loss of office; or
- supply members' pre-emption rights when shares are issued.

Validity of Meetings

To validly constitute a meeting, there must be a Chairperson and a quorum.

Chairperson

A Chairperson must preside over meetings. The 2006 Act lays down the default rule that a member may be elected at the meeting by resolution to be

---

[1] *Mayson, French and Ryan on Company Law* (26th Edition, Oxford University Press, 2009–2010).

its chair, but states that this provision is subject to any provisions in the Articles as to how that person is to be chosen. The position of a Chairperson is an important and onerous one, for he or she will be in charge of the meeting and will be responsible for insuring that its business is properly conducted. As Chairperson, he owes a duty to the meeting, not the board of directors, even if he is a director. He should see that the business of the meeting is efficiently conducted and that all shades of opinion are given a fair hearing. This may entail taking snap decisions and points of order, motions, amendments and questions, often deliberately designed to harass him, and the validity of any resolution may depend upon the correctness of his ruling.

In *National Dwellings Society v. Sykes* (1894), Chitty J. stated:

> "Unquestionably, it is the duty of the chairman, and his function, to preserve order, and to take care that the proceedings are conducted in a proper manner, and that the sense of the meeting is properly ascertained with regard to any question which is properly before the meeting."

Quorum

A quorum is the minimum number of persons who must be present in order for a meeting to commence business. As Lord President Clyde said in *Neil M'Leod and Sons Ltd* (1967), "... a meeting is not properly constituted if only one individual is present, for there is no one for him to meet". The quorum for meetings will be set by the Articles of Association but may be two or more (except for private companies with only one member). Proxies can attend and vote on behalf of members. Only private company proxies have the right to speak. If there is no quorum, no valid meeting is held and no valid decisions are taken. The voting procedure is normally a show of hands, followed by a poll if necessary. A show of hands is used for simple, non-contentious issues. Every member or proxy present has one vote only on a show of hands, but if a poll is demanded, every member has a vote for every share held.

Method of Voting

Show of Hands or Poll

Sections 282–284 of CA 2006 provide for two methods of voting. The first is that of a *show of hands*. Voters in favour of a resolution are asked to raise their hands. Each hand is counted. Each vote can be counted only once. Where a contentious issue is being decided, or where the outcome of a show of hands is unclear, members may wish to call for a *poll* or a *secret ballot*. The poll may be demanded by not less than five members (unless the Articles permit a smaller figure). A poll overrides a vote on a show of hands. The default rule, under section 284(3), is that, in a poll, every member has one vote for every share held.

Proxy Voting

A proxy is the name given to a person appointed by a shareholder to attend, speak and vote on their behalf at a general meeting. Any member of a company that has a share capital, provided he is entitled to attend and vote at a general or class meeting of the company, has a statutory right to appoint another person as his proxy to exercise all or any of his rights to attend and to speak and vote at a meeting of the company. There are different types of proxies as listed below:

- **General Proxy** This can give the power to represent the member at more than one general meeting.
- **Special Proxy** The authority only covers one meeting. The proxy formally indicates who is appointed as proxy. The proxy can be the Chairperson or another individual, often a solicitor or an accountant. If the member is a company proxy, it must be signed by two directors and sealed.
- **The Two-Way Proxy** This entitles the proxy to vote for or against a particular motion in accordance with the member's wishes. Results may then enable the proxy to act as he so wishes in other matters which may arise at the meeting.

Minutes of Meetings

Every company is required to keep minutes, which are formal, written records of the proceedings of its general meetings (section 355 of CA 2006) and meetings of directors (section 248 of CA 2006). Minutes of directors' meetings and all general meetings must be kept at the registered office; the members can inspect those of general meetings. When the minutes are signed by the Chairperson, they are primary evidence of what happened. The records must be kept for at least ten years from the date of the resolution, meeting or decision. A failure to comply with this requirement brings the risk of criminal sanctions.

References

- Derek French, Stephen Mayson and Christopher Ryan, *Mayson, French and Ryan on Company Law* (26th Edition, Oxford University Press, 2009–2010).
- Paul L. Davies, *Gower and Davies' Principles of Modern Company Law* (8th Edition, Thomson, Sweet & Maxwell, 2008).

- Gary Bagnell, Denis Boyd, Norma Davison, Eithne Harkness, Sheena McCormick, David Moore and Richard Steele, *Legal Aspects of Business Start-Up* (SLS Legal Publications (NI) 1992).

REVIEW QUESTIONS

(See Suggested Solutions at the end of this textbook.)

Question 12.1

Liston and Partners, a firm of Chartered Accountants, have recently been appointed as Receivers to a Belfast-based hotel, the Boston Isle Hotel Ltd. ('Boston Isle Hotel'). The appointment is as a consequence of a fixed charge on the hotel's business premises, and a floating charge on the goodwill of the business in favour of the People's Bank of Belfast. The majority shareholder in the Boston Isle Hotel knows little about company law and comes to you for advice.

To effect the administration, Liston and Partners propose to call a meeting of the shareholders to inform them that they have received an offer for the purchase of the business as a going concern from a rival hotel.

Requirement: In relation to this proposed meeting, discuss the following:
 (i) The notice requirements to call an extraordinary general meeting in a private company.
(ii) The methods by which voting can be effected at company meetings.

(Source: Chartered Accountants Ireland, CAP 1, Summer 2010, Extract: Q2(b))

Question 12.2

In the context of company auditors, explain the procedure in relation to their appointment and their removal.

(Source: Chartered Accountants Ireland, CAP 1, Autumn 2008, Extract: Q3(a))

Question 12.3

Fiona has worked for Cruise Publications Limited since 2000 as an accounts assistant. Twelve months ago, Cruise Publications was taken over by another company, Parkway Publications Ltd. Since this takeover Fiona has been experiencing problems with her new manager who wants her to change certain aspects of her employment contract. One of the new tasks that Fiona's manager wishes to add to her job description is the preparation of the company's annual return. Fiona has never completed an annual return and is unsure as to what it involves.

Requirement:
(a) List any FOUR pieces of information included in an annual return, and state how frequently it should be lodged at the Registrar of Companies (Companies House).
(b) Outline the date on which the annual return must be filed and give any TWO consequences of failure to file an annual return.

> (Source: Chartered Accountants Ireland, CAP 1, Law for Accountants (NI), Autumn 2012, Extract: Q3(b)(i) and (ii))

Question 12.4

Allen Enterprises Limited ('Allen') is an online gambling company. In the first three years of operation, Allen's turnover was less than £7.3 million and therefore the company was eligible for an audit exemption. This year Allen's turnover is in excess of £10 million and Allen's accountant has informed the directors that the accounts will need to be audited before presentation to the shareholders at the annual general meeting (AGM).

Requirement: Last month Allen's directors appointed Paddison Chartered Accountants ('Paddison') as Allen's auditor. Paddison has been asked to prepare an explanatory note for Allen's shareholders that:
(a) Outlines the role of an auditor and their requisite qualifications.
(b) Lists any THREE powers available to an auditor when conducting an audit.
(c) States the procedure necessary to effect the removal of an auditor.

> (Source: Chartered Accountants Ireland, CAP 1, Law for Accountants (NI), Summer 2013, Extract: Q4(a)(i)–(iii))

Question 12.5

Following the death of his great uncle Nelson, Cranston inherited 75,000 £1 ordinary shares in Finest Cuisine Catering Ltd ('Finest'). This is the first time that Cranston has owned company shares and has been given share certificates. He knows nothing about company law or how companies operate.

Last week he received a notification from the Company Secretary of Finest informing him that an extraordinary general meeting (EGM) of the company was being requisitioned and that this meeting would consider the sale of 100,000 £1 ordinary shares in the company to a new private investor, Hamilton.

Hamilton has offered to pay a share premium of £0.30 on every £1 share purchased. In addition, this notice also stated that a special resolution was being proposed to avoid pre-emption so that these shares could be offered directly to Hamilton and an ordinary resolution was being proposed to appoint Hamilton as a non-executive director in the company (if he was successful in acquiring these shares). Cranston does not understand the meaning of any of these terms and seeks your advice.

Requirement: Explain the difference between an ordinary resolution and a special resolution under any TWO headings.

(Source: Chartered Accountants Ireland, CAP 1, Law for Accountants (NI),
Summer 2014, Extract: Q3(e))

Question 12.6

Marcus and Isabella run a furniture shop in County Antrim called MI Ltd ('MI'). MI has recently appointed Heron Accountants ('Heron') as its accountant. You are an employee of Heron and are attending a meeting with your manager and Marcus and Isabella. Your manager has asked you to be prepared to discuss the following issues with Marcus and Isabella.

Requirement:
(a) Define the criteria required to obtain audit exemption.
(b) Outline any FOUR items that should be within an auditor's report.

(Source: Chartered Accountants Ireland, CAP 1, Law for Accountants (NI),
Autumn 2014, Extract: Q4(c)(i) and (ii))

Question 12.7

Lismount Ltd ('Lismount') began life as a small family-run recycling plant in 1970. Over the last 45 years, it has grown from employing five people to now employing over 500 people across Northern Ireland. The five directors of Lismount are considering floating the business on the stock exchange to raise additional share capital. The directors come to you for advice on the benefits of doing so. You advise them that if they do become a public limited company (plc), they will have to hold an annual general meeting (AGM).

Requirement: Outline any FIVE items that would normally be discussed at an annual general meeting of a public limited company.

(Source: Chartered Accountants Ireland, CAP 1, Law for Accountants (NI),
Summer 2015, Extract: Q3(a))

Question 12.8

Golfing Mania Ltd ('Golf') is a family-run golf shop business based in Newcastle. Golf was established in 1985 by Mr O'Connor Senior. In 2014, due to the expansive growth of the business, Mr O'Connor Senior decided to change the status of the business from a partnership to a company. As their auditor, you are due to meet with Mr O'Connor Senior and his three sons to discuss with them some of the management requirements of the company under the Companies Act 2006.

The first item on the agenda is an explanation of all the accounting records the O'Connors are expected to keep because of the company status and their obligations in relation to the annual return.

Requirement:
(a) List any THREE items generally contained on an annual return AND state how often the annual return should be delivered to the Registrar of Companies.
(b) Define an auditor.

> (Source: Chartered Accountants Ireland, CAP 1, Law for Accountants (NI), Summer 2015, Extract: Q4(a) and (b))

Question 12.9

Titan Publishing Ltd ('Titan') was established in 2005. Sam is the executive director but, due to his declining health, he has decided to resign his position and also to dispose of his shareholding.

Sam wants to transfer his shareholding in the company to his son Joe. However, Joe was prosecuted for fraud last year and so the other directors are opposing this as they believe that Joe's connection to the company may negatively impact on its commercial reputation.

To ensure that Sam does not transfer his shares to Joe, the remaining directors of Titan are now considering altering the company's Articles of Association to state that the right of voluntary pre-emption should be applied to all share transfers.

Requirement:
(a) A lawful alteration of the Articles of Association requires a special resolution of the members:
  (i) Explain the procedure that should be followed and the majority required to pass the resolution.
  (ii) Give two additional examples of decisions that require a special resolution.

(b) Determine the validity or otherwise of the proposed alteration to Titan's Articles of Association.
(c) If this proposed alteration is not effected, review whether the remaining directors of Titan can refuse to register the transfer of Sam's shares to Joe.
(d) Peter is the company secretary of Titan, but has never had the need to call an extraordinary general meeting (EGM) within the company and is unsure as to his duties in this regard.
   (i) Outline any FOUR duties of Peter as Company Secretary.
   (ii) Discuss the various methods by which voting can be effected at a company meeting.
   (iii) Jessica, one of the shareholding directors, is unable to attend this meeting but wishes to exercise her vote in relation to the proposed alteration of the Articles of Association. Advise her on any action she may take and the procedure that she should follow.

(Source: Chartered Accountants Ireland, CAP 1, Law for Accountants (NI), Autumn 2015, Extract: Q2(b)–(e))

Question 12.10

Tom is aware that companies have obligations in relation to maintenance of books of accounts, but is unsure as to the exact nature of these obligations.

Requirement: Advise Tom on the rules in relation to the maintenance of accounts AND comment on the period that the law requires that these accounts are maintained for.

(Source: Chartered Accountants Ireland, CAP 1, Law for Accountants (NI), Autumn 2015, Extract: Q3(d))

CHAPTER 13

COMPANY DIRECTORS AND THEIR DUTIES

Introduction

A director is an officer of the company and, together with the managers and the Company Secretary, is involved in the management of the company. The director is in a fiduciary relationship with the company, i.e. under a duty to act in the best interest of the company.

There are no formal qualifications that an individual must have in order to be a director. Anyone can become a director, provided:

- they have not been restrained by a court Order from becoming a company director under the Company Directors Disqualification (Northern Ireland) Order 2002 (2002 No. 3150 (N.I. 4));
- they are not an undischarged bankrupt;
- they are not subject to UK government restrictions; and
- they are aged 16 or over.

Every company must have at least one director who is a 'natural legal person' and all public companies must have at least two directors.

In this chapter we will examine the different types of directors that a company can have, how directors can be appointed and removed from office and the duties that directors owe to a company. As we shall see, prior to 2006, directors' duties were simply laid down in common law. However, the Companies Act 2006 (CA 2006) sought to codify these duties.

Types of Directors

There are a number of different categories of directors:

- executive and non-executive directors
- alternate directors
- shadow directors
- de facto directors
- associate directors
- managing directors
- nominee directors

Executive Directors

Executive directors are directors who are also employees (usually full time) of the company. An executive director will usually hold an important position in the day-to-day running of the company, such as financial controller or marketing director. If someone is appointed as a full-time working director, it is usual that he will enter into a service contract with the company. This will be done at the same time as his formal appointment to the board of directors.

Non-Executive Directors

Non-executive directors do not have any executive function in the company's management but they are involved in company board meetings. Non-executive directors are common in large companies and public companies where they bring independent expert knowledge, and perhaps publicity, to the company. It should be noted that a non-executive director will have the same statutory duties (which are discussed below) and obligations as any other type of director. However, the court does have the discretion to apply different standards in examining a level of skill and the standard of the duty of care that a non-executive director can be expected to demonstrate. This can be seen in the case of *Re Stephenson Cobbold Ltd* (2001). In this case, the court refused to disqualify a non-executive director. Even though the director was a cheque signatory, he was not involved in deciding which creditors would be paid where preferential treatment had been given.

It should be noted that neither the term 'executive' nor 'non-executive' are recognised by CA 2006. However, both terms are commonly used in practice.

Alternate Directors

The Companies Act 2006 does not provide for alternate directors but it is very common for a company's Articles to give each director the right to appoint an 'alternate'. In essence, alternate directors are substitute directors who can be appointed to attend and vote at board meetings and in substitution for another director. Alternate directors are still subject to all the statutory obligations and responsibilities of other directors. An alternate director is not entitled to receive remuneration.

Shadow Directors

Under section 251 of CA 2006, a 'shadow director' is defined as a person in accordance with whose instructions or directions the directors are accustomed to act (excluding persons giving advice in a professional capacity such as accountants, solicitors, tax specialists, etc.). Hence, behind the formally appointed board, there may be a controlling shareholder, secure creditor or banker, on whose instructions the board is accustomed to act.[1]

In effect, this means that a shadow director has all the powers of a director but he is never officially appointed as a director. A shadow director is subject to the same rules as an ordinary director and, therefore, the same statutory obligations which apply to ordinary directors also apply to shadow directors.

In *Re Hydrodam (Corby) Ltd* (1994), Millett J. said:

"to establish that a defendant is a shadow director of a company it is necessary to allege and prove: (1) who are the directors of the company, whether de facto or de jure; (2) that the defendant directed those directors how to act in relation to the company or that he was one of the persons who did so; (3) that those directors acted in accordance with such directions; and (4) that they were accustomed so to act. What is needed is, first, a board of directors claiming and purporting to act as such; and, secondly, a pattern of behaviour in which the board did not exercise any discretion or judgment of its own, but acted in accordance with the directions of others."

With effect from 26 May 2015, section 89 of the Small Business, Enterprise and Employment Act 2015 (SBEEA 2015) makes shadow directors subject to the same statutory duties and responsibilities of directors as stated in sections 170 to 177 CA 2006, where and to the extent that they are so capable of applying. According to the explanatory notes to SBEEA 2015, the starting point for shadow directors is that the general duties apply unless they are not capable of applying section 90. The SBEEA 2015 notes that a person is not deemed to be a shadow director simply by reason only that the directors act upon their advice in a professional capacity.

De Facto Director

A de facto director is a person who, although not formally appointed as a director, holds himself out to be a director, occupies the position of director and deals with matters that could be properly discharged only by a director. In the case of *Re Hydrodam (Corby) Ltd* (1994), the distinction given by the judge was that a de facto director was a person who assumes to act as a director, is held out by the company as a director and who claims or purports to be a director without validly being appointed.

---

[1] Martha Bruce, *Rights and Duties of Directors* (9th Edition, Tottel Publishing, 2009).

The following points may be relevant in determining who is a de facto director:
- To determine whether someone has assumed responsibility to act as a director, the court may have to determine in what capacity the director was acting.
- The court will in general also have to determine the corporate governance structure of the company so as to decide in relation to the company's business whether the defendant's acts were directorial in nature.
- The court is required to look at what the director actually did and not any job title actually given to him.

Associate Director

'Associate director' is a term given to a senior executive in a company who does not have a seat on the board of directors. This term has no legal standing as such. Persons who are given the title of an associate director should not hold themselves out as directors to third parties. For example, in the case of *SMC Electronics Ltd v. Akhter Computers Ltd* (2001), an employee who was not a director was given the title of Director of Power Supply Unit Sales. The director was also described as a director on the company's notepaper. This employee entered into a contract which the company was subsequently unable to repudiate. The court held that a third party would reasonably have assumed that the employee had authority to enter into such a contract.

The authority to bestow the title of 'associate director' upon employees will be provided in the company's Articles of Association. If the Articles do allow the appointment of associate directors, the Articles should be very clear that the board of directors has authority to define and limit the powers of associate directors.

Managing Director

The Managing Director is the director responsible for the day-to-day operations of the company. A Managing Director is usually the Chief Executive. A Managing Director usually has overall responsibility for the company's operations. Furthermore, he or she often has the authority to manage and take decisions on the day-to-day running of the company. The specific responsibilities of a Managing Director include tasks such as putting in place effective systems of control and risk management; monitoring operational and financial performance against plans, targets and budgets; achievement of performance targets; building an effective executive management team; monitoring the actions and performance of executive directors; maintaining a dialogue with the Chairman of the Board and representing the company to customers, suppliers, institutions, etc.

Nominee Director

Nominee directors are directors appointed to a company by a large influential outsider, normally a major creditor such as a bank, or a major shareholder. A nominee director must act in the best interests of the company and should not put the appointer's interests before those of the company.

Minimum and Maximum Number of Directors

Under section 154 of the Companies Act 2006, a private company must have at least one director and a public company must have at least two directors. At least one director must be a natural person (section 155(1) CA 2006). This requirement is met if the office of director is held by a natural person as a corporation sole or otherwise by virtue of an office (section 155(2) CA 2006). The Small Business, Enterprise and Employment Act 2015 (SBEEA 2015), amends section 155 to require that all directors must be natural persons, subject to certain exceptions, but this amendment is not expected to come into force until October 2016.

If it appears to the Secretary of State that a company is in breach of sections 154 or 155, he or she may give the company a direction under section 156. The direction must specify:

"(a) the statutory requirement the company appears to be in breach of,

(b) what the company must do to comply with the direction, and

(c) the period within which it must do so.

That period must not be less than one month or more than three months after the date on which the direction is given."

The company's Articles may specify a minimum number of directors. CA 2006 does not prescribe a maximum number of directors, but the company's Articles may impose a maximum.

Appointment of Directors

On initial registration, the company must send to the Registrar of Companies particulars of the first directors with their signed written consents to act. Their identities are disclosed in **Form 21**, which is the form required for the appointment of directors. With effect from 10 October 2015, section 100 SBEEA 2015 replaced the requirement for the consent to act in sections 12(3) and 167(2) CA 2006 with a requirement for the company or, in the case of the formation of a new company, the subscribers to the Memorandum of Association, to make a statement that the person has consented to act. The statement of truth is not filed at Companies House, but it should be kept on file (preferably with the company books). Upon receipt of the statement, Companies House writes to a new director and informs them that their appointment is being recorded on the public register. Companies House will also make the new director aware of their legal obligations and directors' duties. If a new director does not consent to being a director, the onus is on him or her to apply to Companies House for removal of their appointment.

Subsequent appointments must follow the procedure in the Articles. The company must also maintain a second register giving particulars of its directors. Both registers are open to inspection by members of the public so the public can obtain information about who the directors are. This enables people to find out who controls what otherwise might appear to be faceless companies and facilitates enforcement of the obligations to which directors are subject, whether by creditors, the public authorities or others. However, in order to protect directors as appropriate, CA 2006 now provides that the register should contain service addresses for the directors rather than details of their residential addresses. The service address can, for example, be a residential address or stated simply as "the company's registered office". The company must also keep a separate register of the directors' residential addresses.

Removal and Retirement of Directors

A director can be removed from office in one of three ways:
1. retirement
2. resignation
3. dismissal.

Retirement

The Companies Act 2006 contains no general requirement for directors to retire by rotation at each annual general meeting (AGM). However, such a requirement is normally included in the company's Articles of Association. Indeed, the modern Articles of Association require all directors to retire at the first AGM. At subsequent AGMs, any new directors appointed should retire and offer themselves for re-appointment at the AGM following their appointment. From the third AGM onwards, every director who was not appointed at the two previous general meetings should retire.

However, the above provisions are not practical in a small private limited company as directors and shareholders are usually the same people. Such companies often choose to exclude retirement and rotation provisions as they do not consider them necessary.

Resignation

A director is permitted to resign from his appointment at any time so long as he serves the appropriate period of notice contained within his contract. Once notice is given, it cannot be withdrawn except by agreement with the company.

A company's Articles of Association may also specifically state that a director is no longer entitled to hold office if, for example, he becomes bankrupt, suffers from a mental disorder or is absent from meetings of the directors without the consent of the board. Furthermore, legislation states that a director must vacate his office if he is made bankrupt or disqualified by the court.

Once a director resigns or is required to vacate office, the remaining directors must ensure that the following procedures are carried out in order to effectively disclose the change of directors correctly:

1. hold a meeting of the directors to record the resignation or report the reason why the director is required to vacate office;
2. submit a form to the Registrar of Companies (Companies House) to report the resignation;
3. record the resignation in the register of directors;
4. notify the company's bank and insurers of the change;
5. arrange for company stationery to be reprinted where directors' names are disclosed; and
6. check whether a minimum number of directors is required by the Articles and that the resignation does not cause the numbers to fall below the minimum.

Dismissal

A company may remove a director before the expiration of the director's period of office, notwithstanding anything in the Articles or any service agreement between the company and the director. A company's Articles exclude this provision. However, they can permit removal of a director by alternative means.

Since the dismissal of a director is potentially a contentious matter, the director may have the right to damages for breach of contract, for wrongful dismissal or for unfair dismissal if they were an employee of the company and/or if the company did not follow the correct procedure in dismissing the director.

The following steps should be taken when removing a director:

1. Special notice must be received by the company from a member which details the member's intention to bring a resolution to remove a director. This notice must be given at least 28 days before the meeting at which the resolution is to be proposed.

2. If the resolution is received in time, directors should ensure that the proposed resolution is included in the notice of the next AGM. If this is not possible, members can requisition directors to hold a general meeting to consider the resolution. If this is the case, they must hold a general meeting within 21 days of receiving the requisition and special notice.

3. The director who is to be removed should be sent a copy of the special notice. If this director wishes to exercise his right to make written representation to the members and attend the general meeting, the director must ensure that he is permitted to do so. If the ordinary resolution to remove the director is approved, directors should ensure the procedures detailed in the paragraph above are followed.

Directors' Duties

The Companies Act 2006 transformed the law relating to directors' duties. Prior to CA 2006, directors' duties were based on the equitable principles of fiduciary duty that applied to directors and on the common law of negligence. However, CA 2006 has now codified all of these duties into a statutory basis. As a result, CA 2006 now contains seven general duties of directors:

- to act within powers (section 171 CA 2006);
- to promote the success of the company (section 172 CA 2006);
- to exercise independent judgement (section 173 CA 2006);
- to exercise reasonable care, skill and diligence (section 174 CA 2006);
- to avoid conflicts of interest (section 175 CA 2006);
- not to accept benefits from third parties (section 176 CA 2006); and
- to declare interests in proposed transactions or arrangements (section 177 CA 2006).

Each of these statutory duties is owed by a director to the company and not to the shareholders.

Duty to Act within Powers

Under section 171 of CA 2006, a director is required to act within his powers under the company's constitution and only exercise his powers with a purpose for which they were conferred. To do otherwise renders any act of the director voidable. In the case of *Re Cameron's Coalbrook Steam Coal, & Swansea & Lougher Railway Co, Bennett's Case* (1854), Lord Justice Turner said:

> "... in the exercise of the powers given to them ... Directors must, as I can see, keep within the proper limits. Powers given to them for one purpose cannot, in my opinion, be used by them for another and different purpose. To permit such proceedings in the part of Directors of companies would be to sanction not the use but the abuse of their powers. It would be to give effect and validity to an illegal exercise of a legal power."

This is the basis of the equitable principle that a director of a company has the duty to exercise the company's powers for the purposes for which they were given.

Duty to Promote the Success of the Company

This duty replaces the common law duty of loyalty. The duty requires a director to act in the way he or she considers, in good faith, would be most likely to promote the success of the company for the benefit of the members as a collective body, not just the majority shareholders, or any particular shareholder. In doing so, a director must have regard to six factors:

- the likely consequences of any decision in the long term;
- the interest of the company's employees;
- the need to foster the company's business relationships with suppliers, customers and others;
- the impact of the company's operations on the community and the environment;
- the desirability of the company maintaining a reputation for high standards of business conduct; and
- the need to act fairly as between members of the company.

This duty is based on the equitable fiduciary duty espoused by Lord Green in *Re Smith & Fawcett Ltd* (1942). In this case, it was stated that the directors of a company must act:

"... bona fide in what they consider – not what a Court may consider – is in the interests of the company and, not for any collateral purpose ...".

The requirement to promote the success of the company now formalises the need for directors who consider and balance the interests of the company's members with those of other stakeholders when deciding what action should be taken to fulfil this duty.[2]

The decisions taken by a director and the weight given to the factors are a matter for his good faith and judgement. Fundamentally, the decisions are a subjective matter and some degree of objectivity is implied by the need to exercise reasonable skill, care and diligence.

Duty to Exercise Independent Judgement

A director must exercise independent judgement under section 173 CA 2006. This duty is based on the equitable principle that it is legitimate for directors

---

[2] Bruce (2009), *op. cit.*

of a company to exercise their powers independently and to enter into agreements acting as directors if they consider that to do so is in the interests of the company. Under section 173(2) CA 2006, a director's duty to exercise independent judgement is subject to restrictions contained in any agreements entered into by the company or in the company's constitution, including resolutions of the shareholders.

Under this duty, directors may be in breach if they fail to take appropriate advice – for example, legal advice. That said, a director cannot abdicate his duty, under this section, by slavishly trying to rely on the advice. Obtaining outside advice does not absolve directors from exercising their judgement on the basis of such advice.

Duty to Exercise Reasonable Care, Skill and Diligence

Under section 174(2) CA 2006, a director must exercise such reasonable skill, care and diligence as would be exercised by a reasonably diligent person with:

> "(a) the general knowledge, skill and experience that may reasonably be expected of a person carrying out the functions carried out by the director in relation to the company, and
> (b) the general knowledge, skill and experience that the director has."

This duty is based on the director's common law duty of skill and care. The main case in this area was *Re City Equitable Fire Insurance Company Ltd* (1925). In this case, liquidators of a company sued directors for negligence on account of the manner in which they had made certain investments. As a result of these investments, the company lost £1.2 million in assets. The main reason for this loss was due to the deliberate fraud perpetrated by the Managing Director of the company. In this case, the directors were absolved from liability due to the fact that the Articles limited their liability for breach of duty. However, the case established three key principles. First, the duty to exercise skill, care and diligence is a subjective duty. It is based on the knowledge and experience of the particular director. Secondly, directors can delegate or leave the running of the business to the management of the company. Finally, a director's duty of care is owed at board meetings only. A director should attend board meetings regularly.

Duty to Avoid Conflicts of Interest

A director has a statutory duty to avoid any situations in which he has, or can have, a direct or indirect interest that conflicts, or may possibly conflict, with the interests of the company (section 175 CA 2006).

The duty does not apply to a conflict of interest arising in relation to a transaction or arrangement between a director and the company. Furthermore, the duty does not arise if the situation cannot reasonably be regarded as likely to give rise to a conflict of interest. The company should consider a director's conflicts of interest on a case-by-case basis. Approval should be given in accordance with the general directors' duties as set out in CA 2006 – in particular, the need to promote the success of the company.

There are three options that a company can consider if a conflict of interest arises:
1. excluding the director from the relevant information and discussion on the matter;
2. excluding the director from the board in relation to the matter; or
3. requiring that the director resigns.

Duty not to Accept Benefits from Third Parties

A director has the statutory duty not to accept a benefit from a third party that is given because of the position held by the director or because of anything the director has done in his capacity as a director. Effectively, this means that the duty applies only to benefits conferred on the director because he is a director and will not be breached if accepting the benefit cannot reasonably be regarded as likely to give rise to a conflict of interest. Benefits from associated companies are excluded. Otherwise, all third-party benefits, of any description, whether financial or not, have to be authorised by the company shareholders.

Companies should ensure that they have well-devised policies on any question that could arise with regard to corporate hospitality and gifts to directors.

Duty to Declare Interests in Proposed Transactions or Arrangements

A director has a duty to disclose the nature of any interest in a proposed transaction or arrangement to the rest of the board before the transaction is approved. There is no need to make a disclosure if the interest "cannot reasonably be regarded as likely to give rise to a conflict of interest" or if the directors are already aware of the director in question's interest.

Common Law Duties of Directors

The general statutory duties introduced by the Companies Act 2006 were introduced in an effort to codify the common law position as it was before 1 October 2007. The aim of CA 2006 was to replace the corresponding common law rules and equitable principles, which had long been established in common law as the fiduciary duty and a duty of skill and care. Common law required directors operating and making decisions as a board to:
- act in good faith in the best interests of the company;
- use powers conferred on them for the proper purpose;
- avoid conflicts of interest; and
- exercise whatever skill they possessed, with reasonable care, when acting in the company's interest.

That said, the common law duties, and the case law that developed around common law duties, should not be ignored, as they remain important for interpretation and application of the general duties.

Duty to Act in Good Faith

The case of *Smith v. Fawcett Ltd* (1942) established that a board has a duty to act in good faith in what they consider to be the best interests of the company. They should not use their powers for the benefit of third parties or anyone else. If a director is found to have acted honestly, but not in the best interests of the company, he is said to be in breach of the duty to act in good faith. This was seen in the case of *Re W & M Royth Ltd* (1967). In this case, a director, who was in poor health, entered into a service contract providing for a widow's pension. However, the director was held not to be acting bona fide in the interests of the company and so the contract was declared void.

Duty to Exercise Powers for a Proper Purpose

This common law duty provided that directors should act within the powers given to them by the company's Memorandum and Articles of Association. Should a director fail to act within these powers, these actions may be *ultra vires* or constitute a breach of duty or both. Even if a director is acting in good faith in the interests of the company, directors should still use their powers for the purposes for which they were intended. For example, in the case of *Hogg v. Cramphorn Ltd* (1967), directors issued shares with special voting rights to trustees of a scheme set up for the benefit of the company's employees in order to forestall a takeover offer. It was held that, although the directors had acted in good faith, they had breached their duty to the company by the improper use of their power to issue shares.

Duty to Avoid Conflicts of Interest

Under this common law duty, a director should not put himself in a position where there is an actual or potential conflict between his personal interest and his duty to the company. A conflict arises if a director seeks to exploit the assets or opportunities of a company for his own benefit. For example, in the case of *Cooke v. Deaks* (1916), the director shareholders of a railway company negotiated a contract on its behalf but then subsequently took the contract for themselves. They passed a resolution in a general meeting renouncing any legal claims against themselves. A minority shareholder sued to set aside the transaction. The court held that the contract belonged to the company. It further held that to allow the directors to retain the profits "would be to allow a majority to oppress the minority". This case was reaffirmed in the case of *Regal Hastings Ltd v. Gulliver* (1942). In this case, a company owned a cinema and the directors decided that it should acquire two others with a view to selling all three as a going concern. A subsidiary was formed to take lease of the other two. In order to provide the subsidiary with sufficient paid-up capital to satisfy the lessors, the directors took up a number of shares in the subsidiary themselves. They then sold the shares and put the money into the subsidiary. Consequently, the directors made a huge profit. The buyers issued proceedings against the directors claiming that the profit belonged to the company. The court held that the directors, in the course of their management of a company, can avail of opportunities and special knowledge. However, they must account to the company for that profit even if there is nothing improper in what they do and the company does not suffer.

Duty of Skill and Care

This common law duty imposes upon directors the duty to exercise whatever skill they possess and to do so with reasonable care. The leading case on the nature and extent of the duty of skill and care is that of *Re City Equitable Fire Insurance Co. Ltd* (1925). The facts of this case are discussed above.

Disqualification of Directors

The Company Directors Disqualification (Northern Ireland) Order 2002 has been amended by the Company Directors Disqualification (Amendment) (Northern Ireland) Order 2005 (2005 No. 1454 (N.I. 9)), and also by the Small Business Enterprise and Employment Act 2015; a court may disqualify a person from being a director, liquidator, administrator, receiver or manager of a company, and from being concerned in the promotion or management of any company.

There are eight grounds on which a court can make such an Order. These are as follows:

1. where a person is convicted of an indictable offence in connection with the promotion, formation, management or liquidation of a company or with the receivership or management of a company's property;
2. where it appears that a person has been persistently in default in relation to provisions of company legislation;
3. where it appears in the course of winding up a company that a person has been guilty of fraudulent trading, carrying on business with intent to defraud creditors or for fraudulent purpose;
4. where a person is found to be unfit to be concerned in the management of a company;
5. where a director was involved in certain competition violations;
6. where a director has participated in wrongful trading under Articles 177 and 178 of the Insolvency (Northern Ireland) Order 1989 (1989 No. 2405 (N.I. 19)), as amended by the Insolvency (Northern Ireland) Order 2005 (2005 No. 1455 (N.I. 10));
7. where a director has been convicted of a company-related offence overseas; or
8. where a director has instructed a disqualified director.

The latter two grounds were introduced by the SBEEA 2015.

A court is under an obligation to make an Order if any of these situations occurs:

1. the person has been a director of a company which has at any time become insolvent;
2. a director's conduct as a director of a company makes him unfit to be concerned in the management of a company;
3. the nature and extent of harm the misconduct has had; or
4. the director's track record in running failed companies.

The latter two were introduced by the SBEEA 2015.

The Disqualification Period

In *Re Seven Oaks Stationers Retail Ltd* (1991), the Court of Appeal set the guidelines for disqualification of directors. It stated that:

"... the top bracket of disqualification for periods over 10 years should be reserved for particularly serious cases. These may include cases where a director who has already had one period of disqualification imposed on him was to be disqualified yet again. The minimum bracket of 2–5 years' disqualification should be applied where the disqualification is mandatory but the case is, relatively, not very serious. The middle bracket of disqualification from 6–10 years should apply for very serious cases which do not merit the top bracket."

Applying for a Disqualification Order

In order to obtain a disqualification Order against a person, an application should be made to the appropriate court by the Secretary of State. Administrators, receivers and liquidators have a statutory duty to report to the Department for the Economy directors of companies in whose affairs they have become involved and where they believe the necessary conditions for a Disqualification Order have been fulfilled. The Secretary of State then decides whether to proceed the application to court for an Order. Any application must be made within three years of the date on which a company became insolvent.

Authority of Directors

A company is an artificial person and therefore cannot make contracts or enter into transactions itself. It therefore acts through the medium of agents and all directors are agents of the company. The law of agency has already been discussed in **Chapter 9**, but it will now be considered as it relates to directors.

An agent can act only within what is known as the agent's authority. As we have seen in **Chapter 9**, there are two basic kinds of authority:
- actual authority; and
- ostensible/apparent authority.

Actual Authority

Actual authority is the authority given to an agent of a company to bind the principal to a particular contract. A board of directors has actual authority to bind a company. This is stated in the case of *Freeman & Loughier v. Buckhurst Park Properties (Mangal) Ltd* (1964):

"... an actual authority is a legal relationship between principal and agent created by consensual agreement to which they alone are parties. Its scope is to be ascertained by applying ordinary principles of construction of contracts, including any proper implications from the express words used, the usages of the trade, or the course of business between the parties. To this agreement, the contractor is a stranger; he may be totally ignorant of the existence of any authority on the part of the agent. Nevertheless, if the agent does enter into a contract pursuant to the actual authority, it does create contractual rights and liabilities between the principal and the contractor."

On that basis, an individual director may have authority to bind a company but this authority must be permitted by the Articles of Association. If an agent acts outside the limits of his actual authority, the company, as its principal, is bound by all contracts he enters into.

Ostensible Authority

Ostensible or apparent authority is the authority of an agent as it appears to others.

In the case of *Armagas Ltd v. Mundogas SA* (1986), the court described ostensible authority as authority which "comes about where the principal, by words or conduct, has represented that the agent has actual authority, and the party dealing with the agent has entered into a contract with him in reliance on that representation". Based upon this description, it therefore can be said that ostensible authority arises were a company makes a representation to a third party which conveys to the third party that the director has authority to bind the company and the third party enters into the agreement with the director in reliance upon that statement.

For example, in the case of *Freeman & Loughier v. Buckhurst Park Properties (Mangal) Ltd* (1964), the director of a company entered into a contract with a firm of architects. On a later date, the company wanted to get out of the contract and relied on the fact that the director in question was just an ordinary director and so did not have authority to bind the company. However, the director had called himself the Managing Director and the other directors had permitted him to do so. This therefore amounted to representation from the company that he had authority to bind the company and the company was held to be bound to the contract he had signed.

The rule in Turquand's case

The *Turquand* case (*Royal British Bank v. Turquand* (1856)) provided authority for the rule that outside third parties are obliged to presume that actions carried out within a company are done and carried out according to correct procedures, as required by the Articles of Association. In this case, the Articles of a company provided that its directors could borrow above a certain sum of money only if they were authorised by an ordinary resolution at a company meeting. However, the directors, in this case, borrowed in excess without approval and later argued that the loan was invalid. It was held by the court that the loan was valid. As borrowing was within the company's general powers, the court decided that the bank had no way of establishing if an ordinary resolution had been passed in the case. As the bank were 'outsiders', they were entitled to assume that all internal procedures had been carried out correctly, such as the taking of votes. On that basis, the court ruled that the loan was valid and had to be repaid by the company.

This rule is now covered by section 40 of CA 2006, which states that any limitation in the company's constitution on the power of its directors to bind the company is ineffective. This would seem to render the rule in *Turquand's* case no longer relevant. However, section 40 does not operate in favour of a person who is not acting in good faith. That said, it seems unlikely that a court would give a person the benefit of the rule in *Turquand's* case if they had not been acting in good faith.

References

- Derek French, Stephen Mayson and Christopher Ryan, *Mayson, French and Ryan on Company Law* (26th Edition, Oxford University Press, 2009–2010)
- Paul L. Davies, *Gower and Davies' Principles of Modern Company Law* (8th Edition, Thomson Sweet & Maxwell, 2008).
- Martha Bruce, *Rights and Duties of Directors* (9th Edition, Tottel Publishing, 2009).

REVIEW QUESTIONS

(See Suggested Solutions at the end of this textbook.)

Question 13.1

Edward is an executive director of Giselle Ltd ('Giselle'), an accessories manufacturing company, and is employed under a contract of service. Fairways Fabric has been a supplier to Giselle for the past five years. Two months ago Edward ordered a large quantity of fabric from Fairways Fabric and billed it to the company's account. However, there is no record of this order arriving at the company. Upon examination the company discovers that this order was sent to a different delivery address, which is in fact Edward's home address. The company undertakes an investigation of this incident and discovers that Edward has been using the company account to order goods to establish a rival accessories manufacturing business from his home. Upon making this discovery, Giselle removes Edward as a director and is refusing to pay for the fabric supplied by Fairways Fabrics.

Requirement: Discuss the main fiduciary duties that directors owe the company and determine whether Edward has breached these duties and the likely penalties that can be imposed where a breach occurs.

(Source: Chartered Accountants Ireland, CAP 1, Summer 2010,
Extract: Q3(c))

Question 13.2

You have been approached by your manager who has indicated that he will be taking you along to a presentation that he will be giving to an audit client. The presentation is entitled "The Challenges Facing Directors in the 21st Century". In order to assist him in preparing for this presentation, your manager has asked you to draft a memo for him.

Requirement: In your memo, discuss any FOUR of the possible six types of director that a company can have.

(Source: Chartered Accountants Ireland, CAP 1, Summer 2009,
Extract: Q1(a))

Question 13.3

You are approached by a business client, a venture capitalist, who has recently been invited to become a non-executive director of a Northern Ireland manufacturing company, and who is completely unaware of the nature and extent of his obligations in this role.

Requirement: Your client has requested that you prepare a memo outlining to him the following:
(a) The distinction between an executive and non-executive director.
(b) An outline of the duties imposed upon a company director in relation to their interaction with the company.

(Source: Chartered Accountants Ireland, CAP 1, Summer 2010,
Extract: Q3(a) and (b))

Question 13.4

Rose, Hyacinth and Petunia are the sole shareholders and directors of Daffodils and Dandelions Ltd, a company that specialises in providing floral displays for corporate clients. Rose has been delegated the position of managing director of the company by the board.

Daffodils and Dandelions Ltd has been trading successfully for the past eight years and recently the directors have been considering moving the business to larger premises. Last week, they looked at a vacant store in Belfast's city centre. They all agreed that the store was an ideal location, but both Hyacinth and Petunia considered the cost of the lease excessive and decided to keep looking for a more cost-effective solution.

Rose was very disappointed with Hyacinth and Petunia's decision, and after two weeks of viewing other premises, and having found nothing suitable, she signed a lease with the proprietors of the city-centre store on behalf of the company, without consulting with her co-directors. When Hyacinth and Petunia discover that Rose has ignored their wishes and signed the lease, they are extremely annoyed. They are considering removing Rose as a company director and replacing her with Lilly.

Requirement: Explain to Hyacinth and Petunia the procedure necessary to effect the removal of Rose as company director and the appointment of Lilly in her place.

(Source: Chartered Accountants Ireland, CAP 1, Law for Accountants (NI), Summer 2011, Extract: Q4(a))

Question 13.5

Arlington Ltd is a Belfast-based manufacturing company. In 2010, the company experienced significant financial problems and, as a consequence, it has accumulated considerable unpaid debts. In April 2011, an application was made to the High Court by one of the creditors of the company to have it placed in compulsory liquidation on the grounds that the company cannot pay its debts as they fall due. This application was granted and the Official Receiver was appointed as the Compulsory Liquidator. Since the commencement of his appointment, the Official Receiver has discovered the following irregularities:

1. In January 2011, Ethan, one of the directors of Arlington, purchased new haulage vehicles on behalf of the company at a cost of £100,000. However, the Articles of Association of Arlington state that the directors are prohibited from creating credit contracts on behalf of the company in excess of £50,000 without first calling a meeting of the board of directors and obtaining its authorisation. According to Arlington's Company Secretary, no such meeting has taken place.

2. In February 2011, when the company was already insolvent, the managing director of Arlington borrowed £40,000 from the Bank of Belfast to finance the purchase of a new piece of machinery in an attempt to diversify the product base of the company and generate new business. However, this strategy was not successful and resulted in a net loss for the company of £60,000.

3. In February 2011, Ryan, the procurement director of Arlington, authorised an order with a supplier, Florida Ltd, for £200,000. Two weeks after the order was placed, Ryan spent two weeks on holiday at a five-star hotel, in Florida, courtesy of Florida Ltd.

Requirement:
(a) Evaluate whether the credit contract created by Ethan on behalf of Arlington is valid and binding upon the company, or whether it can be invalidated based on Ethan's lack of authority to create this contract.
(b) Discuss the general duties of directors, as set down by the Companies Act 2006, and assess whether the actions of the managing director of Arlington, in borrowing £40,000 from the Bank of Belfast, and the actions of Ryan, amount to a breach of any of these duties.
        (Source: Chartered Accountants Ireland, CAP 1, Law for Accountants (NI),
                            Autumn 2011, Extract: Q1(a) and (b))

Question 13.6

Brendan and Barbara are a husband-and-wife team who have been running a successful hairdressing business, in the form of a partnership, for the last 10 years. They now want to expand the business and to open branches across Northern Ireland. To support this they are considering converting their partnership to a limited company. They now seek advice in relation to the following matters.

Requirement:
(a) They wish to know the people who are ineligible to act as a director of a company. List any FOUR people who are ineligible to act as a company director and state the minimum number of directors that a Northern Ireland company must have.
(b) Explain the difference between an executive and non-executive director.
(c) Identify and explain briefly any FIVE duties of a director as laid down by the Companies Act 2006.
        (Source: Chartered Accountants Ireland, CAP 1, Law for Accountants (NI),
                                        Summer 2012, Extract: Q1)

Question 13.7

Regal Airways Limited ('Regal') was dissatisfied with the quality of passenger meals being provided by its catering contractor and, as a result, the directors took a decision to look for alternative caterers. After much debate and following some lobbying from one of Regal's directors, Sam, they decided to offer the contract to Dragon Catering Services ('Dragon').

Two months after this decision was taken, it came to the attention of Regal's board of directors that Sam's sister is the managing director and that she has a 50% ownership interest in Dragon. Following further investigation, Regal's directors also discovered that Sam holds a 25% ownership interest in Dragon and the remaining 25% is held by Sam's brother-in-law. Following this discovery, Regal is considering taking legal action against Sam for breach of his statutory duties and is also considering removing him as a company director of Regal.

Requirement:
(a) Explain the statutory duties in relation to directors' disclosure obligations regarding contracts. Determine whether the actions of Sam amount to a breach of his statutory duties to Regal.
(b) Discuss the procedure with which Regal must comply in order to effect a lawful removal of Sam as company director.
(Source: Chartered Accountants Ireland, CAP 1, Law for Accountants (NI), Autumn 2013, Extract: Q4(a))

Question 13.8

Porter was an executive director and de facto managing director of Cupcake and Coffee Ltd ('Cupcake'), a nationwide coffeehouse chain, since the company's incorporation in 2001. Last month at an extraordinary general meeting of the company, a resolution was passed removing Porter as a company director. The rationale for this decision is that the company discovered that Porter had lodged a number of cheques payable to Cupcake into his personal bank account. It was also noted that Porter had entered into a number of profitable leases with Cupcake, using a company which, on paper, was owned by his brother, to disguise his true identity. Since his removal, Porter has received a letter from the Secretary of State notifying him that an application has been brought to the High Court seeking his disqualification as a company director. Porter has contacted you for advice in this regard.

Requirement: Write a memo to Porter that:
(a) Explains the effect of a Disqualification Order.
(b) States any SIX grounds upon which such an Order can be imposed.
(c) Advises him on the effect of acting in breach of a Disqualification Order.
(Source: Chartered Accountants Ireland, CAP 1, Law for Accountants (NI), Summer 2014, Extract: Q3(c)(i)–(iii))

Question 13.9

Simon and John are owners of, and partners in, a local heating business called Green Heating Partnership ('GHP'). GHP has been in operation for

10 years but due to the growth of the business in the last two years, they are now changing the status of the business to that of a company and are calling the business Green Heating Limited ('GHL').

Simon and John, now executive directors of GHL, appoint you as the auditor of GHL. They want to meet to discuss with you their obligations as directors under the Companies Act 2006. Among other things that they want to discuss with you are the directors' report and directors' duties. You remind them that one of their first obligations as directors is to prepare their directors' report (section 415(1) CA 2006). You also discuss with them the statutory duties of directors that were introduced in addition to directors' common law duties.

Requirement:
(a) State any FOUR items that should be included in a directors' report.
(b) State any FOUR statutory duties of directors under the Companies Act 2006.
   (Source: Chartered Accountants Ireland, CAP 1, Law for Accountants (NI),
   Summer 2015, Extract: Q2(a) and (b))

Question 13.10

The directors of Chancery Furniture Ltd ('Chancery') were anxious because of declining sales figures, and decided to import a range of reclining sofa chairs. They were able to purchase this furniture at a discounted price, but they decided to sell the furniture at a 25% mark-up in order to boost sales. Though they were made aware in advance of the purchase that a number of the reclining sofa chairs were defective, they failed to disclose this information to the public when selling the sofas. Two weekends ago, they put the sofas out for sale and by the end of the first day they had sold 20 sofa chairs. However, last weekend, the directors were contacted by all 20 purchasers who informed them that the reclining sofa chairs were faulty and all of the purchasers had fallen off the chairs and had ended up in casualty. One purchaser suffered a broken hip, five purchasers suffered fractured arms, six purchasers suffered a fractured leg and the remainder suffered minor sprains.

As a result, all of the consumers are now threatening joint legal action against the directors for breach of the Consumer Protection (Northern Ireland) Order 1987.

As a consequence of the actions of the directors of Chancery, the shareholders have requisitioned a meeting to remove two of the executive directors of the company and have decided to appoint a non-executive director to the board. They have asked you for advice in relation to these matters.

Requirement:
(a) Outline the procedure that must be followed to effect a lawful removal of a company director.
(b) Explain the role of a non-executive director of a company.

(Source: Chartered Accountants Ireland, CAP 1, Law for Accountants (NI), Autumn 2015, Extract: Q4(c)–(d))

Chapter 14

LOAN CAPITAL AND INSOLVENCY

LOAN CAPITAL

Introduction

As discussed in the previous chapter, a company can finance itself not only through the issue of shares but also through loans, i.e. the company incurs debt, which is known as 'loan capital'. The first half of this chapter will examine the law relating to the loan capital in a company.

A company has an implied power to borrow money, although an express power to borrow is also usually given in the company's Memorandum of Association. It is not unusual for this express power to set a limit on the company's borrowing by stating a fixed sum beyond which the company cannot borrow.

In addition, it is usual for lenders of money to a company, within the contract for the loan, to stipulate a form of security against property of the company if the loan is not repaid on time. This security is given either in the form of fixed charges over land or fixed assets and floating charges. This chapter will examine such charges.

The second part of the chapter will look at the law relating to company insolvency. An insolvency situation arises when a company can no longer continue as a 'going concern' and the end result is usually the liquidation of the company. This part of the chapter will explain a voluntary and compulsory liquidation as well as considering the process of administration and a company voluntary arrangement, which are both alternatives to winding up.

Debentures

Most loans are by way of debentures. A debenture is a document acknowledging a debt by a company. There is no legal definition of a debenture. However, section 738 of the Companies Act 2006 states that the term 'debenture' includes "debenture stock, bonds and any other securities of a company, whether or not constituting a charge on the assets of the company".

Furthermore, the courts have also not given the term debenture a precise meaning. Mr Justice Chitty lamented over a century ago:

"I cannot find any precise definition of the term, it is not either in law or commerce as a strict technical term or what is called a term of art."

Types of Debentures

Three types of debentures exist:
- **Single Debenture** An example of a single debenture is a bank loan or an overdraft and this is the most common type of debenture.
- **Series of Debentures** These are a group of separate loans. For debentures issued in a series, it is usual to provide expressly that they are to rank *pari passu*, i.e. equally. This is because loans rank in priority according to the time at which they are made. If such an express provision was not made, the debentures and the series would rank for priority of payment and security according to the date of issue. Alternatively, if they were all issued on the same day, they would rank in numerical order.
- **Debenture Stock** Debenture stock is used by large PLCs to raise money from the public. A number of lenders subscribe for debentures. The loan is then treated as part of an overall stock figure.

The Debenture Trust Deed

A 'debenture trust deed' is a legal document. It can be used for a series of debentures or for debenture stock. The charge securing the debentures is made in favour of trustees who are appointed to act on behalf of all debenture holders. Trustees are usually appointed and paid for by the company.

Debentures can be secured or unsecured. However, most debentures are secured as it provides the debenture holder with a better prospect of being repaid if a company becomes insolvent. The three most common forms of granting security are:
- legal and equitable mortgages;
- pledges; and
- charges.

Mortgages

A mortgage gives a creditor security interest in a particular piece of property without the creditor taking possession of the property. Mortgages can either be legal or equitable.
- **Legal Mortgage** In a legal mortgage, the legal title to a property is transferred to a creditor on the condition that it will be given back when the obligation is met. If the mortgagee defaults in repayment of a mortgage, the mortgagor may be able to sell the property.

- **Equitable Mortgage** This is a more common type of mortgage. In such a mortgage, the mortgagor transfers the equitable interest in the property to the mortgagee (for example, by depositing the title deeds of the property with the bank). If the mortgagee defaults in payment, the mortgagor has the option of selling the property.

A Pledge

A pledge is a means of making a person's goods security by giving possession of the goods to a creditor on the condition that the possession will be returned when an obligation is met.

Charges

A loan can be secured either by a fixed or floating charge.

Fixed Charge

A fixed charge is a charge on a specific asset owned by a company. The company cannot deal with that asset unless it has the permission of the chargee. Fixed charges are often called specific charges.

Floating Charge

In contrast, a floating charge is a general charge over a class of the company's assets, such as plant, machinery and tools, or stocks of goods for sale. A floating charge confers on the chargee the right to take for payment of the secured debt only when the floating charge crystallises. In effect, a floating charge hovers over all of the company's assets and becomes effective only at the moment of crystallisation (for example, the winding-up of a company). The benefit of a floating charge over a fixed charge is that until a floating charge crystallises, i.e. converts to a fixed charge, a company may buy, sell, replace and otherwise deal with assets of the company throughout its normal course of business transactions without making reference to the chargee. In a fixed-charge situation, reference must always be made to the chargee.

Crystallisation of Floating Charges

A floating charge will crystallise in one of the following four situations:
1. if a winding up of the business commences;
2. if a company ceases business;
3. if an event occurs for which the charge provides for automatic crystallisation; or
4. if a company defaults and the debenture holder takes steps to enforce the security either by appointing a receiver or by applying to the court to do so.

The effect of a floating charge crystallising is that it automatically fixes and settles onto the class of assets that it has been attached to. The crucial feature of a floating charge is that the rights of the charge holder are dormant up until the moment of crystallisation. Upon crystallisation, the chargee's equitable rights come into play.

Priority of Charges

Charges must be paid in order of priority. These are as follows:

1. **Fixed Charges** Fixed charges rank according to the order of creation. If two fixed charges over the same factory were created on 1 January and 1 February respectively, the charge created on 1 January would take priority over the February charge.
2. **Preferential Debts** Preferential debts are defined in Article 4 of the Insolvency (Northern Ireland) Order 1989 and include debts due to HMRC social security contributions, contributions to occupational pension schemes and employee remuneration.
3. **Floating Charges** A floating charge created before a fixed charge will take priority over the latter only if, when the latter was created, the fixed charge had notice of the floating charge.

Note, however, that two floating charges take priority according to the time of their creation.

Fixed-charge Receiverships

As discussed above, a fixed or floating charge can be created over an asset or a group of assets. A fixed-charge receiver can be appointed by a lender with a mortgage, charge or other security over specified assets. The function of a fixed-charge receiver is to go into a company, sell off the charged assets and pay off the principal and interest due on the debenture.

How a Fixed-charge Receiver is Appointed The starting point for the appointment of a fixed-charge receiver is a review of the loan facility and/ or security pursuant to which the appointment was made. If a loan is repayable on demand, a lender can start the process of appointing a fixed-charge receiver by serving a letter of demand on the borrower at any time. However, if the debt is not paid following demand, a fixed-charge receiver is appointed under the terms of the appointment document, which would be laid out under the terms of the loan. An appointment of a fixed-charge receiver is effective from the time of signature of an acceptance by or on behalf of the receiver.

The Effect of an Appointment of a Fixed-charge Receiver When a fixed-term receiver is appointed, any floating charges immediately crystallise. Directors cannot make management decisions in relation to the asset over which the charge relates. The job of the receiver is then to sell the charged asset for the best price in the circumstances. Within 28 days of being appointed as a fixed-charge receiver, a receiver must issue a notice to all known creditors confirming his appointment. The receiver must also sign, within three months, a statement to the registrar company and debenture holder detailing the events leading up to his appointment and the details relating to the disposal of the assets in question.

COMPANY INSOLVENCY

The second half of this chapter will now examine the law relating to company insolvency. The legislation governing company insolvency is the Insolvency (Northern Ireland) Order 1989 (1989 No. 2405) and the Insolvency (Northern Ireland) Order 2005 (2005 No. 1455).

Liquidation

Liquidation is the process by which the life of a company or a partnership is brought to an end. Its property is administered for the benefit of its members and creditors. At the end of a liquidation process, a company or a partnership will cease to exist. The liquidation procedure will ensure that the company's affairs have all been dealt with and all its assets are realised. At the end of the liquidation process, a liquidator will apply to have a company removed from the Registrar of Companies.

Article 102 of the Insolvency (Northern Ireland) Order 1989 lays out seven grounds on which a company may be wound up by the High Court:
1. the company has passed a special resolution deciding that the company should be wound up by the court;
2. the company has been registered as a public limited company but has not been issued with a trading certificate;
3. the company is an old public company which has failed to re-register;
4. the company has not commenced business within a year of incorporation or has suspended its trading for a whole year;
5. at the time at which a moratorium for the company under Article 14A comes to an end, no voluntary arrangement approved under Part II has effect in relation to the company;
6. the company cannot pay its debts; or
7. the company should be wound up because the court forms the opinion that it would be just and equitable to wind up the company.

The grounds listed as 6 and 7 above are the two most common on which a company is wound up by the High Court and will be considered now.

Company's Inability to Pay its Debts

Further to Article 102(f) of the Insolvency (Northern Ireland) Order 1989, a company is deemed unable to pay its debts if:

- a creditor for more than £750 has served on the company a written demand for payment and, within the next three weeks, the company has neither paid the debt nor given security for its payment;
- judgment has been obtained against the company for a debt (normally in excess of £750) and enforcement via the Enforcement of Judgments Office has resulted in a Certificate of Unenforceability;
- the court is satisfied that the company is unable to pay its debts as they fall due; or
- the court is satisfied that the value of the company's assets is less than the amount of its liabilities, taking into account its contingent and prospective liabilities.

The Just and Equitable Ground

Further to Article 102(g) of the Insolvency (Northern Ireland) Order 1989, the court can make an Order that a company be wound up if the circumstances of justice or equity so demand. Article 102(g) allows a company to be wound up on just and equitable grounds. This can cover the following situations:

- if the main object of a company has failed as a company;
- if the main purpose for which the company was formed has been fulfilled or has failed or if the company is engaging in acts which are outside the objects of a company;
- if there is deadlock in the management of the business because the directors cannot agree on matters; or
- where the company is in a quasi-partnership and the mutual confidence between the parties has broken down. This is illustrated in the case of *Ebrahimi v. Westbourne Galleries Ltd* (1973) (a case which was discussed in **Chapter 11**) as the company was a quasi-partnership and there was a justifiable lack of confidence in the management.

There are two types of liquidation:

- the first is a *compulsory liquidation*, which begins with a court Order; and
- the alternative is a *voluntary liquidation*, which is the most common type of liquidation and which occurs when the members of the company pass a resolution to wind up the company.

Each type of liquidation will now be considered in detail below.

1. Compulsory Liquidation

In a compulsory liquidation situation, a winding-up petition is presented to the High Court under one of the grounds listed in Article 102(g) (as stated above) by a creditor of the company. This petition will state that the company owes the creditor a sum of money that the company is unable to pay.

The Official Receiver The Official Receiver is an officer of the High Court and therefore a civil servant. He is appointed by the High Court to handle a compulsory liquidation and so he is a liquidator. His role is to inform a company's creditors and shareholders that the company is being wound up. However, if there are significant assets involved in the winding up of a company, the Department of Enterprise, Trade and Industry (DETI; from May 2016, the Department for the Economy) can appoint an insolvency practitioner instead of the official receiver to manage the affairs of the company while it is being wound up.

Insolvency Practitioners As stated above, sometimes the Department of Enterprise, Trade and Investment or the creditors or shareholders of a company can appoint insolvency practitioners to manage the liquidation of the company. Insolvency practitioners are usually accountants or solicitors who are qualified practitioners under one of the recognised professional bodies for insolvency.

The role of either the insolvency practitioner or the official receiver is effectively to realise the company's assets, pay the fees and charges arising from liquidation and thereafter share out any surplus funds to creditors. Occasionally, surplus funds may be available for distribution to shareholders but this is very rare.

Appeals against a Winding-up Order There are a number of instances when winding-up proceedings can be stopped but, in reality, these are very rare. First, winding-up orders can be stopped if the court cancels a winding-up order. A company can apply to the court for the winding-up order to be rescinded if the company believes that the court did not hear all the relevant facts when making the winding-up order. An application to have a winding-up order rescinded should be made within seven days of the order being made. The application to have the winding-up order stopped is very onerous and a stringent approach is adopted by the High Court in deciding whether or not to grant the application.

Secondly, a company can appeal against a winding-up order. As a result of an appeal, the court can make the decision to rescind the winding-up order.

Appeals against a winding-up order must be made within four weeks of the Order being made.

Finally, a liquidator, official receiver, creditor or shareholder can apply to the court to have liquidation proceedings 'stayed', either permanently or temporarily. If liquidation proceedings are stayed permanently, the result is that directors regain control of the company. Applications to stay liquidation proceedings can be made any time after a winding-up order has been made.

Effects of an Order for Compulsory Liquidation Once an order for compulsory liquidation has been made by the court, all floating charges crystallise, the employees of the company are automatically dismissed and the roles of the company's directors all but cease. The liquidator appointed will assume the powers of management previously held by directors. Moreover, any legal proceedings in progress against the company are automatically halted once the order for compulsory liquidation is passed. Furthermore, no further legal proceedings may be commenced after this date.

Under Article 111 of the Insolvency (Northern Ireland) Order 1989, within 21 days of the making of the compulsory liquidation order, a statement of affairs must be delivered to the liquidator or official receiver that has been verified by one or more officers of the company, i.e. the directors or Company Secretary. This statement will show the assets and liabilities of the company, it will list the creditors and it will stipulate any security that the creditors may hold.

At this stage, the role of the official receiver or liquidator is to investigate, under Article 112 of the Insolvency (Northern Ireland) Order 1989, the causes for the failure of the company and it must consider generally the promotion, formation, business dealings and affairs of the company. If the official receiver deems it appropriate, he or she may make a report to the court on these matters. Such a report is evidence of the facts stated in the report.

Furthermore, within 12 weeks of the winding-up order, the official receiver must decide whether to summon meetings of creditors and contributories. If the official receiver decides not to do so, he must inform the court, the creditors and the contributories. The purpose of this meeting is to give the creditors and contributories the opportunity to appoint their own nominee as a permanent liquidator to replace the official receiver and also to appoint a liquidation committee to work with the liquidator. The purpose of this committee is to assist the liquidator and act as the link between the company and the liquidator.

That said, if an official receiver has reason to believe that there is little interest among the creditors and that the creditors will be unable to appoint a liquidator, he can dispense with this meeting but he must inform the court, the creditors and the contributories of the decision. Furthermore, at a later stage, he can be required to call a meeting if at least 25% in value of the creditors require him to do so. If no meeting is held, or a meeting is held and no liquidator is appointed, the official receiver thereafter continues to act in the capacity of a liquidator. However, if the creditors do hold a meeting and decide to appoint their own nominee, this person automatically becomes liquidator. The person appointed to act as liquidator must be a qualified insolvency practitioner. A notice of the order for compulsory liquidation and of the appointment of a liquidator is given to the Registrar of Companies and must be published in *The Belfast Gazette*.

Completion of Compulsory Liquidation Once a liquidator completes his tasks, he is under an obligation to make a report to the Registrar of Companies. The Registrar will examine the accounts presented. Once the accounts have been registered, the company will automatically be dissolved three months after this date. A liquidator can make an application to the High Court asking for the deferral of this date and that the dissolution of the company should take place with an Order for the High Court. Equally, the official receiver can also apply to the Registrar of Companies for an early dissolution of the company if its realisable assets will not cover its expenses and no further investigation is required.

2. Voluntary Liquidation

Voluntary liquidation is the second type of liquidation method open to a company and is the most common type of liquidation. As shareholders own a company, only the shareholders of a company can put the company into a voluntary liquidation. There are two types of voluntary liquidation:
  • members' voluntary liquidation; and
  • creditors' voluntary liquidation.

Members' Voluntary Liquidation A members' voluntary liquidation takes place when the shareholders of a company decide to put the company into liquidation. The directors, or a majority of the directors, must make a declaration of solvency before such a liquidation can be passed. This declaration must contain the latest practicable statement of the company's assets and liabilities and it must further state that, after enquiry, in their opinion, the company will be able to pay its debts within a period of not more than 12 months. This declaration must be made no more than five weeks before the passing of the resolution for the voluntary winding up. A resolution for a voluntary winding up must be made at a general shareholders' meeting. This resolution must also appoint one or more liquidators to the company. If it subsequently transpires that the company was not solvent, the liquidation automatically becomes a creditors' voluntary liquidation.

Creditors' Voluntary Liquidation A creditors' voluntary liquidation occurs if the majority of directors do not make a declaration of solvency or if the company is insolvent. In this instance, the shareholders vote for a voluntary liquidation by holding a general meeting of the company and passing a resolution for voluntary winding up. At this meeting, an authorised insolvency practitioner is appointed. Furthermore, a meeting of the creditors of the company must also be called and, at this meeting, all creditors should receive details of the company's financial affairs. The creditors are given authority to nominate a liquidator to wind up the company.

Once a liquidator has been appointed, he or she takes control of the company's affairs and, as with a compulsory liquidation, all powers of the directors cease. The role of the liquidator essentially becomes the same as the role of the liquidator in a compulsory liquidation in that the liquidator is under a duty to dispose of all of the company's assets and, after paying the costs and expenses of the liquidation, distribute any remaining money to creditors.

In a voluntary liquidation, company directors are under a duty to provide information about the company's affairs to the liquidator and attend interviews with the liquidator as and when reasonably required. Moreover, the directors are also under a duty to look after and hand over the company's assets to the liquidator, together with all books, records, bank statements, insurance policies and any other papers which relate to the assets and liabilities of the company.

A voluntary liquidation ends when the company is dissolved once a final meeting has been held by the liquidator. In any instance, the length of a liquidation always depends on the circumstances of the individual case. However, once the process has been completed, the company is dissolved and ceases to exist.

It should be noted that a members' voluntary liquidation can be converted into a creditors' voluntary liquidation if a liquidator decides that the company will be unable to pay its debts in full from the period stated in the directors' declaration of solvency. In order to do so, a liquidator must hold a meeting of creditors no later than the 28th day after the day upon which it formed the opinion that the debts could not be paid in full. Creditors must be sent out notice of a creditors' meeting no less than seven days before the day of the meeting and a notice must be published in *The Belfast Gazette*. At the meeting, the liquidator will also make out a statement of the company's affairs.

Administration

The concept of administration in Northern Ireland came into force through the Insolvency (Northern Ireland) Order 1989, as amended by the Insolvency (Northern Ireland) Order 2005 (Consequential Amendments) Order (Northern Ireland) 2015 (2015 No. 159). The purpose of an administration is to try to rescue a company and to achieve a better result for the company's creditors as a whole than would be likely if the company were wound up. An administration is, in effect, an alternative to liquidation and acts as a last rescue remedy for the company. Once an administration order is passed by the court, it is no longer possible to petition a court for a winding-up order against the company. Similarly, once an order for winding up has been made, an administration order cannot be granted.

In order to put the company into administration, a party must petition the court for an administration order. Such a party can either be the company itself (that is, a majority of the members), the directors of the company, or one or more creditors of the company. It should be noted that individual members cannot apply to the court for an administration order. A court will grant an administration order if it is satisfied that the company is, or is likely to be, unable to pay its debts and the court is satisfied that the administration order is likely to achieve the purpose of rescuing the company. The application to the court will also name the person the applicants want to be the administrator.

Once an application for administration is made, a company, as stated above, cannot be wound up. Furthermore, no charge, hire purchase or retention of title clause can be enforced against the company without the consent of the court. In addition, no other proceedings can be commenced or proceeded with against the company without the consent of the court. This is called a 'moratorium'.

Administrator's Duties

An administrator has a number of legal duties. First, he must take custody or control of all the property of the company. Secondly, he must send a notice of his appointment to the company immediately, to the Registrar of Companies within 14 days, and to all the creditors within 28 days.

In addition, the administrator can require, within 21 days, a statement of affairs from officers or employees, giving details of the assets, debts and liabilities of the company, the names and addresses of creditors and securities held by creditors.

Furthermore, within three months of the administration order, the administrator must send to the Registrar, the creditors and the members, a statement of proposals for achieving the purpose of administration. He must lay the statement before a meeting of creditors. The purpose of the meeting is to approve the proposals.

If the creditors' meeting does not approve the proposals, the court may discharge the administration order or make any order it thinks fit. Furthermore, if the meeting approves the proposals, it may appoint a committee of creditors. The committee may require the administrator to attend before it and give such information as it may reasonably require. Any creditor or member may apply to the court for an order on the grounds that the company is or has been managed by the administrator in a manner unfairly prejudicial to the creditors or members or that any other act or admission of the administrator is or would be so prejudicial. The court may make any order it thinks fit.

Variation of Court Order

An administrator may apply to the court at any time to discharge or vary an administration order on the following grounds:
1. it appears to him that the purpose of the administration order has been achieved or is incapable of achievement; or
2. he has been instructed to apply to the court by the meeting of creditors.

The court may discharge or vary the order and make any other order it thinks fit. If the order is discharged or varied, the administrator must, within 14 days, send a copy of the order of discharge or variation to the Registrar.

End of Administration

An administration period ends when:
1. the administration has been successful;
2. 12 months have elapsed from the date of the appointment of the administrator;
3. the administrator applies to the court to end the appointment;
4. a creditor applies to the court to end the appointment; or
5. a 'just and equitable' winding-up petition is granted.

An administrator automatically vacates office after 12 months of his appointment. That said, the time period can be extended by court order or by consent from the appropriate creditors. Alternatively, the administrator may apply to the court if he thinks:
1. the purpose of administration cannot be achieved;
2. the company should not have entered into administration; or
3. the administration has been successful (if appointed by the court).

Company Voluntary Arrangement

A company voluntary arrangement (CVA) is another alternative to liquidation proceedings. The purpose of a CVA is to allow a company to come to a mutual agreement with all its creditors regarding the payment of its debts over a period of time. There are three instances when a CVA can arise: it can be proposed by an administrator when he or she is administrating the company, by a liquidator when the company is being wound up or by the company directors at any stage. It should be noted that it cannot be proposed by the creditors themselves or by a company's shareholders.

If a CVA is going to take place, it is usual for the company to apply to the court for a moratorium, which will prevent any creditors of the company from taking action against the company. That said, in an administration situation, a moratorium will automatically be imposed (as discussed above).

If a CVA has been proposed, an insolvency practitioner will report to the court as to whether a meeting of creditors and shareholders should be held to consider the proposal. If a meeting is held, the creditors should take a vote as to whether the proposal should be approved. If 75% or more of the creditors agree to the arrangement, the terms of the arrangement become binding on all those creditors who had notice of the meeting. The insolvency practitioner who nominated the CVA to the court ultimately becomes responsible for insuring that the terms of the arrangement are carried out.

Once the terms of the arrangement have been fulfilled, the company's obligations to the creditors bound by the CVA are discharged and the company can thereafter continue trading.

References

- Derek French, Stephen Mayson and Christopher Ryan, *Mayson, French and Ryan on Company Law* (26th Edition, Oxford University Press, 2009–2010).
- Paul L. Davies, *Gower and Davies' Principles of Modern Company Law* (8th Edition, Thomson, Sweet & Maxwell, 2008).

REVIEW QUESTIONS

(See Suggested Solutions at the end of this textbook.)

Question 14.1

Russell has recently been appointed as the auditor of Buzaar Enterprises Ltd ('Buzaar'). In the course of the audit he discovered numerous financial irregularities, such as the failure by Stanley, the company accountant, to keep the books of account on a continuous and consistent basis, incorrect valuation of work in progress, failure to make sufficient bad debt provisions, and the omission of a significant contingent liability from the company's accounts. On discovery of these irregularities, Stanley resigned and a new accountant, Sarah, has been appointed.

Russell has advised Sarah that Buzaar is in significant financial difficulty and has recommended that the company be put into administration.

Requirement: Discuss the nature of administration, assess the key functions of an administration, and outline the potential outcomes of an administrator's proposals.

(Source: Chartered Accountants Ireland, CAP 1, Autumn 2009, Extract: Q4(b))

Question 14.2

MST Services Ltd is a construction company in Northern Ireland. In the last 12 months, the company has experienced severe difficulties trading. Several creditors have issued petitions on the grounds of the company's insolvency.

Requirement:
(a) Describe the two main statutory grounds for creditors seeking a compulsory liquidation.
(b) Outline the procedure for creditors to seek a liquidation.
(c) Outline the consequences of an order for compulsory liquidation.
(d) Explain the differences between a compulsory and voluntary liquidation.

(Source: Chartered Accountants Ireland, CAP 1, Summer 2009, Extract: Q3)

Question 14.3

Vincent has recently been appointed as the liquidator of Messing Construction Ltd. In the course of the liquidation, he discovered that one of the company's directors, Wilbur, had borrowed £400,000 three months previously from the People's Bank on behalf of the company and used the money to pay off another loan with the Prudential Bank. The loan with the Prudential Bank was secured by a personal guarantee by Wilbur to the value of £500,000.

Vincent has also discovered that two months prior to liquidation, Messing Construction Ltd paid substantial dividends, in the amount of £200,000, to its only two shareholders and directors, Wilbur and Wilma. At the time of the payment the company was in severe financial difficulty, which Wilbur hid by falsifying the value of the company's net assets.

(a) Identify any THREE grounds upon which the Court may appoint a compulsory liquidator to a company.
(b) Outline the effects of an Order for Compulsory Liquidation.

> (Source: Chartered Accountants Ireland, CAP 1, Law for Accountants (NI), Summer 2011, Extract: Q1(c) and (d))

Question 14.4

Outline the duties of an Official Receiver throughout a winding-up process.

> (Source: Chartered Accountants Ireland, CAP 1, Law for Accountants (NI), Autumn 2011, Extract: Q1(c))

Question 14.5

ABC Ltd is a private company in Northern Ireland. In order to finance the purchase of a number of motor vehicles for the business, ABC Ltd has obtained a loan from its bank. In order to do so, it had to stipulate a form of security over a number of the company's motor vehicles. The charge secured is that of a floating charge.

Requirement Explain to ABC Ltd the meaning of the term 'floating charge', the occasions when such a charge will crystallise and the effect of a floating charge crystallising.

> (Source: Chartered Accountants Ireland, CAP 1, Law for Accountants (NI), Autumn 2011, Extract: Q4(a))

Question 14.6

Peacock Books Limited ('Peacock') is a private limited company owned and managed by James and John, the sole directors and shareholders of the company. Peacock has been experiencing a downturn in its business in recent years.

In April 2013, HMRC made an application to the High Court for the compulsory liquidation of Peacock on the grounds that it cannot pay its debts. The Court granted this application and Robert Barry was appointed as the insolvency practitioner to manage the liquidation. On liquidation, the assets of the Peacock were valued at £300,000, but the liabilities were valued at £485,000. These liabilities comprise, among other things:
1. Unpaid employee remuneration of £30,000.
2. HMRC debts of £20,000.
3. A loan of £40,000 in favour of Provincial Bank secured on the stock by a floating charge, created on 21 September 2004 and registered on 4 October 2004.

4. A loan for £100,000 in favour of Bank of Galway secured on the stock by a second floating charge, created on 24 September 2004 and registered on 26 September 2004.
5. A loan of £30,000 from James's father.
6. A mortgage of £165,000, secured on Peacock's business premises in favour of Trinity Bank plc, created and registered in March 2000.
7. Unpaid trade creditors in the amount of £ 40,000.

Requirement: As a trainee accountant in the firm acting as insolvency practitioner to Peacock, you have been asked to draft a memo to James and John that:
(a) Outlines the characteristics of a floating charge.
(b) Lists the priority of payment of a company's debts upon liquidation.
(c) Lists the priority of the debts due to the creditors in 1–7 above.

(Source: Chartered Accountants Ireland, CAP 1, Law for Accountants (NI), Summer 2013, Extract: Q2(a)(i)–(iii))

Question 14.7

Baxter Manufacturing plc ('Baxter') was incorporated in 2005 with an authorised share capital of 5,000,000 £1 ordinary shares. At incorporation, 1,000,000 of these shares were issued and since then Baxter has not issued any further capital.

Upon incorporation, Mark purchased 300,000 Class A ordinary shares. At the point of subscription, Mark was only required to pay £0.50 for every £1 share purchased and since incorporation, Mark has made no other payment on foot of these shares.

Unfortunately, in recent years, Baxter has experienced a significant decline in sales and its most recent financial statements highlighted that the company had incurred a trading loss of £200,000. In addition, Baxter is also carrying a retained loss of £500,000 from previous trading periods. As a consequence of these losses, it is now insolvent and the board of directors has decided to put the company into liquidation. Baxter has contacted you for advice in relation to this situation.

Requirement:
(a) Write a response to Baxter that:
    (i) Outlines the potential liability of Mark on the liquidation of Baxter.
    (ii) Outlines the steps involved in a creditors' voluntary liquidation, assuming Baxter's shareholders vote for this type of liquidation.

(b) One of Baxter's creditors has threatened to bring an action to the High Court for the compulsory liquidation of BAXTER if he is not paid immediately. Discuss any TWO grounds upon which the Court may order the compulsory liquidation of a company.

(Source: Chartered Accountants Ireland, CAP 1, Law for Accountants (NI), Autumn 2013, Extract: Q2(a)(iii) and (iv) and (b))

Question 14.8

Aunty Em's Catering School Ltd ('Aunty Em') has been trading successfully since 1963. Since its incorporation, its founder and primary shareholder, Emilia, has acted as the company's managing director. Emilia celebrated her 75th birthday last year and at this stage she decided to sell the business. She received an offer from the Dingle Catering School Ltd ('Dingle'), proposing to purchase all of the assets of Aunty Em for £2.5 million. Emilia accepted this offer and has been advised by her solicitor to effect a members' voluntary liquidation of Aunty Em in order to distribute the £2.5 million to the company's shareholders. Emilia does not understand the meaning of the term 'members' voluntary liquidation' and seeks your advice.

Requirement:
(a) State the main prerequisite to effect a members' voluntary liquidation.
(b) Explain the procedure that must be followed to effect a members' voluntary liquidation.
(c) State the alternative type of voluntary liquidation that may be available.

(Source: Chartered Accountants Ireland, CAP 1, Law for Accountants (NI), Summer 2014, Extract: Q4(a)(i)–(iii))

Question 14.9

Robert and Matthew own a property business called RM Ltd ('RM'). RM is struggling to pay its debts and has sought the assistance of an insolvency practitioner for financial advice. No petition has yet been brought in the High Court for a compulsory liquidation of RM.

Requirement:
(a) Explain the role of an insolvency practitioner to RM Ltd.
(b) Name and briefly describe TWO alternatives to a compulsory liquidation that the insolvency practitioner could discuss with RM Ltd.

(Source: Chartered Accountants Ireland, CAP 1, Law for Accountants (NI), Autumn 2014, Extract: Q3(c)(i) and (ii))

Question 14.10

A company owned by Simon and John is showing a loss at the year end. Simon and John want to discuss all options in relation to this company and want to know what would happen if this company were to be placed into compulsory liquidation.

Requirement:
(a) Identify any THREE grounds by which a company can be wound up by the High Court in Northern Ireland.
(b) Explain the compulsory liquidation process to Simon and John.

(Source: Chartered Accountants Ireland, CAP 1, Law for Accountants (NI), Summer 2015, Extract: Q2(c) and (d))

CHAPTER 15

SHARES AND SHARE CAPITAL

Introduction

In this chapter we will examine the concept of shares and shareholders in a company. An important source of finance to a company limited by shares is the capital it receives from the issuing of shares to members. As a result of holding shares in a company, shareholders are permitted to receive a share of the profits through issues of share dividends. There are a number of different types of shares, which will be considered in this chapter, that a shareholder can purchase. Maintaining the balance of share capital in a business is very important and is often referred to as 'capital maintenance'. The second part of this chapter, therefore, will look at the rules relating to capital maintenance.

Shares and Shareholders

A share "is essentially a unit of account for measuring a member's interest in a company".[1] In the case of *Borelands Trustee v. Steel Brothers and Coal Ltd* (1901), a share was defined as an "interest of a shareholder in the company, measured by a sum of money, for the purpose of liability in the first place and of interest in the second". Any capital contributed for shares is called share capital.

By contributing capital to a company, a shareholder essentially becomes a member in the company and accrues a number of rights called membership rights. These include, but are not limited to, the right to:
- a dividend, if a dividend is declared;
- attend and vote at general meetings of a company;
- propose resolutions;
- be informed of notices under the Companies Act 2006;
- receive a share in any surplus of assets if a company is wound up.

Types of Share Capital

Share capital represents company funds. There are a number of ways of measuring share capital and these are set out below.

---

[1] *Mayson, French and Ryan on Company Law* (26th Edition, Oxford University Press, 2009–2010).

Issued or Allotted Share Capital

Issued share capital is the total value of the shares which a company has issued. When a shareholder takes shares from a company, it is called issuing the shares. Public companies must have a minimum allotted share capital of £50,000.

Paid-up Share Capital

Paid-up share capital is the amount of capital contributed for shares which are issued but excluding the share premium. Sometimes when shares are issued, the amount that is contributed under the contract for the allotment of shares is greater than the nominal value of the shares itself. The difference in this amount is called the 'share premium'. The amount of any share premium is credited to a separate share premium account.

Called-up Capital

This is the total amount called up by the company on the shares allotted plus any amount which is due to be contributed by members. Such amounts can arise because a company is due to receive further contributions from partly paid shareholders. It can also arise if members agree to pay for their shares in instalments and these instalments are due on later fixed dates.

Types of Shares

A number of different types of shares can be issued by a company.

Ordinary Shares

Ordinary shares are also known as 'equity shares'. Section 560(1) of the Companies Act 2006 (CA 2006) defines an 'ordinary share' as one in which there is no prior limit on the amount which the shareholder may receive in a distribution, either by way of an annual dividend or by way of distribution of surplus assets on winding up. Hence, an ordinary shareholder or member will have the right to share in the profits of a company provided such profits are available for distribution. Furthermore, if a company is insolvent and unable to pay all of its creditors in full, in an insolvency situation, an ordinary shareholder will receive nothing.

Preference Shares

Preference shares are relatively common. The holder of preference shares usually has the right to an annual fixed dividend which is normally expressed as a percentage of the nominal value of the shares, e.g. 10% of £1 preference shares. In any given year, if a dividend cannot lawfully be paid out because there are no distributable profits, the preference dividend usually accumulates (i.e. rolls forward until it can be paid lawfully). Generally, once the preference shareholders have been paid their fixed dividends, they are not able to participate in any additional dividend paid out to the ordinary shareholders unless such rights are expressed in the company's Articles.

In addition to the above, preference shareholders are entitled to a return of their initial capital investment on a winding up in priority to any capital paid to ordinary shareholders. Generally, once they are repaid their initial capital contribution in full, the preference shareholders are not able to participate in any surplus capital paid out to ordinary shareholders. This issue is important in a solvent liquidation where there may be substantial amounts to return to investors.

Finally, given their relatively secure position, preference shareholders do not tend to have voting rights at general meetings of members in respect of their preference shares.

Redeemable Shares

Although there is a general restriction on a company buying its own shares (as discussed later in this chapter), a private limited company is able to issue redeemable shares, i.e. shares that can be bought back at a date in the future at the election of either the company or the shareholder or both unless a company's Articles exclude this right (section 684 CA 2006) and provided strict statutory controls are adhered to on redemption.

Redeemable shares are a method of attracting short-term finance (the holder knows at the outset that membership can only be for a defined period). These types of shares are particularly attractive to short-term venture capitalists who often play a key role in starting new businesses.

Bonus Shares

These are shares which can only be issued out of profits to existing shareholders. They are issued in proportion to a shareholder's existing shareholding and can be issued only if shares are fully paid up.

Issue of Shares

The issue of shares should not be confused with share transfers (see below). Share issues or allotments involve a contract whereby a company issues new shares to new or existing shareholders. It is the company that receives the consideration (cash or non-cash) and the shareholder who receives the shares. As stated, the main purpose of the share issue process is for a company to raise finance to employ in the business.

Any issue of new shares will affect the control that existing shareholders have over the affairs of the company. For example, if a shareholder has three of the four shares currently in issue, he has control over the affairs of the company (i.e. 75% of votes). However, if the directors decide to issue another 11 shares to another shareholder, the first shareholder's control has shrunk to 20% and, assuming the shareholder has no seat on the board of directors and cannot block their proposals, the shareholder has lost any significant control over the company. Directors have common law duties not to issue shares for any improper purpose (i.e. to deliberately dilute the control of a difficult shareholder).

Authorisation of Share Issues

Sections 549 and 550 CA 2006 allow directors of a private limited company, with only one class of shares, to allot shares freely unless they are prohibited from doing so by the company's Articles. This will apply in most cases, as small companies tend to have only one class of shares.

However, if a company has more than one class of shares, directors must have the authority to allot shares (section 551 CA 2006). This authority can come from two places: either expressly in the Articles or from a resolution of the members. It can only last for five years and it must state the maximum number of shares to which it relates and the date on which it expires. The resolution passed at a shareholders' meeting will need to be filed with the Registrar of Companies (section 29(1)(e) CA 2006).

Return of Allotment of Shares

On all share issues, a return of allotment and a statement of capital need to be filed with the Registrar so that details of the current issued share capital appear at Companies House. The company's internal statutory books also need updating.

Under Article 3 of the the Companies (Shares and Share Capital) Order 2009 (2009 No. 388), a return of allotment must state:
1. the number of shares allotted;
2. the amount paid up and the amount (if any) unpaid on each allotted share (whether on account of the nominal value of the share or by way of premium); and

3. where the shares allotted are fully or partly paid up (as to the nominal value or any premium paid on them) otherwise than in cash, the consideration for the allotment.

The statement of capital must state:
1. the total number of shares of the company;
2. the aggregate nominal value of those shares;
3. for each class of shares:
   - the particulars of the rights attached to the shares,
   - the total number of shares of that class,
   - the aggregate nominal value of shares of that class, and
4. the amount paid up and the amount (if any) unpaid on each share (whether on account of the nominal value of the share or by way of premium).

Share Certificates

A company is under an obligation to have share certificates for all the shares allotted and paid within two months after the allotment of a company's shares (section 769 CA 2006). However, this rule does not apply if shares are allotted through CREST (see below).

A record of ownership of a company's shares is its register of members. Companies must provide their shareholders with share certificates. These provide evidence of ownership of the shares. In 1996, a computer system was introduced to deal with shares on the London Stock Exchange. This system is known as 'CREST'. If title to a share is recorded in CREST, there is no need for a share certificate to be issued in respect of the share, as it is said to be 'uncertificated' or 'dematerialised'.

A share certificate must state the name and address of a member. It should also certify that the member is a registered holder of a specified number of shares of a certain class. It should further state whether the shares are fully paid up or, if partly paid, how much of their nominal value has been paid up.

Share Transfers

Share transfers, which should not be confused with share issues, are concerned with the sale (or gift) of existing shares from one outgoing shareholder to a new incoming shareholder. The company itself is not a party to the contract and receives no consideration (the payment for the shares going to the old shareholder who has disposed of his capital asset). *Share transmissions*, on the other hand, occur automatically in law on death, to the deceased's personal representatives, or on bankruptcy, to a trustee.

The transfer of shares is incomplete until a stock transfer form has been completed, the transferee is registered as a member of the company in the Companies Register of Shareholders (as discussed above) and the appropriate stamp duty has been paid on the shares.

Restrictions on Transfer

In order to help maintain members' control, the Articles of a private company usually contain either a pre-emption clause, i.e. that no shares shall be transferred to an outsider as long as a member can be found to purchase them at a fair price, determined in accordance with the Articles, or a power vested in the directors to refuse to register a transfer (section 561 CA 2006). Each member must be offered a number of shares which allows their proportionate holding in the company to be maintained. Such an offer is called a "rights issue" and the purpose of such issues is to maintain members' control of a company and to prevent, as far as possible, the control of the company being taken away from the existing members.

In *Ocean Coal Co. v. Powell Duffern Steamed Coal Co.* (1932), the plaintiff and defendant each held half of the shares of the Taff Merthyr Steam Company. The Articles of this company stated that, if a member wished to sell his shares to an outsider, he must first offer them to other shareholders at the price at which it was proposed to sell to the outsider. The defendant wished to sell 135,000 shares, but the plaintiff only wished to buy 5,000 at the proposed price. It was held that he could not do so. The plaintiff either had to accept or reject the offer to sell the full 135,000 shares.

The Power to Refuse To Register Transfers

Directors have no power to refuse to register transfers unless such power is given to them by the company's Articles. Moreover, the power to refuse a transfer must be exercised within a reasonable timeframe. For example, in the case of *Popely v. Planarrive Ltd* (1997), the prospective transferee and directors had fallen out because the transferee had recently fathered children outside of marriage, and the directors were his wife, her children and his nephew. It was held that the directors were not obliged to stand down because they had personal feelings about him and that a reasonable board would have been likely to refuse registration also.

In addition, in the case of *Re Hafner* (1943), it was held that the directors acted in bad faith by not allowing a transfer to take place. They refused registration simply on the basis that, if the transferee became a member, he would query the "bloated emoluments", i.e. serious overpaying of the directors, and the present directors wanted to avoid such queries.

Share Prospectus

Unlike private companies, public limited companies (PLCs) can offer their shares and debentures directly to the public. This usually occurs when the company is floated on the stock exchange and the public can trade in shares. If, however, a public limited company is issuing shares to the public, it is under an obligation to supply a prospectus or a set of listing particulars. This prospectus is basically a statement of fact about the company. The purpose of the prospectus is to permit potential shareholders to find out more about the company and make a reliable and informed decision on whether to subscribe for shares in that company.

The types of information which a prospectus will usually contain are:
1. the assets and liabilities of the company;
2. its financial position;
3. profits and losses;
4. prospects of the company and whether there is any guarantor; and
5. rights attached to the shares in question.

The Prospectus Directive was implemented in the UK by the provisions of the Financial Services and Markets Act 2000.

CAPITAL MAINTENANCE

As stated at the beginning of this chapter, there are two main ways in which a company can generate the money it requires to continue in business. This can be done by borrowing and generating loan capital or by encouraging investment in a company through share capital. It is a long-established principle of company law that the share capital of a company cannot be returned by that company to its members throughout the company's lifetime. A company's share capital must be maintained. Shareholders who trade in the company's shares and provide the company with credit are entitled to assume that the pool of assets, represented by the nominal value of the share capital fund, will remain intact and be available for distribution to them to settle their debts in whole or in part when the company is wound up and its life is brought to an end.[2]

Furthermore, the capital in a company should be used only for the purposes defined in a company's objects clause. Capital should not be used for any unlawful or improper purpose. Capital maintenance rules govern any activity, permitted under statute, that seeks to reduce the share capital of a company. These rules will be examined now.

---

[2] *Mayson et al.* (2009–2010), *op. cit.*

Capital Maintenance Rules and Public Limited Companies

A company, which is registered as a public limited company (PLC), on its original incorporation is not permitted to do business or borrow money unless it has been issued with a trading certificate under section 761 CA 2006. This trading certificate will only be issued, by the Registrar of Companies, to the public company if it has allotted shares with a nominal value at least equal to the authorised minimum of £50,000. If a public company issues shares partly paid, at least one-quarter of the nominal value, under section 586(1) CA 2006, must be paid on or before allotment unless the shares are being allotted in pursuance of an employee share scheme (section 586(2) CA 2006). Furthermore, it should be noted that the nominal value of any shares allotted to an employee share scheme do not count towards the £50,000 unless one-quarter of their nominal value and the whole of any share premium have been paid up.

If a public company wishes to reduce its capital, it must adopt a special resolution and this resolution must be confirmed by the court (section 641(1) CA 2006). The court, in considering whether or not to approve the resolution for the reduction of capital, will consider the interests of all existing creditors and ensure that their interests are protected. The court will further assure itself that the procedure by which the resolution was carried out was formally correct. Moreover, a court will also satisfy itself that the cause of the reduction of the share capital of the plc was presented in a proper manner to all the members of the company, allowing them to make an informed choice in deciding to reduce the share capital. Finally, a court will also consider the public interest.

Any resolution to propose a reduction of capital will be refused by the court if the scheme is unfair. A court will decide whether or not any scheme is fair as between different classes of shareholders or between different shareholders of the same class. For example, in the case of *Re Old Silk Stone Collieries Ltd* (unreported), a company's business had been nationalised. The Board had adopted a policy of overturning capital to shareholders as and when it became available. Throughout this process, two reductions of share capital had been approved. On each occasion, the preference shareholders had been promised that they would not be bought out entirely but rather would be kept on as members of the company so that they would be entitled to claim compensation under a special scheme thought to be available to preference stockholders. The company proposed a third reduction. It was intended that this reduction would return all remaining capital to the preference shareholders so that they would no longer be members of a company and could no longer claim compensation. However, the Court of Appeal decided that this reduction was unfair and therefore did not approve the scheme.

Capital Maintenance and Private Companies

There are a number of capital maintenance rules which apply specifically to private companies. These rules relate to:
1. the issue of redeemable shares;
2. reduction of share capital;
3. distribution of profits;
4. purchase of own shares by the company; and
5. financial assistance for the purchase of own shares by a company.

Each of these rules will now be considered.

1. The Issue of Redeemable Shares

Section 684(1) CA 2006 permits a limited company to issue redeemable shares. Redeemable shares provide a shareholder with temporary membership of a company. This membership will terminate after a fixed period or when the company so chooses, depending on the terms of redemption of the shares. At the end of this fixed period, the shares are redeemed, with repayment of the nominal value of the shares, and the shares are subsequently cancelled (section 688).

Once the redeemed shares have been cancelled, a company is obliged, under section 688 CA 2006, to reduce its issued share capital by the nominal value of the cancelled shares. The amount of the nominal value of the cancelled shares should then be transferred to a new capital account called the capital redemption reserve. Furthermore, a company must give notice to Companies House, within one month of redeeming any of its shares, with a statement of capital.

2. Reduction of Share Capital

Section 641 CA 2006 provides that a company can reduce its share capital, in any way, by a special resolution which must be supported by a solvency statement and/or, if the reduction is confirmed, by the court. Prior to CA 2006, specific authorisation in a company's Articles was required to reduce share capital but this is no longer the case and the company is now able to reduce its share capital unless its Articles contain a specific restriction against this.

Section 643(1) lays out the detail which must be contained in a solvency statement issued by a company that wants to reduce its share capital. This solvency statement is a written statement that each of the directors has formed the opinion that, at the date of the statement:
  • there is no ground on which the company could be found unable to pay, or otherwise discharge, its debts; and

- the company will be able to pay, or otherwise discharge, its debts as they fall due during the following year.

If it is intended to wind the company up within that year, the directors must be of the opinion that the company will pay and discharge its debts in full within 12 months of the commencement of winding up.

No later than 15 days after the resolution has been passed to permit a reduction of capital, a copy of the solvency statement must be sent to Companies House, together with a statement of capital. No reduction can take effect until both of these documents have been registered with Companies House. Moreover, a statement by the directors, confirming that the solvency statement was made within 15 days of the reduction resolution being passed, must also be sent to Companies House. Directors of a company should note that it is an offence to submit a solvency statement to Companies House without having reasonable grounds for the opinions expressed in the statement.

3. The Distribution of Profits

The payment of profits of a company to members of a company is called a 'dividend'. Lord Cranworth, in the case of *Henry v. Great Northern Railway Co.* (1857), described a dividend as "each person's portion of the amount to be divided". All dividends should be paid in cash to members, unless the Articles of the company provide otherwise. Dividends must be declared by an ordinary resolution. A dividend cannot be paid unless directors have made a recommendation to do so, nor can a dividend exceed the amount recommended by directors.

A private company can only make a distribution out of profits available for the purpose of distributing (section 830(1) CA 2006). A company's profits available for distribution are, under section 830(2) CA 2006:

> "its accumulated, realised profits, so far as not previously legalised by distribution or capitalisation, less its accumulated, realised losses, so far as not previously written off in a reduction or reorganisation of capital duly made".

4. Purchase of Own Shares by a Company

A company cannot purchase its own shares from existing shareholders, and it cannot agree to subscribe for new shares in itself (section 658(1) CA 2006). That said, there are a number of statutory exceptions to this rule:
1. A company is able to purchase (or buy back) its own shares whether they are issued as redeemable or not, provided that the company's Articles do

not contain a restriction on the ability of the company to buy back its own shares (section 690 CA 2006).

2. The shares to be bought back by a company must be fully paid up (section 691 CA 2006). After the buy back has been completed, these shares are cancelled and the issued share capital of the company is reduced accordingly. Furthermore, after this process has been completed, there must remain at least one member of a company holding a share other than shares which are issued as redeemable.

Once shares are bought back, there are certain administrative matters to be dealt with. For example, section 707 CA 2006 requires a company to submit a return to the Registrar of Companies within 28 days of the buy back, which states the number and nominal value of those shares and the date of buy-back. In addition, a copy of the special resolution approving the contract for a buy-back will have to be delivered to a registrar. Moreover, the company must keep a copy of the contract for the purchase of the shares, or a memorandum of its terms, for 10 years from completion of the purchase of all of the shares at its registered office (section 702 CA 2006). Generally, the shares in question must be bought back out of assets representing distributable profits of the company or out of the proceeds of a fresh issue of shares (section 692 CA 2006). If the company's distributable profits are used to finance the buy-back, then capital must be maintained in the amount by which the company's share capital is diminished and the buy-back must be transferred to the capital redemption reserve.

5. Financial Assistance for Purchase of Own Shares

The Companies Act 2006 does not prohibit a private company from giving financial assistance for the acquisition of its own shares. However, if the subsidiary is a public company, it may not assist the acquisition of shares in its private holding company.

Shareholder Protection and Remedies

Under the rule in *Foss v. Harbottle* (1843), when a wrong is done to a company, minority shareholders are precluded from suing to redress that wrong. *Foss v. Harbottle* established the principle that action must be brought in the name of the company.

In this case, Mr Foss and Mr Turtan, who were members of a statutory company called The Victoria Park Company, made allegations that the defendants had made secret profits as promoters of the company. They further alleged that the defendants had breached their fiduciary duties to the company by causing it to enter into improper and fraudulent transactions. Mr Foss and Mr Turtan brought an action against the alleged wrongdoers "on behalf of themselves and all other proprietors of shares except the Defendants". The court decided in this case that the company was the proper vehicle for bringing an action when a company suffers a wrong. *Foss v. Harbottle* therefore established three principles:

1. the company is a separate legal person able to sue in its own right;
2. shareholders of a company should not bring proceedings to overturn a decision of the company – *Foss v. Harbottle* established that the majority rules in a company; and
3. a court will not interfere with the internal management of companies acting within their powers. This is called the "internal management principle".

There appear to be three reasons for the courts' decision not to hear a claim by a member of a company concerning the affairs of the company. First, it would seem that the courts do not want to become involved in disputes about business policy. Secondly, the courts appear to want disputes among members to be settled by members themselves in a general meeting where the majority should prevail. Thirdly, the courts also fear a multiplicity of claims. As Lord Justice Melish in *MacDougall v. Gardiner* (1875) said:

"... looking to the nature of these, looking at the way in which their Articles are formed and ... some Directors may have been irregularly appointed, some Directors as irregularly turned out, or something or other may have been done which ought not to have been done according to the proper construction of the Articles. Now, if that gives a right to every member of the company to file a bill to have the question decided, then if there happens to be one cantankerous member, or one member who loves litigation, everything of this kind will be litigated; whereas if the bill must be filed in the name of the company, then, unless there is a majority who really wish for litigation, the litigation will not go on. Therefore, holding that such suits must be brought in the name of the company does certainly tend to stop litigation."

Derivative Actions – Exception to the Foss v. Harbottle *rule*

Under section 260 CA 2006, shareholders are permitted to bring claims on behalf of the injured party, so-called derivative claims, "in very limited circumstances". Derivative claims are claims whereby the minority can bring an action against those who control a company. Section 260 contains a tripartite definition of a derivative claim:

1. it must be brought by a member of the company (or a person who is not a member to whom shares in the company have been transferred or transmitted by operation of law; for example, as a result of the bankruptcy or death of a member);
2. the cause of action must be vested in the company; and
3. the relief must be sought on behalf of the company (as opposed to the member).

Hence, a derivative claim is brought by a member of a company to enforce the company's rights.

The cause of action in respect of which a derivative claim may be brought arises from an actual or proposed act or omission which involves negligence, default, breach of duty or breach of trust by a director, former director or shadow director of the company. Furthermore, a section 260 cause of action may be made against a director, or another person, or both. Additionally, section 260 provides that the derivative action may be brought in respect of a cause of action arising before or after the person seeking to bring a derivative claim became a member of the company because the cause of action is vested in the company rather than the individual member.

A derivative claim is commenced by issuing a claim form under the Civil Procedure Rules. There is no requirement to obtain the leave of the court prior to issuing the claim form. A member of a company making a claim must obtain leave to continue the claim in order to ensure that claims that are motivated by reasons other than promoting the success of the company, or that are otherwise without merit, are dismissed by the court at the earliest possible opportunity without the involvement of the company itself (section 261(1) CA 2006). The onus is on the member who is making the application to provide the evidence to make out a *prima facie* case for obtaining such permission. If the court determines that such a case is not made out, then the court is required to dismiss the application. The court may make any consequential Order that it considers appropriate; for example, a costs order against the applicant. The purpose of these requirements is to constitute a deterrent element to potential claimants.

In determining what is or is not conduct that will promote the success of the company, the court will take into account (section 263(3) CA 2006):
- whether the member is acting in good faith in seeking to continue the claim;
- the importance that a persona acting in accordance with the duty to promote the success of the company would attach to the continuing claims;

- whether the act or omission giving rise to the cause of action could be, and in the circumstances would be, likely to be authorised or ratified by the company;
- whether the company has decided not to pursue the claim; and
- whether the act or omission in respect of which the claim is brought gives rise to a cause of action that the member could pursue in its own right rather than on behalf of the company.

Unfairly Prejudicial Conduct of the Company's Affairs

Part 30 of the Companies Act 2006 (sections 994–999) provides the grounds on which a member can apply to court to remedy conduct of a company's affairs "that is unfairly prejudicial to the interests of its members generally or of some part of its members" or "that an actual or proposed act or omission of the company ... is or would be so prejudicial".

The meaning of "unfairly prejudicial" was considered in *Re A Noble & Sons Clothing Ltd* (1983). The court decided in this case that a member must show that:

> "the value of his or her shareholdings are being seriously diminished or at least seriously jeopardised by reason of a course of conduct on the part of those persons who have de facto control of the company".

Moreover, in *Re Saul v. Harrison & Sons plc* (1995), the court said that:

> "unfairly prejudicial are general words and they should be applied flexibly to meet the circumstances of the particular case ... the conduct [being complained of] must be both prejudicial (in the sense of causing prejudice or harm to the relevant interest) and also unfairly so; conduct may be unfair without being prejudicial or prejudicial without being unfair, and it is not sufficient if the conduct satisfies only one of those tests."

The test for "unfairly prejudicial" is objective and this was highlighted in the case of *O'Neill v. Phillips* (1999). In this case, O'Neill joined Pectel Ltd (a construction company) when it was wholly owned by Mr Phillips. O'Neill started as a manual worker, but worked his way through the ranks. In 1985, he was given 25% of the shares and appointed to the board. He then took over the day-to-day management of the company and Phillips resigned as a director. The company prospered for a few years. Phillips waived his entitlement to 25% of the profits so that O'Neill received 50%. Discussions took place with a view to O'Neill being allotted additional shares to bring his holding up to 50% in the event of the company's net asset value reaching set targets. However, a recession set in and the company began to struggle. Phillips became critical of O'Neill's management and, in 1991, took on the role of managing director (although O'Neill remained on the board) and told O'Neill that his profit share would reduce to 25%. O'Neill brought a petition under section 459 of the Companies Act 1985 complaining of the termination of his profit-share arrangements and the repudiation of an alleged agreement to allot additional shares to him. In 1994, after three years of litigation, Phillips offered to buy his shares. O'Neill rejected the offer for various reasons, including the fact that Phillips did not intend to pay O'Neill's legal costs. The Court of Appeal found in favour of O'Neill, but the decision was overturned in the House of Lords. O'Neill's petition failed on the grounds that Phillips had not acted unfairly. O'Neill's claims to extra profits and shares were conditional on the performance of the company. As Phillips had not acted unfairly, there was no need to consider his offer to buy out O'Neill.

Another case dealing with the concept of "unfairly prejudicial" was that of *Re London School of Electronics* (1986). In this case, the petitioner owned 25% of the company (LSE) and City Tutorial Colleges Ltd (CTC) owned 75%. Two directors of LSE were also directors and members of CTC and caused LSE to transfer many of its students to CTC. It was held that the petitioner was unfairly prejudiced by the loss of revenue from students who transferred to CTC. CTC was ordered to buy out the shares of the petitioner, valued on the basis that the students had not transferred.

A petitioner of a section 994 claim should specify the relief sought by him or her. If a section 994 petition is successful, the court may make such order as it thinks fit under section 996 CA 2006. The court may:
- regulate the conduct of the company's affairs in the future;
- require the company to refrain from or cease performing the act complained of by the petitioner (or require the company to do something where the petitioner has complained of an omission);
- authorise civil proceedings to be brought in the name of and on behalf of the company;
- require the company not to make any, or any specified, alteration in the Articles; or
- provide for the purchase of shares belonging to any members by other members of the company itself.

The most common Order is probably for the petitioner's shares to be bought out.

Section 459 petitions under the old Companies Act were very unpopular with judges and so section 994 applications under the Companies Act 2006 will probably be equally unpopular. Mr Justice Harman described unfair prejudice petitions as being notorious for their length and unpredictability and involving "enormous and appalling costs" as a result of the volume of documents produced. He took the view that the normal remedy should be action under the company's constitution. Only future case law on the matter will demonstrate the court's views on such applications.

References

- Derek French, Stephen Mayson and Christopher Ryan, *Mayson, French and Ryan on Company Law* (26th Edition, Oxford University Press, 2009–2010).
- Paul L. Davies, *Gower and Davies' Principles of Modern Company Law* (8th Edition, Thomson, Sweet & Maxwell, 2008).
- Andrew McGee, *Share Capital* (Butterworths, 1999).

REVIEW QUESTIONS

(See Suggested Solutions at the end of this textbook.)

Question 15.1

Twin brothers, Henry and George, have just inherited £500,000 each from the estate of their late aunt Florence. Henry has decided that he wants to invest the money in the stock market and is planning on investing in a bio-technology company, Fringe plc ('Fringe'). George plans on re-investing the money in his own company, Delicious Desserts Ltd.

Requirement: (a) Fringe failed to reach its target profits by April 2009. Consequently, when Henry came to buy shares in Fringe, the company offered him the opportunity to buy the shares at a discount of 30%; so instead of paying £1 per share, Henry will only have to pay 70 pence per share.

Discuss the rules regarding issuing shares at a discount, and determine whether Henry would have any liability for the 30 pence discount per share, if the company went into liquidation.

(b) George plans on loaning his £500,000 to Delicious Desserts Ltd to allow the company to buy its own shares and reduce its issued capital. However, George has been advised by his solicitor that rules on capital maintenance restrict a company from buying its own shares, except in limited circumstances.

Outline these limited circumstances to George and explain to him the procedure required to reduce Delicious Desserts Ltd's issued share capital.

(Source: Chartered Accountants Ireland, CAP 1, Autumn 2009,
Extract: Q1(b) and (c))

Question 15.2

Vincent has recently been appointed as the liquidator of Messing Construction Ltd. In the course of the liquidation, he discovered that one of the company's directors, Wilbur, had borrowed £400,000 three months previously from the People's Bank on behalf of the company and used the money to pay off another loan with the Prudential Bank. The loan with the Prudential Bank was secured by a personal guarantee by Wilbur to the value of £500,000.

Vincent has also discovered that two months prior to liquidation, Messing Construction Ltd paid substantial dividends, in the amount of £200,000, to its only two shareholders and directors, Wilbur and Wilma. At the time of the payment the company was in severe financial difficulty, which Wilbur hid by falsifying the value of the company's net assets.

Requirement: Assess whether or not the payment of the dividend would be viewed as an unlawful distribution and the ramifications for both Wilbur and Wilma if the dividend payment is deemed unlawful.

(Source: Chartered Accountants Ireland, CAP 1, Law for Accountants (NI),
Summer 2011, Extract: Q1(b))

Question 15.3

Aengus is a minority shareholder, holding 26% of the company's issued capital, in Heaton Health Stores Ltd. The other company shareholders are Ryan and Griffin, who each hold 37% of the company's shares. Ryan and Griffin are also the company's directors.

The company has recently received an offer from its main competitor, Healthy Solutions Ltd, to buy out the company. Ryan and Griffin are keen to accept this offer, but Aengus is against it. Without Aengus's support, the proposed buy-out cannot go ahead as takeover law requires 75% approval before the minority will be compelled to sell their shares.

In order to facilitate the buy-out, Ryan and Griffin call a directors' meeting and alter the company's Articles of Association to remove the right of pre-emption. They also pass a resolution to issue another 500 shares and each of them purchases 50% of the new issue to increase their shareholding to 40% each respectively. They then call a shareholder meeting and pass a resolution to accept the buy-out offer from Healthy Solutions Ltd.

Requirement: Aengus is furious about this situation and seeks your advice in relation to the following:
(a) Define the term 'pre-emption' in this context.
(b) Determine whether the right of pre-emption would be classified as a condition or a warranty.
(c) Aengus feels that his rights as a minority shareholder have been oppressed and he now wishes to bring a derivative claim. Explain the concept of a derivative claim and the remedies available to Aengus if such a claim is successfully established.

(Source: Chartered Accountants Ireland, CAP 1, Law for Accountants (NI), Summer 2011, Extract: Q3(b)–(d))

Question 15.4

The Joe Glass Partnership operates a successful recycling business based in Belfast. The partnership has recently become a client of your firm. You have been brought along by the firm's senior partner to a meeting with Joe Glass. Joe explains to you that every year he prepares a business plan for the partnership. One of his goals for the next financial year is to expand the business into a public limited company, but he is unsure of the advantages and disadvantages of changing his corporate form. If the company is incorporated, Joe indicates that he wants to issue shares on the stock market. Joe Glass has heard of a share prospectus but is unsure of the purpose of this document or its contents.

Requirement:
(a) Explain the purpose of a share prospectus and outline any THREE pieces of information usually contained in a prospectus.
(b) Joe is aware that the rules on capital maintenance will apply if the company is incorporated as a public limited company. In this regard he is considering issuing 500,000 £1 redeemable ordinary shares and seeks your advice in this regard.
　(i) Explain any TWO characteristics of an ordinary share.
　(ii) Define a redeemable share.
　(iii) Explain any TWO rules in relation to the redemption of shares by a company.

(Source: Chartered Accountants Ireland, CAP 1, Law for Accountants (NI), Autumn 2012, Extract: Q1(b) and (c))

Question 15.5

Following the death of his great uncle Nelson, Cranston inherited 75,000 £1 ordinary shares in Finest Cuisine Catering Ltd ('Finest'). This is first time that Cranston has owned company shares and has been given share certificates. He knows nothing about company law or how companies operate.

Last week he received a notification from the company secretary of Finest informing him that an extraordinary general meeting (EGM) of the company was being requisitioned and that this meeting would consider the sale of 100,000 £1 ordinary shares in the company to a new private investor, Hamilton, who has offered to pay a share premium of £0.30 on every £1 share purchased. In addition, this notice also stated that a special resolution was being proposed to avoid pre-emption so that these shares could be offered directly to Hamilton and an ordinary resolution was being proposed to appoint Hamilton as a non-executive director in the company (if he was successful in acquiring these shares). Cranston does not understand the meaning of any of these terms and seeks your advice.

Requirement:
(a) Explain the meaning of the term 'share premium', commenting also on how the share premium is accounted for in a company's accounts.
(b) Explain to Cranston any THREE items which will be included on a share certificate.
(c) Define the meaning of the term 'pre-emption' in the context of an issue of shares.

(Source: Chartered Accountants Ireland, CAP 1, Law for Accountants (NI), Summer 2014, Extract: Q2(a)–(c))

Question 15.6

Lismount Ltd ('Lismount') began life as a small family-run recycling plant in 1970. Over the last 45 years, it has grown from employing five people to now employing over 500 people across Northern Ireland. The five directors of Lismount are considering floating the business on the stock exchange to raise additional share capital. The directors come to you for advice on the benefits of doing so. You advise them that if they do become a public limited company (plc), they will have to hold an annual general meeting (AGM).

While the family are keen to increase the share capital of the business, they also want to be assured that they can reduce the share capital at a later stage. You advise Lismount that if they become a plc, there are special rules governing the reduction of share capital.

Requirement: Outline the procedure to reduce the share capital of a public company.

(Source: Chartered Accountants Ireland, CAP 1, Law for Accountants (NI), Summer 2015, Extract: Q3(b))

Question 15.7

Titan Publishing Ltd ('Titan') was established in 2005. Sam is the executive director but, due to his declining health, he has decided to resign his position and also to dispose of his shareholding. Sam wants to transfer his shareholding in the company to his son Joe. However, Joe was prosecuted for fraud last year and so the other directors are opposing this as they believe that Joe's connection to the company may negatively impact its commercial reputation.

To ensure that Sam does not transfer his shares to Joe, the remaining directors of Titan are now considering altering the company's Articles of Association to state that the right of voluntary pre-emption should be applied to all share transfers.

Requirement: Define the meaning of the term 'pre-emption'.

(Source: Chartered Accountants Ireland, CAP 1, Law for Accountants (NI), Autumn 2015, Extract: Q2(a))

CHAPTER 16

MARKET ABUSE AND MONEY LAUNDERING

Introduction

In this chapter, we will look at the issues of market abuse and money laundering. In the first part of the chapter, market abuse and the forms of insider dealing that constitute market abuse, will be defined. In the second part, we will look at the issue of money laundering and the legislation that governs money laundering in the UK.

MARKET ABUSE AND INSIDER DEALING

The Stock Exchange is the forum in which companies buy and sell shares and other securities. As with any forum for buying and selling, people will only buy and sell if they believe the prices of the shares are an accurate reflection of their worth. People who work with shares on a daily basis naturally are in a position to deal with company shares long before outsiders have the opportunity to purchase them. This is referred to as 'insider dealing'. Insider dealing by officers, employees, directors or shareholders is legal if the trading is done in a way that does not take advantage of information which is not available to the public. However, if any of these individuals use privileged information which they receive on the shares in an advantageous way for themselves, this is known as fraud on other investors. It is a breach of trust and lowers public confidence in the market. Such acts constitute market abuse.

The three main pieces of legislation incorporating all the law on market abuse and insider dealing within the UK are:
- The Criminal Justice Act 1993;
- The Financial Services and Markets Act 2000; and
- The Market Abuse Directive (2003/6/EC).

The Criminal Justice Act 1993 – Insider Dealing

The Criminal Justice Act 1993 (the Act) created two insider dealing offences. The first offence, the *dealing offence* (under section 55 of the Act), is aimed at those who deal in particular kinds of securities and, in specified circumstances, on the basis of inside information:

> "An individual is guilty of insider dealing if he has information as an insider and deals, in specified circumstances, in securities which are price-affected in relation to that information."

Hence, a person deals in securities if he acquires or disposes of them or procures, directly or indirectly, an acquisition or disposal of the securities by any other person. The terms 'acquire' and 'dispose' include agreeing to deal either of those things when entering into, or discharging, a contract creating the relevant security.

The second offence, the *"tipping offence"* (under section 52), is committed either by disclosing inside information or by encouraging another to deal in particular kinds of securities and in specified circumstances.

> "An individual is guilty of insider dealing if he has information as an insider and either encourages another person to deal in securities which are price-affected in relation to the information knowing or having reasonable cause to believe that the dealing would take place in specified circumstances or if he discloses the information to another person otherwise than in the proper performance of the functions of his employment, office or profession."

In both cases, for there to be an offence it must be shown that the information an individual is passing on, or the information on which he is basing his encouragement, is inside information in the sense defined by the Act.

Persons and Dealings to Whom the Act Applies

Definition of 'Inside Information' Inside information means information which:
1. relates to particular securities or to a particular issuer of securities or to particular issuers of securities and not to securities generally or to issuers of securities generally;
2. is specific or precise;
3. has not been made public; and
4. if it were made public, would be likely to have a significant effect on the price of any securities. For this purpose, a price includes value.

Definition of 'Insider' A person has information from an inside source if he has it through being a director, employee or shareholder of an issuer of securities or through having access to the information by virtue of this employment, office or profession, or if the direct or indirect source of his information is such a person. It is not necessary for the information to originate from the issuer of the price-affected securities. An employee of an unrelated company (for example, a researcher in an investment bank) may become an insider by virtue of information, relevant to the fortunes of a particular company, which he uncovers in the course of his employment.

To commit the offence of insider dealing, an individual, who does not himself have the information by direct access, must know that the direct or indirect source of the information was a person of the sort described above who did have such direct access through his position. On this basis, it would not be sufficient for the prosecution to establish that the defendant knew, for example, that the direct or indirect source of the information was a director, employee or shareholder of a particular company if he did not also know that the inside information had come to that director, employee or shareholder through his being in that position.

Defences to Insider Dealing

General Defences   Under section 53 of the Act, an individual has a defence to a charge of *insider dealing* if he can show that:
1. he did not at the time expect the dealing to result in a profit attributable to the fact that the information in question was price-sensitive information in relation to the securities;
2. at the time, he believed on reasonable grounds that the information had been disclosed widely enough to ensure that none of those taking part in the dealing would be prejudiced by not having the information; or
3. he would have done what he did even if he had not had the information.

It is a defence to an allegation of *disclosing inside information* for the defendant to show that:
- they did not expect any person, because of the disclosure, to deal in the securities;
- they did not expect the dealing to result in a profit attributable to the fact that the information was price-sensitive information in relation to the securities;
- they did not expect there to be a profit or avoidance of loss;
- they had reasonable grounds to believe that the information had been disclosed widely enough to ensure that those taking part in the dealing would be prejudiced by having the information; or
- they would have done what they did even if they did not have the information, for example, where securities are sold to pay a pressing debt.

Territorial Scope

The territorial scope for insider dealing is as follows:
- if it was committed by a person within the UK at the time when he is alleged to have done any act constituting or forming part of the alleged dealing;
- if the regulated market in which the dealing is alleged to have occurred is declared by the Treasury to be a market which is to be treated as regulated in the UK; or
- if the relevant professional intermediary was within the UK at the time when he is alleged to have done anything by means of which the offence is alleged to have been committed.

The tipping offence can only be committed:
- by someone within the UK at the time he is alleged to have disclosed the information or encouraged the dealing; or
- if the recipient of the information or encouragement was within the UK at the time of receipt.

Penalties

The maximum penalties given by statute are seven years' imprisonment and/or an unlimited fine.

The Financial Services and Markets Act 2000

On 1 December 2001, the Financial Services and Markets Act 2000 (FSMA 2000) introduced a statutory prohibition on market abuse which supplements the criminal offences of insider dealing and market manipulation.

The reason for the introduction of FSMA 2000 was the government's view that existing criminal and regulatory sanctions (and in particular the provisions relating to insider dealing) did not effectively address all forms of abusive conduct. As a result, the concept of market abuse represented a considerable expansion in the scope of the law. Further, it was widely considered that the criminal law standard of proof was too high for the effective policing of the UK markets.

There are now five categories of market abuse as a result of FSMA 2000:
1. Misuse of information by knowingly buying shares in a takeover target for a general disclosure of the proposed takeover. This is similar to insider dealing.
2. Market distortion. This is the process of interfering with the normal process of shared prices moving up and down in accordance with the supply and

demand for shares. An example of this would be dealing on the exchange just before the exchange closes with a sole purpose of positioning the share price at a distorted level.

3. Creating a false or misleading impression about supply and demand or prices and values of investments. An example of this would be posting an inaccurate story on an internet bulletin board.

4. Recklessly making a statement or forecast that was misleading, false or deceptive.

5. Engaging in a misleading course of action for the purpose of inducing another to exercise or refrain from exercising rights in relation to investments.

An offence of market abuse is a criminal offence punishable by an unlimited fine and/or imprisonment for up to seven years.

The Market Abuse Directive

The Market Abuse Directive (2003/6/EC) is one of a number of EU initiatives implementing the financial services action plan for completing the single market for financial services. The aim of the Directive is to promote clean and efficient markets, regulated in a harmonised way throughout the EU. To this end, the Directive requires Member States to outlaw insider dealing and market abuse and to provide for timely disclosure of price-sensitive information to market users.

MONEY LAUNDERING

Introduction

Money laundering is a separate issue and concept to insider dealing and market abuse. Money laundering has a wide definition: it includes all forms of handling or possessing criminal property, including possessing the proceeds of one's own crime and facilitating any handling or possession of criminal property. Criminal property has a wide definition but can include money or money's worth, securities, tangible property and intangible property. Money laundering activity can also range from a single act – for example, for being in possession of the proceeds of one's own crime – to complex and sophisticated schemes involving multiple parties and multiple methods of handling and transferring criminal property, as well as concealing it and entering into arrangements to assist others to do so. All businesses and individuals need to be fully alert to the risks of clients, their counterparties and others laundering money in any of its possible forms.

The three main pieces of legislation governing the UK Anti-Money Laundering (UK AML) regime are:

- Terrorism Act 2000 (TA 2000);
- Proceeds of Crime Act 2002 (POCA 2002); and
- Money Laundering Regulations 2007 (the 2007 Regulations), which revoked the Money Laundering Regulations 2003.

Money Laundering Offences

Sections 327–329 of the Proceeds of Crime Act 2002 (POCA 2002), as amended by the Serious Organised Crime and Police Act 2005 (SOCPA 2005) and the Crime and Courts Act 2013, defines money laundering offences. The first category of principal money laundering offences relates to laundering the proceeds of crime or assisting in the process. Under section 327, it is an offence to conceal, disguise, convert or transfer criminal property, or remove criminal property from England and Wales, or from Scotland or Northern Ireland. Secondly, if an individual enters into or becomes concerned in an arrangement which he knows or suspects facilitates (by whatever means) the acquisition, retention, use or control of criminal property by or on behalf of another person, he is guilty of money laundering (section 328 of POCA 2002). Thirdly, if someone acquires, uses or has possession of criminal property, except where adequate consideration has been given for the property (section 329), he is also guilty of the offence.

Anyone can commit any one of these offences. Conviction of any of these offences is punishable by up to 14 years' imprisonment and/or an unlimited fine.

However, none of these offences are committed if:

1. the persons involved did not know or suspect that they were dealing with the proceeds of crime;
2. a report of the suspicious activity is made promptly to a Money Laundering Reporting Officer (MLRO) or direct to the National Crime Agency under the provisions of section 338, POCA 2002, or, if no report is made, there was a reasonable excuse for this failure;
3. the Act is committed by someone carrying out a law enforcement or judicial function; or
4. the conduct giving rise to the criminal property was reasonably believed to have taken place outside of the UK and the conduct was in fact lawful under the criminal offence of the place where it occurred.

To prove knowledge, the prosecution has to prove a suspect knew that the money or property originated from the proceeds of crime; for example, monies received from the sale of drugs or monies obtained by deception. Suspicion does not have to be clear or firmly grounded and targeted on specific facts, but must be more than merely fanciful (see *R v. Da Silva* (2006)).

Knowledge or suspicion catches both 'front-line' criminals and those facilitating or benefiting from crime; for example, professional individuals laundering for criminals, couriers, and partners or family members living a lavish lifestyle.

Offences Relating to Failure to Report Money Laundering

There are four offences concerned with a person's action or inaction upon discovering potential money laundering. These are:

1. **Failure to Disclose** A person working in a business in the regulated sector knows or suspects, or has reasonable grounds for knowing or suspecting, that another person is engaged in an offence under sections 327 to 329 POCA 2002 but fails to disclose that knowledge or suspicion to a relevant officer (section 330).

2. **Failure to Disclose (Nominated Officers)** A person nominated to receive disclosures under section 330 working in the regulated sector (the MLRO) knows or suspects, or has reasonable grounds to know or suspect, money laundering, as a consequence of his or her role of person nominated to receive disclosures under section 330, and fails to make the necessary disclosure under section 338 as soon as practical after the information comes to him or her (section 331). It is a defence for the MLRO if he or she has a reasonable excuse for not disclosing the information.

3. **Tipping Off** A person working in a business in the regulated sector knows or suspects that another person's suspected involvement with money laundering is under investigation or in contemplation of investigation, and regardless makes a disclosure to any person likely to prejudice any investigation (section 333A).

4. **Prejudicing the Investigation** A person knows or suspects that a money laundering investigation has or is about to be commenced in respect of another and he or she makes a material disclosure to any other person which is likely to prejudice the investigation, or interferes with relevant material (section 342). This offence can be committed by both regulated and non-regulated individuals.

Note: The failure to disclose offence can only be committed by a person in the regulated sector. In practice, the simple rule exists so that a regulated person can avoid committing a 'failure to report' offence by informing their MLRO of their suspicion and not telling anyone else about it.

Money Laundering Obligations

The Money Laundering Regulations 2003 imposed a number of obligations on practitioners in an effort to tackle money laundering. Some of these are set out below.

Identification and Record-keeping Procedures

Relevant persons have an obligation to obtain and verify a customer's identity on the basis of documentation or information obtained from a reliable and independent source. Regulation 14 of Money Laundering Regulations 2007 states that this should be completed before establishing a business relationship or carrying out an occasional transaction. Identification or verification evidence must be kept for at least five years after the date on which all activities taking place in the course of a one-off transaction (or series of transactions) have been completed.

Reporting

There is a requirement for relevant persons (other than individuals who neither employ nor act in association with other people) to appoint a 'nominated officer' (a money laundering reporting officer (MLRO)) with responsibility for internal and external reporting structures. The nominated officer is responsible for receiving internal disclosures of knowledge or suspicion of criminal activity from staff members and making external reports to the National Crime Agency (NCA), which is the UK's financial intelligence unit (UKFIU). The NCA took over this role from the Serious Organised Crime Agency (SOCA) on 7 October 2013. The nominated officer is also responsible for receiving internal disclosures under the Proceeds of Crime Act 2002 (POCA 2002) (sections 337 and 338) and the Terrorism Act 2000 (TA 2000) (sections 21A and 21B).

Reports of suspicions of money laundering activity are made via a suspicious activity report (SAR). A report is normally made to the NCA, which considers the information provided and either gives or refuses consent to complete the transaction. If consent is given, the transaction can be completed without any risk of committing a proceeds of crime offence. If consent is refused, the transaction cannot be completed and the MLRO still has to take appropriate steps to avoid committing an offence of tipping off.

The MLRO's Responsibilities

Every accountancy firm must appoint a money laundering reporting officer (MLRO). The MLRO is responsible, under delegation from senior management, for oversight of the firm's compliance with the Financial Conduct Authority (FCA) rules and guidance on AML systems and controls. As a result, in practice, the MLRO's responsibilities are likely to include the following:

- Identifying the money laundering risks the firm is exposed to and appropriately documenting the firm's money laundering risk profile.
- Establishing the nature of the firm's AML systems and controls.

- Developing and appropriately documenting the firm's risk management policies and processes, as well as carrying out regular assessments of their adequacy.
- Appropriate measures to ensure that procedures for identifying new customers do not unreasonably deny access to the firm's services to potential customers who cannot reasonably be expected to produce detailed evidence of identity.
- Ensuring staff are trained on AML, which includes making sure that staff training is offered, that staff training records are kept, and that the training is of an appropriate standard and scope to ensure that staff are aware of their AML obligations and are alert to money laundering risks.
- Providing information to senior management. This will include providing a formal report to senior management, at least annually, on the operation and effectiveness of the firm's AML systems and controls. The Joint Money Laundering Steering Group's (JMLSG) guidance recommends that firms should consider whether or not to prepare reports more frequently. This will depend on the complexity of the firm and the specific AML risks it is exposed to. Guidance on the suggested content of an MLRO report was prepared by the British Bankers' Association (BBA), in conjunction with the FSA, in 2002. An updated version was made available on the JMLSG's website in December 2006.
- Taking appropriate measures to ensure that money laundering risk is taken into account in the firm's day-to-day operations, including in relation to the development of new products, the taking-on of new customers, and changes in the firm's business profile.
- Ensuring the firm stays up to date with, and acts on, national and international findings on deficiencies in the AML regimes of other jurisdictions. This will entail monitoring government reports, the findings of the Financial Action Task Force (FATF), FATF-style regional bodies and other international findings, such as those of the International Monetary Fund (IMF) or the World Bank (WB).
- Ensuring the firm is aware of, and acts on, alerts relating to money laundering risk from regulators and other relevant bodies. These alerts include FCA statements and final notices.
- Where the MLRO is also the nominated officer for the purposes of the MLRs, POCA and TACT, he or she will also be required to receive internal reports of possible money laundering or terrorist financing, consider internal reports in the light of all the information available to him or her, and determine whether the information in the reports give rise to a

knowledge or suspicion of money laundering or terrorist financing, and if so, report this promptly to the NCA.

The MLRO's criminal liability emerges from both the offences under POCA and regulation 45 of the MLRs. Under regulation 45, the MLRO can be subject to criminal sanctions for failing to put in place the following relevant regulations prescribed by the MLRs:

- customer due diligence measures (regulation 7(1), (2) or (3));
- ongoing monitoring of business relationships (regulation 8(1) or (3));
- verifying the identity of a customer before conducting a transaction (regulation 9(2));
- failing to cease transactions where customer due diligence measures cannot be undertaken (regulation 11(1)(a), (b) or (c));
- carrying out enhanced due diligence measures (where appropriate) (regulation 14(1));
- keeping relevant transactional records (regulation 19(1), (4), (5) or (6));
- putting in place adequate policies and procedures, including anti-money laundering procedures (regulation 20(1), (4) or (5));
- ensuring that employees receive appropriate anti-money laundering training (regulation 21); and
- failing to follow a direction made under regulation 18 (made by HM Treasury).

The Privilege Reporting Exemption

The privilege reporting exemption excludes a relevant professional adviser (defined as an accountant, auditor or tax adviser who is a member of a professional body which tests applicants for membership for competency, imposes and maintains professional and ethical standards for its members, and sanctions non-compliance with those standards) from the obligation to report where the knowledge or suspicion of money laundering offences is gained in privileged circumstances. Not all relevant persons are relevant professional advisers. (Members of Chartered Accountants Ireland are within the scope of the exemptions.)

There are two types of privileged circumstances, namely legal advice and litigation. Examples of where the privilege reporting exemption might apply include:

- advice on taxation matters, where the tax adviser is giving advice on the interpretation or application of any element of tax law and in the process is assisting a client to understand his tax position;

- advice on legal aspects of a takeover bid (e.g. on Companies Act legislation);
- assistance to clients by taking witness statements from the client or from third parties in respect of litigation; and
- representing a client at a tax tribunal.

What Defences are Available to Failure to Report Charges?

A person in the regulated sector can avoid committing a money laundering offence by disclosing any information that gives rise to knowledge or suspicion of a money laundering offence to the relevant officer (section 330 of the Proceeds of Crime Act 2002) and subsequently keeping that disclosure confidential (section 333A).

There is an obvious conflict for persons working within the regulated sector. A failure to act in accordance with their client's instructions is potentially a breach of contract and regulatory principles, and could lead to civil claims.

This conflict was considered in the case of *Shah and another v. HSBC Private Bank (UK) Ltd* (2012). HSBC made a number of suspicious activity reports in respect of transactions requested by their client, Shah. HSBC subsequently delayed making the requested transactions while awaiting consent from the National Crime Agency. As a result, Shah's assets in Zimbabwe were seized and he lost over US$300 million. Shah's damages claim was dismissed in the High Court. The court ruled:
- the test for suspicion remains as per the test from *Da Silva*; a suspicion does not have to be clear or firmly grounded;
- there will be no liability for loss when a report is made in good faith; and
- terms could be implied into a contract where:
  - the bank could refuse to execute instructions in the absence of appropriate consent where money laundering was suspected; and
  - the bank would not provide information in circumstances where there was a risk of tipping off.

Reporting Obligations under the Proceeds of Crime Act 2002

The flowchart below provides a short summary of the steps individuals should take when determining whether a suspicious activity report (SAR) needs to be made to their MLRO and on to the NCA under POCA relating to suspected money laundering.

Figure 16.1: Reporting Obligations under the the Proceeds of Crime Act 2002

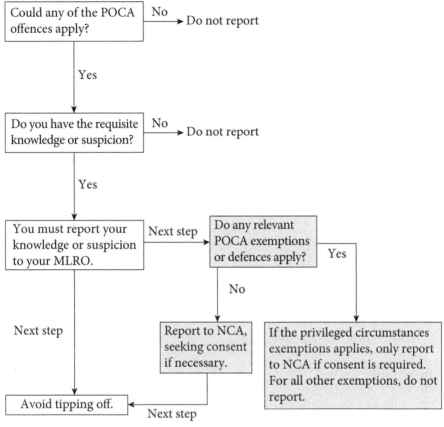

Note: The steps in the shaded boxes apply to MLROs only.

Conclusion

It is evident that the 2007 Regulations introduced some important aspects to the AML regime in the UK. Clearly, time and resources are likely to be required in meeting the requirements to identify beneficial owners and PEPs. That said, the obligations on relevant persons have not changed dramatically. Overall, practitioners should take steps to ensure that efficient and effective policies and procedures are in place to combat money laundering.

References

- Brenda Hannigan, *Insider Dealing* (2nd Edition, Longman).
- The Consultative Committee of Accountancy Bodies, *Anti-Money Laundering Guidance for the Accountancy Sector* (August 2008) – see www.ccab.org.uk/.

- Flowchart in **Figure 16.1** produced by Jon Gale, a senior associate in the dispute resolution department at Ashurst LLP, designed to help bank staff comply with their reporting obligations under the POCA 2002.

REVIEW QUESTIONS

(See Suggested Solutions at the end of this textbook.)

Question 16.1

You are approached by a business client, a venture capitalist, who has recently been invited to become a non-executive director of a Northern Ireland manufacturing company, and who is completely unaware of the nature and extent of his obligations in this role.

Requirement: Your client has requested that you prepare a memo outlining to him the following: as your client regularly buys and sells shares on the stock market, he seeks your advice on the law relating to insider trading in Northern Ireland. Your memo should also include a discussion of the sanctions that can be imposed where a case of insider trading is proved.

(Source: Chartered Accountants Ireland, CAP 1, Summer 2008, Extract: Q3(c))

Question 16.2

Allen Enterprises Limited is an online gambling company. In the first three years of operation, Allen's turnover was less than £7.3 million and therefore the company was eligible for an audit exemption. This year Allen's turnover is in excess of £10 million and Allen's accountant has informed the directors that the accounts will need to be audited before presentation to the shareholders at the Annual General Meeting (AGM). Last month Allen's directors appointed Paddison Chartered Accountants ('Paddison') as Allen's auditor.

During the course of the audit, Paddison discovered that a client named Mr Fit made a £2,000 bet every month on a horse with long odds. Every month, Mr Fit's bet generated winnings in excess of £20,000. In 2012, Mr Fit, having not lost one bet, netted winnings of £263,000 from successful bets. Paddison is now suspicious that Mr Fit may not be real and that the directors may be using Allen to launder money.

Requirement:
(a) Define the term 'money laundering' and explain any TWO ways in which this offence can be committed.

(b) Outline the legal obligations imposed upon auditors where a suspicion of money laundering occurs.

(Source: Chartered Accountants Ireland, CAP 1, Law for Accountants (NI),
Summer 2013, Extract: Q4(b)(i) and (ii))

Question 16.3

Buckley is the CEO of a waste management company, Premier Waste Disposal Limited ('Premier'), which has contracts with a number of financial institutions around Ireland. Last year, a number of Buckley's collection drivers were unable to attend work due to heavy snow that had left a number of roads closed. Consequently, Buckley decided to complete a number of the collections himself. Whilst collecting paper for shredding from the Bank of Belfast, Buckley noticed a document in the shredding bag marked 'Confidential – Department of Finance Memo'. Buckley took this document from the shredding bag and (back in his office) he opened the document and read its contents. The document stated that Balantine Pharmaceuticals plc ('Balantine') was being investigated for Revenue fraud, and the document contained instructions to the bank granting the Department of Finance the right to review all of Balantine's bank accounts.

After Buckley read the memo, he contacted his accountant and asked him if any of his personal and pension investments included shares in Balantine. His accountant reviewed Buckley's investment portfolio and told Buckley that he had approximately £100,000 invested in Balantine. Upon hearing this, Buckley told the accountant to sell these shares immediately. When the accountant asked him why, Buckley stated that he had a bad feeling about Balantine. The accountant complied with Buckley's request and sold the shares.

Three months after selling Buckley's shares in Balantine, the accountant saw a news story that Balantine was being investigated on suspicion of Revenue fraud. Following the disclosure of this story, the value of Balantine's shares fell 48%. Upon hearing this news story, the accountant became suspicious as to whether Buckley was engaging in 'insider trading' at the time he requested his shares to be sold in Balantine.

Requirement:
(a) Define the term 'insider trading' and explain what is meant by 'inside information'.
(b) List the various classes of people that are considered insiders for the purpose of the law regarding insider trading.

(c) Outline the criminal sanctions that can be imposed where a person is found guilty of insider trading. Comment also upon whether you consider Buckley to be guilty of insider trading.

(Source: Chartered Accountants Ireland, CAP 1, Law for Accountants (NI), Autumn 2013, Extract: Q3(a)(i)–(iii))

CHAPTER 17

THE REGULATION OF CHARTERED ACCOUNTANTS

Introduction

The Chartered Accountants Regulatory Board (CARB) was established by Chartered Accountants Ireland (the Institute). The purpose of CARB is to regulate all of its members in accordance with the laws of the Institute. Furthermore, CARB is also responsible for developing standards of professional conduct while ensuring that all members, member firms, affiliates and students are compliant with the bye-laws of the Institute.

Complaints and Disciplinary Procedures

If a member or a member firm breaches a bye-law or regulation, fails to comply with the standards of professional conduct and/or brings discredit on themselves, the Institute or the accountancy profession, they ultimately become liable for disciplinary action by CARB. There are a number of disciplinary bodies within CARB that deal with members who either have complaints made against them or who do not meet the standards reasonably to be expected of members of the profession. The relevant bodies are:

- The Conduct Committee
- Disciplinary Tribunals
- Appeal Tribunals
- Independent Review Committees.

The CARB Disciplinary Process

A new disciplinary process was introduced by CARB in October 2015, which is reflected in this chapter. Key new features of the process worth mentioning at this point include:

- New grounds for liability to disciplinary action – in effect, the grounds will be reclassified and liability will arise in respect of misconduct, poor professional performance and failure to respond or co-operate with CARB or the Institute.
- New decision-making powers for the Head of Professional Conduct – in less serious cases, the Head of Professional Conduct is empowered to make a decision as to whether or not the member, member firm, student or affiliate has a case to answer in respect of an allegation. Such decisions will be subject

to oversight by members of the Conduct Committee. Complainants will have the right to have findings of "no case to answer" reviewed independently.

- A new order to be known as an 'unpublished caution' – this order can be imposed following a finding of "case to answer" by the Head of Professional Conduct.
- The renaming of the 'Complaints Committee' as the 'Conduct Committee', which will focus on more serious, higher risk and complex cases.
- Regarding sanctions, it will not be necessary to hold a hearing before a Disciplinary Tribunal where a member consents to the imposition of an order for exclusion or suspension from membership. The same applies in respect of suspension or removal of affiliate status.
- New provisions to allow cases to be resolved through settlement – parties will be entitled to seek to conclude proceedings by way of settlement agreement at any time prior to the final decision in a case. Details of settlement agreements will be published in all cases.
- New provisions allowing orders to be made on an interim basis in matters of public concern – interim orders suspending membership or imposing conditions in public concern cases may be imposed in exceptional circumstances, where it has been established that it is necessary in the public interest to do so.
- A new approach to dealing with bankrupt and otherwise insolvent members.

Conduct Committee

Upon receiving a complaint against a member of the Institute, a case manager is required to assess the nature of the complaint. This initial complaint can come from either a member of the public, another accountant, another client, etc., and he or she is known as 'the complainant'. Any complaint made must be assessed. Many complaints are resolved at the initial stages as, very often, they involve misunderstandings.

In the normal course, the purpose of this stage is for a case manager to investigate and to prepare a report on the matter, supported by the available evidence, for the consideration of the Head of Professional Conduct or the Conduct Committee. A decision will then be taken as to whether or not there is a case to answer in respect of the matter.

If it is established that there is a case to answer, it can exercise one of five options:

- First, the matter is referred to a Disciplinary Tribunal for a hearing.

- Secondly, it can offer a consent order, which is a disciplinary penalty that must have the agreement of the member.
- Thirdly, it can invite the individual concerned to accept an unpublished caution.
- Fourthly, the matter can be deferred to permit the Conduct Committee to gather further necessary information to enable it to make a decision.
- Fifthly, take no further action.

Interim Orders Where the Conduct Committee has decided that a disciplinary matter is a matter of public concern, the Conduct Committee or any special investigator appointed may (directly or through the Head of Professional Conduct) request that the Convenor or Deputy Convenor refer an application to a disciplinary tribunal seeking the imposition of an interim order. The Convenor or Deputy Convenor shall appoint a disciplinary tribunal to hear each interim order application. For the avoidance of doubt, a disciplinary tribunal, or any member of a disciplinary tribunal, which has heard an application for an interim order, shall not be precluded from hearing the formal allegation (if any).

As soon as practicable after its appointment, the Disciplinary Tribunal shall give to the case presenter and the member, member firm, student or affiliate concerned notice of the time and place appointed for the hearing of the application.

The Disciplinary Tribunal shall notify the member, member firm, student or affiliate concerned of their right to appear and/or be represented before the Disciplinary Tribunal by a practising lawyer and/or Chartered Accountant and/or by such other person or persons as a Disciplinary Tribunal may permit.

Hearings relating to applications for the imposition of interim orders shall be conducted in private. Subject to the rights of the case presenter, the member, member firm, student or affiliate to appear and be represented and the right of an oversight authority to appoint an observer, the Disciplinary Tribunal may, in its absolute discretion, determine who may attend such hearing.

Having heard the application and any submissions of the member, member firm, student or affiliate concerned, the Tribunal may make an interim order if it is satisfied that the order is appropriate and justified in all of its circumstances having regard to the public interest, Disciplinary Bye-Law 6 and any guidance issued by the board from time to time.

The case presenter, member, member firm, student or affiliate concerned may apply to have any interim order imposed reviewed on the grounds of a change in circumstances since the order was made. Any application for review should be made in writing to the Head of Professional Conduct.

Appealing Interim Orders A member, member firm, student or affiliate may appeal against any interim order made on the grounds that:
1. the interim order is excessive; and/or
2. the interim order is flawed because of a serious procedural or other irregularity in the proceedings before the Disciplinary Tribunal.

An individual wishing to appeal an interim order must, within 14 days from the date of service of the notice, give notice to the Head of Professional Conduct stating the grounds of appeal. For the avoidance of doubt, an interim order takes effect immediately unless the Disciplinary Tribunal determines otherwise.

Appeals against interim orders are conducted in private. An Appeal Tribunal may at its absolute discretion:
1. grant the appeal;
2. confirm or revise the interim order if it is satisfied that the order is necessary and justified in all the circumstances having regard to public interest, Disciplinary Bye-Law 6 and any guidance issued by the board from time to time.

Disciplinary Tribunals

The purpose of a Disciplinary Tribunal is to hear cases referred to it by the Conduct Committee. Generally speaking, Tribunals will hear more serious cases involving misconduct. The convenor of the Disciplinary Panel appoints a Disciplinary Tribunal to hear the case in full and it is generally conducted in public. Members of the Disciplinary Tribunal are drawn from a disciplinary panel. A Disciplinary Tribunal is comprised of two non-accountants (including a lawyer as chairperson); the third member is an accountant. The role of the Disciplinary Tribunal is to give the respondent (i.e. the person against whom the complaint is made) the opportunity to attend and be heard at the hearing of the formal allegation made against them; be represented by counsel, a solicitor or a member of the Institute; cross-examine witnesses called by the person or persons presenting the formal allegation; adduce documentary evidence on their behalf; call witnesses to give evidence on their behalf and make such submissions to the Tribunal as they deem appropriate. Furthermore, the Disciplinary Tribunal will give the persons bringing the complaint the opportunity also of attending and being heard at the hearing, adducing documentary evidence, calling witnesses to give evidence, cross-examining witnesses called by the respondent and making any other submissions that are deemed appropriate to the Disciplinary Tribunal.

If the Disciplinary Tribunal finds that the formal allegation has been proven in accordance with the standard of proof required, it will make a ruling to that effect. If it finds that the formal complaint has not been proven, it will dismiss the complaint. In both scenarios, the Tribunal must give reasons for doing so.

If a formal allegation is proven against the respondent, the respondent can, for example, be excluded from membership, be suspended from membership, have his practising certificate withdrawn, be ineligible for a practising certificate, have his insolvency licence withdrawn, be reprimanded or be fined.

Appeals

Decisions made by the Disciplinary Tribunal are subject to a right of appeal by the respondent on certain grounds. The Appeal Tribunal will give the appellant making the appeal (i.e. the respondent at the Disciplinary Tribunal stage) the opportunity to attend and be heard at the hearing of the appeal and, if the appellant so desires, to be represented at the hearing by counsel or by a solicitor or by a member of the Institute. The Appeal Tribunal has the authority to affirm, vary or rescind any finding or Order of the original Disciplinary Tribunal in respect of which the appeal was brought. Furthermore, it may substitute any other finding or Order which it considers appropriate. An Appeal Tribunal can also make an Order for costs against either party if it deems such Order appropriate.

As at the Disciplinary Tribunal stage, at the appeal hearing the appellant will have the opportunity to attend and be heard, be accompanied by a solicitor, counsel or member of the Institute, hear the evidence put forward by or on behalf of the Conduct Committee, cross-examine witnesses called, produce documentary evidence, call witnesses to give evidence on his or her behalf and finally make any other submissions to the Appeal Tribunal which it deems appropriate.

An Appeal Tribunal can hear appeals against a finding or Order of the Disciplinary Tribunal on the grounds that the finding is wrong, the Order is excessive, the finding or Order is flawed because of a serious procedural rule or other irregularity in the proceedings, or that the award of costs against the applicant is excessive. However, it should be noted that no appeal to the Appeal Tribunal can be made solely on the question of costs. Any appeals to the Appeal Tribunal should be heard as soon as reasonably practicable after the receipt of notice of the appeal.

Settlements

It should be noted that settlement negotiations can be entered into at the discretion of the Head of Professional Conduct and at any stage throughout the investigation process. All settlement negotiations are conducted on a 'without prejudice' basis. Proposed terms of settlement must be considered and approved by a settlement approver.

CARB's Standard Disciplinary Process

The figure below summarises CARB's Standard Disciplinary Process.

Figure 17.1 CARB's Standard Disciplinary Process[1]

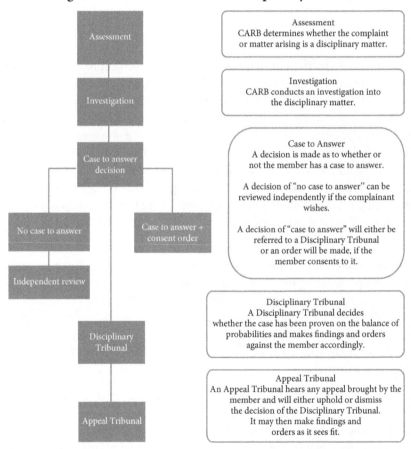

---

[1] Source of material and figure: the website of the Chartered Accountants Regulatory Board (www.carb.ie) Disciplinary Regulations effective 5 October 2015.

Judicial Review and Other Legal Rights

It should be noted that the disciplinary processes of CARB can be subject to the rules of judicial review. If the member or complainant believes that the processes of CARB were not followed or carried out with due regard to a person's rights, a member or complainant can take an application for judicial review to the High Court. Moreover, it should be noted that the processes carried out by CARB do not, in any way, infringe on a complainant's right to either sue an accountant in contract or tort or any other legal form or avenue appropriate for the complainant.

Matters of Public Concern

Where the Conduct Committee of CARB decides that a matter which has been brought to its attention gives rise to, or includes, questions of public concern, one of four approaches may be adopted:
1. If the case relates to a Republic of Ireland matter of public concern, the Conduct Committee will engage with the Irish Auditing and Accounting Supervisory Authority (IAASA) to determine whether IAASA intends, under company law, to investigate the case itself.
2. If the case relates to a UK matter of public concern, the Conduct Committee will engage with the Financial Reporting Council (FRC, see below) to determine whether it intends, under the provisions of the FRC scheme, to investigate the case itself.
3. If neither IAASA nor the FRC undertake to investigate the matter, the Conduct Committee may arrange for the matter to be investigated by a Special Investigator. The Special Investigator will report to the Conduct Committee whether or not, in his or her opinion, there is a case to answer. Where the Special Investigator certifies that there is a case to answer, the Conduct Committee will immediately refer the matter by way of a formal allegation.
4. If neither IAASA nor the FRC undertake to investigate the matter, the Conduct Committee may direct that the matter be investigated by a case manager under the direction of the Head of Professional Conduct in accordance with ordinary process.

The Financial Reporting Council

The Financial Reporting Council (FRC) was initially established in 2003, in the UK, following the collapse of Enron and Arthur Andersen. It is an independent regulator whose role is to promote high-quality corporate governance and reporting in order to foster investment in the UK. Effectively, it promotes the *UK Corporate Governance Code* and the *UK Stewardship Code*. Its functions are threefold:

1. it sets standards for corporate reporting, audit and actuarial practice and monitors and enforces accounting and auditing standards;
2. it oversees the regulatory activities of the actuarial profession and the professional accountancy bodies; and
3. it operates independent disciplinary arrangements for public interest cases involving accountants and actuaries.

The FRC underwent further reform in 2012 and three divisions were set up to support it in carrying out its functions:
- the Codes and Standards Committee;
- the Conduct Committee; and
- the Executive Committee.

The Codes and Standards Committee advise the FRC on maintaining an effective framework of UK codes and standards for governance. It carries out this function through its Accounting, Actuarial and Audit and Assurance Councils. The Conduct Committee is responsible for the FRC's conduct work, it has the power to commence an inquiry, to determine the scope of any such inquiry and to appoint members to its Monitoring Committee and Case Management Committee. Lastly, the Executive Committee is responsible for advising the FRC on its strategic direction and providing day-to-day oversight of the work of the FRC. It supervises the implementation of the FRC business plan and advises the FRC Board on budget, business plan, Board agenda and management of the organisation.

Given that the FRC has the power to deal with cases of potential misconduct that raise or appear to raise important issues affecting the public interest in the UK, it should be noted that on 8 December 2014, the FRC published The Accountancy Scheme and The Accountancy Regulations and The Actuarial Scheme and The Actuarial Regulations.[2] Both Schemes and supporting Regulations updated existing independent disciplinary arrangements applying to members and member firms of the participating accountancy and actuarial bodies. The Schemes and Regulations contain the detailed rules that govern how cases are dealt with by the FRC.

In brief, the stages of the disciplinary process are:
- decision to investigate (in some cases following preliminary enquiries);
- investigation;
- decision on whether to bring disciplinary proceedings against any firm or individual;
- referral to disciplinary tribunal;
- tribunal hearing;
- determination and imposition of sanction and/or cost orders.

---

[2]   See www.frc.org.uk/Our-Work/Enforcement/Enforcement/Schemes.aspx

The FRC can start a disciplinary investigation in one of two ways:
1. the professional bodies can refer cases to the FRC;
2. the FRC may decide of its own accord to investigate a matter.

The Conduct Committee will consider each case identified or referred to it, and decide whether or not the criteria for an investigation are met.

Investigations are conducted by Executive Counsel within the Enforcement Division. The decision about whether to bring disciplinary proceedings rests with the Executive Counsel, a legally qualified officer of the FRC. If disciplinary proceedings are to be commenced, Executive Counsel will file a complaint with the Conduct Committee. The Conduct Committee will instruct the Convener to appoint a Disciplinary Tribunal.

Transparency is provided for in the disciplinary Schemes at various stages of the disciplinary process. All decisions made by the Conduct Committee, Executive Counsel and Tribunals are publicised unless the Conduct Committee considers publication would not be in the public interest.

The disciplinary arrangements contribute to the achievement of the FRC's mission by:
- safeguarding the public interest by protecting the public, maintaining public confidence in the accountancy and actuarial professions, and declaring and upholding proper standards of conduct by accountants and actuaries;
- providing a demonstrably fair and independent system for investigating, and where appropriate, taking disciplinary action in significant public interest cases of potential misconduct;
- imposing appropriate sanctions where misconduct has been proved; and
- seeking to deter future misconduct.

(Significant changes relating to statutory audit, the FRC and the RSBs were due to take effect in June 2016.)

REVIEW QUESTIONS

(See Suggested Solutions at the end of this textbook.)

Question 17.1

Russell has recently been appointed as the auditor of Buzaar Enterprises Ltd ("Buzaar"). In the course of the audit he discovered numerous financial irregularities, such as the failure by Stanley, the company accountant, to keep the books of account on a continuous and consistent basis, incorrect valuation of work in progress, failure to make sufficient bad debt provisions, and the omission of a significant contingent liability from the company's accounts. On discovery of these irregularities Stanley resigned and a new accountant, Sarah, has been appointed.

As Stanley is a Chartered Accountant, Russell has referred a complaint against Stanley to the secretary of the Chartered Accountants Regulatory Board Conduct Committee.

Requirement: Outline to Stanley the various findings/outcomes that may be reached, and the penalties that may be imposed, by the Chartered Accountants Regulatory Board Conduct Committee, if this complaint is upheld.

(Source: Chartered Accountants Ireland, CAP 1, Autumn 2009, Extract: Q4(c))

Question 17.2

You have been approached by your manager who has indicated that he will be taking you along to a presentation which he will be giving to an audit client. The presentation is entitled "The Challenges Facing Directors in the 21st Century". In order to assist him in preparing for this presentation, your manager has asked you to draft a memo for him.

Many of this client's employees are Chartered Accountants and therefore your manager also intends to discuss, as part of his presentation, the Chartered Accountant Regulatory Board.

Requirement: Discuss in your memo, the situation whereby Chartered Accountants can become liable for disciplinary action, and the procedure for investigating complaints.

(Source: Chartered Accountants Ireland, CAP 1, Summer 2009, Extract: Q1(c))

Question 17.3

Your firm has acquired a new client, BlueSky Ltd. You are part of the team on the first audit of Bluesky Ltd. One of your tasks is to audit the travel expenses incurred by the company's management team in the past year. In doing so, you discover that Gary, the company's accountant, made numerous claims for trips abroad, which he claimed were work related. Further investigation has revealed that these trips were personal holidays and completely unrelated to his work. The firm's solicitor has advised that there could be both civil and criminal proceeding against Gary based on his fraudulent claims.

As Gary is a Chartered Accountant, Bluesky Ltd has reported his fraudulent actions to the Chartered Accountant's Regulatory Board (CARB).

Requirement:
(a) Explain the role of CARB and list the THREE grounds under which members and member firms become liable to disciplinary action by CARB.
(b) List TWO sanctions that can be imposed by a Disciplinary Tribunal of CARB.

(Source: Chartered Accountants Ireland, CAP 1, Law for Accountants (NI),
Autumn 2012, Extract: Q2(b))

Question 17.4

Lismount Ltd ('Lismount') began life as a small family-run recycling plant in 1970. Over the last 45 years it has grown from employing five people to now employing over 500 people across Northern Ireland.

The directors come to you for advice on various matters and tell you that their finance director, Shane, a qualified chartered accountant, has been making fraudulent travel claims against the company for the last six months. The amount fraudulently claimed has been in excess of £100,000. You tell the directors that they must now report this matter to the Chartered Accountants Regulatory Board (CARB) for investigation.

Requirement: Outline the process by which a complaint will be investigated by CARB.

(Source: Chartered Accountants Ireland, CAP 1, Law for Accountants (NI),
Summer 2015, Extract: Q3(c))

CHAPTER 18

CORPORATE GOVERNANCE

What is Corporate Governance?

The concept of corporate governance came to the fore in US law journals in the 1970s and is therefore said to be an import from America into the UK.[1] However, it was not until 1990, when Sir Ian Cadbury chaired the committee on the financial aspects of corporate governance, that the concept came into its own in the UK. In the now famous *Cadbury Report*, in 1992, corporate governance was defined as:

"the system by which business corporations are directed and controlled".

This definition has now been used in subsequent corporate governance reports and has been widely adopted by many as the definition of corporate governance.

The Rise of Corporate Governance in the UK

The need for Corporate Governance in the UK came about as a result of a series of corporate collapses and scandals in the late 1980s and early 1990s, including the collapse of the BCCI (Barings) Bank and the Robert Maxwell pension fund scandal. As a result of these, the business community recognised the need for a corporate governance framework in the UK. This led to the setting up, in 1991, of the Committee on the Financial Aspects of Corporate Governance. It was chaired by Sir Ian Cadbury and produced what has become known as the *Cadbury Report*, which was published in 1992. The report addressed issues and concerns relating to:
* the relationship between chairman and chief executive;
* the role of non-executive directors; and
* the reporting on internal control on companies' positions.

Moreover, a requirement was added to the listing rules of the London Stock Exchange that a company should report whether they had followed the recommendations of the *Cadbury Report*. If they had not done so, they had to explain why; this is known as the 'comply or explain' concept or requirement.

---

[1] See Richard Smerdon, *A Practical Guide to Corporate Governance* (3rd Edition, Sweet & Maxwell, 2007).

Since 1992, the *Cadbury Report* has been added to and amended with the publication of subsequent corporate governance reports. The *Greenbury Report* (1995) set out recommendations on the remuneration of directors. Following this, the *Cadbury Report* and *Greenbury Report* were combined together and updated in the 1998 *Combined Code*. Furthermore, the *Turnbull Guidance* was issued in 1999 with the aim of providing directors with advice on how to develop sound systems of internal control. In 2003, the *Combined Code* was updated again as a result of the Enron scandal in the US. Other changes were made to the *Combined Code* in 2006 and 2008. In 2010, the *Combined Code* became the *UK Corporate Governance Code*, which has since been updated in 2012 and 2014. At all times, however, the 'comply or explain' approach, first set out in the *Cadbury Report*, has been maintained.

The Regulation of Corporate Governance

Corporate governance in the UK is regulated by a number of factors, as set out below.

The Financial Reporting Council

The Financial Reporting Council (FRC) has two main subsidiaries: the Accounting Standards Board and the Financial Reporting Review Panel. These were formed in 1990 in order to promote best practice and financial reporting. The powers of the FRC broadened with the publication of the *Cadbury Report* in 1992. In 2003, it assumed responsibility for drafting the revised *Combined Code* of 2003. The stated aim of the FRC is to "promote confidence in corporate reporting and governance". In pursuit of this, its five objectives are to promote:
- high-quality corporate reporting;
- high-quality auditing;
- high standards of corporate governance;
- the integrity, competence and transparency of the accountancy profession; and
- its effectiveness as a unified independent regulator.

Statute

There are a number of parts and sections of the Companies Act 2006 (CA 2006) (see **Chapters 11–15**) that have a direct effect on corporate governance. These are Part 10 (directors), Part 11 (derivative claims), Part 12 (Company Secretaries), Part 13 (resolutions and meetings), Part 15 (accounts and reports) and Part 16 (audit). All of these parts of CA 2006 are likely to have an effect on corporate governance. However, due to the fact that CA 2006 has been implemented over a phased period, with the last phase of implementation only taking place in October 2009, it is too early to tell the exact significance of these parts and sections upon corporate governance.

Codes of Best Practice (The *UK Corporate Governance Code*)

The *Combined Code* of best practice was first published in 1998 and brought together the relevant parts of the *Greenbury* and *Cadbury* reports and the *Hampel Report* into one combined code of best practice. Since then, the *Combined Code* was updated in 2003, 2006, 2008 and 2010. In 2010, the *Combined Code* became the *UK Corporate Governance Code*, which has since been updated in 2012 and 2014. Its development is now considered in the section below.

The Development of the UK Corporate Governance Code

Beginning with the *Cadbury Report* in 1992, a number of reports and codes have made the *Combined Code* into what it is today. These reports and codes are as follows:

- *Cadbury Report* (1992)
- *Greenbury Report* (1995)
- *Hampel Committee Report* (1998) – *Combined Code* (1998)
- *Turnbull Report* (1999)
- *Higgs Report* and the revised *Combined Code* (2003)
- *Smith Report* (2003)
- *Combined Code* (2006)
- *Combined Code* (2008)
- *UK Corporate Governance Code* (2010)
- *UK Corporate Governance Code* (2012)
- *UK Corporate Governance Code* (2014)

The Cadbury Report (1992)

As stated above, the *Cadbury Report* was the first step in the process towards the regulatory regime of corporate governance. The *Cadbury Report* established that governance was not a matter for legislation, but that a code of best practice should be set up. This code comprised 19 provisions and 14 notes dealing with board and committee structures, remuneration and financial reporting, and the appropriate relationship with auditors. Among other things, the key recommendations of the *Cadbury Report* were:

1. the appointment of non-executive directors;

2. the appointment of an audit committee to achieve greater control of financial reporting; and
3. the improved management of the board.

The Greenbury Report (1995)

The *Greenbury Report* was brought about by the rise of the 'fat cats' concept.[2] This was a situation where senior executives of newly privatised companies were paying themselves excessive remuneration packages. The key recommendations of the report were the appointment of a nomination committee responsible for appointments to the Board and the appointment of a remuneration committee to determine directors' remuneration and other pay issues. It was also recommended that the remuneration committee should prepare an annual report, which should be included in the annual accounts, and distributed to shareholders.

The Hampel Committee Report (1998) – the Combined Code (1998)

A committee on corporate governance was established under the Chairmanship of Sir Ronald Hampel in 1995. Hampel's final report was issued in January 1998. A criticism of the *Cadbury* and *Greenbury* reports was that they had established a 'box-ticking' mentality or approach to governance. It was soon recognised that, although companies could tick every box of the codes, they could still be fundamentally flawed. The purpose of the Hampel Committee's report was that there should be a move away from the box-ticking mentality and that the 1992 and 1995 reports should be combined. The result of the *Hampel Report* was the *Combined Code* (1998). The recommendations of the *Combined Code* were:
- consolidation of the recommendations of earlier reports into one combined code;
- improved communication with shareholders;
- a redress of the balance between implementing controls and achieving business success by allowing companies the discretion to apply corporate governance principles in the manner most suited to their organisation and to explain deviations from 'best practice' to shareholders through their annual accounts.

The Turnbull Report (1999)

In September 1999, the Institute of Chartered Accountants in England and Wales (ICAEW) published a report on internal controls in response

---

[2] Smerdon (2007), *op cit.*

to the *Combined Code*. This became known as the *Turnbull Report* after its Chairman, Nigel Turnbull. The *Turnbull Report* recommended a number of guidelines for companies to introduce effective internal controls:

- giving directors, rather than operational managers, the responsibility for risk management and maintaining a sound system of internal controls;
- basing internal controls on a risk-based approach; and
- embedding such controls on the company's operations, the procedures for identifying and reporting control weaknesses, so that appropriate remedial action can be taken.

The Higgs Report and the Revised Combined Code (2003)

The *Higgs Report* came about as a result of the Enron scandal in 2002. This report was commissioned to examine the roles and effectiveness of non-executive directors and the report was particularly critical of many non-executives and their lack of independence. This report made a number of changes to the *Combined Code* as follows:

- a non-executive director should normally serve only two three-year terms, with annual re-election after nine years;
- a time commitment should be set for non-executive directors;
- non-executive directors should meet as a group at least once a year;
- after 10 years in office, a non-executive director ceases to be independent;
- a full-time executive director should not take on more than one non-executive directorship;
- a senior independent director should be identified and available to communicate with shareholders; and
- there should be a formal recruitment, retirement and executive development programme.

In and around the same time, the US passed the Sarbanes–Oxley Act in July 2002, which was their response to the Enron collapse. The essential features of this Act were:

- rules requiring better internal monitoring for potential fraud by a company's board and executives;
- the imposition of responsibilities on outside professionals such as lawyers and auditors to report misfeasance;
- provision for more disclosure, especially of firms' internal control structures; and
- rules on the conduct of corporate insiders, such as prohibition of loans to executives.

The Smith Report (2003)

The purpose of the *Smith Report* was to examine the independence of auditors following the collapse of Arthur Andersen and Enron in the US. In particular, it recommended that an audit committee should have at least three members, all independent non-executive directors. At least one member of the audit committee should have significant, relevant and recent financial experience. The roles and responsibilities of the committee should be set out in written terms of reference, containing at least the requirements of the *Combined Code* of 2003.

The UK Corporate Governance Code

The *Combined Code* was revised again in 2006 and once again in 2008. A small number of changes were made to the versions of the Code in both instances. However, the financial crisis of 2008 and 2009 triggered a further widespread reappraisal of the *Combined Code*. Sir David Walker, in the UK, was asked to review the governance of banks and other financial institutions. The report was published in June 2010 and the *UK Corporate Governance Code* 2010 (formerly the *Combined Code*) was published in June 2010. It sets out standards of good practice in relation to board leadership and effectiveness, remuneration, accountability and relations with shareholders.

Since 2011, the FRC has issued annual assessments of the impact of the *UK Corporate Governance Code* and the *UK Stewardship Code* (discussed below). Work prompted more specifically by the financial crisis also continued, with a number of new requirements introduced in 2012 and through an inquiry led by Lord Sharman, commissioned by the FRC in the same year to identify steps to improve consideration by companies and auditors regarding going concern and liquidity risks, and to recommend measures necessary to improve the existing reporting regime. The final *Sharman Report* was issued in 2013, its main conclusion being that both directors and auditors need to put greater focus on robust management of risks to going concern and in doing so consider the full business cycle of the company concerned. Consequential changes were introduced in the *UK Corporate Governance Code* of 2014 and supplementary guidance, introducing new requirements relating to risk assessment and mitigation, and the monitoring of internal controls and assessing going concern. This was matched by new disclosure requirements setting out the board's views on the longer-term viability of the company and the period they have considered for this purpose.

Principles of the UK Corporate Governance Code

The *UK Corporate Governance Code* sets out the principles of good governance under five headings as shown in **Table 18.1**.

Table 18.1 The Main Principles of the *UK Corporate Governance Code*

Section A: Leadership

1. Every company should be headed by an effective board which is collectively responsible for the long-term success of the company.

2. There should be a clear division of responsibilities at the head of the company between the running of the board and the executive responsibility for the running of the company's business. No one individual should have unfettered powers of decision-making.

3. The chairman is responsible for leadership of the board and ensuring its effectiveness on all aspects of its role.

4. As part of their role as members of a unitary board, non-executive directors should constructively challenge and help develop proposals on strategy.

Section B: Effectiveness

1. The board and its committees should have the appropriate balance of skills, experience, independence and knowledge of the company to enable them to discharge their respective duties and responsibilities effectively.

2. There should be a formal, rigorous and transparent procedure for the appointment of new directors to the board.

3. All directors should be able to allocate sufficient time to the company to discharge their responsibilities effectively.

4. All directors should receive induction on joining the board and should regularly update and refresh their skills and knowledge.

5. The board should be supplied in a timely manner with information in a form and of a quality appropriate to enable it to discharge its duties.

6. The board should undertake a formal and rigorous annual evaluation of its own performance and that of its committees and individual directors.

7. All directors should be submitted for re-election at regular intervals, subject to continued satisfactory performance.

Table 18.1 *(Continued)*

Section C: Accountability

1. The board should present a fair, balanced and understandable assessment of the company's position and prospects.
2. The board is responsible for determining the nature and extent of the principal risks it is willing to take in achieving its strategic objectives. The board should maintain sound risk management and internal control systems.
3. The board should establish formal and transparent arrangements for considering how it should apply the corporate reporting, risk management and internal control principles and for maintaining an appropriate relationship with the company's auditors.

Section D: Remuneration

1. Executive directors' remuneration should be designed to promote the long-term success of the company. Performance-related elements should be transparent, stretching and rigorously applied.
2. There should be a formal and transparent procedure for developing policy on executive remuneration and for fixing the remuneration packages of individual directors. No director should be involved in deciding his or her own remuneration.

Section E: Relations with Shareholders

1. There should be a dialogue with shareholders based on the mutual understanding of objectives. The board as a whole has responsibility for ensuring that a satisfactory dialogue with shareholders takes place.
2. The board should use general meetings to communicate with investors and to encourage their participation.

These main principles of the *UK Corporate Governance Code* are designed to achieve:
- well-directed and balanced activity by the board, with clear leadership by the board's chairman, focused on the long-term success of the company;
- the contribution of appropriate skills, knowledge and time to achieve that success;
- effective identification and management of risks, together with clear and understandable reporting;
- safeguards on remuneration so as to ensure alignment of executive directors with the company's long-term success; and
- meaningful dialogue with shareholders.

Each of the main principles is supported by specific provisions setting out the steps ordinarily required to achieve the aim of the principle concerned. Key provisions of the code can be summarised as follows:

Leadership (Section A) The board's role consists of entrepreneurial leadership within a prudent framework of controls, ensuring appropriate resources are available. The board is also to set the company's values and standards and ensure that its obligations to its shareholders and others are understood and met. Steps to achieve this include ensuring that:

- the board meets sufficiently regularly to discharge its duties effectively;
- there is a formal schedule of matters reserved for its decision;
- the annual report provides information to shareholders (and others) on how the board operates; and
- appropriate insurance cover for directors is in place.

In addition, the *UK Corporate Governance Code* stresses the importance of a clear division between responsibility for the operation of the board and responsibility for the running of the company's business. To this end, the code both requires an appropriate balance between executive and independent non-executive directors (setting out criteria for determining independence) and states clearly that responsibility for running the board lies with the chairman, who is to be independent on appointment and who should not combine the role with that of chief executive. Specifically, the chairman is responsible for:

- setting the board's agenda;
- ensuring there is adequate time for discussion, in particular of strategic issues;
- encouraging openness and debate; and
- ensuring that directors receive accurate, timely and clear information.

Non-executive directors, for their part, are to bring appropriate scrutiny to bear on the performance of management and reporting of performance. As part of doing so, one of the independent non-executive directors is to be appointed as the '**senior independent director**' and in that role should:

- act as a sounding board for the chairman;
- be available to shareholders who wish to raise concerns.

Effectiveness (Section B) The board is to be of a size sufficient to meet the needs of the business (without becoming unwieldy) and is to include an appropriate combination of executive and non-executive directors such that no individual or small group can dominate its decision-making. In support of this aim:

- shareholders (and others) are to be provided with information as to which directors are considered independent, together with explanatory information for that conclusion in circumstances in which contraindications exist, such as recent employment by the company, close family ties with the company's advisor, directors or senior employees, or when a director represents a significant shareholder;

- at least half the board is to consist of independent non-executive directors and the code sets out criteria against which independence is assessed;
- there should be a nomination committee (with a majority of independent non-executive directors) to lead the process for board appointments, which are to be made on merit, against objective criteria and with due regard for diversity (including gender) as a safeguard against inappropriate 'group think', with regular opportunities for re-appointment;
- terms and conditions of appointment of non-executive directors are to be made available for inspection (and thereby comment);
- directors are to update their skills and knowledge on a continual basis, with review by the chairman as to their training and development needs;
- new directors are to be given a full, formal and tailored induction, including opportunities to meet major shareholders;
- directors are to have access to independent professional advice;
- the chairman is to act on the result of the required annual evaluation of board performance, both by recognising strengths and addressing weaknesses, including, if appropriate, making changes in board membership;
- in the case of larger companies, an external facilitator should be involved at least every three years ('larger' companies are those within the London FTSE 350 and those listed on the Irish Main Securities Market and having a market capitalisation of €750 million or more); and
- the non-executive directors are to evaluate performance of the chairman.

Accountability (Section C) The board's overall responsibility is presentation of the "fair, balanced and understandable assessment of the company's position and prospects". In doing so, each annual report of the company is to contain:

- a confirmation from the directors that they consider the standard of "fair, balanced and understandable" has been met;
- an explanation of how the company generates or preserves value over the longer term (taking into account the direction given by the FRC's *Guidance on Risk Management, Internal Control and Related Financial and Business Reporting* (2014)) in addition to a statement as to whether the directors consider it appropriate to adopt the going-concern basis of accounting in preparing the company's financial statements;
- a confirmation from the directors that they have carried out a robust assessment of the principal risks facing the company, together with a description of those risks and how they are being managed or mitigated; and

- an explanation of how the directors have assessed the longer-term prospects of the company, the period they have considered for this purpose (which the FRC guidance indicates is likely to be considerably in excess of a year), and whether they have a reasonable expectation that the company will be able to continue in operation and meet liabilities over that period.

In addition, the 2014 version of the *UK Corporate Governance Code* also introduced a requirement for ongoing monitoring of risk management and internal control systems, supplementing the requirement of earlier codes for an annual review of those systems.

Section C of the *UK Corporate Governance Code* also establishes that companies should establish an audit committee of at least three independent non-executive directors (or two, for smaller companies), with at least one member having recent and relevant financial experience, and with written terms of reference covering at least the matters set out in **Table 18.2**. In addition, it requires the committee:

- to review arrangements for staff of the company to raise concerns in confidence regarding possible improprieties, whether regarding financial reporting or other matters; and
- if there is no internal audit function, to make an annual assessment of whether this is appropriate.

Table 18.2 Role and Responsibilities of the Audit Committee

The *UK Corporate Governance Code* (paragraph C.3.2) indicates that the audit committee's terms of reference, which are to be in writing and available on the company's website, should include:

- to monitor the integrity of the financial statements of the company and any formal announcements relating to its financial performance, reviewing significant financial reporting judgements contained in them;
- to review the company's internal financial controls and, unless expressly addressed by a separate board risk committee composed of independent directors, or by the board itself, to review the company's internal control and risk management systems;
- to monitor and review the effectiveness of the company's internal audit function;
- to make recommendations to the board, for it to put to the shareholders for their approval in general meeting, in relation to the appointment, re-appointment and removal of the external auditor and to approve the remuneration and terms of engagement of the external auditor;

Table 18.2 *(Continued)*

- to review and monitor the external auditor's independence and objectivity and the effectiveness of the audit process, taking into consideration relevant UK professional and regulatory requirements;
- to develop and implement policy on the engagement of the external auditor to supply non-audit services, taking into account relevant ethical guidance regarding the provision of non-audit services by the external audit firm; and to report to the board, identifying any matters in respect of which it considers that action or improvement is needed and making recommendations as to the steps to be taken; and
- to report to the board on how it has discharged its responsibilities.

How the audit committee discharged its responsibilities is to be set out in a separate section of the annual report, which is to include:
- significant issues considered in relation to the financial statements and how these were addressed;
- the committee's assessment of the external auditor; and
- if the external auditor provides non-audit services, an explanation of how auditor objectivity and independence are safeguarded.

Again, while not set out in the *UK Corporate Governance Code* itself, the auditor has a role and is specifically required by the revised ISA (UK and Ireland) 700 to comment if this section does not appropriately address matters communicated by the auditor to the audit committee.

Remuneration (Section D) The board is to establish a remuneration committee with a majority of independent non-executive directors that is responsible for setting the remuneration of executive directors and the chairman. The committee is to use careful judgement to determine remuneration levels, with the aim of promoting the long-term success of the company. Performance-related elements are to be transparent, and the code indicates that the remuneration arrangements should also:
- include provisions to enable the company to recover sums paid or withhold payment in specified circumstances;
- avoid termination payments that reward poor performance and take a robust line regarding directors' obligations to mitigate loss; and
- in the case of non-executive directors, exclude share options or other performance-related elements (unless shareholder approval is obtained in advance).

To help support appropriate decisions, the chairman should ensure that the remuneration committee chairman keeps principal shareholders informed regarding remuneration, and that shareholders are invited to approve all new and amended longer-term incentive schemes.

Relations with Shareholders (Section E) As can be seen, a number of elements in earlier sections of the code are designed to support an open and effective dialogue with shareholders. The final section of the code underpins these by requiring that:

- the chairman ensure that views of shareholders are communicated to the board as a whole;
- non-executive directors are provided with opportunities to attend meetings with major shareholders;
- the annual report sets out steps taken by board members to develop an understanding of the views of major shareholders;
- arrangements for general meeting include clearly set resolutions and appropriate arrangements to facilitate proxy voting;
- when a significant proportion of votes is cast against a resolution, the company explains what actions it intends to take to understand the reasons behind that result; and
- the chairmen of the audit, remuneration and nomination committees are available to answer questions at the annual general meeting.

The UK Stewardship Code

The term 'stewardship' is used in a wide range of contexts to indicate the proper use of resources. In the context of commercial enterprises, effective stewardship involves acting to promote long-term success in such a way that companies, investors and the economy as a whole benefit. The term was used in the *Cadbury Report* primarily in describing the duties of directors to act as good stewards of the company's resources; however, while primary responsibility lies with the company's board, which oversees management, investors also have a part to play in publicly listed companies by holding the board to account for the fulfilment of its responsibilities.

The *UK Stewardship Code* aims to support constructive involvement by institutional investors, such as pension funds, insurance companies, investment trusts and asset managers, in supporting effective governance by holding the board to account for the fulfilment of its responsibilities. While following the *UK Stewardship Code* is voluntary, the FRC encourages institutional investors to become signatories of this code and to publish on their website a description of how they have applied its principles or, if the *UK Stewardship Code* is not fully applied, disclose reasons why.

Principles of the *UK Stewardship Code* *The UK Stewardship Code sets* out seven principles, requiring institutional investors to:

1. publicly disclose their policy on how they will discharge their stewardship responsibilities;
2. have a robust policy on managing conflicts of interest;
3. monitor their investee companies;
4. establish clear guidelines on when and how they will escalate stewardship activities; these include (but are not limited to) circumstances in which investors have concern about the company's strategy, performance, governance, remuneration or approach to risks;
5. be willing to act collectively with other investors where appropriate;
6. have a clear policy on voting and disclosure of voting activity; and
7. report periodically on their stewardship and voting activities.

Steps by which institutional investors may monitor investee companies are also set out in the code and include: keeping abreast of the company's performance and factors that could affect that performance; considering whether the company adheres to the spirit of the *UK Corporate Governance Code*; and attending general meetings. Investors should also endeavour to identify at an early stage any issues that may result in a significant loss in investment value, raising concerns as appropriate with the company's board.

Conclusion

No doubt this latest amendment to the *UK Corporate Governance Code* will not be the last. As the economic crisis continues to unfold, the role of the FRC will be to continually monitor corporate governance and the Code will be subject to constant analysis and review. However, the FRC will commission further research as and when necessary.

References

- Richard Smerdon, *A Practical Guide to Corporate Governance* (3rd Edition, Sweet & Maxwell, 2007).
- Vaeni Mac Donnell, *An Introduction to Business Law* (2nd edition, Chartered Accountants Ireland, 2015).

SOLUTIONS TO REVIEW QUESTIONS

Solution to Question 1.1

In a criminal action the State brings the prosecution on behalf of the public via the police and the Public Prosecution Service. The penalties are usually imprisonment and/or a fine, although community service and probation are alternatives.

A civil action, by comparison, is a private matter usually brought by the injured party with a view to their receiving compensation.

Solution to Question 1.2

European Regulations have a direct effect on members of the EU and are binding in their entirety from the date they come into effect.

European Directives are not binding in their entirety and the EU member states have to enact separate legislation to bring them into force.

Solution to Question 1.3

An Act of Parliament originates from a proposal usually by a member of the government that is introduced to the House of Commons as a bill. The first draft is published and introduced to the House on a first reading. It then proceeds to a second reading, which involves a general debate on its merits. Thereafter, the bill goes to Committee Stage, which involves a more in-depth analysis, consultation and amendment. Once the committee is satisfied with the contents, the bill passes to the Report Stage. If approved by a majority in the House of Commons, it proceeds to a similar process in the House of Lords. The bill must be approved by both Houses of Parliament if it is to become law and comes into force as an Act on the day on which it receives Royal Assent.

Solution to Question 1.4

(a) The High Court is a predominately civil court, located in Belfast, which deals with cases valued in excess of £30,000. It is presided over by the Lord Chief Justice, three Lord Justices of Appeal, 10 High Court Judges and seven High Court Masters. It consists of three divisions: the Queen's Bench, Chancery and Family.

(b)
- Queen's Bench cases: claims in contract and tort, including personal injury litigation;
- Chancery cases: includes claims of a commercial and proprietary nature, including bankruptcy.
- Family cases: matrimonial proceedings such as divorce, as well as cases involving child welfare, residence and adoption.

Solution to Question 1.5

The primary source of EU law is the Treaties of the European Union. Legislation passed by the European Union is known as a 'secondary' source of EU law. Article 189 of the EC Treaty defines the various types of secondary legislation – Regulations, Directives or Decisions:
- Regulations: Regulations are pieces of legislation which are directly applicable in all Member States automatically without the need for implementing legislation at a national level. They have general application and are binding in their entirety. The purpose of regulations is to obtain uniformity throughout the member states; for example, the EU Regulation on insolvency provides for mutual recognition of insolvency proceedings throughout Europe.
- Directives: Directives tend to be more aspirational than practical pieces of legislation as they establish a legal principle that member states are then required to incorporate into national legislation within a specified period of time. For example, there are a number of EU Directives aimed at ensuring equal treatment and equal opportunities. They are addressed to the Member States and do not have immediate binding force until the necessary changes or implementing legislation has been made by the national legislature.
- Decisions of the Court of Justice of the European Union (CJEU): Decisions of the CJEU on the interpretation and application of EU law are a form of common law and are not only binding on the parties to the case but also establish a precedent for future cases. They may be addressed to a state, an individual or an institution and can assist in clarifying general principles of EU law in practice.

Solution to Question 1.6

The courts structure within Northern Ireland:
- The Supreme Court – the highest court in the UK. Based in London and presided over by Lord Chancellor with a staff of 12 Justices of the Supreme Court, the Supreme Court acts as the ultimate appeal court for all courts throughout the UK.
- Court of Judicature of Northern Ireland – comprises the Court of Appeal, the High Court and the Crown Court – presided over by the Lord Chief Justice of Northern Ireland.
- Court of Appeal – comprises Lord Chief Justice and three other judges.
- High Court of Justice – deals with the hearing of more important civil cases as well as some appeals from inferior courts

- Crown Court – sits at 13 venues in Northern Ireland and is the court for more serious trials.
- The Subordinate Courts – County Court, Small Claims Court and Magistrates' Court. The County Court deals with everyday civil disputes. The Small Claims Court deals with cases less than £3,000, while the Magistrates' Court deals with less serious criminal offences.

Solution to Question 1.7

Distinction between civil and criminal law:

1. Definitions: civil law is deemed to be private law and it generally concerns disputes between individuals, where one person sues another person for a wrong, whereas criminal law is deemed to be public law, which involves the state imposing codes of conduct and prosecuting an individual for breaching that code.
2. Title of the Proceedings/Parties: a civil claim is called an action and the parties are known as the plaintiff and the defendant, whereas a criminal case is called a prosecution and the parties are known as the prosecution and the defence (accused).
3. Objectives: the main objective of civil law is compensation and ceasing the unwanted conduct, whereas criminal law's objective is punishment (as well as incapacitation, retribution, deterrence and rehabilitation).
4. Tests: for a civil court to find a defendant liable, the test is the balance of probabilities; for a criminal court to find a defendant guilty the test is beyond all reasonable doubt.
5. Commencement of Proceedings: in civil law an action is initiated by way of pleadings; in criminal law a prosecution is initiated by the State/People/Director of Public Prosecutions either through a summons or an indictment.
6. Representatives: the representative of the State in civil cases is the Attorney General, whereas the representative of the State in criminal cases is the Director of Public Prosecutions.
7. Remedies: the main civil remedies are damages, injunctions, court orders, an account for profits, etc., whereas the main criminal remedies are fines, imprisonment, probation orders, community service orders, etc.

Examples: examples of civil law are contract law, the law of tort, family law and company law. Examples of crimes include a fatal offence (murder/manslaughter), non-fatal offence (assault/false imprisonment), property offence (theft/robbery) and sexual offence (rape/sexual assault).

Solution to Question 1.8

(a) Jurisdiction of the High Court: Claims for more than £30,000 are brought in the High Court.
(b) The High Court of Justice deals with the hearing of the more important civil cases as well as appeals from some inferior courts. The High Court consists of

the Lord Chief Justice, three Lord Justices of Appeal, 10 High Court Judges and seven High Court Masters. The division in which a case in the High Court is dealt with depends on the type of subject matter involved. There are three divisions of the High Court.

The first division is the Queen's Bench Division. This division is for claims in contract or tort and for all matters not assigned by legislation to another division.

The second division is the Chancery Division. This is for types of claims dealt with as equity business in the County Courts and for bankruptcies and claims involving breach of copyright, etc.

The third division is the Family Division, which is for every type of claim concerning family matters, including the awardship of children, determination of a person's legitimacy and the administration of the property of a mental patient.

Solution to Question 1.9

Precedent: a precedent can be defined as a judgment that is cited as an authority to justify a similar decision in a later case involving similar legal issues.

In relation to the hierarchy of the Courts, the precise rules of precedent are:
- a decision of a superior court is binding upon an inferior court;
- a decision of an inferior court will not bind a superior court;
- courts of similar authority have neither the power to bind or over-rule each other; and
- a decision of a foreign court will not bind a national court, although it may act as persuasive authority.

Solution to Question 1.10

The structure of the High Court within Northern Ireland:
- The High Court of Justice is a predominantly civil court, located in Belfast, which deals with cases valued in excess of £30,000.
- The High Court consists of the Lord Chief Justice, three Lord Justices of Appeal, 10 High Court Judges and seven High Court Masters.
- These 10 other judges are officially called 'Puisne' judges, meaning a judge inferior in rank to the Lord Chief Justice. They may sit in any of the divisions of the High Court, although some judges are seen as particularly expert in one or other divisions.

Three classifications of cases heard in the High Court:
- Queen's Bench Division – claims in contract or tort and for all matters not assigned by legislation to another division.
- Second division is called the 'Chancery Division' which is for types of claim dealt with as equity business in the County Courts and for bankruptcies and claims involving breach of copyright.
- Third division is the Family Division – every type of claim involving family matters.

Solution to Question 1.11

The role and structure of the European Court of Human Rights is outlined below.

The European Court of Human Rights (which sits in Strasbourg) should not be confused with the European Court of Justice (which sits in Luxembourg). The Court of Human Rights has the job of interpreting the European Convention for the Protection of Human Rights.

The Court structure has three different types of bodies: Committees, Chambers and a Grand Chamber.

The bulk of the Court's work is carried out in Chambers. Committees of three judges appointed from the chamber have powers to strike out applications or declare them inadmissible.

The Chambers include, as a member, the judge elected in respect of the state party whose conduct is being challenged or a substitute nominated by that state. Should the case before it raise a serious question affecting the interpretation of the Convention, or be likely to result in a decision inconsistent with previous judgments of the Court, the matter can, if none of the parties object, be referred to a Grand Chamber. A Grand Chamber of 17 judges includes the President of the Court, his/her deputies and the Presidents of the Chambers. A case can also be referred to the Grand Chamber after judgment at the request of one of the parties. The case is referred to the Grand Chamber under this provision by a five-judge panel whose decision to reject is not appealable. The Grand Chamber can also hear a request from the Committee of Ministers of the Council of Europe for an advisory opinion on 'legal questions concerning the interpretation of the convention and the protocols'.

Solution to Question 1.12

Rules of Statutory Interpretation:
1. the Literal Rule: this rule gives words their plain, ordinary and everyday meaning – although this may lead to injustice, such as in *Whitely v. Chappell* (1868);
2. the Golden Rule: this rule is only applied in instances of absurd application of literal rule, and it interprets the statute within its broader context, such as in *Adler v. George* (1964); and
3. the Mischief Rule: this rule examines the former law before the statute was passed to ascertain the mischief or remedy that the statute was intended to fix.

Solution to Question 2.1

The standard of care is measured against the 'reasonable man test' based on foreseeability and proximity. In essence, a person falls below the appropriate standard, and is negligent, if he or she fails to do what a reasonable person would in the circumstances. If the defendant is a specialist or professional, he or she will be judged by the reasonable standards of that profession, taking account of industry norms, accepted practice and the level of expertise. The role of the financial controller is to oversee internal accounts and practices; failure to adequately insure company assets means that the controller could be liable for negligence.

Solution to Question 2.2

In determining whether Martin has been negligent it must first be established as to whether or not he had a duty of care. The case of *Donoghue v. Stevenson* (1952) established that a person must take reasonable care to avoid acts or omissions that could reasonably be expected/foreseen as likely to harm another person.

In this case, anyone relying on the accounts of Acme Enterprises Ltd, and in particular the company, its shareholders and creditors will suffer harm from the inflated accounts. This is a reasonably foreseeable outcome and under the principles of the above case, Martin did have a duty of care to those people.

In addition, Martin is expected to comply with certain professional standards in relation to audit procedure which he has not complied with by not actually attending the stock takes.

If Martin had attended the stock takes then the directors would not have been able to falsify the figures so easily and the accounts would have given a true and fair view. Therefore Martin is clearly a significant contributory factor to the loss suffered by the creditors. While it is the directors who falsified the accounts, they would not have been able to do this if Martin had carried out his role as auditor properly.

It is therefore clear that Martin breached the professional requirements of his profession and also the common law duty of care towards users of the accounts. As a result, Martin can be held liable for the losses suffered by the company.

Solution to Question 2.3

Remoteness of Damages: This is a device used by the Court to determine whether or not the level of damage caused by the breach could have been reasonably foreseen; if the courts determine that the level of damage caused by the breach was too remote and could not have been foreseen by a reasonable person, they will not hold the defendant liable. This means that although the defendant's breach may have caused the damage, the defendant will not be held accountable for all of the damage because the damage resulting from the breach is so unexpected or 'remote' that the court considers it unfair to hold the defendant accountable for a level of damage he could not have foreseen. This test is known as the 'reasonably foreseeable' test and was developed in *The Wagon Mound* (1961). (**Note**: A practical application of this case law analysis to the question scenario will suffice for an adequate assessment.)

Solution to Question 2.4

Contributory negligence arises where a person contributes to their own injuries by failing to exercise reasonable care in relation to their own personal safety or the safety of their property; the Court views it as a breach of duty of care towards oneself.

The defence is governed by the Law Reform (Miscellaneous Provisions Act (Northern Ireland) 1948, which allows for the apportionment of damages where contributory negligence arises, based on the degree of fault of the respective parties. The defence may also arise by a failure to mitigate damages, such as in *Jones v. Livox Quarries* (1952) and in *Froom v. Butcher* (1976). In allowing a defence of contributory negligence the Court will take into consideration the age and experience of the person, as well as the actions of a 'reasonable person'. In our scenario the defence may apply to reduce Peter's compensation if his failure to wear the regulation work boots, as required by health and safety law, exacerbated his injuries.

Solution to Question 2.5

The original test to determine whether a duty of care exists is based on the decision of Lord Atkins in *Donoghue v. Stevenson* (1932) and is known as the 'neighbour principle'. The current test was established in *Caparo Industries Plc v. Dickman* (1990) and is a three-tier test which asks:
1. Was the harm reasonably foreseeable?
2. Was there a relationship of proximity between the parties (*Ward v. McMaster* (1988)); and
3. Considering the circumstances, is it fair, just and reasonable to impose a duty of care?

Solution to Question 2.6

Factors the Court will take into consideration in determining whether the instructions given by the kitchen manager are in breach of the required standard of care in respect of negligent actions include:
- The probability of the accident – the higher the probably of an accident, the higher the standard of care it carries. In *Bolton v. Stone* (1951) the miniscule probability of an accident relieved both defendants of liability.
- The gravity of the threatened injury – the higher the gravity, the higher the standard imposed. In *Paris v. Stepney Borough Council* (1951), because the gravity of the injury was high, the failure of the defendant to take reasonable measures to reduce a risk breached the standard of care.
- The social utility of the defendant's actions – the motivation behind the defendant's conduct may be a factor in determining negligence (*Watt v. Hertfordshire County Council* (1954); and
- The cost of eliminating the risk – where the risk is low and the cost is high, failing to eliminate a risk completely may not amount to negligence. However, where the risk or gravity is high, cost is not a factor. In *Donaldson v. Irish Motor Racing Club* (1959) the Court held that the organisers of a motor race were relieved from liability based on the fact that it was impracticable to eliminate the risk completely.

Conclusion: the instructions given by the kitchen manager on behalf of Aunty Em's Catering School Ltd to keep using the blow torch are in breach of the required standard of care, as the probability and gravity of the potential injury were both high. Therefore, the standard of care exercised should have been high to prevent injury.

Solution to Question 3.1

The enforceability of the contract and/or the validity of the revocation will be determined by whether the acceptance of the offer was effectively communicated before the telephone call retracting the offer.

Jacob's letter of acceptance was issued by post. The postal rule, established by case of *Adam v. Lindsell* (1818), provides that a letter of acceptance is validly communicated when it is posted rather than when it is received.

As a general rule, revocation is only effective on communication to the offeree.

The contract in this scenario was formed at the point at which Jacob posted the letter, thus rendering the later revocation invalid.

Solution to Question 3.2

Consideration is a necessary element of a contract which represents the exchange of something of value between the parties as an integral part of the implementation of their agreement.

Past consideration occurs when a promise is made after the benefit of the contract has already been provided/obtained without any inducement or agreed exchange.

The promise of £5,000 payment to Sheila took place after she had performed the task and acted to her detriment and is therefore not legally enforceable.

Solution to Question 3.3

The main elements of a contract are as follows:
1. Offer – the terms and conditions on which one party is prepared to entered into a legally binding agreement with another party;
2. Acceptance – the party receiving the offer confirms their agreement to the terms and conditions being offered;
3. Consideration – the exchange of something of value between the parties;
4. Intention to create legal relations and legal capacity to enter into a legally binding agreement – in other words, the parties must intend to be bound by the agreement, be of sound mind and have reached the age of majority.

A valid contract has not been entered into between the parties in this case as there is no evidence of consideration.

Solution to Question 3.4

For a contract to be valid, it must contain three parts: offer, acceptance and consideration.

The price on the stall of £1,500 is an invitation to treat by the stallholder to the world. James makes a verbal offer to the stallholder to buy the book for £1,000. In making a counter-offer of £1,300 to James, the stallholder has rejected James's offer. The offer in this case is therefore the £1,300 made by the stallholder to James. The first part of the contract is therefore in place.

The second part of the contract is acceptance. James has told the stallholder that he will contact his bank and that if he can get the money from his bank he will buy the book. This is only a conditional acceptance by James of the stallholder's offer of £1,300. However, without an unconditional acceptance and until the consideration has been paid by James, no contract is in place.

James did not ask the stallholder to withdraw the book from the stall until his return, nor did he pay a deposit to secure exclusivity until later in the day.

As all the elements of a contract were not in place, the stallholder was entitled to sell the book to someone else. His offer to James was terminated by the elapse of time as well as by not being fully accepted by James; therefore James cannot sue for breach of contract.

Solution to Question 3.5

(a) The concept of contractual frustration is engaged when an agreement cannot be completed due to unforeseen circumstances outside of the contracting parties' control. Fulfilment of the contract becomes impossible or unworkable.

Four situations where the Court is likely to uphold a claim of frustration:
- where the sole purpose of the contract is invalidated (the traditional example of this is the case of *Krell v. Henry* (1903) which centred around a flat rented to view the King's coronation which was unexpectedly postponed due to the King's ill health).
- the death of one of the contracting parties (a high-profile example being the cancellation of concerts in London following the death of Michael Jackson in 2009);
- natural disasters or environmental catastrophes prevent the fulfilment of the contract (an example being flight cancellations as result of ash cloud and volcanic activity in Iceland in 2010);
- government intervention and/or civil unrest that prevents the contract from being completed (for example government warnings not to travel to a foreign country for security reasons during and in the immediate aftermath of civil unrest in holiday destinations such as Egypt and Greece).

(b) (i) A restraint of trade clause is a term commonly found in contracts of employment that seek to establish exclusivity between the parties by restricting a party's ability to work with/for a competitor for a certain period of time to prevent any loss to the principal business.

   (ii) The court will consider the reasonableness of the restraint of trade clause on a case-by-case basis by reference to the agreed duration, geographical constraints, nature of the industry, the degree of specialism involved, the structure of the business, the role carried out by the employee and the understanding of the parties within the context of any written contract or verbal agreements. If the court considers the clause to be contrary to public policy, unlimited in its duration/geographical restriction or otherwise excessive, it will render the clause void.

(iii) The Court is likely to consider the clause in this instance to be valid as a definitive period and location has been given, neither of which are excessive.

Solution to Question 3.6

An order for specific performance is an order compelling the parties of a transaction to honour their obligations under a contract. It is most commonly encountered in the context of land law and the sale of property, when one party is compelled to complete the transaction. A court would not grant such an order if any of the following grounds were apparent:

1. one of the parties is a minor;
2. the contract is for personal services, such as employment, and the court cannot supervise performance;
3. in circumstances where honouring the contract would cause undue hardship to the one or other of the parties and damages would suffice to compensate the loss; and
4. where there is an issue regarding the conduct of the parties and it would be unjust or inequitable to reinstate the contract.

There is likely to be a legitimate reason why the supplier in this scenario is unable to adhere to the agreed price on a long-term basis (e.g. increased production costs). If such reasons are evident, it would be inequitable to force the supplier to honour the original contract as it would cause undue hardship and could threaten the solvency of the company. It is therefore unlikely that the court would make an order for specific performance, particularly when a one-off monetary compensation would provide an immediate and fair resolution.

Solution to Question 3.7

(i) Within the area of business law, it is common for contracts to contain restraint of trade clauses. Such clauses are commonly found in employment contracts but they are also found in commercial contracts whereby a vendor of a business can restrict a buyer's liberty to compete with the vendor. The courts view such clauses as contrary to public policy and will render them void unless parties take steps to justify that they are reasonable and in the interest of their business. The question of what is reasonable is considered on a case-by-case basis, as the clause must go no further than is reasonable for the protection of the employer's business.

In an employment contract, it is not uncommon or illegal for an employer to restrict a former employee from working within a fixed geographical area or from working for a rival business of the former employer for a period of time after the employee's contract ceases. However, the restrictions must not be excessive. What is excessive depends on the nature of the work in question and the structure of the business.

In *Norbrook Laboratories Limited v. Smith* (1987) an international manufacturer of pharmaceutical products employed the defendant, a chemist, who signed a confidentiality agreement promising not to take up any employment in which he might disclose confidential information within one year of the end of his employment with the plaintiff. The defendant announced his intention to take up work as a chemist for another international company and the plaintiff sought an injunction to prevent him from doing so. It was held by the Northern Ireland Court of Appeal that the injunction should be granted as the agreement was reasonable in relation both to the parties and to the public. In arriving at this decision, the Court considered the worldwide scope of the plaintiff's business, the competition the plaintiff faced and the fact that defendant would be putting himself into a position to pass confidential information to the plaintiff's rivals.

(ii) Any logical analysis of the clause and sensible application of whether or not it is valid or invalid would be awarded marks.

(iii) An injunction is a discretionary equitable remedy of the court, requiring a party to stop or refrain from doing a particular act. Injunctions can be perpetual or they can be granted on a time-specific basis. Types of injunction include:
- interim injunction;
- interlocutory injunction;
- perpetual injunction;
- Mareva injunction.

Solution to Question 3.8

(i) **Frustration** This is where a contract cannot be completed as agreed due to some unforeseeable factor outside the control of the contracting parties. The circumstances where a claim of frustration will be upheld include:
1. when the subject matter of the contract is destroyed – in *Taylor v. Caldwell* (1863) the destruction of a music hall by a fire four days before a performance was due to take place was held to amount to frustration;
2. where government interference prevents performance of the contract – in *Ross v. Shaw* (1917) a contract to purchase yarn from a mill in Belgium could not be lawfully performed once the mill was occupied by German troops during World War I and the contract was deemed frustrated;
3. where performance of the contract becomes illegal;
4. in contracts of personal service, the death or incapacity of one party will amount to frustration – in *Flynn v. Great Northern Railway Company* (1953) the employment contract of a van driver was deemed frustrated when medical evidence proved that he would not be able to return to his job;
5. an inordinate delay or interruption of the contract – such as the contract for the construction of the M50 motorway following the delays caused by the discovery of an old Viking burial site;
6. commercially different circumstances (this scenario arose in a number of coronation cases, including *Krell v. Henry* (1903), when the coronation

procession of Edward VII had to be cancelled due to the King's illness; consequently many arrangements made in which persons obtained the right to view the procession from hotels and rooms overlooking the route came before the English courts – and the courts ruled that the contracts were frustrated); and

7. where a particular event, which is the sole reason for the contract, fails to take place.

(ii) A Government Order is outside the control of Rossmore, meaning they cannot comply with the conditions of the contract any longer. Therefore, the contract is likely to be frustrated.

Solution to Question 3.9

Contract Formation To create a contract an offer must be met by acceptance and supported by consideration. In reviewing the scenario of this case it is clear that an offer was made by the CEO of the college to all of the lecturing staff. An offer can be defined as a clear and unambiguous statement of the terms and conditions under which the parties are willing to contract. In this scenario the offer can be classified as a unilateral offer (where the promise is made 'in return for' the doing of the act). When an offer is made it must be accepted to create a valid contract.

Acceptance can be defined as the final and unequivocal expression of agreement to the terms of an offer. To constitute a valid acceptance, the response must be a mirror image of the offer. In the case of a unilateral offer, acceptance can take place by performance. Relevant case law relating to unilateral offers and acceptance by performance includes *Carlill v. Carbolic Smoke Ball Company* (1893).

It is obvious from the scenario that both Anne's and Frank's actions constitute acceptance by performance to the offer. However, as the offer was only made to the lecturing staff, Frank's actions cannot be classified as valid acceptance as his actions do not mirror the offer. In conclusion, the only valid contract that exists is between Dylan Accounting College and Anne, and the CEO cannot revoke the offer as performance has already taken place.

Solution to Question 3.10

(i) Methods of contractual discharge include the following:
- Performance of contractual obligations – the general rule is that contractual obligations are only discharged by complete and exact performance.
- Agreement – this may arise pursuant to a condition precedent or subsequent, or, where neither exist, the agreement must be supported by consideration.
- Notice – this may arise as per the terms of the contract, subject to minimum notice being prescribed by legislation, or based upon what the court considers reasonable in the circumstances.
- Breach of a contractual condition – this breach may be anticipatory or actual.
- Operation of the law – this may arise upon (a) death, (b) bankruptcy, (c) insanity or (d) frustration.

(ii) Bella's contract has been discharged by operation of the law based on a frustrating event, where government intervention has prevented performance of the contract (the fire inspection report preventing use of the premises as a bakery in their present condition). The legal consequences of this frustrating event is that the loss lies where it falls.

Solution to Question 3.11

Rules relating to Incorporation of Exemption Clauses In order for an exclusion clause to be incorporated into a contract, the 'contracting' party must have actual notice of the clause (by signature, in an unsigned document or by a notice) before the contract is created.

The only exception to this rule arises in the context of a course of dealing, where the contracting party frequently creates this contract and is assumed to have knowledge of the existence of the clause by their course of regular dealing.

Conclusion This clause does not exclude Aunty Em's Catering School Ltd in respect of this loss as this clause was not brought to the student's attention before she created this contract by actual notice and she cannot be classed as a regular contracting party based on the information provided.

Solution to Question 3.12

(a) **Contractual Capacity** Certain categories of persons are deemed, by the law, as being incapable to make contracts. For example, sane and sober adults are perceived as having the capacity to enter into contracts. Minors and people with a mental disorder, on the other hand, are said to be incapable of entering into a contract. If a minor or someone with a mental disorder enters into a contract, this person is said to lack the capacity to enter into a contract and therefore the resulting contract is declared as either void or voidable.

Conclusion Anton and Aaron are under 18 and are therefore minors. Minors are defined by the Age of Majority Act (Northern Ireland) 1969 as any person under the age of 18. The Act states that they have limited contractual capacity. Any contract made by an infant/minor is generally regarded as being void and therefore this contract is void.

(b) The main elements of a valid contract are:
   1. Offer: one party makes an offer. An offer can be described as the terms and conditions on which the offeror is prepared to enter a contract.
   2. Acceptance: the second party must accept the offer (as made by the offeror) and distinguish between offer and invitation to treat.
   3. Consideration: there must be consideration exchanged. Consideration has to be something of value and in general will comprise money or money's worth.

4. Capacity: the parties to the contract must have the capacity to enter into the contract, e.g. have the appropriate intellectual capacity and be of the age of majority.
5. Intention: there must be an intention to create legal relations

Conclusion All of these factors must be met for the contract to be enforceable, i.e. recognised by the court as giving rights and obligations to the parties to the contract. All elements are present, as an offer made by BCG that has been accepted by Mr Elis. Both parties have the capacity to enter into a contract and there was an intention by both parties to create legal relations. Therefore, a valid contract exists.

Solution to Question 3.13

The main elements of a valid contract are:
1. Offer: one party makes an offer. An offer can be described as the terms and conditions on which the offeror is prepared to enter a contract.
2. Acceptance: the second party must accept the offer (as made by the offeror) and distinguish between offer and invitation to treat.
3. Consideration: there must be consideration exchanged. Consideration has to be something of value and in general will comprise money or money's worth.
4. Capacity: the parties to the contract must have capacity to enter into the contract, e.g. have the appropriate intellectual capacity and be of the age of majority.
5. Intention: there must be an intention to create legal relations.

Conclusion All of these factors must be met for the contract to be enforceable i.e. recognised by the court as giving rights and obligations to the parties to the contract. All elements present as an offer made by Bill and accepted by Mid Ulster Computer Services (MUCS). Consideration of £1,500 not paid but has been offered. Both parties have capacity to enter contract and there was an intention by both parties to create legal relations. Therefore, a valid contract exists.

Solution to Question 3.14

(a) **Restraint of Trade Clause** This is a clause where one party to the contract agrees to restrict his liberty in the future to carry on trade with other persons, not parties to the contract. Generally, they arise in the context of employment contracts, exclusive service contracts, contracts with vendors of businesses and solus agreements.

(b) In general, the Court only allow these clauses where they are:
1. protecting a legitimate interest (such as trade secrets, confidential information);
2. reasonable between the parties (in terms of both geographical and time restrictions); and
3. not contrary to public interest (unduly restrictive or anti-competitive).

(c) The Court may conclude that the restraint is valid as PFA are protecting a valid interest (confidential customer information). The restraint is not unreasonable in terms of time (six months) or geography (30-mile radius of Belfast), and is not anti-competitive. However, as PFA terminated Harrison's contract, the clause is null and void and has no legal effect.

(d) The Court will never grant an Order for Specific Performance in the following contracts:

1. contracts for personal services: these would include employment contracts, or contracts to perform at a specific concert/event as such an order would be analogous to forced labour and can be futile;
2. contracts to advance money;
3. where the court cannot supervise performance of the contract (where constant supervision by a court is required);
4. where one of the parties is an infant/minor;
5. where the contract is neither fair nor just;
6. where the Order would cause hardship;
7. where the conduct of the party seeking specific performance is questionable, or
8. where damages are an adequate remedy.

(e) **Order against Redmound** It is unlikely that Harrison will obtain such an Order against Redmound as damages will adequately compensate for these losses.

(f) **Payment** It is unlikely that Harrison will be ordered to pay Redmound for work already completed as Redmound committed a repudiatory breach of contract. By doing this they forfeited the right to any compensation for work already completed; as their performance was neither perfect or exact, their abandonment of the contract means that remedies are negated.

Solution to Question 4.1

(a) The Consumer Rights Act 2015 sets out a number of implied terms which are contained in every contract for sale:
  • that the seller has title to the goods in sale;
  • that the goods match the description;
  • that, where goods are being sold in bulk, all goods are of the standard of any sample; and
  • that the goods are fit for their intended purpose.

In James's case, the goods neither match their description nor are they fit for purpose. The book should contain all of the pages set out in the contents and, further, as it is an academic text, it is important that all of the pages are in fact there. The principle of *caveat emptor* or 'buyer beware' cannot apply, as the defects in the book were not made known to him before the purchase.

Had the book been for sale in a 'seconds' bin or had a notice on it to warn that it was not a full and complete copy, it would be different as he would have had prior notice of the defect.

James is therefore entitled to either a replacement book or a refund from the shop.

(b) Under the Consumer Protection (Northern Ireland) Order 1987, a producer will be liable for damage caused by a defective product. A product is defective when it does not meet the safety standards that the consumer is entitled to expect.

Solution to Question 4.2

The General Consumer Council of Northern Ireland was set up in 1985 and has a general duty to promote consumer interests. To this end, it has powers to carry out research, provide information and investigate matters of consumer concern. It consists of a part-time Chairperson, a deputy Chairperson and 12 others members. There is supporting staff of 26 employees. The members represent a wide range of organisations and interests, such as the Trade Union movement, advice centres, local authorities and women's groups. These representatives make up a central body of consumer opinion watching over consumer interests and speaking on consumers' behalf to the Government. The Council liaises closely with the National Consumer Council as well as the Consumer Councils for Scotland and Wales. The Council regularly commissions and publishes reports on matters such as buying a home, private rented housing for students, remedies for consumer complaints, etc.

Solution to Question 4.3

(a) (i) Definition of a **defective product** – this is defined as arising where the product fails to provide the safety that a person is entitled to expect, taking all circumstances into account – such as the presentation of the product, the intended use of the product and the time the product was put into circulation.

Definition of a **producer** – this includes any person who:
- is a manufacturer of a finished product,
- makes themselves out to be a producer by putting their own brand mark or other distinguishing mark on the goods supplied to them, **or**
- is someone who has imported the product into a Member State of the European Union.

(ii) A producer is entitled to rely on the following defences under the Consumer Protection (Northern Ireland) Order 1987 where such a defective product claim is made:
1. The defect in the product is an inevitable consequence of compliance with a requirement imposed by statue or a European Union obligation.
2. The person being sued did not supply the defective product to another person.
3. The product supplied was not supplied in the course of the supplier's business.
4. The product was not defective when it left the supplier's hands.
5. The state of scientific and technical knowledge at the relevant time was not such that the producer might be expected to have discovered the defect.

6. The defect constituted a defect in a product in which the product in question had been comprised and was wholly attributable to the design of the subsequent product.
7. More than 10 years have elapsed since the product was first supplied.

Solution to Question 4.4

(a) In order to successfully bring a claim against a manufacturer for product liability, the plaintiff must show that the product contained a defect and that the plaintiff suffered damage. A plaintiff must also establish that the damage was caused by the product. The last hurdle for a plaintiff to overcome is that he or she must show that the defendant was a producer or importer of the product. Furthermore, it should be noted that the supplier can also be held liable in the event that he is unable to identify the producer or importer if he is requested to do so.

(b) Defences:
1. The defect in the product is an inevitable consequence of compliance with a requirement imposed by statue or a European Union obligation.
2. The person being sued did not supply the defective product to another person.
3. The product supplied was not supplied in the course of the supplier's business.
4. The product was not defective when it left the supplier's hands.
5. The state of scientific and technical knowledge at the relevant time was not such that the producer might be expected to have discovered the defect.
6. The defect constituted a defect in a product in which the product in question had been comprised and was wholly attributable to the design of the subsequent product.
7. More than 10 years have elapsed since the product was first supplied.

Solution to Question 5.1

(1) A typical lease will contain: the identity of the parties, the date of commencement of the lease, a description of the property/premises, confirmation of the rent including the amount to be paid and the method and frequency of payment as well the term of the tenancy, how it can be brought to an end and requisite notice periods.

(2) Six typical covenants of a tenant to the landlord:
- to keep the premises in good repair;
- not to assign or sub-let the lease without authority from the landlord;
- to permit the landlord to re-enter at reasonable times for the purpose of inspections and repair;
- to use the premises for specified purposes only, e.g, residential use only;
- to pay rent in full and on time;
- to deliver up possession at the end of the tenancy.

Four typical covenants given by the landlord to a tenant:
- to allow the tenant to have quiet enjoyment of the property;
- to repair and maintain the structure of the premises;
- to pay rates and service/water charges, if applicable;
- to keep the premises insured (unless covenanted by the tenant).

Solution to Question 5.2

A rent review clause is significant as it enables the parties to regulate the level of rent that is payable on a periodic basis during the course of the lease and allows adjustments to be made by reference to market conditions and with the assistance of an independent expert/valuer so that fairness is achieved between the parties.

Solution to Question 5.3

Terms of a commercial lease: (1) names of the parties, (2) commencement date, (3) duration, (4) recitals – purpose of the lease, (5) the amount of the rent, and payment terms, (6) description of the premises, (7) the notice period to terminate the agreement, (8) the intended use of the premises, as well as any restrictive covenants, (9) the penalties in event of late/non-payment, (10) insurance obligations, etc.

Solution to Question 5.4

Terms normally included within a commercial lease are:
1. Rent Review Clauses One of the most important aspects of a commercial lease is that of rent – it is prudent to consider whether it is appropriate to review the amount of rent during the term of a lease, together with the frequency of review. A balance must be struck here.
2. Service Charge Clauses If any common area is used by a tenant, there will need to be a service charge arrangement. This will usually be contained in the lease and provides for a sum of money to be paid each year by the tenant into a communal fund for the upkeep of the common areas. This may be a stated percentage, or in line with the consumer price index.
3. Alienation (Assignment and Sub-letting) This is the legal term used for assignment or subletting by the tenant of the lease to a third party.
4. Insurance Clause This will provide that the landlord will seek and maintain an insurance policy but that he will recover the insurance premiums from the tenant. It will generally also provide that the insurance policy may not be ended without the tenant being informed and it is often included in the service charge.

Solution to Question 6.1

Application for planning permission should be submitted to the divisional Planning Service Office for the area where intended works are to be carried out. Each local office forms part of a central planning operation and is therefore bound by general planning policy. Notification of applications published in Press and Planning Service notifies neighbouring occupiers should they wish to object to the application.

In making a determination on grant or refusal of planning permission, the Planning Service will refer to the relevant planning policy documents.

The applicant can appeal to the Planning Appeals Commission, which is an independent body. Appeals may only be made by or on behalf of the person who made the application. There is no third-party right of appeal. The appeal must be made within six months of the date of refusal of planning permission.

If successful, planning permission may be granted either in outline or in full. If granted in full, the applicant has permission to carry out works, but this is subject to reserved matters. If permission is granted in outline, it will be essential to obtain subsequent permission, which will deal only with the specifically reserved matters in the outline permission. If planning permission is conditional, then any conditions imposed must be reasonably related to the permitted development and must also be reasonable.

Full planning permission is valid for only five years after it has been granted. After that, a fresh application has to be made. Though works have to be started within that five-year period, they do not have to be completed.

In the case of outline permission, approval of reserved matters must be sought within three years and work must have begun within five years of outline permission or two years of final approval, whichever is the later.

If building occurs without planning permission, or if any condition of the planning permission is breached, the Town and Country Planning Service has the power to issue an enforcement notice outlining the procedure to be followed to remedy the breach.

The Town and Country Planning Service has four years from the date of the works to issue an enforcement notice, a four-year time limit that applies only if the breach relates to an operational development or if there has been a change of use to a single dwelling.

Solution to Question 7.1

(i) Redundancy is a type of dismissal. The legal definition is found in Article 174 of the Employment Rights (Northern Ireland) Order 1996 which states as follows:

"an employee who is dismissed shall be taken to be dismissed by reason of redundancy if the dismissal is wholly or mainly attributable to —
(a) the fact that his employer has ceased or intends to cease —
   (i) to carry on the business for the purposes of which the employee was employed by him, or
   (ii) to carry on that business in the place where the employee was so employed, or

(b) the fact that the requirements of that business —
   (i) for employees to carry out work of a particular kind, or
   (ii) for employees to carry out work of a particular kind in the place where the employee was employed by the employer, have ceased or diminished or are expected to cease or diminish".

(ii) The first step in any redundancy procedure is to identify the criteria which will be used to select employees for possible redundancy and, taken a step further, the criteria which will be applied in the final decision-making process. Consultation with employees at an early stage is essential to ensure that the procedure is fair. Employers are under a statutory obligation to consider alternatives to redundancy including possible redeployment and employees should be made aware of any such opportunities.

Solution to Question 7.2

Grounds which qualify as automatic, unfair dismissal include:
- pregnancy;
- religion, race or political opinion of the employee;
- where an employee has exerted the right to be paid minimum wage;
- trade union membership.

A redundancy payment is determined by reference to the employee's age and length of service. If Dermot is aged between 22 and 40 he will be entitled to one week's pay for every year of service (10 weeks' pay). If aged 41 or above, he will be entitled to 1.5 week's pay for every year of service (15 weeks' pay).

Solution to Question 7.3

(a) The law in relation to lawful dismissal and unfair dismissal is set out in the Employment Rights (Northern Ireland) Order 1996, which establishes that an employee has the right not be unfairly dismissed (in the majority of cases, employees must have one year's continuous service to qualify for this right).

A dismissal is lawful if an employer has just cause to dismiss an employee. Fair reasons for dismissal include incapability, misconduct, redundancy or retirement.

An employer must also follow disciplinary and dismissal procedures to ensure that all relevant information is taken into account and that the employee has an opportunity to respond to any allegations made against him/her.

A three-step procedure is normally involved:
   (i) Fact-finding investigation and correspondence issued to the employee, giving written notice of the procedures being invoked against them and the reasoning behind the action;

(ii) Meeting between the employee and the management to discuss the action being taken and to inform them of the outcome of the fact-finding and ultimate decision;

(iii) The outcome is confirmed in writing and the employee is offered an opportunity to appeal the decision.

An employee must also be given adequate notice in accordance with the statutory requirements and their contract of employment.

Unfair dismissal gives rise to a legal cause of action. A dismissed employee who feels that he has been dismissed without due cause or process can apply to an Industrial Tribunal to examine the reasoning and procedures behind the dismissal within three months of the effective date of termination. The onus will then be on the employer to show that the reason for the dismissal was fair and that they acted reasonably in all of the circumstances surrounding the decision to dismiss. The tribunal has the power to order the employee to be reinstated, re-engaged or compensated.

(b)

(1) The express terms of an employment contract are as follows:
- Job title and description
- Provision of pay and benefits (e.g. pension entitlements or expenses)
- Holiday entitlements and hours of work
- Grievance and dispute resolutions procedures
- Company rules and regulations.

(2) Employees' implied duties:
- To act in good faith
- To exercise due care and attention in carrying out their duties.

Employers' implied duties:
- To maintain a safe working environment
- To indemnify their employees.

Solution to Question 7.4

An employment contract will usually contain some or all of the following key provisions:

- Job title and description of duties and standard weekly hours to be worked;
- Details of salary, including bonuses and benefits such as pension, medical insurance, company car, etc.;
- Details of holiday entitlements;
- Details of the company's disciplinary and grievance procedures;
- Restrictive covenants such as non-compete and non-solicitation on leaving the company;
- Confidentiality provisions;
- A provision assigning any intellectual property created during employment to the company;

- Other company rules and policies such as maternity entitlements, data protection, retirement, redundancy procedures etc., which are often found in a Company Handbook.

Solution to Question 7.5

There are a number of tests to determine whether a person is an employee or an independent contractor. It is important in Peter's case as a number of employment rights, and in particular the right to redundancy payments, apply to employees only and not to independent contractors.

Despite what is stated in the contract between the parties, the court will look behind the contract at all elements of the relationship between the parties.

The criteria they will use include:

- **The level of control that the employer exercises over the person** An independent contractor is given a task to do but can carry it out any way they wish. An employee will be obliged to comply with all orders given to them and must carry out the work when and how instructed, in addition only employees are required to comply with a company's policies.
  In Peter's case the company exercises a large amount of control over him. He must comply with reasonable instruction and comply with company policy. In addition, the company provides his office, equipment and even pays for his training. These indicate he is an employee.
- **How the person is paid** An employee is paid a weekly or monthly salary and the company is responsible for the deduction and payment of tax and National Insurance. An independent contractor, on the other hand, submits invoices for payment and is responsible for their own tax and National Insurance payments. Peter submits invoices and pays his own tax, which indicates that he is an independent contractor.
- **Benefits** Independent contractors do not receive any kind of benefits such as pension or medical insurance. The fact that Peter receives these benefits indicates that he is in fact an employee.
- **Non-compete** An employee will be required to work only for their employer and enter into restrictive covenants. Independent contractors would not normally enter into such restrictions as often in practice they will work for a number of companies at any one time. The fact that Peter has been required to enter into non-compete restrictions indicates that he is an employee.
- **Period of employment** Independent contractors are usually on short- or fixed-term contracts, which usually last only for the duration of a specific project.
  Peter has been employed for 12 years and appears to have worked only for the company during that time. This indicates that he is an employee.

Based on the above, it appears that, despite the terms of his contract and the method of pay, Peter is in fact an employee and is therefore entitled to redundancy payments for the 12 years he has been employed by the company.

Solution to Question 7.6

(a) Four duties owed by an employer to an employee are to:
- pay remuneration;
- provide a safe system of work;
- indemnify the employee for any loss incurred in carrying out their role, and
- identify the terms and conditions of employment.

(b) The four main sources of employment contracts are:
- Primary legislation
- Collective agreements
- Custom and practice
- Staff handbooks.

Solution to Question 7.7

Three remedies are available for unfair dismissal: reinstatement, reengagement and compensation. Although the emphasis within the legislation is on securing the reinstatement or reengagement of the dismissed employee, there is in fact no legal right for an employee to get his or her job back. Few awards of reinstatement or re-engagement are made in practice, due to the logistical difficulties and the breakdown in the relationship between the employer and the employee.

Reinstatement This takes effect as if an employee had never been dismissed. Therefore, it involves full restoration of pay and other benefits, seniority and pension rights, etc.

Reengagement This occurs in situations where the tribunal thinks that reinstatement is not practicable. It allows the employer to offer the employee a different but comparable job, or another suitable job.

Compensation Compensation is generally the type of award made by the Industrial Tribunal, particularly where the employer and employee consider that reinstatement or reengagement would be unworkable. There are two elements to a compensatory payment. The first is the basic award that aims to compensate the employee for the loss of his or her job and is calculated in the same way as a redundancy award. The second aspect of the award is discretionary, and is based on future loss.

Solution to Question 7.8

(a) The prerequisites for bringing an unfair dismissal tribunal claim are that the individual must actually be an employee, as opposed to being a self-employed independent contractor, and he or she must also have had one year's continuous service with their employer.

(b) Tests that an Industrial Tribunal will look at to establish whether or not someone is an employee for the purposes of an unfair dismissal claim:

The Control Test Developed during the 19h Century, the determining factor of this text was said to be the degree of control exercised by the employer. Could the employer tell the worker not only what to do, but also how to do it? Did he or she control the manner of performance? In the case of *Walker v. Crystal Palace* (1910), a professional footballer was held to have a contract of employment with the club.

The Organisation (or Integration) Test A test suggested first by Lord Denning in the 1950s requires one to ask: "Is the individual integrated into the organisational structure?" If so, he or she is more likely to be an employee. The less degree of integration there is, the greater the likelihood of self-employment. This test was approved in *Whittaker v. Ministry of Pensions* (1967) where the plaintiff was held to be an integral part of the organisation and therefore entitled to be treated/classed as an employee.

The Economic Reality Test Is it possible for a worker to be closely integrated into an organisation and to be closely controlled, and yet to remain a self-employed worker rather than an employee? This question was asked in *Market Investigations v. Ministry of Social Security* (1968). The issue was whether a part-time market researcher employed to carry out specific and time-limited assignments was employed under a contract of service or a contract for services. It was concluded that she was employed by the company on a series of contracts of service. She was not in business "on her own account", even though she could work for other employers.

The Multiple Factor Test As examined in the case of *Ready Mixed Concrete v. Ministry of Pensions* (1967) there is no one factor that can establish whether a contract of service exists or not. In different situations, different factors can assume greater or lesser importance. All relevant factors must be taken into account.

No Right to Arrange for a Substitute The right to arrange for a substitute is not necessarily inconsistent with a contract of employment. In *McFarlane v. Glasgow City Council* (2001) the question was whether a contract which provided for gym instructors working in council leisure centres was a contract of employment or not. The instructors were permitted to arrange for a replacement from the register maintained by the council if they were unable to work a particular shift. The Employment Appeals Tribunals held that this did not prevent the contract being a contract of employment. It was enough that the dominant obligation was to do the work personally.

A Mutual Obligation to Provide Work and to Accept the Work There must be 'a mutual obligation' between the parties. In *O'Kelly v. Trust House Forte plc* (1983) a 'regular casual' made a claim for unfair dismissal. Although he had worked for the hotel at functions for many years, the work was seasonal and irregular. There was no mutual obligation to provide or to accept work. It was said by the Court of Appeal to be custom and practice in the industry that casual workers were not to be considered employees working under a contract of employment. There was no right to claim unfair dismissal. This idea of 'mutuality of obligation' means that casual workers are unlikely ever to be employees.

(c) Students will be expected to weigh up the characteristics of an employee versus a contractor. The fact that Sarah worked set hours and was told what to do would point towards her being an employee. However, the fact that the contract says 'contract for services' indicates she is self-employed. So long as students apply a convincing rationale for an answer, he or she will be awarded the marks.

Solution to Question 7.9

Outline and explain the principles of natural justice that employers should follow when subjecting employees to disciplinary actions.
(a) Three principles of natural justice that employers should follow when subjecting employees to disciplinary actions:
   - The opportunity to state a case This involves the holding of a hearing, the purpose of which should be twofold: (1) to allow the employer to find out whether or not misconduct has been committed; and (2) to give the employee a chance to explain the conduct or provide any mitigating circumstances.
   - The right to know the case against you The rules of natural justice require an employee to know the case he or she has to meet at a disciplinary hearing. The allegation or allegations must be specific. Any evidence against the employee should be made available to him or her or at the start of the hearing or preferably beforehand.
   - Avoidance of bias A fundamental tenet of many legal systems is that you cannot be a judge in your own case. The person conducting the disciplinary hearing should not have a direct interest in the outcome of the proceedings and should not be or appear to be biased or impartial.
(b) Constructive Dismissal Constructive dismissal is where an employee believes that they have no other option but to resign from their employment because of the actions of their employer. The conduct of the employer must be sufficiently serious as to entitle the employee to resign from their employment. In this instance, the onus lies on the employee to prove that what has happened amounted to a dismissal.
(c) As far as pre-requisites to bring a claim for constructive dismissal are concerned, the person bringing the claim must be an employee and they must have at least one year's service.
(d) Conclusion The actions of Fiona's employer are likely to be classified as grounds for a claim for constructive dismissal as they are attempting to penalise Fiona for a failure to alter her contract.

Solution to Question 7.10

Failure by an employer to comply with health and safety legislation is normally a criminal offence. Article 31 of the Health and Safety at Work (Northern Ireland) Order 1978 imposes a range of penalties. On summary conviction in a magistrate's court, penalties are by way of fines only. On conviction on indictment, the penalty is up to two years' imprisonment and/or an unlimited fine.

Solution to Question 7.11

Grounds that may constitute fair dismissal include only: (1) lack of competence, (2) lack of capability, (3) lack of qualifications, (4) redundancy, (5) misconduct, (6) illegality (employee could not continue to work in the job he or she held without contravention of a duty or restriction imposed by law).

The standard procedure to effect a fair dismissal is in three steps, as follows:
- the employer informs the employee in writing about the basis of the charge and invites him or her to a meeting to consider a response;
- the employee must attend the meeting and be informed afterwards of the decision and of the right to appeal;
- if an appeal meeting is held, afterwards the employer must inform the employee of the final decision.

If Cherry follows these three steps when dismissing Edward, they will have complied with the rules of natural justice and will ensure his dismissal is unlikely to be unfair if challenged by Edward.

Solution to Question 7.12

Duties an employer owes to an employee pursuant to the health and safety legislation are as follows:
1. a duty to provide reasonably competent fellow employees;
2. a duty to provide a safe plant and appliances, equipment, tools and machinery;
3. a duty to provide a safe system of work, training and supervision, protective clothing, etc.

Conclusion Regal have breached their duty by not providing the injured employee with protective clothing.

Solution to Question 7.13

(a) Redundancy Article 174 of the Employment Rights (Northern Ireland) Order 1996 defines a redundancy as a dismissal which is wholly or mainly due to the fact that the business in which the employee works has or will cease to exist, the business has or will cease to exist in the place in which the employee works, or the requirements of the business for employees to carry out work of the particular kind carried out by the employee either generally, or in the place where the employee works, have ceased or diminished or are expected to cease or diminish.

(b) Eligibility requirements to obtain a statutory redundancy payment are as follows:
- being employed under a contract of service; and
- having been employed by the employer for at least two years.

(c) Conclusion Porter is not entitled to a statutory redundancy payment in these circumstances. His position is still available; therefore this is not a genuine redundancy. In reality, he has been dismissed for gross misconduct.

Solution to Question 7.14

Items that should be contained within a contract of employment include:
- names of employer and employee;
- date of commencement of employment and relationship with previous employment;
- date the contract is issued;
- scale or rate of remuneration;
- intervals at which remuneration is paid (e.g. weekly, monthly);
- any terms and conditions relating to hours of work;
- holiday entitlement;
- sickness notification rules and procedures;
- pensions and pension schemes;
- length of notice that the employee must give and is entitled to receive;
- job title or description;
- date of expiry of a fixed-term contract;
- place of work;
- details of applicable collective agreements;
- disciplinary rules and grievance procedures.

Solution to Question 8.1

Under the Data Protection Act 1998, an employer will be considered to be a data processor as they hold information on their employees. The Act requires:
- that information is only obtained that is fairly required for specific and lawful purposes;
- that the information is used only for the purpose for which it was collected;
- that the information is kept secure and confidential; and
- that the information is only retained for as long as it is legitimately needed.

Solution to Question 8.2

The rules on data processing are follows. Personal data must:
- be processed fairly and legally;
- be processed for limited purposes and in an appropriate way;
- be relevant and not excessive for the purpose;
- be accurate and up-to-date;
- not be kept longer than is necessary to fulfil that purpose;
- be processed in accordance with the rights of the individual;
- be kept securely;
- only be transferred to countries that have suitable data controls.

(*Note:* the answer should be in memo format to attain full marks.)

Solution to Question 8.3

The Data Protection Act 1998 imposes the following obligations upon data controllers:
1. to ensure that data is only kept for one or more specified, lawful purposes;
2. to ensure that data is used in a manner compatible with its purpose;
3. to implement appropriate security measures to safeguard data;
4. to ensure that retained data is accurate and up-to-date;
5. to ensure that retained data is adequate, relevant and not excessive;
6. to ensure that data is not retained for longer than necessary; and
7. to provide a right of access to individuals/employees.

Conclusion Cherry Cottage Ltd has breached its security obligations and therefore may be liable under the terms of the Act.

Solution to Question 8.4

(a) The eight principles of the Data Protection Act are as follow:
    1. personal data should be processed fairly and lawfully;
    2. personal data should be obtained only for limited purposes;
    3. personal data should be adequate, relevant and not excessive;
    4. personal data should be accurate and, where necessary, kept up to date;
    5. personal data processed shall not be kept for longer than is necessary for that purpose or those purposes;
    6. personal data shall be processed in accordance with an individual's rights;
    7. personal data should be secure; and
    8. personal data should not be transferred to other countries without adequate protection.

(b) The procedure to make a Data Subject Access Request (DSAR) is as follows:

A DSAR must be made by a data subject in writing. Before complying with the DSAR, employers are entitled to request a fee of £10.00 and such information as may reasonably be necessary to satisfy themselves as to the identity of the individual making the DSAR in an order to locate the information sought. If the employee concerned is still working for the employer, there is unlikely to be any uncertainty about their identity – though the employer should still make sure that the request is from the employee and not for, for example, from an inquisitive colleague. Employers must respond within 40 days of the receipt of a request or within 40 days of receipt of the £10 fee.

Solution to Question 9.1

Directors are agents of the company. If a director acts outside his authority, but third parties act in good faith believing that he/she is acting in accordance with the objectives of the company, the company can still be bound by the director's actions if the board of directors has given the impression that the director has their full authority. This impression can be inferred by conduct or from the ordinary course of business of the company which is likely to be sufficient in terms of this scenario to confer responsibility on Giselle Ltd to pay for the supplies ordered by Edward.

Solution to Question 9.2

As a director, Rose has both implied and apparent authority to enter into a contract on the company's behalf, but if she is acting contrary to express instruction, the law of agency will apply to protect innocent third parties from the fact that she is holding herself out to have actual authority.

In the case of *SMC Electronic Ltd v. Akhter Computers Ltd* (2003), an employee who was a director in name/title only was deemed to have entered into a valid contract with a third party as the court held that it was reasonable for the third party to assume that he had authority to enter into such a contract. Applying this case to the facts of this scenario, it is likely that the lease agreement would be considered valid.

Solution to Question 9.3

A contract of agency can be terminated:
1. By the action of the parties:
    (a) where a single transaction is completed,
    (b) by notice of revocation of the agreement,
    (c) by the efflux of time,
    (d) by mutual agreement, or

2. By operation of the law:
    (a) upon the death of the principal or agent,
    (b) insanity,
    (c) bankruptcy, or
    (d) the occurrence of a frustrating event.

3. Completion of the Agency Agreement.

Conclusion This agreement should be terminated by mutual agreement or notice (as it is not a single transaction, there is no efflux of time and operation of the law does not apply).

Solution to Question 9.4

Agency by estoppel is where the principal allows a third party to believe that the person is his agent or where the actions of the principal have postulated this fact. This situation may arise where a person acted as agent in the past and continues to act as such after the agency relationship has been terminated. Case examples include: *Panorama Developments (Guildford) Limited v. Fidelis Furnishing Fabrics Limited* (1971) and *Freeman & Lockyer v. Buckhurst Park Properties (Mangal) Limited* (1964).

In these circumstances the agent does not have actual authority, but instead the agent has apparent or ostensible authority.

Conclusion Cupcake and Coffee Ltd is legally obliged to pay the £3,000 due to the Aromatic Coffee Company as Porter acted as an agent of Cupcake and Coffee Ltd. In this situation the Aromatic Coffee Company had no reason to believe that he was acting outside the scope of his duties and for his own personal interest. The only option available to Cupcake and Coffee Ltd is to seek recompense of this £3,000 from Porter.

Solution to Question 10.1

Four methods to dissolve a partnership are as follows:
- by agreement of the parties;
- by order of the court upon the application of one of the partners;
- on the expiration of a fixed term under the partnership agreement; and
- upon completion of the purpose or venture upon which the partnership was based.

Solution to Question 10.2

(a) A Partnership Deed regulates the relationship between the partners and deals with the resolution of various matters which will arise during or at the conclusion of the partnership term. It will generally deal with the following:

- details of the firm – its name and place of business;
- the capital contributed by each partner;
- details of all property to be owned by the partnership;
- the date the partnership commences and its term;
- profit and loss distribution – not always in equal proportions;
- the duties, rights and obligations of the partners;
- procedure for dissolving the partnership – sale or winding up;
- procedure for a person leaving (death, bankruptcy or retirement) or joining the partnership;
- dispute resolution.

(b) There are three statutory duties under the Partnership Act 1890:

- duty to disclose;
- duty not to compete; and
- duty to account.

(c) A partnership can be dissolved by:

- Expiry of its stated term;
- By notice of the partners;
- By the death or bankruptcy of a partner;
- If a partner is found guilty of misconduct; and
- If the partnership can only continue to trade at a loss.

Solution to Question 10.3

(a) The main benefits of continuing to trade as a sole trader include:
- the business model is personal, informal and flexible;
- ultimate control of the business rests with Bertie and the assets are owned by Bertie personally;
- no statutory registration, filing requirements, formal permission or licence required to trade as sole trader; therefore, there are no cost implications.

The main disadvantages of continuing to trade as a sole trader include:
- a sole trader has unlimited personal liability for the debts of business and Bertie's personal assets could be at risk if the business fails;
- the business is dependent upon Bertie – it has no fixed duration and there is no natural succession plan, unlike a partnership which can make provision for this, or a company, which has perpetual succession.

(b) Four terms which should usually be included in a partnership agreement are:

1. the date of commencement and proposed duration of the partnership;
2. a description of the main business and purpose of the partnership;
3. provision for the allocation of profit and losses;
4. the procedure to be adopted on the death, retirement or bankruptcy of a partner.

(c) A limited liability partnership (LLP) is similar to a limited company. The partnership itself has a separate legal identity and unlimited liability for its debts, while the liability of the individual partners is limited to the amount of their capital contribution.

Two or more people can apply to be incorporated as an LLP to the Registrar of Companies. LLPs have similar requirements for governance and accountability as limited companies. To be incorporated, subscribers to an LLP must file an LLP registration form with the Registrar of Companies and pay the appropriate registration fee. A partnership agreement or deed to regulate the position is also advisable.

The registration form will include the following key information: the name of LLP; location of registered office (in Northern Ireland) and address; names and addresses of all LLP members; names of designated members who take responsibility for the LLP's publicity requirements; contributions made by each member; proposed duration of the partnership and a statement confirming the intention to form an LLP.

(d) The Partnership Act 1890 contains the following three provisions to govern the termination of a partnership.
- by agreement of the parties (section 32);
- by operation of law (section 33 and 34);
- by order of a court (section 35).

Solution to Question 10.4

A deed of partnership (partnership agreement) regulates the relationship between the partners and deals with the resolution of various matters which will arise during or at the conclusion of the partnership term.

A partnership agreement generally contains the following:
- details of the firm – its name and place of business;
- the capital contributed by each partner;
- details of all property to be owned by the partnership;
- the date the partnership commences and its terms;
- profit and loss distribution – not always in equal proportion;
- the duties, rights and obligations of the partners;
- procedure for dissolving the partnership – sale or winding up.

Solution to Question 10.5

To: Partners, Maddox Consultancy Solutions
From: Management Consultant
Date: September 2015
Subject: Partnership queries

Dear Partners,

Please find below my responses to your recent queries.

(a) Dissolution of a Partnership This may arise: (1) by agreement of the parties (section 32 of the Partnership Act 1890); (2) by operation of the law (section 33 and 34) – through the expiration of its term, completion of the partnership's purpose, a partner giving notice that he or she wants to end the partnership, through death of one or more of the partners, bankruptcy, illegality, frustration or a change of a partner's share in the partnership; or (3) by order of a court (section 35) – through insanity, incapacity, conduct prejudicial to the business of the partnership, breach of duties, where the partnership can only be carried on at a loss or in any circumstances that the court considers it just and equitable.

In this situation, Maddox could either effect the dissolution by agreement or by an order of the court based on Martin's act of misconduct.

(b) Priority of Debts on Dissolution Once the value of the partnership property is realised, the proceeds are applied in the following order: (1) all debts to outsiders; (2) all monies advanced by partners beyond their original capital contribution; and (3) all capital contributions of the individual partners:
- any residue is divided between the partners in the same proportion as they shared in profits (section 44 of the 1890 Act);
- if there is a deficit, then this has to be made good out of any profits held back from previous years, out of the partners' capital, or by the partners individually in the proportion to which they were entitled to a share in profits.

If you require further information, please contact me directly.

Regards

Management Consultant

Solution to Question 11.1

Section 21 of the Companies Act 2006 states that Articles of Association can be altered by special resolution, which must be notified to the Registrar of Companies within 15 days (section 26).

Solution to Question 11.2

The Veil of Incorporation ensures that the company and its directors are treated as separate legal entities. It can be lifted by the court in exceptional circumstances if deemed to be in the public interest and if there is evidence of abuse by company directors; for example, the company has been formed for an improper purpose (*Re Bugle Press Ltd* (1969)) or is being exploited by individual directors to evade their liabilities, e.g. in the cases of *Re H and Others* (1996), where the company was being used for fraudulent evasion of excise duty.

Solution to Question 11.3

(a) The main advantage of operating as a limited company as opposed to as a partnership is that a company is a separate legal entity and the members' liability is limited to the amount paid up by them on their shares.

The main disadvantage is that a limited company must make certain information publicly available, including the annual accounts, by filing these with the Registrar of Companies.

(b) To establish and trade as a public limited company, the following steps must be taken:
1. File the following with the Registrar of Companies:
   - Memorandum of Association – this sets out the name, place of business, the main objects of the company, the authorised capital of the company, the names and addresses of the first subscribers, and the number of shares taken by each subscriber;
   - Articles of Association – this document deals with the internal running of the company such as directors, meetings, share dealings, etc.;
   - Form 21 – sets out first directors, secretary and the registered office of the company; and
   - Form 23 – sworn certificate that the statutory formation requirements have been complied with.
2. Once these have been received, the Registrar of Companies will issue a Certificate of Incorporation.
3. A public company must also have a Trading Certificate in order to trade, which it can apply for on receipt of the Certificate of Incorporation.

Solution to Question 11.4

(a) A 'promoter' is someone who is actively involved in the formation of the company. This role not only involves co-ordinating the procedural steps to be taken to meet the statutory requirements of formation at the Registrar of Companies (Companies House) but can also involve seeking investment and start-up capital and issuing a company prospectus.

(b) The five main documents to be lodged at Companies House include:
   1. Memorandum of Association
   2. Articles of Association
   3. Application for Registration
   4. Statement of the Company's proposed officers
   5. Statement of Compliance.

Solution to Question 11.5

(a) A promoter is said to be anyone involved in the planning, incorporation or initial running of a company other than persons involved in a professional capacity (hence, solicitors, accountants, etc., will not be considered promoters). The role of a promotor would typically include the initial procedural steps to form a company, seeking out investment and inviting suitable people to be the company's directors.

(b) A pre-incorporation contract is a contract that is attempted to be formed prior to a company being formed. If a company attempts to make a contract on behalf of the company, prior to the company being formed, it is not binding on the company. The person who purports to act on behalf of the company is personally liable on the contract unless there is some provision to the contrary.

(c) A promoter can avoid liability for a pre-incorporation contract:
   - by avoiding entering the contract until the company has been incorporated;
   - by entering into an agreement 'subject to contract' with the effect that there is no binding agreement until the company itself enters into one;
   - where the promoters become the first directors of the company, they can ensure that the company does in fact enter the pre-arranged contract.

Solution to Question 11.6

(a) The vast majority of companies in Northern Ireland are private companies limited by shares. Private limited company shares cannot be offered to the public and the shares of a private company cannot be listed on a stock exchange. In contrast, a public company's shares can be offered to the public and they can be listed. A public company's name must end with the words 'Public Limited Company' or the abbreviation 'plc'.

(b) The company is required to pass a special resolution with a 75% majority to effect this alteration in business form.

(c) There is a provision within the Companies Act 2006 for the dissenting minority to object to re-registration as a private company. Holders of 5% or more of the nominal value of the public company's issued share capital can apply to the Court for the cancellation of the special resolution to request re-registration as a private company. However, they can only do so on the provision that they did not consent to or vote in favour of the resolution. Such an application has to be made within 28 days of the passing of the resolution. A court has the power to either cancel or confirm the resolution, once it hears the section 98 application.

Solution to Question 11.7

Advantages of a Company Status over Partnership Status:
- A company is a legal entity with perpetual succession.
- A company can own property, make contracts and sue or be sued in its own right. A company is protected by the 'veil of incorporation'.
- A company is liable for torts committed by the company as a separate legal person.
- A company is vicariously liable for torts committed by any of its directors or employees.
- A member of a company cannot bind the company by his or her acts.
- A company is subject to limited liability.
- A company has greater ability to raise finance and expand than a partnership.

Disadvantages of Company Status as Compared with Partnership Status
- The routine administration of a company is burdensome and costly.
- Owners' disclosure provisions force much of a company's internal business into the public domain. A company thereby loses the privilege of informality and privacy.

Solution to Question 11.8

(a) **Articles of Association and Memorandum of Association:**

Articles of Association formerly governed the legal internal relationship (rules, constitution) between the company and its members. Under the Companies Act 2006, it is now the prominent document. It contains the regulations for the running of a company and the rights and duties of its members – procedures for share transfers and altering share capital, meetings, the election of directors, voting rights, secretary appointments, procedures relating to the payments of dividends, procedures for the accounts and audit of the company, procedures relating to company liquidation and company borrowing.

A **Memorandum of Association** is a legal document that must be filed with the Registrar of Companies before a company can be incorporated. Prior to the Companies Act 2006: it governed the external relationship between the company and third parties; it contained the name of the company, registered address, objectives of the company, statement of share capital, etc. Now the Memorandum has been simplified considerably. It simply has to state subscribers to a company. It must also state that subscribers agree to become members upon formation.

(b) **Changing the Articles of Association**

Section 21 of the Companies Act 2006 states that Articles can be altered by special resolution, which must be notified to the Registrar of Companies within 15 days (section 26).

Solution to Question 11.9

The courts may lift the veil of incorporation at their absolute discretion in order to establish:

- that the company is a sham; for example, if the company is being used to enable a person to evade his legal obligations (*Guilford Mortor Company v. Horn* (1933));
- the evasion of liability including tax liabilities (*Re H & Others* (1996));
- that a company is being used to conceal the nationality of a company (*Unit Construction Limited v. Bullock* (1960));
- in a time of war, whether or not the company is controlled by an enemy (*Re FG Films Limited* (1953));
- the reality behind a small company that is more akin to a partnership – Quasi Partnership (see *Ebrahini v. Westbourne Galleries Limited* (1973)). Conclusion: Robert Barry's legal action against Bastian Publications Ltd is likely to be successful, as the company was formed for illegal purposes – in order to siphon off the assets of Peacock Books Ltd prior to its liquidation – and the Court may decide that both companies are in fact the same economic entity.

Solution to Question 11.10

(a) Types of companies: the various options available to Jane are as follows:

Unlimited Liability Company In such a company, the members of the company are not liable to creditors of the company directly. In the event, however, that the company becomes insolvent, the members' liability is to the company as a separate person. The main reason for having an unlimited company is that the company is exempt from the many disclosure requirements to the Registrar of Companies.

Limited Companies The vast majority of companies are limited companies. In a limited company, the liability of the members, if the company is wound up, is limited to a fixed amount agreed with the company when they become members. If a company is applying for registration of a limited company, they must make a choice between liability limited by shares or liability limited by guarantee. The vast majority of limited companies are limited by shares.

Private Companies The vast majority of companies in Northern Ireland are private companies limited by shares. Private limited company shares cannot be offered to the public and the shares of a private company cannot be listed on a stock exchange.

Public Companies In contrast, a public company's shares can be offered to the public and they can be listed. A public company's name must end with the words 'public limited company' or the abbreviation 'plc'. The principal reason for forming a public limited company lies in the benefit of obtaining capital from the public due to the fact that shares are listed. The minimum nominal value requirement for members to contribute in a public company is £50,000. By contrast, there is no minimum nominal value for authorised share capital in a private company.

(b) (i) In choosing the name of a company, a number of factors have to be taken into consideration by virtue of the Company, Limited Partnership and Business (Sensitive Words and Expressions) Regulations 2014 and the Company, Limited Partnership and Business (Names and Trading Disclosures) Regulations 2014. First, a limited company's name must indicate whether it is a public or private company. Characters that are permitted to be included in a company's name are those of the Latin alphabet, or Arabic numerals, punctuation marks and some signs and symbols. In addition, a company cannot be registered by a name that would be a criminal offence. Similarly, there are provisions that prevent companies being registered with similar names. This is because the goodwill and reputation that is attached to an existing businesses name can be damaged by a new company using the same or a similar name. This is known as the 'tort of passing off' and can be restrained by an injunction. For example, in the case of *Hendriks v. Montagu* (1881), the Universal Life Assurance Society obtained an injunction to prevent Montagu and his associates registering a company with the name Universe Life Assurance Association Limited.

(ii) Conclusion: John is likely to be successful in his application for an injunction.

(c) (i) Until 30 September 2009, every company had to state its objects in the old-style Memorandum of Association and every company was restricted to pursuing its stated objects. The effect of this was that if a company's objects were restricted by its Memorandum of Association, a company could not exercise beyond these powers. If a company did do anything outside of its objects, the company was said to be acting *ultra vires* or beyond the power of the company, and the acts were therefore void.

(ii) This *ultra vires* doctrine was the cause of great hardship and injustice to innocent third parties dealing with a company that was acting *ultra vires*. Accordingly, in an effort to protect third parties dealing with a company, an attempt to reform the *ultra vires* doctrine was made by section 9 of the European Communities Act 1972. This later became Article 45 of the Companies (Northern Ireland) Order 1986 and it has now been repealed again within the Companies Act 2006.

The present position is that companies are now permitted to have an objects clause that simply states that the company aims to carry on business as a general commercial company. This has greatly cut down the likelihood of transactions being found to be *ultra vires*.

Solution to Question 11.11

(a) **Separate legal personality/corporate personality** This concept means that a company has a separate legal status from its members and in reality has a distinct personality from the natural persons who set up the company. This was first recognised in the case of *Salomon v. Salomon & Co Ltd* (1897).

This separate personality means that a company:
- can own its own property;
- can enter in contractual relations with either natural persons or other companies;
- can commit crimes and be held responsible for such crimes;
- has perpetual existence; and
- can be sued or sue other persons.

This separate personality also gives the shareholders of the company the ability to have limited liability for company debts.

(b) **Differences between public and private limited companies.**

	Public limited company	**Private limited company**
Subscription	Requires a minimum of two shareholders.	Requires a minimum of one member.
Capital	A public company must have a minimum issued share capital of £50,000, 25% of which must be fully paid.	A private company can trade with a minimum of one £1 share if it is a single member private company or two £1 shares if it is a private limited company.
Trading	A public company can only trade upon receipt of a trading certificate from the Registrar of Companies. This document evidences everything about the company that makes it public.	Upon receipt of the Certificate of Incorporation a private company can commence trading.
Transfer of Shares	A public company can sell its shares freely on the market.	There is a prohibition against offering shares to the public in a private limited company.
Stock Market	A public limited company can be listed on the stock market.	A private company cannot be listed on the stock market.
Registration	In a public limited company the application for registration must state that it is a public limited company.	In a private limited company the application for registration must state that it is a private limited company.

Solution to Question 12.1

(i) The notice requirement to call an extraordinary general meeting in a private limited company is 14 days.
(ii) The general method of voting is by show of hands, and each share carries one vote. A poll or secret ballot can, however, be requested, which will override the show of hands.

Solution to Question 12.2

The first auditors are usually appointed by the directors and each year thereafter are appointed by the shareholders at the AGM.

The auditors can be removed by ordinary resolution of the shareholders at any shareholders' meeting such as the AGM.

Solution to Question 12.3

(a) Annual Return   The general information included in the annual return is: (1) the name of the company and its address, (2) the location where the register of members is kept, (3) details pertaining to shares and company debt, (4) details of company members and their particular shareholdings, (5) the company's registered number, (6) the date of the return, (7) the financial year, and (8) particulars of the directors and Company Secretary.

An annual return should be delivered at least once every 12 months (section 854(1) CA 2006).

(*Note*: after June 2016, confirmation statements will replace annual returns – see **Chapter 12**.)

(b) Return Date A company's directors and Secretary are responsible for ensuring that they deliver the annual return to the Registrar of Companies within 28 days after the anniversary of incorporation of a company or of the anniversary of the 'made up date' of the last annual return. The made up date is the date at which all information in an annual return must be correct. The made up date is the anniversary of incorporation of the company or the made up date of the previous annual return registered at the Registrar of Companies.

Non-compliance This is an offence; the company may be fined; the company and its officers may be prosecuted; the company risks losing its audit exemption or being struck off the register.

Solution to Question 12.4

(a) The Role of an Auditor An auditor is an independent professional expert appointed by a company to prepare an independent report on the financial affairs of the company (i.e. to audit the company), and to present this report to the shareholders at the annual general meeting. This report must give a true and fair view of the company's affairs at the end of the year. An auditor must be appointed for each financial year. To be qualified to act as an auditor a person must be: (1) a member/qualified by a recognised accountancy body, (2) registered with the UK register of auditors, and (3) independent (not subsequent to disqualification).

(b) Powers of the Auditor (1) to access all written information regarding financial affairs of the company, (2) to ask questions/request explanations by the company's officers, (3) to call an EGM, (4) to be heard at company meetings on any matter that affects him in his role as auditor, and (5) to receive notice of all company meetings.

(c) A company may, by ordinary resolution, passed at a meeting at any time, remove an auditor from office. However, the auditor, unlike a director, may not be removed prior to the expiration of the term of office other than by resolution of the shareholders. If management wishes to remove the auditor prematurely, it must do so by means of a proposal to the shareholders.

Solution to Question 12.5

Resolutions The main differences between **ordinary** and **special** resolutions are:

	How they are passed	Notice to members
Ordinary resolution	Simple majority.	No specific notice **except** to remove a director/auditor, which requires 28 days' notice.
Special resolution	75% approval.	Minimum notice for all meetings is 14 days, even if special resolution proposed.

Solution to Question 12.6

(a) In order to qualify for the exemption from audit in a particular financial year, the company has to meet two conditions.

First, it must meet the criteria for being classified as a 'small company' for the purposes of the Act's accounting rules. This means meeting two out of three criteria relating to the size of the company's balance sheet, turnover and workforce over a period of two years. These figures are not more than:
- £3.26 million for balance sheet total,
- £6.5 million for turnover, and
- 50 for employees.

Secondly, the company must meet the specified turnover and balance sheet tests in the financial year for which it claims audit exemption.

(b) Items that should be within an auditor's report include the following.
- An **introduction** identifying the accounts that were the subject of the audit. The introduction should describe the scope of the audit identifying the

auditing standards used and the financial reporting framework used in the preparation of the accounts.

- The report should state clearly whether, in the auditor's opinion, the accounts have been **prepared in accordance with the Companies Act 2006** and, where appropriate, in accordance with Article 4 of EC Regulation 1606/2002.
- The report must also state whether or not, in the opinion of the auditor, the report gives **a true and fair view** of the company's or, in the case of group accounts, the group's financial affairs. The report should further state whether the directors' report is **consistent with the accounts**.
- If the auditor is of the opinion that the company has not kept adequate accounting records, a statement to that effect should be given and if the company has not provided the auditor with all the information they need to complete the report, a statement to that effect should also be given.
- The auditor's report must also be **either unqualified or qualified** and include a reference to any matters to which the auditor wishes to draw attention by way of emphasis without qualifying the report. The auditor will qualify the report either where there has been a limitation on the scope of the auditor's work or where there is a material disagreement between the company and the auditor about the accounts.

Solution to Question 12.7

The following matters would usually be discussed at an annual general meeting (AGM):
- the annual accounts and reports for the most recent financial year of the company, which the directors lay before the company;
- the auditor's term of office ends at the end of the meeting and the auditor can be reappointed or a new auditor appointed instead;
- the accounts for the financial year must be accompanied by a directors' report, which will contain the directors' recommendation of the dividend to be paid to shareholders (a resolution will be proposed that the amount recommended be paid as dividend);
- in companies whose Articles require directors to retire by rotation, some directors will retire at each AGM and will have to be re-elected or replaced; and
- the New Model Articles for public companies state that a person appointed to be a director by the other directors must retire at the AGM following appointment. As a result, he cannot continue in office unless re-appointed by the members.

Solution to Question 12.8

(a) An annual return generally contains information about:
- details of all the company's directors (corporate or individual);
- details of the Company Secretary (where one has been appointed);
- the registered office address;
- shareholders and share capital; and
- the type of company it is (e.g. private or public).

Every company must deliver an annual return to the Registrar of Companies at least once every 12 months (section 854(1) CA 2006). The company's director(s) and the Company Secretary (where applicable) are responsible for ensuring that they deliver the annual return to the Registrar of Companies within 28 days after the anniversary of incorporation of a company or of the anniversary of the made up date of the last annual return. (*Note:* after June 2016, confirmation statements will replace annual returns – see **Chapter 12.**)

(b) **An auditor** is a person who makes an independent report to a company's members as to whether the company has prepared its financial statements in accordance with the Companies Act 2006 and the applicable financial reporting framework. A company's auditor is required to report on the accounts for a financial year of the company. The case of *Re Allen, Craig & Co (London) Limited* (1934) stated that it is sufficient if an auditor delivers the report to the Company Secretary. They are not required to personally deliver it to all members of the company.

Solution to Question 12.9

(a) (i) Alteration of the Articles of Association must be made by a special resolution of the members (sections 21 and 283 CA 2006). Therefore, a meeting must be called providing the shareholders with notice to effect this alteration. The notice period will depend on the type of meeting being called rather than the resolution. The resolution must be passed by a 75% majority.

   (ii) Examples of decisions requiring special resolution include decisions to:
   - amend the company's Articles of Association;
   - re-register from private to public or public to private;
   - approve a substantial property transaction with a director;
   - approve compensation to a director or shadow director of company for loss of office; and
   - supply members' pre-emption rights when shares are issued.

(b) Conclusion The proposed alteration to Titan's Articles of Association is valid as the directors are acting bona fide and in the best interests of the company.

(c) Directors have no power to refuse to register transfers unless such power is given to them in the company's Articles. Power to transfer must be exercised reasonably, in good faith, acting in the best interests of the company as a whole. The courts will usually uphold this discretion unless there is evidence of *mal fide* on the part of the directors, such as in *Re Hafner, Olhausen v. Powderly* (1943) and *Re Banfi Ltd v. Moran* (2006).

Conclusion The directors can refuse to effect the transfer of shares as they are acting bona fide and in the best interests of the company.

(d) (i) The Company Secretary's duties are:
   1. maintaining the company's statutory register;
   2. filing accurate returns with the Registrar on time;
   3. organising and minuting company and board meetings;

4. ensuring accounting records meet statutory requirements;
5. ensuring annual accounts are prepared and filed in accordance with statutory requirements;
6. monitoring statutory requirements of the company; and
7. signing company documents as required by law.

(ii) Voting at meetings is governed by a company's Articles of Association. The general rule is that voting takes place first by a show of hands and a result is declared by the chairperson of the meeting. This declaration is deemed conclusive. After a show of hands, not less than five members can demand a poll (secret ballot). The results of the poll take precedence over the show of hands. Poll voting depends upon the number of shares held by each shareholder. The right to conduct a poll cannot generally be excluded by the Articles.

(iii) Jessica should appoint a **proxy**. This is the appointment of a person to attend, vote and speak on behalf of a shareholder at a meeting. Jessica must ensure that she has completed the required form to nominate a person as her proxy and that it is received by the company at least 48 hours prior to the meeting.

Solution to Question 12.10

A company is under a duty to keep up-to-date accounting records sufficient to:
- show and explain the financial transactions of the company;
- disclose, with reasonable accuracy at any time, the financial position of the company;
- enable the directors to ensure that any accounts required to be prepared comply with the requirements of the Companies Act 2006; and
- these accounting records include the:
  ○ balance sheet/statement of financial position as of the last day of the financial year,
  ○ a profit and loss account,
  ○ the directors' report, and
  ○ the auditor's report.

These accounts need to be kept for a minimum period of six years from the date to which they relate (if public) and three years (if private).

Solution to Question 13.1

The fiduciary duties of a director centre upon acting in good faith in the best interests of the company and prioritising the company over any personal gain. A director must therefore avoid all potential conflicts of interest. The exercise of a director's authority must also be in accordance with the company's Memorandum and Articles of Association. Edward has breached these duties by acting in competition with the company. A director can be removed from office by an ordinary resolution of the shareholders or subject to disqualification proceedings.

Solution to Question 13.2

Four possible types of director:
- Executive Director – director responsible for day-to-day workings of the company;
- Non-Executive Director – director who sits at board meetings but is not involved in the day-to-day management of the company;
- Alternate Director – title given to a person who is nominated by a director to act in his or her absence;
- Shadow Director – an individual who can influence the decisions taken by the directors and as a result the directors are accustomed to act in accordance with his or her instructions.

Solution to Question 13.3

To: Client
From: Accountant
Date: Summer 2008

Dear Mr X

(a) Further to our recent meeting in relation to the role and duties of a director, my comments are as set out below:

1. An executive director normally manages the day-to-day running of a company and is usually also an employee of the company. By comparison, a non-executive director is not involved in the day-to-day management of the company but rather has been appointed to the board due to their relevant knowledge and skill and advises the board on strategic matters. They are not usually an employee, and usually act in a consultative capacity.
2. All directors of a company, regardless of their status as executive, non-executive or shadow director, will have the same duties and responsibilities to the company.

(b) There are three main types of duty:
- Statutory duties – which are imposed by legislation and in particular the Companies Act 2006. These include:
  - duty to disclose any substantial property transactions involving them in a personal capacity and/or as a director of the company;
  - duty to disclose any personal interests they may have in any contracts with the company;
  - duty to keep proper company registers.
- Fiduciary duties – these duties are now also contained in the Companies Act 2006 and include:
  - duty to prepare accounts;
  - duty to avoid conflicts of interest.

- Duty of due care and skill – which means that directors must act with the care, skill and diligence that would reasonably be expected of someone with their experience and knowledge.

This is a complex area and there are substantial personal liabilities for any director found to be in breach of any of the above duties.

Solution to Question 13.4

To remove Rose as a company director, a member of the company (either Hyacinth or Petunia) must issue a special notice to confirm their intention to bring a resolution for her removal and request a general meeting to consider the resolution. Notice must be given to the company at its registered office 14 days prior to the meeting. Rose is entitled to make both written and oral representations. It is important to ensure compliance with wider employment legislation to avoid any inference of unfair dismissal. The outcome of the general meeting must be communicated to the Registrar of Companies.

The appointment of Lilly in Rose's place must comply with the company's Articles of Association. Notice of the appointment must be given to the Registrar of Companies in accordance with section 167 of the Companies Act 2006.

Solution to Question 13.5

(a) Whether the credit contract created by Ethan is valid and binding can be assessed with reference to the rule in section 40 CA 2006 and the case of *Royal British Bank v. Turquand* (1856). Section 40 states that any limit placed on a director's ability to bind the company is ineffective. The *Turquand* case was decided prior to the introduction of the Companies Act 2006. It confirmed that where an innocent third party contracts with a company in good faith, they are entitled to presume that internal procedures have been observed without making further enquiry. However, it is important to note that this rule does not apply in cases where it is clear that the third party had notice of an irregularity and should have taken steps to verify the position; for example, where there are suspicious circumstances, such as arose in *AL Underwood Limited v. Bank of Liverpool & Martins* (1924) where a company director lodged cheques payable to the company into a personal bank account.

The emphasis within both the legislation and the case law is on protecting innocent third parties. It would appear that the third party in Ethan's case was dealing at arm's length without knowledge of Ethan's authority or lack thereof. It is therefore unlikely that Ethan's lack of authority would be sufficient to invalidate the credit contract in the circumstances of this case.

(b) While there are no formal qualifications required to become a director, there are high expectations regarding a director's conduct. The Companies Act 2006 contains seven general duties that must be adhered to once an individual is appointed:

- to act within his or her powers under the company's constitution (section 171 CA 2006);
- to promote the success of the company (section 172 CA 2006);
- to exercise independent judgement (section 173);
- to exercise reasonable care, skill and diligence (section 174 CA);
- to avoid conflicts of interest (section 175);
- not to accept benefits from third parties (section 176); and
- to declare interests in proposed transactions or arrangements (section 177).

Beyond these formal, statutory duties, directors are required to act with the upmost integrity and to act in good faith.

The managing director's actions are in clear breach of the duty to exercise reasonable care, skill and diligence as he borrowed funds at a time when he knew, or ought to have known, that the company was insolvent and would not be able to repay the loan, which resulted in a further loss to the company. His actions could result in director's disqualification proceedings for reckless trading and, arguably, trading whilst insolvent. He may also be held personally accountable for the loss incurred.

Ryan's actions are highly questionable as he appears to have accepted a holiday as a gift/reward/incentive from a supplier contrary to the provisions of section 176 CA 2006, which, in itself, results in an associated breach of the duty to declare interests in proposed transactions and the duty to avoid conflicts of interest.

Solution to Question 13.6

(a) In order to be a director, there are no formal qualifications that an individual must have. Anyone can become a director provided:
- they have not been restrained by a court order from becoming a company director under the Company Directors Disqualification (Northern Ireland) Order 2002;
- they are not an undischarged bankrupt;
- they are not subject to UK Government restrictions; and
- they are aged 16 years or more.

Every company must have at least one director who is a 'natural legal person' and all public companies must have at least two.

(b) **Executive directors** are directors who are involved in the operational management of the business providing continuous attention to the affairs of the business. They are generally also employees of the company, usually full time. An executive director will usually hold an important position within the day-to-day running of the company, such as financial controller or marketing manager. In such a situation the executive director holds two distinct positions and holds different responsibilities in each position.

Non-executive directors are directors who are only involved in the company at board level, As members of the board, deciding the strategic direction of the company is core to their role. They do not have another function within the company, i.e. they are not involved in the operational running of the business. Non-executive directors are appointed due to their expert knowledge, experience, attainment or skills. Part of their role is to act as monitors of the executive directors (by ensuring that they are acting within their powers and the company's objectives) and to provide the board of directors with additional expertise and an objective viewpoint.

(c) The Companies Act 2006 Act contains seven general duties of directors:
   - the duty to act within his or her powers under the company's constitution (CA 2006 s171);
   - the duty to promote the success of the company (CA 2006 s172);
   - the duty to exercise independent judgement (CA 2006 s173);
   - the duty to exercise reasonable care, skill and diligence (CA 2006 s174);
   - the duty to avoid conflicts of interest (CA 2006 s175);
   - the duty not to accept benefits from third parties (CA 2006 s176); and
   - the duty to declare any interest in proposed transactions or arrangements (CA 2006 s177).

Duty to act within his powers under the company's constitution   Under section 171 CA 2006, a director is required to act within his powers under the company's constitution and only exercise his powers with a purpose for which they were conferred. Exercising power for a purpose outside the scope for which the power has been given makes any act of the director voidable.

Duty to promote the success of the company   This duty replaces the common law duty of loyalty. The duty requires a director to act in the way he considers, in good faith, would be most likely to promote the success of the company for the benefit of the members as a collective body, not just the majority of the shareholders, or any particular section of shareholders. In doing so, a director must have regard to six specified factors:
   - the likely consequences of any decision in the long term;
   - the interest of the company's employees;
   - the need to foster the company's business relationships with suppliers, customers and others;
   - the impact of the company's operations on the community and the environment;
   - the desirability of the company maintaining a reputation for high standards of business conduct; and
   - the need to act fairly as between members of the company.

Duty to exercise independent judgement   A director must exercise independent judgement under section 173 CA 2006. This duty is based on the equitable principle that it is legitimate for directors of a company to exercise their powers independently and to enter into agreements acting as directors if they consider that it is in the interests of the company. Under section 173 CA 2006, a director's duty to exercise independent judgement is subject to restrictions contained in any agreements entered into by the company or in the company's constitution, including resolutions of the shareholders.

Duty to exercise reasonable care, skill and diligence   Under section 174 CA 2006, a director must exercise such reasonable skill, care and diligence as would be exercised by a reasonably diligent person with:
- the general knowledge, skill and experience that could reasonably be expected from the person carrying out the director's functions; and
- the director's actual general knowledge, skill and experience.

This duty is based on the director's common law duty of skill and care.

Duty to avoid conflicts of interest   A director has a statutory duty to avoid any situations in which he has, or can have, a direct or indirect interest that conflicts, or possibly may conflict, with an interest of the company (CA 2006 section 175). The duty does not apply to a conflict of interest arising in relation to a transaction or arrangement with a director in the company. Further, the duty does not arise if the situation cannot reasonably be regarded as likely to give rise to a conflict of interest. The company should consider directors' conflicts of interest on a case-by-case basis. Approval should be given in accordance with the general director's duties as set out in the Companies Act 2006, in particular the need to promote the success of the company.

Duty not to accept benefits from third parties   A director has the statutory duty not to accept a benefit from a third party that is given because of the position held by the director or because of anything the director has done in his capacity as a director. Effectively this means that the duty applies only to benefits conferred on the director because he is a director and will not be breached if accepting the benefit cannot reasonably be regarded as likely to give rise to a conflict of interest. Benefits from associated companies are excluded. Otherwise, all third-party benefits, of any description, whether financial or not, have to be authorised by the company shareholders.

Duty to declare interests in proposed transactions or arrangements   A director has a duty to disclose to the rest of the board the nature of any interest in a proposed transaction or arrangement before the transaction is approved. There is no need to make a disclosure if the interest "cannot reasonably be regarded as likely to give rise to a conflict of interest", or if the directors are already aware of the director's interest.

Solution to Question 13.7

(a) Disclosure Obligations and Contracts a director has a duty to avoid any situations in which he has, or can have, a direct or indirect interest that conflicts, or may possibly conflict, with the interests of the company (section 175 CA 2006). The duty does not apply to a conflict of interest arising in relation to a transaction or arrangement between the director and the company. The three options a company can consider if a conflict of interest arises are: (1) exclude the director from the relevant financial information and discussion on the matter; (2) exclude the director from the board in relation to the matter; (3) require that the director resigns. In this scenario Sam has breached his statutory duty as he failed to disclose a substantial conflict and used his power as a director to ensure that the contract was awarded to his sister's company.

(b) Removal of a Director The following steps should be taken when removing a director:
1. Special notice must be received by the company, from a member, which details the member's intention to bring a resolution to remove a director. This notice must be given at least 28 days before the meeting at which the resolution is to be proposed.
2. If the resolution is received in time, directors should ensure that the proposed resolution is included in the notice at the next AGM. If this is not possible, members can requisition directors to hold a general meeting to consider the resolution. If this is the case, the general meeting must be held within 21 days of receiving the requisitions and special notice.
3. The director who is to be removed should be sent a copy of the special notice. If the director wishes to exercise his right to make written representation to the members to attend the general meeting, the director must ensure that he is permitted to do so.

Solution to Question 13.8

To: Porter
From: AN Other
Date: May 2014
Subject: Disqualification Orders

Following your letter from the Secretary of State notifying you that an application has been brought to the High Court seeking your disqualification as a company director, I have provided you with the requested information.

(a) Effect of a Disqualification Order This is an Order brought against directors, auditors, company officers, liquidators or receivers, which disqualifies them from taking part in the promotion, formation or management of any company, either directly or indirectly, for up to five years, or any other such period as the court may direct.

(b) Grounds upon which a Disqualification Order can be imposed:
1. Where a person is convicted of an indictable offence in connection with the promotion, formation, management or liquidation of a company or with the receivership or management of a company's property.
2. Where it appears that a person has been persistently in default in relation to provisions of company legislation.
3. Where it appears, in the course of the winding up of a company, that a person has been guilty of fraudulent trading, carrying on business with intent to defraud creditors or for any fraudulent purpose.

4. Where a person is found to be unfit to be concerned in the management of a company.
5. Where a director was involved in certain competition violations.
6. Where a director has participated in wrongful trading under Articles 177 and 178 of the Insolvency (Northern Ireland) Order 1989 as amended by the Insolvency (Northern Ireland) Order 2005.

(c) Effect of acting in breach of a Disqualification Order A person who acts while disqualified faces the following consequences:
   • being guilty of a criminal offence;
   • incurring personal liability for the debts of the company if it becomes insolvent during, or within 12 months of, the Disqualification Order; and
   • being liable to imprisonment.

If you require additional clarification on any of the points above please contact me.

Solution to Question 13.9

(a) Directors of a company are under an obligation to prepare a directors' report for each financial year (section 415(1) CA 2006). If the company in question is a parent company, the directors prepare group accounts and therefore the Directors' Report must be a group directors' report (section 415(2)). The directors' report will contain, among other things:
   • the names of all persons who were directors of the company during the financial year;
   • a corporate governance statement;
   • a statement outlining the principal activities of the company or group in the course of the year; and
   • the amount that should be paid by way of dividends for the year, together with a business review.

(b) Statutory duties of directors under the Companies Act 2006 include:
   • the duty to act within their powers under the company's constitution (section 171);
   • the duty to promote the success of the company (section 172);
   • the duty to exercise independent judgement (section 173);
   • the duty to exercise reasonable care, skill and diligence (section 174);
   • the duty to avoid conflicts of interest (section 175);
   • the duty not to accept benefits from third parties (section 176); and
   • the duty to declare any interest in proposed transactions or arrangements (section 177).

Solution to Question 13.10

(a) **The Procedure to Effect a Lawful Removal of a Director** Since the dismissal of a director is potentially a contentious matter, the director may have the right to damages for: breach of contract, wrongful dismissal, or unfair dismissal if they were an employee of the company and/or if the company did not follow the correct procedure in dismissing the director.

The following steps should be taken when removing a director:

1. Special notice must be received by the company from a member, which details the member's intention to bring a resolution to remove a director.
2. This notice must be given at least 28 days before the meeting at which the resolution is to be proposed.
3. If the resolution is received in time, the directors should ensure that the proposed resolution is included in the notice of the next AGM. If this is not possible, members can requisition the directors to hold a general meeting to consider the resolution. If this is the case, they must hold a general meeting within 21 days of receiving the requisition and special notice.
4. The director who is to be removed should be sent a copy of the special notice.
5. If this director wishes to exercise his right to make written representation to the members and attend the general meeting, the director must ensure that he is permitted to do so.
6. If the ordinary resolution to remove the director is approved, directors should ensure that the steps at 1–5 above are followed.

(b) **Non-executive Directors**

- are directors appointed to manage the business on a transient basis;
- are more involved in strategic management at board level, and are not involved in the operational running of the company;
- are appointed due to their expert knowledge, experience, attainment or skills;
- act as monitors of the executive directors (by ensuring that they are acting within their powers and the company's objectives); and
- provide the board of directors with additional expertise and an objective point of view.

Solution to Question 14.1

Administration is a rescue mechanism used as an alternative to liquidation to afford an insolvent company the opportunity to achieve the following possible outcomes: recover from financial crisis, be sold as a 'going concern' or obtain greater return for creditor by completion of work in progress or realisation of the company's assets.

An administrator is a qualified, licensed Insolvency Practitioner and is regarded as an officer of the court when exercising his or her functions, which include assessing the company's viability and obtaining a full statement of its financial affairs, responding to the urgent needs of the company such as issues relating to employees and identifying the most effective realisation of the company's assets.

Within three months of the making of an administration order, the administrator must send to all creditors details of his proposals for achieving the purpose or purposes specified in the order and must summon a meeting of the creditors to consider them. The meeting may approve the proposals, with or without modifications, or may decline to do so, in which case it is open to the court to discharge the administration order.

Solution to Question 14.2

(a) Article 102 of the Insolvency (Northern Ireland) Order 1989 sets out the grounds for compulsory liquidation. The primary basis for a winding-up order is that the company is unable to pay its debts as they fall due, evidenced by the fact that it has failed to comply with a statutory demand, that a certificate of unenforceability has been issued by the Enforcement of Judgments Office or that its assets are insufficient to meet its debts. Alternatively, the Court has a wider discretion to determine that it is just and equitable for the company to be wound up.

(b) A winding-up petition is issued in the High Court and can be presented by either the company itself usually through its directors or by a creditor, served on the company's registered office and advertised in the *Belfast Gazette* 14 clear days prior to the hearing of the petition before the Bankruptcy and Companies Master.

(c) An order for compulsory liquidation has immediate effect. The Official Receiver is automatically appointed as liquidator to deal with the company's creditors and preserve/realise the company's assets on their behalf. A statement of the company's affairs verified by the director/Company Secretary Setting out the company's assets, liabilities (both secured and unsecured) and financial circumstances of the company is required. The company's bank account is frozen and an investigation is made into the trading activities of the company particularly any transfers or transactions. Any employees are automatically dismissed and any floating charge crystallizes.

(d) A major difference between compulsory and voluntary liquidation is the effective date of commencement. In a voluntary winding up, liquidation commences the day the resolution is passed, while a compulsory winding up is not effective until the date of the hearing and court order.

Another significant difference relates to the role of the Official Receiver. In the case of a compulsory liquidation, the Official Receiver automatically adopts the role of liquidator but in a voluntary winding up members or creditors can select an insolvency practitioner as liquidator directly.

Solution to Question 14.3

(a) Article 102 of the Insolvency (Northern Ireland) Order 1989 sets out the grounds upon which the Court can make a winding-up order and appoint a compulsory liquidator, including:
   • the company is unable to pay its debts as they fall due;
   • the winding up of the company would be just and equitable;

- the company has ceased to trade and has been inactive for over a year or has never actually traded.

(b) A winding-up order/order for compulsory liquidation has a number of immediate effects:
  - the Official Receiver is automatically appointed to assume responsibility for the company's affairs and steps will be taken to realise all moveable assets and secure all immoveable assets and property pending further realisation;
  - the powers of the directors cease;
  - the winding up will be advertised;
  - all floating charges crystallise;
  - all company accounts and bank facilities will be frozen and withdrawn;
  - all pending legal action by/against the company is suspended;
  - employees are automatically dismissed;
  - the affairs of the company and the factors giving rise to its winding up will be investigated;
  - a statement of affairs itemising the company's assets and liabilities will be prepared; and
  - consideration will be given to the need for a meeting of creditors to appoint an external insolvency practitioner to assume the role of liquidator.

Solution to Question 14.4

The Official Receiver is a senior civil servant appointed by the High Court to oversee and manage the liquidation of a company. He is regarded as an officer of the Court and assumes the role of liquidator to realise and distribute the company's assets for the benefit of creditors.

On his appointment, the Official Receiver must take steps to protect, insure and value the company's assets. He may instruct an agent to attend the business premises/registered office and will seek to obtain all available books, records and accounts. He is required to advertise the winding up of the company and will require the directors to attend for interview to complete a statement of affairs for the company within 21 days.

One of the Official Receiver's key duties is to investigate the failure of the company and to report any misconduct to the Department for the Economy to consider whether disqualification proceedings should be taken against the directors.

The Official Receiver is obliged to report to creditors at various stages in the process but must, within 12 weeks of his appointment, decide whether to summon a meeting of creditors to establish a creditors' committee or appoint an external insolvency practitioner. Thereafter, he will liaise with creditors to obtain details of their claims and can accept or reject the claims as he deems appropriate. Ultimately, he will take steps to sell all realisable assets and, if possible in the circumstances of the winding up, will calculate and distribute a dividend to creditors from the net proceeds of sale.

Once the Official Receiver completes his tasks, he is obliged to notify the Registrar of Companies to enable the company to be formally dissolved.

Solution to Question 14.5

A 'floating charge' is a fluid form of security that allows a company to borrow against a class of both current and future assets such as plant, machinery, equipment, vehicles, tools or inventory. By definition, the charge 'floats' over the assets in question and only becomes effective when the charge crystallises. The lender's right to repossess/recover the assets is dormant until crystallisation, which, in turn, allows the company to buy, sell, replace and otherwise deal with assets on a routine basis without reverting to the lender.

A floating charge will crystallise in one of the following four situations:
1. if the company goes into liquidation;
2. if the company ceases to trade;
3. if a company defaults on agreed repayments;
4. if an event occurs for which the charge provides for automatic crystallisation.

When a floating charge crystallises, it automatically settles onto and attaches to the agreed class of assets. In essence, the charge converts from a floating charge to a fixed charge. Upon crystallisation, the lender's equitable rights are engaged and steps can be taken to realise the security by recovering and selling the assets. The lender may seek to appoint a receiver or administrator under the terms of the charge for this purpose.

Solution to Question 14.6

(a) A 'floating charge' is created when a company borrows money and secures that borrowing on a non-specific company asset. The charge was defined in *Re Yorkshire Woolcombers Ltd* (1903) as a charge on an asset both present and future, which changes in the ordinary course of business. A floating charge does not attach to the asset until the charge crystallises; crystallisation can arise on default on the debenture, company liquidation, receivership or the cessation of business, or, alternatively, on a pre-determined future date. Upon crystallisation, the floating charge becomes affixed to the charged asset over which it previously floated. (When a floating charge is created, the borrower retains the ability to deal with the asset in the normal course of business.) The priority of a floating charge upon crystallisation is that it is only paid after the fixed charges and the preferential debts have been discharged.

(b) The priority of payment of a company's debts upon liquidation is as follows: fixed charges, preferential debts and floating charges (in that order).

(c) The listed debts will be paid as follows:
1. fixed charges: £165,000 mortgage in favour of Trinity Bank;
2. floating charges: the loan of £40,000 and then the loan of £100,000 (they are paid in order of creation and not registration);
3. the unpaid salaries of £30,000;

4. unsecured debts: HMRC debts of £20,000, £40,000 to trade creditors and £30,000 unsecured loan from James's father.

Solution to Question 14.7

(a) (i) Mark's Liability upon Liquidation As Mark purchased partly paid shares, he is obliged to pay the unpaid balance when called (depending upon the terms of the issue) or upon liquidation (whichever occurs first); therefore, he is obliged to pay the balance (£300,000 × £0.50 = £150,000) when the company is put into liquidation.

    (ii) The steps involved in a **creditor's voluntary liquidation**:
1. A company that is unable to make a declaration of solvency because of insolvency may initiate a creditors' voluntary liquidation.
2. The members of the company must pass a resolution to liquidate the company.
3. An authorised Insolvency Practitioner is appointed. A meeting of the creditors must also be called. At this meeting, all creditors should receive details of the company's financial affairs and the creditors are given authority to nominate a liquidator to wind up the company.
4. When a liquidator is appointed, he or she takes control of the company's affairs. The liquidator is now under a duty to dispose of all the company's assets and, after paying the costs and expenses of the liquidation, distribute any remaining money to creditors.
5. The company's directors are under a duty to provide information about the company's affairs to the liquidator and attend interviews with the liquidator as and when reasonably required.
6. A voluntary liquidation ends when the company is dissolved once a final meeting has been held by the liquidator.

(b) Grounds for Compulsory Liquidation (See **Solution to Question 14.10(a)** below.)

Solution to Question 14.8

(a) Prerequisite to Effect a Members' Voluntary Liquidation The directors or the majority of the directors must make a declaration of solvency before such a liquidation can be passed.

(b) The procedure to effect a members' voluntary liquidation is as follows:
- A members' voluntary liquidation takes places when the shareholders of a company decide to put the company into liquidation.
- The directors, or a majority of the directors, must make a declaration of solvency before such a liquidation can be passed;
  - this declaration must contain the latest practicable statement of the company's assets and liabilities, and
  - it must further state that, after inquiry, in their opinion, the company will be able to pay its debts within a period of not more than 12 months.

- ○ This declaration must be made no more than five weeks before the passing of the resolution for the voluntary winding up.
- A resolution for a voluntary winding up must be made at a general shareholder's meeting.
- The resolution for a voluntary winding up must also appoint one or more liquidators of the company.
- If it subsequently transpires that the company was not solvent, the liquidation automatically becomes a creditors' voluntary liquidation.

(c) An alternative type of voluntary liquidation would be a creditors' voluntary liquidation.

Solution to Question 14.9

(a) Insolvency Practitioners are usually accountants or solicitors who are qualified practitioners under one of the recognised professional bodies for insolvency. The role of the Insolvency Practitioner, if appointed by RM Ltd, is to effectively realise RM's assets, pay the fees and charges arising from compulsory liquidation and thereafter share out any surplus funds to creditors.

(b) Two alternatives to a compulsory liquidation are:
- Voluntary Liquidation A voluntary liquidation can either be a members' voluntary liquidation (which takes place when the shareholders decide to put the company into voluntary liquidation) or a creditors' voluntary liquidation (when the company's creditors appoint a liquidator). In both situations a liquidator is appointed and he or she takes control of the company's affairs.
- Administration An 'administration' tries to rescue a company and achieve a better result for the company's creditors than if it were wound up. An administration is an alternative to liquidation and is a last-action rescue remedy for the company. The company can continue to trade while an administration is being carried out.

Solution to Question 14.10

(a) Article 102 of the Insolvency (Northern Ireland) Order 1989 lays out seven grounds on which a company may be wound up by the High Court:
  1. The company has passed a special resolution deciding that the company should be wound up by the Court.
  2. The company has been registered as a public limited company, but has not been issued with a trading certificate.
  3. The company is an old public company that has failed to re-register.
  4. The company has not commenced business within a year of incorporation or has suspended its trading for a whole year.
  5. At the time at which a moratorium for the company under Article 14A comes to an end, no voluntary arrangement approved under Part II has effect in relation to the company.

6. The company cannot pay its debts.
7. The company should be wound up because the Court forms the opinion that it would be just and equitable to wind up the company.

(b) The compulsory liquidation process is as follows. Once an order for compulsory liquidation has been made by the Court:

- All floating charges crystallise.
- The employees of the company are automatically dismissed.
- The role of the company's directors all but ceases.
- The appointed liquidator will assume the powers of management previously held by the directors.
- Legal proceedings in progress against the company are automatically halted once the order for compulsory liquidation is passed. No further legal proceedings may be commenced after this date.
- Under Article 111 of the Insolvency (Northern Ireland) Order 1989, within 21 days of the making of the compulsory liquidation order, a statement of affairs must be delivered to the liquidator or Official Receiver verified by one or more officers of the company, i.e. the directors and company secretary. This statement will show the assets and liabilities of the company; it will list the creditors; and it will also stipulate any security that the creditors may hold.
- At this stage, the role of the Official Receiver or liquidator is to investigate, under Article 112 of the 1989 Order, the causes for the failure of the company and it must also consider, in general, the promotion, formation, business dealings and affairs of the company. If the Official Receiver deems it appropriate, he or she may make a report to the Court on these matters. Such a report is evidence of the facts stated in the report.
- Within 12 weeks of the winding-up order, the Official Receiver must decide whether to summon meetings of creditors and contributories. If the Official Receiver decides not to do so, he must inform the Court, the creditors and the contributories. The purpose of this meeting is to give the creditors and contributories the opportunity to appoint their own nominee as a permanent liquidator to replace the Official Receiver and also to appoint a liquidation committee to work with the liquidator. The purpose of this committee is to assist the liquidator and act as the link between the company and the liquidator.
- If an Official Receiver has reason to believe that there is little interest among the creditors in appointing a liquidator and that the creditors will be unable to appoint a liquidator, he can dispense with this meeting but he must inform the Court, the creditors and the contributories of the decision. Furthermore, at a later stage, he can be required to call a meeting if at least 25% in value if the creditors require him to do so. If no meeting is held, or a meeting is held and no liquidator is appointed, the Official Receiver thereafter continues to act in the capacity of liquidator. However, if the creditors do hold a meeting and decide to appoint their own nominee, this person automatically becomes liquidator. The person appointed to act as liquidator must be a qualified insolvency practitioner.

- A notice of the Order for Compulsory Liquidation and of the appointment of a liquidator is given to the Registrar of Companies and must also be published in the *Belfast Gazette*.

Solution to Question 15.1

(a) The general rule is that shares cannot be acquired for anything less than their full market value as it could distort the capital of the company. The exceptions to this rule are limited to shares issued for non-cash consideration or shares offered without having to pay a sales commission.

If an individual has notice that they are purchasing shares at a discount to their true market value, contrary to the general prohibition, and the company goes into liquidation, the shareholder will be liable for the differential. Henry would therefore be liable for 30p in each share obtained at a discount if Fringe plc went into liquidation.

(b) Both private and public companies can reduce their share capital by passing a special resolution and seeking the endorsement of the court.

The Companies Act 2006 provides for a new, simplified procedure for effecting a reduction of capital which removes the need for court approval. A special resolution will still be required and the directors must make a declaration of solvency confirming that the company is able to pay its debts.

Alternatively, instead of reducing the share capital directly, a company can do any of the following, the net result of which is to reduce the capital of the company:
- Cancelling further liability on partly-paid shares
- Paying back to members capital that is not needed
- Reducing the value of the company's shares to reflect capital losses
- Redeeming redeemable shares
- Buying back ordinary shares that have been issued.

Under the current legislation, a company can only buy its own shares if the Articles of Association contain express authority enabling it to so. The purchase can be by means of a 'market' purchase on a recognised stock exchange as authorised by an ordinary resolution or an 'off-market' purchase (outside of the recognised stock exchange as authorised by a special resolution). By contrast, the Companies Act 2006 provides that a company has the right to purchase its own shares unless expressly prohibited by the Articles of Association.

Solution to Question 15.2

A dividend is a payment of a share of a company's profit after taking account of the company's losses in accordance with section 830 of the Companies Act 2006 and, therefore, by its very nature can only be justified when a company is trading profitably. In this case, it is clear that Messing Construction Ltd was insolvent and trading at a loss when the dividend was paid and, by implication, that the dividend was unlawful as it was paid in an effort to defeat or defraud creditors.

If, indeed, the dividend is deemed to be unlawful, Wilbur and Wilma would be liable to repay the proceeds to the liquidator for the benefit of creditors.

Falsifying records, trading while insolvent, mismanaging a company and engaging in fraudulent activity would not only have potential implications in criminal law but, in the context of a liquidation, are likely to result in an application to have both Wilbur and Wilma disqualified as directors for up to 15 years.

Solution to Question 15.3

(a) 'Pre-emption', in this context, refers to the right of an existing member to first refusal of new shares before they are offered to outside third parties as prospective new members.
(b) The right to pre-emption is likely to be a contractual condition, as it is fundamental to the shareholders' agreement.
(c) A derivative claim is an action initiated by a majority shareholder seeking redress on behalf of the company generally against an act or omission of negligence by those in control of the company's affairs, as prescribed by section 260 CA 2006. If the claim is successful, the Court can be make any Order it sees fit to ensure that restitution is made, including providing for the costs incidental to the application, ordering compensation for any loss, or restoring the position to what it would have been had the impugned actions not taken place.

Solution to Question 15.4

(a) A prospectus is essentially a statement of fact about a company. Its purpose is to allow potential shareholders to discover more about the company and make a reliable and informed decision on whether to subscribe for shares in that company.

The pieces of information that a prospectus will usually contain are:
1. assets and liabilities of the company;
2. the company's financial position;
3. profits and losses of the company;
4. prospects of the company and whether there is any guarantor; and
5. rights attached to the shares in question.

(b) (i) Characteristics of ordinary shares:
  1. These are shares owned by the equity shareholders of a company. These shareholders are risk-takers as they are the last to be paid upon the liquidation of the business. If there are no funds available on liquidation, they receive no return on capital.

    2. They do, however, bear the possibility of capital growth. In effect, they have a right to a share of any available assets/funds upon winding-up if funds are available.

    3. They receive a return called a 'dividend' but its payment is completely dependent upon company performance – if profits are available for distribution and the directors declare a distribution, then ordinary shareholders may receive a dividend.

    4. Ordinary shareholders generally have the ability to influence company policy by exercising voting rights at meetings (AGM/EGM) relating to company business.

(ii) Redeemable shares are shares (ordinary or preference) issued by a company that are then redeemed (bought back) by the company at a future date; their redemption is usually contingent on certain events taking place.

(iii) Rules relating to the redemption of shares:

    1. Redeemed shares can be cancelled upon redemption (which results in a reduction of issued capital and the transfer of an equivalent amount to the capital redemption reserve fund); and

    2. Notice must be given to the Registrar of Companies, within one month of redeeming shares, with a statement of the company's capital.

Solution to Question 15.5

(a) Share premium arises where a company issues shares above their par/nominal value – the excess in value is the premium. In relation to company accounts, this premium must be credited to the share premium account.

(b) The following items can be included on a **share certificate**:

    1. A share certificate must state the name and address of the member who holds the relevant shares.

    2. It should also certify that the member is a registered holder of a specified number of shares of a certain class.

    3. It should further state whether the shares are fully paid up or, if partly paid, how much of their nominal value has been paid up.

(c) Pre-emption In accordance with section 561 CA 2006, a company that is allotting ordinary shares must first offer them to existing shareholders in the same proportion as their existing holding. This is known as 'pre-emption'. This pre-emption right allows shareholders to keep their level of shareholding constant.

Solution to Question 15.6

Procedure to Reduce the Share Capital of a Public Company Section 641 CA 2006 provides that a company can reduce its share capital, in any way, by a special resolution, which must be supported by a solvency statement "and/or if the reduction is confirmed by the Court".

Section 643(1) lays out the detail that must be contained within a solvency statement issued by a company that is planning to reduce its share capital. This solvency statement is a written statement that each of the directors has formed the opinion that, at the date of the statement:

- there is no ground on which that company could be found unable to pay, or otherwise discharge, its debts; and
- the company will be able to pay, or otherwise discharge, its debts as they fall due, during the following year.

If it is intended to wind up the company within a year of the date of the solvency statement, the directors must be of the opinion that the company will pay and discharge its debts in full within 12 months of the commencement of winding up.

No later than 15 days after the resolution has been passed to permit a reduction of capital, a copy of the solvency statement must be sent to the Registrar of Companies (Companies House) together with a statement of capital. No reduction can take effect until both of these documents have been registered with the Registrar of Companies. Moreover, a statement by the directors, confirming that the solvency statement was made within 15 days before the reduction resolution was passed, must also be sent to the Registrar of Companies. Directors of a company should note that it is an offence to submit a solvency statement to the Registrar of Companies without having reasonable grounds for their opinions expressed in the statement.

Solution to Question 15.7

Pre-emption   Pursuant to section 561 CA 2006, a company that is allotting shares must first offer them to existing shareholders in the same proportion as their existing holding. This right is known as the right of **pre-emption**. This right may also arise in respect of the sale of shares.

Solution to Question 16.1

You had also asked about the law relating to insider trading. This is defined in the Criminal Justice Act 1993 as dealing in securities when you have information that will affect the price of the securities and make a profit as a result of using that information.

Inside information is price-sensitive information which you have as a result of your position as a director, employee or shareholder of a company.

Dealing in securities is buying or selling shares on a regulated stock market. To be found guilty you have to have either dealt in the securities yourself or encouraged others to do so.

If you pass the inside information to a third party but they do not actually trade, you may still be found guilty of an offence.

The penalties for insider dealing include prison and an unlimited fine.

Solution to Question 16.2

(a) 'Money laundering' is the way in which criminals attempt to turn cash and other assets obtained from criminal activities into assets that appear to have been obtained legally through the financial services system and through established businesses. Sections 327 and 329 of the Proceeds of Crime Act 2002 (POCA 2002), as amended by the Serious Organised Crime and Police Act 2005 (SOCPA 2005), define money laundering offences. The first category of principal money laundering offence relates to laundering the proceeds of crime or assisting in the process. Under section 327, it is an offence to conceal, disguise, convert or transfer criminal property or remove criminal property from England, Wales, Scotland or Northern Ireland. Secondly, if an individual enters into, or becomes concerned in, an arrangement that he knows, or suspects, facilitates (by whatever means) the acquisition, retention, use or control of criminal property by, or on behalf of, another person, he is guilty of money laundering (section 328 POCA 2002). Thirdly, if someone acquires, uses or has possession of criminal property, except were adequate consideration has been given for the property (section 329 POCA 2002), he is also guilty of the offence.

(b) Auditor's reporting obligations where a suspicion of money laundering occurs. The auditor is legally obliged to report any suspicion of money laundering to the National Crime Agency via a suspicious activity report.

Chartered accountants must also report any suspicion to a Chartered Accountants Ireland Money Laundering Reporting Officer (MLRO). The MLRO then reports the matter to the relevant criminal authorities, if appropriate; the member of Chartered Accountants Ireland is prohibited from telling their client that they have reported the suspected offence.

Solution to Question 16.3

(a) Definition of 'insider trading' The Criminal Justice Act 1993 created two insider trading offences. The first offence, the 'dealing offence', was aimed at those who deal in particular kinds of securities and, in specified circumstances, on the basis of inside information: "an individual is guilty of insider dealing if he has information as an insider and deals, in specified circumstances, in securities which are price effected in relation to that information". The second offence, the 'tipping offence', is committed either by disclosing inside information or by encouraging another to deal in particular kinds of securities and specified circumstances.

Definition of 'inside information' Inside information means information that: (1) relates to particular securities or to a particular issuer of securities or to particular issuers of securities and not to securities generally or to issuers of securities generally; (2) is specific or precise; (3) has not been made public; (4) if it were made public, would be likely to have a significant effect on the price of any securities.

(b) Definition of an 'insider' A person may be defined as an 'insider' as a consequence of (1) their membership of professional bodies (especially those who issue financial instruments), (2) by virtue of their capital holding, (3) through employment or professional duties, or (4) through criminal activity.

(c) Criminal sanctions that can be imposed where a person is found guilty of insider trading: seven years' imprisonment and/or an unlimited fine. Buckley is an insider through employment; it is likely that he will be found guilty as he was aware of:
1. the price-sensitive nature of the information, and
2. that it was confidential and nonetheless he used it to avoid a loss.

Solution to Question 17.1

Upon receiving a complaint against a member of the Institute, the case manager, on behalf of the Conduct Committee, is required to investigate the nature of the complaint. He or she will carry out an initial fact-find, at the end of which the case manager will decide if there is a case to answer. If the Conduct Committee decides that there is no prima facie case to answer, the complainant has the right to have their complaint reviewed by an independent reviewer. If the complainant chooses not to exercise this right, the matter is closed.

However, if the Conduct Committee establishes that there is a case to answer, it can exercise one of five options:
1. First, the matter is referred to a Disciplinary Tribunal for a hearing.
2. Secondly, it can offer a consent order, which is a disciplinary penalty that must have the agreement of the member.
3. Thirdly, it can invite the individual concerned to accept an unpublished caution.
4. Fourthly, the matter can be deferred to permit the Conduct Committee to gather further necessary information to enable it to make a decision.
5. It can take no further action.

It should be noted also that where the Conduct Committee decides the matter is one of public concern, they can refer the matter to a disciplinary investigator for the imposition of an interim order. Interim orders can be appealed.

Solution to Question 17.2

A Chartered Accountant can become liable for disciplinary procedure if they breach the standards of professional conduct or bring the profession into disrepute. The basic procedure involved is as follows:
1. Upon receiving a complaint, a case manager is required to carry out initial fact-find and will decide if there is a case to answer.
2. If there is a case to answer, the Conduct Committee can decide one of five options:
   - First, the matter is referred to a Disciplinary Tribunal for a hearing.
   - Secondly, it can offer a consent order, which is a disciplinary penalty that must have the agreement of the member.
   - Thirdly, it can invite the individual concerned to accept an unpublished caution.

- Fourthly, the matter can be deferred to permit the Conduct Committee to gather further necessary information to enable it to make a decision.
- It should be noted also that where the Conduct Committee decides the matter is one of public concern, they can refer the matter to a disciplinary investigator for the imposition of an interim order. Interim orders can be appealed.

3. If the Conduct Committee decide that the matter should be dealt with by way of a Disciplinary Tribunal, the matter is referred to such a tribunal.
4. The Disciplinary Tribunal decide if the matter is proven or unproven.
5. All decisions made by a Disciplinary Tribunal are subject to a right of appeal by an Appeal Tribunal.

Solution to Question 17.3

(a) CARB is an independent body established to regulate members of Chartered Accountants Ireland ('the Institute') in accordance with the provisions of the Institute's bye-laws. Grounds for disciplinary action by CARB:
1. breach of a bye-law or regulation;
2. failure to comply with standards of professional conduct; and
3. bringing discredit to themselves, the Institute or the accounting profession.

(b) If the Tribunal set up by CARB finds that a formal complaint is proven, in accordance with the standard of proof required, it will make a declaration to that effect. If it finds that a formal complaint is not proven, it will dismiss the complaint. In both cases, the Tribunal must give reasons for doing so.

If a formal complaint is proven, the respondent can be excluded from membership, have their practising certificate withdrawn, be ineligible for a practising certificate, have their insolvency licence withdrawn, or be reprimanded or fined.

Solution to Question 17.4

If a member of Chartered Accountants Ireland breaches a bye-law or regulation, fails to comply with the standards of professional conduct and/or brings discredit on themselves, the Institute or the accountancy profession, they become liable for disciplinary action by CARB. There are a number of bodies within CARB that deal with members who either have complaints made against them or who do not meet the reasonable expectations of the public or the profession. The relevant bodies are:
- The Conduct Committee,
- Disciplinary Tribunals, and
- Appeal Tribunals.

Conduct Committee Upon receiving a complaint against a member of the Institute, a case manager, on behalf of the Conduct Committee, is required to investigate the nature of the complaint. This initial complaint can come from either a member of the public, another accountant, another client, etc., and he or she is known as 'the complainant'. Any complaint made must be investigated, regardless of how trivial it may seem.

A case manager appointed to investigate the complainant will carry out an initial fact-find. This fact-find will be carried out by holding detailed interviews and enquiries with all the relevant parties. At the end of the fact-find, the case manager will decide if there is a case to answer. If the Conduct Committee decides that there is no prima facie case to answer, the complainant has the right to have their complaint reviewed by an independent reviewer. If the complainant chooses not to exercise this right, the matter is closed.

However, if the Conduct Committee establishes that there is a case to answer, it can exercise one of the five options:
- First, the matter is referred to a Disciplinary Tribunal for a hearing.
- Secondly, it can offer a consent order, which is a disciplinary penalty that must have the agreement for the member.
- Thirdly, it can invite the individual concerned to accept an unpublished caution.
- Fourthly, the matter can be deferred to permit the Conduct Committee to gather further necessary information to enable it to make a decision.
- Fifthly, it can take no further action.

Disciplinary Tribunals The purpose of a Disciplinary Tribunal is to hear cases of more serious misconduct referred to it by the Conduct Committee. The convenor of the Disciplinary Panel appoints a Disciplinary Tribunal to hear the case in full and it is generally conducted in public. A Disciplinary Tribunal is comprised of at least two non-accountants (including one lawyer) while the third member is generally an accountant. The role of the Disciplinary Tribunal is to give 'the respondent' (i.e. the person against whom the complaint is made) the opportunity to attend and be heard at the hearing of the formal complaint made against him; be represented by counsel, a solicitor or a member of the Institute; cross-examine witnesses called by the person or persons presenting the complaint; adduce documentary evidence on his behalf; call witnesses to give evidence on his behalf and make such submissions to the Tribunal as he deems appropriate. Furthermore, the Disciplinary Tribunal will also give the persons bringing the complaint the opportunity also of attending and being heard at the hearing, adducing documentary evidence, calling witnesses to give evidence, cross-examining witnesses called by the respondent and making any other submissions that he deems appropriate to the Disciplinary Tribunal.

If a Disciplinary Tribunal finds that the formal complaint has been proven in accordance with the standard of proof required, it will make a declaration to that effect. If it finds that the formal complaint has not been proven, it will dismiss the complaint. In both scenarios, the Tribunal must give reasons for its decision.

Appeal Tribunals All decisions made by a Disciplinary Tribunal are subject to a right of appeal to an Appeal Tribunal. The majority of the members of an Appeal

Tribunal, typically made up of three people, will be persons who are not members of the Institute and at least one of whom should be a lawyer. The Appeal Tribunal will give the appellant making the appeal (i.e. the respondent at the Disciplinary Tribunal stage) the opportunity to attend and be heard at the hearing of the appeal and, if the appellant so desires, to be represented at the Appeal Tribunal by counsel or by a solicitor or by a member of the Institute. The Appeal Tribunal has the authority to affirm, vary or rescind any finding or Order of the original Disciplinary Tribunal in respect of which the appeal was brought. Furthermore, it may substitute any other finding or Order which it considers appropriate. An Appeal Tribunal can also make an Order for costs against either party if it deems such an Order appropriate.

Index